WATCHDOG
OF LOYALTY

WATCHDOG OF LOYALTY

The Minnesota Commission of Public Safety During World War I

CARL H. CHRISLOCK

MINNESOTA HISTORICAL SOCIETY PRESS · ST. PAUL

Frontispiece: Members of the Minnesota Commission of Public Safety sat for a group portrait in their State Capitol meeting room, about 1918. Seated around the table (from left foreground) are Thomas E. Cashman, Anton C. Weiss, Henry W. Libby, Gov. Joseph A. A. Burnquist, Attorney General Clifford L. Hilton, Ambrose Tighe, John F. McGee, and Charles H. March.

This book was supported in part by the Minnesota Historical Society Public Affairs Center, which is funded by the Northwest Area Foundation.

Minnesota Historical Society Press
St. Paul 55101

Manufactured in the United States of America
10 9 8 7 6 5 4 3 2 1

♾ The paper used in this book meets the minimum requirements of the American National Standard for Information Sciences — Permanence for Printed Library Materials, ANSI Z39.48-1984.

Library of Congress Cataloging-in-Publication Data

Chrislock, Carl Henry.
    Watchdog of loyalty : the Minnesota Commission of Public Safety during World War I / Carl H. Chrislock.
        p.   cm.
    Includes bibliographical references and index.
    ISBN 0-87351-263-4 (cloth : alk. paper) — ISBN 0-87351-264-2 (paper : alk. paper)
    1. Minnesota Commission of Public Safety — History. 2. World War, 1914–1918 — Minnesota. 3. Civil rights — Minnesota — History — 20th century. 4. Internal security — Minnesota — History — 20th century. 5. Minnesota — History — 1858– I. Title.
D570.8.C8M63 1991   91-11228
977.6'051 — dc20   CIP

To Karyna,
Marit,
Winston,
and Zora

Contents

Preface

The Minnesota Commission of Public Safety (MCPS), which had a brief but controversial life between 1917 and 1920, was created to control the Minnesota home front during World War I.* According to the statute passed by the state legislature shortly after the United States declared war on Germany, the safety commission was empowered "to do all . . . things non-inconsistent with the constitution or laws of the state of Minnesota or of the United States" that were required to maintain domestic law and order and to assure a decent contribution by the people of Minnesota to the war effort.[1]

The seven members of the safety commission included the governor and the attorney general, both of whom served ex officio, and five appointees. Despite Governor Joseph A. A. Burnquist's role as chairman of the safety commission, he failed to establish himself as its dominant personality. That role was assumed by John F. McGee, a Minneapolis corporation attorney whose extremist rhetoric helped to shape the commission's image as the scourge of anyone remotely suspected of being soft on the war, socialistically inclined, or infected with pacifism. The other commissioners were less vitriolic, but McGee's high visibility — not unlike that achieved by Wisconsin Senator Joseph R. McCarthy more than a generation later — created a perception that McGee rather than the governor was the commission's authentic spokesman.

Early in my research I was impelled to choose between two differing approaches to the history of the Minnesota Commission of Public Safety. The first would have viewed the MCPS operation as an aspect

*The MCPS had no relation to the contemporary Minnesota Department of Public Safety, an agency created in 1970 to oversee such functions as driver and vehicle licensing, liquor licensing, the Minnesota State Patrol, and support services for local law enforcement agencies.

of national home-front mobilization, an approach that would have necessitated a detailed comparison of Minnesota's commission with the other state councils of defense. The second approach, and the one I selected, perceives the MCPS era as a significant chapter in Minnesota political history, an era that profoundly influenced the state's political future.

The rationale for choosing the second approach deserves explanation. To begin with, the MCPS was not a typical state council of defense. Most of the other state councils were created by gubernatorial proclamation in response to a request from the Council of National Defense, the federal agency that coordinated the mobilization effort. The MCPS, on the other hand, was established by a legislative statute that was well on the road to passage by the time the national council's request reached Governor Burnquist. With an exception or two, moreover, the powers of the other state councils were limited; their principal role was to carry out policies formulated by federal authorities. By contrast, the MCPS was endowed with almost dictatorial powers. While the statute was pending in the legislature, the *Minneapolis Journal* noted that it "would gather the sovereign powers of the State in a few responsible hands for quick and effective use in case of need."[2]

While these sovereign powers were in their hands, the safety commissioners spent more time defending the existing socioeconomic order against a rising tide of radicalism on the prairies and a growing labor-union militance in the mines, forests, and working-class wards than they did cooperating with the federal mobilization effort. The MCPS paid considerable lip service to the latter goal, but when state and federal responses to labor-management disputes collided — as they increasingly did in 1918 — the commission covertly resisted implementation of federal policies. It responded similarly to the Nonpartisan League, the radical farmers' movement that entered Minnesota from North Dakota in 1916. Federal authorities sought to co-opt the league, whereas the commission tried to exclude it from the state's political process — not by outlawing it, but by encouraging local officials to ban league activity within their jurisdictions.

Most allusions to the safety commission in historical literature focus on its sponsorship of the intolerant loyalty crusade that was directed against German Americans during 1917 and 1918. This focus is not inappropriate, but the loyalty crusade should be viewed in the context of its relationship to the commission's top objective — defeating trade unionism and the Nonpartisan League. The left wing of organized labor and the Nonpartisan League were opposed to the war before American entry, and "loyalists" perceived a lack of enthusiasm for the war within the ranks of both movements after April 6, 1917. This situation created an opportunity for the MCPS to impeach the loyalty of its domestic enemies and to identify defense of the existing order with patriotic obligation. The efforts of the NPL and the labor movement to link their programs with the claims of patriotism were considerably less successful.

In addition to boasting that its efforts helped save Minnesota for loyalty, the safety commission claimed credit for sponsoring a myriad of "creative" activities relating to home-front mobilization. This study accepts a few of these claims but views many of them with skepticism — the commissioners were not above claiming credit for projects only nominally linked to the MCPS. Much of the credit for the success of such programs as food conservation should be assigned to Alice Ames Winter and the women's network she supervised, which operated with only minimal MCPS supervision.

Ironically, the MCPS legacy was in many respects the antithesis of what the commissioners and their sponsors intended. The commission temporarily helped to block Nonpartisan League access to power and to retard the advance of trade unionism. In the long run, however, bitter memories of the agency's repressive measures — memories that may have exaggerated MCPS culpability but that were assiduously cultivated by those who regarded themselves as its victims — helped to reinforce Minnesota's liberal tradition.

Given the premise that women and men truly learn from history, one may be entitled to hope that this wholly negative image of the Minnesota Commission of Public Safety militates against resort to commission precedents in future crises. Unfortunately, there are no ironclad guarantees. Many Minnesotans, along with a multitude of other Americans, lack a strong sense of history. Moreover, contemporary society is in the grip of cataclysmic change, a milieu extremely vulnerable to the kind of excess that subjects the democratic process to severe strain. Within the political arena, a tendency for slogans and "sound bites" to overwhelm rational discourse inhibits the ability of a democratic system to respond creatively to the enormous challenges of the day. Nevertheless, coming to terms with the less ennobling chapters in our history may provide our cherished democratic values with a margin of safety that sole preoccupation with the "glories" of the past fails to bring. There is, asserted President Václav Havel of the newly named Czech and Slovak Federal Republic in 1990, "no full freedom where full truth is not given free passage."[3]

Acknowledgments

I am profoundly grateful to staff members of the Minnesota Historical Society for their assistance in the production of this book. Early in 1985 Jean A. Brookins, assistant director for publications and research, and Deborah L. Miller, research supervisor, persuaded me to undertake the project. As the research and writing progressed, Miller helped locate relevant sources, served as a sounding board when knotty problems of interpretation arose, and critically read the first-draft chapters as they emerged. Brookins also perused several of the first-draft chapters, and she was always available for counsel and encouragement when the inevitable loneliness afflicting every author threatened to sink morale.

Elaine H. Carte of the Minnesota Historical Society Press, who edited the manuscript, deserves special commendation. Her exceptional editorial skills spotted errors of fact, improved the manuscript from a stylistic standpoint, and, above all, sharpened its focus. Other persons at the Minnesota Historical Society whose contributions warrant recognition include Ann Regan, managing editor, and Alan Ominsky, production supervisor of MHS PRESS; and Faustino Avaloz, Tracey Baker, Ruth Bauer, Dallas R. Lindgren, Steven Nielsen, Alissa Rosenberg, and Ruby Shields of the Library and Archives Reference Department.

In 1986 and 1987 three college undergraduates served very efficiently as my research interns: Georg Leidenberger, then enrolled at Macalester College in St. Paul; and Anne Clausen and Cathy Kleiman, both enrolled at Augsburg College in Minneapolis in the late 1980s.

A grant awarded by the Minnesota Historical Society Public Affairs Center helped defray some of the expenses connected with research and writing. Appreciation is due Dwight and James Pederson for providing me with a haven on the shores of Swede Lake in Polk County, Wisconsin, where much of the writing was done.

Finally, I thank Valborg Gilseth Chrislock, my wife, for not only benignly accepting but positively encouraging my six-year preoccupation with the Minnesota Commission of Public Safety.

WATCHDOG
OF LOYALTY

Minnesota in 1917, showing some of the places that figured in the story of the Minnesota Commission of Public Safety

CHAPTER ONE

The Setting

In April 1917, when the United States entered the Great War, the Minnesota political community was in the early stage of a polarization that shortly would realign state politics. The Minnesota Commission of Public Safety, which came into being in the same month, would play a significant role in this process, not as a mediator between contending factions but as an advocate for one of them.

Ten years earlier such a development could not have been predicted. Since the turn of the century an informal coalition vaguely committed to something called "progressivism" had dominated policy making. For the most part, a politics of consensus animated by the reform spirit of the age had sustained a climate of reasonable tranquility. Specific issues, particularly those concerned with liquor legislation, could spark spirited debate, but strategically wise politicians appropriated the "progressive" label as eagerly as their descendants of the 1980s would cultivate a "conservative" image.

Progressivism, whether in its Minnesota or national embodiments, eludes easy definition. Historians have recognized a myriad of progressive movements, each with its own strategies and priorities. However, one can identify two basic premises underlying progressive culture. First of all, most progressives were supremely confident that American society was capable of surmounting contemporary challenges, either through governmental action or private effort. As popular historian Walter Lord put it, the early years of the century "were good because, whatever the trouble, people were sure they could fix it."[1] Progressives generally rejected the notion that human beings were helpless victims of an inhospitable environment.

The second premise was that a variety of current troubles required "fixing." An accelerating concentration of wealth and economic power was threatening equality of opportunity; unscrupulous bosses were corrupting the political process; urban blight was turning the nation's cities into cesspools; natural resources were being consumed at a rate threatening the future with impoverishment; the children of the poor were suffering unconscionable neglect; and a crass materialism was subverting the values that defined America. Given the attention focused on these perceived evils by novelists, journalists, clergy, and "progressive" politicians, few literate Americans were left unaware of the shortcomings afflicting their society.

But awareness did not translate into despair. Most Americans believed that the combined efforts of settlement houses, social workers — a profession providing an outlet for upper- and middle-class women whose opportunities for fulfillment in other callings were limited — and social-gospel religion, coupled with governmental action, could effect reasonable cures without overturning the system.

At the close of World War I, many of the evils that progressives had sought to exorcise were still highly visible. Corruption still held sway within all levels of government. The gap between rich and poor persisted. Corporate influence on policy making had not significantly diminished. Above all, the idyllic harmony dreamed of by idealistic progressives seemed more elusive than ever. But progressivism had made a difference. Its most productive period — through the administrations of Theodore Roosevelt (1901–09) and William Howard Taft (1909–13) and into Woodrow Wilson's first term — saw several landmark statutes that steered the nation into new public policy directions. The Pure Food and Drug Act and the Federal Meat Inspection Act (both 1906) broadened the federal responsibility for the nation's health. The Hepburn (1906) and Mann-Elkins (1911) acts significantly strengthened federal regulatory authority over transportation, and the Federal Reserve Act (1913) brought some order into the nation's chaotic currency and banking systems. The Sixteenth Amendment (1913) legitimated the progressive income tax, and that same year the Seventeenth Amendment established the direct election of United States senators. Most important, the agitation of the progressive years made many Americans aware of the gap separating the American reality from the American dream.

The progressive movement was largely a spent force by 1920, although some historians have argued that a residual progressivism significantly influenced public policy in the 1920s.[2] Common wisdom generally attributes the decline to World War I. This thesis cannot be lightly dismissed. For one thing, the war reordered the nation's priorities, subordinating domestic reform to victory over Imperial

Germany. For another, issues relating to the war tended to fragment the progressive coalition. A prowar group perceived the conflict as an opportunity to expand progressivism by the sword. Committed antimilitarist progressives stopped short of resisting the war once it was declared, but their enthusiasm for "stomping on the Kaiser" was tempered by a desire to seek an early peace settlement and by an anxiety to prevent wartime hysteria from eroding the nation's basic liberties.

But disagreement on war-related issues was not the only factor imperiling progressive unity in 1917. Internal tensions had plagued the movement for some time. Following enactment of his New Freedom program (tariff reduction, the Federal Reserve Act, and two antitrust measures — the Clayton and Federal Trade Commission statutes) in 1914, President Wilson announced that his "covenant" with the American people, as defined in the campaign of 1912, was fulfilled. Many moderate progressives reacted favorably; from their standpoint, reform had proceeded far enough. The progressive left believed otherwise. It felt that the process of reforming America had just begun. Social justice advocates were clamoring for federal legislation outlawing child labor. Organized labor was seeking to improve its invidious position before the law. Farm organizations were demanding tightened regulation of the commodity markets and a federally funded farm credit system. Feminists were crusading for a constitutional amendment giving women the right to vote. Foes of the liquor trade were accelerating their drive for total prohibition. Not all of these groups supported each other's goals — organized labor was not enthusiastic about prohibition, for example — but their combined impact was sufficient to impress politicians seeking public office. [3]

Wilson changed course as the presidential campaign of 1916 approached. His appointment of Louis D. Brandeis to the United States Supreme Court in early 1916 delighted advanced progressives as much as it enraged conservatives and some moderate progressives. And more was to come. In the spring and summer of 1916, Wilson pushed through Congress much of the program championed by the progressive left. The more important measures included the Federal Farm Loan Bank Act, the Owen-Keating child labor bill, and the Adamson eight-hour railway labor act, a measure that averted a serious transportation strike by writing the railroad brotherhoods' basic demands into law. [4]

Wilson's swing to the left coupled with his capture of the peace issue yielded the Democratic party a narrow victory in the 1916

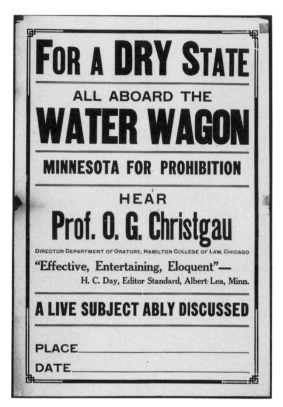

Announcement of a lecture promoting the cause
of prohibition in Minnesota, about 1914

election. Reassuring as this outcome was to the progressive left, it by no means assured smooth passage ahead. The margin of victory was exceedingly thin, and the president's new course — particularly the Adamson Act — had alienated the business community. Precisely how a confrontation between the president and his new allies on the one side and business conservatism on the other would have played out can never be known. The diplomatic crisis with Germany and the declaration of war reordered the nation's priorities. Domestic policy was now a handmaiden of the war effort.

Throughout the first decade and a half of the new century, the Minnesota electorate strongly supported the programs and policies associated with national progressivism. The movement spoke to the

interests of most sectors within the Minnesota political community —
directly to the hopes and fears of upper- and middle-class citizens
and more rhetorically than substantively to the aspirations of the less
privileged. President Roosevelt enjoyed immense popularity both as
president and then as leader of the ill-fated 1912 Progressive (Bull
Moose) party.

Since the late nineteenth century, Minnesota politics had reflected
a sense of regional injury based on a belief that eastern corporate
interests exercised oppressive control over national politics and the
American economy to the detriment of the Midwest. This belief had
helped spawn the Populist movement of the 1890s, which gained acceptance in the state until it alienated Minnesota's business interests,
as well as a large bloc of middle-class voters, by embracing Free Silver
and other radical "heresies." The defeat of Free Silver and the subsequent demise of populism encouraged a refocusing of concern from
the menace of irresponsible radicalism to the sins of the eastern
seaboard corporate complex.[5]

A wave of mergers at the turn of the century created newer and
ever larger industrial and financial conglomerates. The United States
Steel Corporation, founded in 1901, dominated the economy of Minnesota's iron ranges, and the formation that same year of the Northern Securities Company — a step that in effect consolidated the Great
Northern, Northern Pacific, and Burlington railroads into a single
system — rang alarm bells over the whole state.[6]

Antipathy to excessive tariff protections within both the business
and agricultural communities of Minnesota rivaled the hostility directed
against railroad monopoly. The linkage between the tariff question
and progressive idealism may seem tenuous, but Minnesotans perceived high protectionism as a means of levying a toll on the virtuous
West for the benefit of eastern interests. Worse yet, the reasoning went,
high tariff rates threatened the access of such Minnesota products as
wheat and flour to world markets by tempting foreign governments
to retaliate against them. Downward tariff revision was thus a cause
célèbre throughout Minnesota between 1900 and 1910. Another reform
issue commanding attention was the need to restructure the nation's
rigid and highly centralized monetary and banking system, although
no consensus on how this should be accomplished emerged.

Continuity and consensus characterized Minnesota politics
throughout the progressive years. The five governors who served from

John A. Johnson, governor of Minnesota from 1905 to 1909

1899 to 1915 — three Democrats and two Republicans — all professed commitment to progressivism. This three-to-two predominance of Democrats over Republicans in the statehouse might create the misleading impression that Minnesota was a two-party state at the beginning of the twentieth century. It would be more correct to say that nominally the Republicans commanded a substantial majority within the electorate, but as a determinant of voting behavior party loyalty was considerably less important than it had been earlier. The electoral success of the three Democratic governors — John Lind (1899–1901), John A. Johnson (1905–09), and Winfield Scott Hammond (1915) — was in part attributable to internal Republican dissension and in part to their personal strengths. Throughout the period the Republicans controlled the legislature by wide margins, and only two Democrats (Lind and Hammond) won seats in the congressional delegation.[7]

The reform programs championed by Lind, Republican Samuel R. Van Sant (1901–05), and Johnson extended across the public policy landscape. Comprehensive tax reform was a goal cherished by all three. The single most important achievement in this area was ratification in 1906 of the "Wide Open" tax amendment, which liberated the legislature from the onerous restrictions that Minnesota's original constitution had imposed on its power to tax. Adoption of this amendment opened the way for further reforms, including creation of a permanent tax commission to monitor operation of the tax system and to recommend appropriate changes in its structure.

The crowning achievement of the Johnson administration was a revamped insurance code that imposed tighter regulation on this industry. Soon after taking office in January 1905, the governor launched an investigation which disclosed that gross mismanagement had brought a leading Minneapolis insurance firm to the verge of collapse. Personal intervention by Johnson forced an immediate reorganization of the company and stimulated his determination to strengthen the state's insurance statutes. The legislative sessions of 1905 and 1907 acted favorably on the governor's carefully formulated recommendations. Insurance reform was not looked upon as unwarranted interference with private enterprise. On the contrary, most business people regarded it as a prudent safeguard against financial disasters that would severely impair business confidence. Johnson's activism in the insurance area won for him and Thomas D. O'Brien, his insurance commissioner, a nationwide reputation. [8]

The legislatures of 1905 and 1907 adopted other significant reform measures. The 1905 session closed loopholes in the code governing the sale of timber on state lands, a step welcomed by conservationists. A 1907 statute enlarged the powers of the Bureau of Labor, thereby permitting more effective enforcement of existing factory inspection laws. Another 1907 statute conferred on municipalities the authority to own and operate such public utilities as street railways, telephone systems, gas works, and electric light plants. Two years later Johnson's last legislature created a Department of Banking, an important regulatory agency the establishment of which was heartily endorsed by the state's banking community.

Railroad issues also preoccupied the Johnson legislatures. Previous experience with the railroad question had underscored two realities: that an almost obsessive fear of railroad monopoly afflicted nearly everyone in Minnesota; and that the competence of the state to tackle this challenge was limited. When the Northern Securities Company was formed in November 1901 — at a time when railroading virtually monopolized freight and passenger transportation — Governor Van Sant had directed the Minnesota attorney general to institute legal action against the new firm. This brave stance — so consistent with Van Sant's moralistic style — was exceedingly rewarding from a political standpoint. His bid for reelection in 1902 was spectacularly successful, and candidates for public office studiously cultivated an "antimerger" image for the next decade or so. Unfortunately, from a legal standpoint the Van Sant initiative ended in a blind alley: federal rather than state action was required to slay the Northern Securities giant. In February 1902 President Roosevelt instructed his attorney general to proceed against the merger on the grounds that it violated the Sherman antitrust law, a contention accepted by the United States Supreme Court two years later. [9]

Congressional passage of the Hepburn Act in 1906, which broadened the powers of the Interstate Commerce Commission, confirmed the tendency toward federal preemption of railroad regulation. Nevertheless, Minnesota politicians remained determined to do what was constitutionally possible within a shrinking sphere of activity. The 1907 legislature banned free railroad passes, a measure welcomed rather than resisted by the railroad companies; fixed passenger rates at two cents a mile; and classified commodities and set maximum rates for their carriage. Johnson also exerted pressure on the Railroad and Warehouse Commission to exercise its powers more aggressively, although not vigorously enough to satisfy the more militant advocates of railroad reform. [10]

When untimely death terminated Johnson's career on September 21, 1909, several of his goals remained unfulfilled. The legislature had declined to establish a workers' compensation system based on the concept of employer liability. Similarly, it had failed to extend the direct primary to statewide constitutional officers: the 1901 session had applied it to all county officials, state legislators, and congressmen. Several issues relating to iron ore taxation were also pending. Thanks to the vigilance of the new tax commission, mining properties hitherto exempt had been placed on the tax rolls, but the constitutional propriety of occupation and royalty levies remained in dispute. County option — a procedure empowering counties to exclude licensed liquor establishments from within their boundaries by referendum — was also becoming a consequential issue.

Adolph Olson Eberhart, the Republican lieutenant governor who became governor following the death of Johnson, promised to continue his predecessor's policies. The new governor was known to oppose county option, however, and on other questions his position appeared equivocal. Nevertheless Eberhart demonstrated a remarkable ability to survive politically, winning election in his own right in 1910 and reelection in 1912, a feat attributable to a happy combination of luck and astute management by a rejuvenated Republican machine headed by Minneapolis attorney Edward E. Smith, who, according to one political observer, "came as near the definition of a boss as any one ever did in Minnesota." [11]

While an ongoing deadlock between the governor and progressive legislators stymied reform on the state level, a massive reaction against the policies of the Taft administration was gathering momentum throughout the Midwest. The president's handling of the tariff issue initiated a precipitous fall in his popularity that he subsequently failed to reverse. Although the Republican national convention of 1908 adopted a plank that pledged to revise existing rates downward, the bill that Congress considered the next year — the Payne-Aldrich law — did not accomplish this goal. A coalition embracing virtually the entire Democratic membership and a band of insurgent Midwest Republicans (including seven of Minnesota's eight Republican congressmen and both its GOP senators) unsuccessfully opposed the passage of Payne-Aldrich. Taft was known to be unhappy with the bill, but nevertheless he signed it into law. Midwest Republicans felt betrayed. [12]

Taft compounded his difficulties by moving from apologetic defense of Payne-Aldrich to a positive claim that it represented sound public policy. Speaking in Winona, Minnesota, in September 1909, he declared that Payne-Aldrich was the best tariff law ever enacted by the Republican party and praised James A. Tawney, the only Minnesota congressman who had supported the law (and within whose district Taft was speaking). "Western sentiment, Western interest, Western influence in the settlement of this great question receives slight consideration from the president," complained the *St. Paul Dispatch,* a paper hitherto known for its unswerving Republicanism. [13]

A year after Taft's Winona performance, Republican voters in Minnesota's first congressional district rejected Representative Tawney's bid for renomination, an outcome attracting national attention. [14] Adverse reaction to the administration's conservation policies also diminished Taft's popularity. Before long an organized effort challenging the renomination of Taft emerged. At first this effort focused on the declared candidacy of Senator Robert M. La Follette of Wisconsin, but following Theodore Roosevelt's announcement of his own availability in February 1912, the former president appeared to be the insurgents' favorite.

Although the Smith-Eberhart machine did not court identification with the policies of the Taft administration, it could not avoid the spillover effect of the anti-Taft movement. As Republicans prepared to deny renomination to Eberhart at the upcoming party convention, he called the legislature into special session for the purpose of enacting a statewide direct primary law. Although Eberhart's many adversaries in the legislature hesitated to assist his reelection effort, their long championship of the direct primary impelled them to support the recommendation. In short order they passed a primary law and scheduled a statewide election to be held in September. For good measure the session also raised the railroad gross earnings tax from 4 to 5 percent, strengthened the existing child labor law, and enacted a stringent corrupt practices law imposing strict limits on campaign spending. In evaluating the session the *Minneapolis Journal* remarked, "In many ways [it] was the most memorable in the history of the state. In thirteen days the legislature completely revolutionized the state's present political system."[15]

The *Journal* exaggerated. Even when combined with earlier reforms, the changes instituted by the special session were far from revolutionary. Nevertheless, the political process had fallen into a state of "revolutionary" disarray in 1912. After Taft's renomination by the national Republican convention, Theodore Roosevelt and his followers launched the Bull Moose party, placing progressive Republicans who favored Roosevelt but hesitated to forfeit their allegiance to the GOP in a quandary. In Minnesota most Republican officeholders seeking reelection either backed Roosevelt without becoming Bull Moosers or muted their preferences in the presidential race. Among the candidates for major statewide offices, only Eberhart and Senator Knute Nelson tepidly endorsed Taft.

Despite the chaos of the 1912 campaign, the electoral outcome produced few surprises. Four opponents challenged the governor: a progressive Democrat, an eloquent Prohibitionist, a Socialist, and a Bull Mooser who ran behind Roosevelt by more than ninety thousand votes. Eberhart won with about 40 percent of the total vote. The remaining candidates on the statewide Republican ticket also prevailed, most of them more decisively than Eberhart.[16]

The presidential returns generated more happiness within progressive ranks than the gubernatorial outcome. Roosevelt captured Minnesota's twelve electoral votes: his total was 125,999. Wilson, who won the national election with 42 percent of the popular vote, ran a comparatively close second: his count was 106,431. With 64,342 votes, Taft finished a poor third; and Eugene V. Debs, the Socialist contender, received 27,505. Roosevelt carried sixty counties, Wilson twenty-four, Debs two, and Taft none. [17]

Within Minnesota, the aftermath of this powerful mandate in support of further progressive reform was anticlimactic. Minnesota progressives appreciated the skill with which Woodrow Wilson piloted his New Freedom program through Congress, but Adolph Eberhart was no Woodrow Wilson. When the 1913 legislature convened, the deadlock between the governor and the legislators resumed. As political observer Charles B. Cheney recalled, "The [1913] legislature was pretty much anti-Eberhart . . . on general principles." The session's major achievements were a workers' compensation law and the abolition of party designation in legislative races. [18]

As the campaign of 1914 approached, Minnesota progressivism — particularly its Republican sector — took on the appearance of a one-issue movement, that issue being county option. This measure, its proponents argued, would protect the home by reducing the availability of strong drink. It also would strike a blow at the distillery-brewery complex, a nefarious influence that in concert with other corporate interests was corrupting the political process and inhibiting the advance of progressive reform. Why not, the argument concluded, provide the people with a weapon that promised liberation from this monstrous evil?

Support for woman suffrage was also growing in the wake of the 1912 campaign, thanks in part to the Bull Moose embrace of this cause. Most county option progressives supported the vote for women, but county option was their first priority — awarding the vote to women, they promised, would come later. At the same time an active minority opposed to county option, fearing that women electors would most certainly vote the saloon out of existence, stoutly opposed female enfranchisement. The combination of these two factors largely explains why Minnesota's well-organized women's movement was unable to win the vote in advance of ratification of the Nineteenth Amendment in 1920. [19]

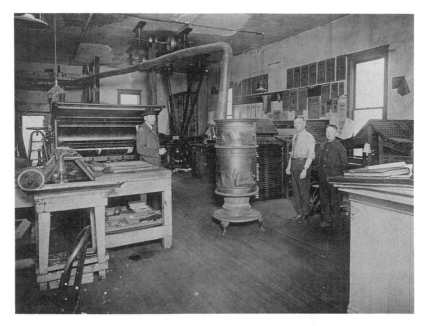

Gunnar B. Björnson, editor, C. S. Johnson, foreman, and Gunnar's son Valdimar, "printer's devil," in the pressroom of the Minneota Mascot, *1919*

Realizing that Eberhart opposed their goal, GOP drys organized under the leadership of Gunnar B. Björnson, editor of the *Minneota Mascot,* and agreed to back William E. Lee, a small-town banker, in the June primary election. The Lee challenge to Eberhart succeeded, but the bitterness generated during the campaign guaranteed that many Eberhart supporters would refuse to vote for Lee in the final election. The outcome of the Democratic primary provided aggrieved Eberhart backers with an attractive alternative to Lee. Congressman Winfield Scott Hammond, the victor, exuded the aura of a scholar statesman. Cheney recalled that he was "dignified, and in personal contacts . . . very reserved." During his four terms in Congress, Hammond had become known as a consistent and effective supporter of progressive causes. [20]

In the final stages of the 1914 campaign, it was impossible to determine whether Hammond was more "progressive" than Lee or the other way around. On most issues of consequence the articulated views of the two contenders were virtually identical. Even on county

option they were not as far apart as the rhetoric of the campaign implied. Lee promised to push vigorously for enactment of a county
option law, whereas Hammond indicated that he would sign such
a law if the legislature saw fit to pass it.

From a purist's standpoint, Lee's stand appeared more forthright.
From a practical point of view Hammond's was more prudent. It
assured him the support of people opposed to county option, while
allowing county option supporters who preferred Hammond over Lee
on other grounds to vote for the former in the belief that he would
not block enactment of a law they favored.

On November 3 Hammond triumphed over Lee by about twelve
thousand votes, not an impressive margin, but one that vindicated
the strategy of the Democratic campaign. When the new governor
assumed office he pleaded for early resolution of the county option
question, which, he maintained, had aroused "a bitterness entirely
unwarranted by its importance from a temperance standpoint or from
any other standpoint." He requested early action "so that other matters of great importance" could be considered. [21]

Legislative deliberation on county option began early in the 1915
session, but final resolution was not accomplished early enough to
permit thoroughgoing consideration of the "other matters of great
importance." As he had promised in the campaign, Hammond signed
the county option law that reached his desk in late February. He
also signed a companion statute, the so-called antiroadhouse law,
which prohibited the licensing of liquor establishments in rural
townships. [22]

Editorial reviews of the 1915 legislature appearing after adjournment of the session tended to be unflattering. However, the *Minneapolis Journal* spoke for many by commenting, "Much may be
forgiven a lawmaking body that passes two such laws as [county option and the antiroadhouse bill]." The *St. Paul Pioneer Press* was less
charitable: it thought that more gubernatorial vigor would have
enhanced the session's productivity. [23] Unfortunately Hammond was
denied the opportunity to sharpen his performance. He died suddenly
on December 30, 1915, a few days short of his first anniversary as
governor.

Early in the century's second decade, the comparative civility that
had marked political discourse during the preceding decade — with
an occasional lapse in the county option controversy — began to show

signs of strain. Potentially, one of the more disruptive conflicts was an ongoing struggle between a radical wing of the farmers' movement and the organized grain trade. In the late nineteenth century farmers had gained the integration of the local cooperative elevator into the marketing system. Unfortunately, this victory turned out to be less significant than initially believed: control of the Upper Midwest grain trade, farmers believed, remained securely in the hands of the Minneapolis Chamber of Commerce (the older name of the Minneapolis Grain Exchange); and membership in the chamber was a privilege denied to farmers and their representatives.[24]

On May 30, 1908, a group of farmers affiliated with the American Society of Equity, meeting in Minneapolis, organized the Equity Cooperative Exchange, an enterprise designed to operate as a terminal marketing agency serving a chain of local cooperative elevators. When George S. Loftus, an idealistic and uncompromising crusader on behalf of the farmers, became sales manager in 1912, the exchange began to prosper sufficiently to alarm the established grain trade. Under the generalship of John G. McHugh, the secretary of the Minneapolis Chamber of Commerce, the grain trade establishment declared war on Loftus and his organization. In the hostilities that followed, both sides exchanged bitter charges. Loftus characterized the chamber as an evil conspiracy organized to rob farmers of their due. McHugh and his fellow believers responded in kind. *Commercial West,* for example, which spoke for the grain trade interests, reacted to Loftus's charges with an equally uncivil broadside: "For such an outfit to presume to attack the integrity of the Chamber of Commerce [is] an exhibit of insincerity like a rogue questioning the motives of an honest man."[25]

Meanwhile, the Nonpartisan League, which was founded in North Dakota in 1915, posed a more serious threat. The NPL, which recruited many Equity supporters into its ranks, proposed to capture all three branches of state government for the purpose of enacting a radical program featuring state ownership and operation of the intermediary sector of the agricultural economy. The strategy for winning power was based on capturing the machinery of a state's dominant political party (in Minnesota and North Dakota, the Republican party) by mobilizing league members for participation in primary elections. Thanks in large part to the inspired leadership of NPL President Arthur C. Townley, this strategy worked beautifully in the 1916 North Dakota election: candidates endorsed by the league won every statewide office but one and captured 81 of the 113 seats in the North Dakota House of Representatives. When the North Dakota legislature convened in January 1917, the "revolution" heralded by the 1916 election got under way.[26]

Even before their stunning North Dakota triumph, Townley and his associates invaded Minnesota. Their initial target was the Red River valley county of Polk, where they launched a recruitment campaign in early July 1916. Although Red River valley grain growers responded enthusiastically to the NPL gospel, the Townleyite invasion came too late in the campaign season to have a significant impact on the election. However, political pulse-takers anticipated that the NPL would be a factor in the future. Shortly after the 1916 election a confidant of Frank B. Kellogg advised the senator-elect that the Nonpartisan League "must be considered in [the plans] made for future work, or there will be additional trouble."[27]

By 1912 developments within the Minnesota labor movement bore some resemblance to the evolving pattern within the militant agricultural sector. During progressivism's golden age, moderate Minnesota Federation of Labor unionists enjoyed a limited rapport with middle-class progressivism: such measures as stricter factory inspection and workers' compensation were fruits of this relationship. County optionists, however, resented the MFL's consistent opposition to their pet measure, and progressives generally were reluctant to support the closed shop. Unionists also resented an alleged insensitivity on the part of middle-class progressives to complaints concerning the unfair labor practices of many Minnesota employers.

Progressivism's inability to identify with basic trade-union goals coupled with MFL reluctance to organize miners and unskilled workers created a gap encouraging radicalization within the labor movement. The Debsian Socialist (Public Ownership) vote rose significantly in Minnesota between 1910 and 1916. In 1912 the Socialists won only about 8 percent of the total vote in the gubernatorial race, but in a few northern counties and within several Minneapolis working-class wards they were emerging as major players in the political process. Thomas Van Lear, Minneapolis's most successful Socialist politician, attracted many middle-class voters on the basis of municipal issues as well when he won the mayoralty in 1916.[28]

Establishment of an Industrial Workers of the World presence within Minnesota, particularly in the northern mines and forests, was another sign of the times. Founded in 1905, the IWW discovered opportunity on the Minnesota iron ranges following collapse of a 1907 strike organized by the Western Federation of Miners that had temporarily halted ore production on the Mesabi Range and allegedly threatened a breakdown of law and order. Although Governor Johnson displayed some sympathy for the plight of the miners, the strike collapsed without achieving any of its declared goals. In the strike's aftermath the mining companies instituted a harsh regimen in the mines that effectively blocked all union activity, and the MFL did not accept organization of the mostly immigrant miners as its responsibility. Finnish-American Wobblies (as IWW activists were called), many of them former miners now excluded from employment in the mines by company blacklists, stepped into the breach by launching an "educational" campaign designed to reinforce the class consciousness of the miners. Soon the area's celebrated Finn halls became centers for propagation of the IWW syndicalist message not only to Finns but also to the other nationality groups inhabiting the range. [29]

The IWW also established a presence in Minneapolis. In 1915 it created the Agricultural Workers Organization, which for a time maintained national headquarters on Hennepin Avenue. The AWO dispatched "job delegates" throughout the midwestern grain belt and also into the lumber mills and camps of northern Minnesota for the purpose of organizing unions for migratory workers. [30]

The rising visibility of left-wing unionism created a dilemma for the moderate leaders of the Minnesota Federation of Labor. On the one hand, it appeared to threaten the long-established effort of the American Federation of Labor and the MFL to win mainstream acceptance of trade unionism. On the other hand, the receptivity of many workers to the radical message challenged MFL claims to leadership of the labor movement. Along with their AFL counterparts, MFL leaders responded to the challenge by stepping up recruitment, chartering several industrial unions, and becoming more aggressive politically. These tactics enjoyed some success. In reporting to the MFL's 1915 convention, President E. George Hall pointed to "a paid up membership larger than the Federation has ever had" and what he believed to be "the largest number of new affiliations for any year in [MFL] history." [31]

Meanwhile the national climate of opinion with respect to trade unionism was changing. Severe governmental repression of strike actions in West Virginia and Colorado, among other places, "horrified the nation," in the words of historian Joseph G. Rayback. An increasing number of Americans "now became convinced that much of the blame for industrial strife could be laid upon the doorsteps of employers, and that a reform in industrial conditions was needed." Closer to home, mounting controversy about taxation of mining properties by local authorities aroused the resentment of middle-class residents of the iron ranges toward the companies. A shared sense of being victimized by a common oppressor was forging a sympathetic bond between range miners and small shopkeepers that had not been evident earlier. [32]

Sympathy for the plight of unorganized workers did not extend into the corporate boardrooms of Minneapolis. On the contrary, Minneapolis business leaders remained more determined than ever to maintain their city's open-shop tradition. This was not attributable to an innate hardness of heart, but to a sense of vulnerability seldom acknowledged in trade publications. The wheat frontier had long since moved into western Canada, and defeat of Canadian Reciprocity in 1911 had denied easier access to that country's wheat. Milling centers less burdened by unfavorable freight rates were threatening Minneapolis's position as the national leader in the flour trade, an honor it had proudly held since the early 1880s. Thanks to depletion of the region's magnificent white pine forests, lumbering, too, was in deep trouble. Finally, the opening of the Panama Canal in 1914 reduced the significance of the Twin Cities as a transportation center serving the Pacific Northwest. [33]

Many years later Minneapolis would revitalize its economy on new foundations blessed with rich potentialities for growth. [34] For the time being the city's business elite sought to sustain growth by rigidly holding the line against wage increases and other benefits, a goal best served by doggedly maintaining the open shop. By contrast, St. Paul accepted the limitations imposed by adverse circumstances and allowed moderate unionism to proceed during these years.

By mid-1915 debates on issues relating to the European war were enlivening political discussion throughout Minnesota. In the weeks immediately following outbreak of the war (early August 1914), many Americans expressed a sympathetic preference for one or another of the belligerents; virtually everyone, however, seemed to agree that the United States should avoid involvement in the conflict. This fundamental conviction continued to hold sway among a majority of Minnesotans and midwesterners down through the final crisis leading to the declaration of war.

Nevertheless, within this broad context a number of controversial issues emerged. Would an embargo on arms, other contraband, and loans be appropriate? Was a higher level of preparedness prudent? And what about neutral rights? Should the United States respond more vigorously to unrestricted German submarine warfare, or were British blockade practices equally reprehensible?

Ethnic loyalty was an important factor shaping the opinions of many Minnesotans on these issues. This was particularly true within the highly organized German-American community, the state's largest non-Anglo group. On August 5, 1914, less than a week after the outbreak of the war, several Minnesota German-American organizations directed an appeal to the Minnesota press requesting suspension of judgment concerning responsibility for the war "until authentic reports . . . are available." The appeal went on to accuse the press of "careless handling of unconfirmed, biased and sensational news matter" and pointedly reminded publishers of the "liberal support" given American newspapers by German Americans. It did "not ask that any partiality be shown Germany or Austro-Hungary" but called for "fair treatment."[35]

Meanwhile, German-American publicists were formulating an interpretation of the European tragedy differing significantly from the message carried by the mainstream American press. An editorial appearing initially in the *Illinois Staats-Zeitung* and subsequently reprinted in other papers — both German- and English-language — under German-American control forcefully reminded German-American citizens of their duties in the current crisis:

> While France fights to regain her German provinces, while England fights to regain her maritime and commercial supremacy, Germany defends herself against them with the one hand, and with the other fights to preserve not only herself but France and England and the civilization of all western Europe from Slavic domination.

This sacred mission placed a heavy burden on the shoulders of German Americans. They "should take the necessary action to make the situation clear to their American fellow citizens; . . . American help for those who fall wounded and helpless, American moral support when peace is negotiated, will be the result."[36]

As a prophecy, the *Staats-Zeitung* editorial failed dismally, but as a call to action it struck a responsive chord. Throughout the period of American neutrality, the crusade to keep America out of the war and to preserve some semblance of German honor united the diverse

Gingerbread house, one of the candy booths at a Red Cross bazaar for German and Austrian widows and orphans, St. Paul Auditorium, 1916. The sign invites "young and old for a sweet treat."

elements within the German-American community as never before. A propaganda effort utilizing every accessible forum was an important component of the crusade, but not the only one. Bazaars in German-American neighborhoods collected generous contributions for the benefit of the Germany-Austria-Hungary Red Cross. Congressmen and senators reported an unprecedented (and intimidating) flow of neutralist correspondence from German-American constituents. And in late 1915 several German-American organizations attempted to organize a boycott against banks participating in a loan to the Western Allies. The effort failed, but its potentialities aroused concern within banking circles. [37]

The spirited German-American neutrality crusade — which appeared to rise in stridency as American relations with Germany deteriorated — created a legacy of ill will that would inflict considerable pain on German Americans following the declaration of war on Germany. For the time being, however, other groups joined the antiwar campaign. Scandinavian-American opinion, particularly within the Swedish sector, remained staunchly neutralist. [38]

Reaction to the German-American neutrality crusade, coupled with a fear that in a perilous world the United States needed more solidarity than its ethnic diversity permitted, sparked a campaign against "hyphenated Americanism" in 1915. Given the size of Minnesota's foreign-born population, this development had ominous implications for the state. An estimated 70 percent of Minnesota's population, according to the state census of 1905, was either foreign-born or the progeny of foreign-born parents. Within this group, which included more than a score of nationalities, persons of German origin were the most numerous; Norwegians and Swedes, whose numerical count was about equal, ranked second and third. A wide gap separated the "big three" — who accounted for 43 percent of the state's population — from the fourth largest group, the Canadians. Irish, Danes, English, Finns, South Slavs (labeled as "Austrians" in the census), and Bohemians (probably also including other Czech people and Bohemians of German descent) followed in that approximate order. [39]

The sheer size of this foreign-born population, and its tendency to settle in both rural and urban ethnic enclaves, encouraged a higher degree of cultural pluralism than seemed consistent with prevailing assimilationist norms. Nevertheless, except for a brief upsurge of anti-foreign agitation in the 1890s, the pre-1914 climate of opinion gave wide latitude to ethnic diversity. Early in the state's history, when more population was perceived as a key to economic development, both government and the private sector had labored mightily to encourage immigration from overseas, particularly from Germany and Scandinavia. Thousands responded to the lure of the American dream. Before many decades had passed, the foreign-born element had established itself as a significant component within the social, economic, and political structure of the state. From time to time the clash of immigrant and old-stock American values on such questions as regulation of the liquor trade, public education, and Sabbath observance generated unpleasant tensions, but politicians found it inexpedient to crusade against groups armed with voting power, and the private sector maintained a healthy respect for immigrant market power.

Outbreak of the hyphenist controversy disturbed the tolerable coexistence that had characterized Minnesota's interethnic relations. Throughout 1915 and 1916 the issue was hotly debated in the press and other forums. Most Twin Cities papers, with the *Minneapolis Journal* in the lead, adopted an antihyphenist line. In a May 29, 1915, editorial entitled "The Hyphen Must Go," the *Journal* deplored the inefficiency of the melting pot within Minnesota and its neighboring states. Throughout the region countless schools, societies, and newspapers still had not adopted English as their language of communication. In the following months the *Journal* returned to this theme time and again. On June 8, 1916, it proclaimed: "A people speaking one language are a unity; speaking two languages, they are a division. Americans in their optimism have felt they could ignore what no other nation can afford to ignore."[40]

The German- and Scandinavian-language press, on the other hand, contended that American culture was as yet unformed: in other words, the proverbial melting pot was still cooking. It followed that so-called 100 percent Americanism was in reality Anglo-Americanism, preoccupied as it was with promoting the universal adoption of the English language. One German-American advocate promised that his people would abandon the hyphen when Anglo-Americans did so. Meanwhile, he added, "Let the exodus of Anglo-Americans start at once! Let all those people go who think that America is a new England."[41]

If ethnicity powerfully influenced attitudes on American foreign policy, so did class. To judge by the editorial line of country newspapers, rural and small-town Minnesota was strongly committed to neutralism. A large Scandinavian and German presence outside the metropolitan areas undoubtedly encouraged this stance, but there were other factors. A sharp rise in the cost of living in 1915 and 1916 reduced the significance of higher prices for agricultural commodities, and farmers seeking to enhance their prosperity by expanding their operations encountered a credit stringency that could easily be attributed to appropriation of available capital by foreign loans. In dismissing the thesis that the war was promoting American prosperity, one small-town weekly paper commented: "It would be nearer the truth to say that some of the munition factories of the United States are making money out of the war. Most everybody else is paying extortionate prices for life's necessities."[42]

During the period of American neutrality, the trade unions were solidly noninterventionist. In a piece appearing on June 26, 1915, the Duluth *Labor World* estimated that a majority of trade unionists favored "peace at any price," a position with which the editor disagreed.[43] Among the factors shaping this attitude, none was more important than a deadly fear of the preparedness program being pushed by advocates of a "firm" policy toward Germany. In early 1916 Henry L. Stimson, an ardent preparedness advocate who had served as secretary of war under Taft and would hold the same position under Franklin D. Roosevelt, regretfully observed that the American worker did not regard "the militiaman as a citizen, training to perform his duty of defending the country in case of real war." Instead the wage earner perceived the guardsman "as a representative of capital, being trained as a policeman against labor."[44]

Obviously, the business elites of the Twin Cities entertained no such fears. Moreover, as the months passed the Minneapolis and St. Paul daily papers (with the notable exception of the *St. Paul Daily News*) moved perceptibly away from the strong neutralist commitment they had articulated in August 1914. Among explanations for this trend, one of the most intriguing was offered in June 1917 by Randolph S. Bourne, the radical essayist of the World War I period. According to Bourne,

> the nerve of the war-feeling centred . . . in the richer and older classes of the Atlantic seaboard, and was keenest where there were French or English business and particularly social connections. The sentiment then spread over the country as a class-phenomenon, touching everywhere those upper-class elements in each section who identified themselves with this Eastern ruling group. . . . [I]n every community it was the least liberal and least democratic elements among whom the preparedness and later the war sentiment was found.[45]

Proliferation of National Security League branches throughout the nation in 1915 facilitated the process described by Bourne. Founded in December 1914, the league soon established itself as a powerful pressure group working for greater armed preparedness and a "tougher" American foreign policy, particularly in dealing with Germany. By the autumn of 1915 business leaders in Minneapolis, St. Paul, and Duluth had sponsored the formation of security league branches within their cities. In defining the goals of the organization, Edward W. Decker, president of the Northwestern National Bank and head of the Minneapolis chapter, expressed a desire "to get at the farmers" and "to break up the insularity of view and get the people thinking about the country as a whole and its situation among the countries of the world." [46]

Establishment of a National Security presence in Minnesota evoked a mixed reaction. Top business leaders extended a warm welcome. Those who spoke for organized labor, including the moderate wing, were less cordial. The *Labor World,* whose editor was a firm supporter of the Wilson administration, wanted to know who was "behind all this propaganda for 'preparedness?'" Duluth, the paper reported, had recently

> entertained one of these itinerant, violent patriots . . . and about twenty of our richest and most influential citizens met him, organized a Security League, contributed some $500 toward his expenses, and were left with the job of "arousing" this particular section of the country to its "danger." [47]

Given the tensions fermenting within the state's political community, the election campaign of 1916 was surprisingly tranquil. The really explosive issues, it seemed, were in a holding pattern that politicians were loath to disturb. From May 1916 through January 1917, relations between the United States and Germany were reasonably free of crisis, thanks to Germany's temporary suspension of unrestricted submarine warfare; and the farmers' movement had not yet achieved sufficient institutional clout to be a major factor.

Outcomes in the major contests appeared to contradict each other. All but one of the incumbent congressmen were reelected despite their unanimous support for the McLemore resolution, which counseled Americans to avoid taking passage on ships bound for war zones. On the other hand, the victory of Frank B. Kellogg in the race for United States senator on a strong preparedness platform appeared to communicate a different message. [48]

Incumbent Republican Governor Joseph A. A. Burnquist (who had succeeded to the office following the death of Hammond ten months earlier) won a smashing victory in his bid for election in his own right, a result attributable to an almost complete disarray within the Minnesota Democratic party. Surprisingly, however, this disarray did not preclude a strong Democratic showing in the presidential contest. Wilson failed to carry Minnesota, but the Republican margin was exceedingly thin: fewer than four hundred votes. Clearly the peace plus progressivism appeal that eked out a narrow Wilson victory nationally also attracted a substantial constituency within Minnesota. Unfortunately, neither peace nor progressivism would fare well in the immediate future.

A Promise Unfulfilled

"**H**armony Reigns in New Legislature," proclaimed the *St. Paul Daily News* on January 2, 1917, the opening day of the state's fortieth legislative session. [1] Before the legislators assembled, some observers had anticipated a lively contest for the speakership of the House of Representatives. Recent Nonpartisan League triumphs in North Dakota, as well as the enthusiastic response of western Minnesota wheat growers to NPL recruitment efforts, encouraged "farmer" legislators to back Magnus Johnson of Meeker County for the speakership. Johnson, who in the 1920s would attract nationwide attention as Minnesota's colorful United States senator, was already a leader of the farmers' movement, having served as an official in several enterprises linked to the American Society of Equity.

Johnson's candidacy failed to gain sufficient momentum, however, to counteract what one journalist called a "stampede" to Ralph J. Parker of Spring Valley, former county attorney for Fillmore County. When this became clear Johnson withdrew from the race, as did another candidate, Charles J. Warner. Before doing so, however, they exacted a price: a promise that Parker would be deferential to the farmers' movement when appointing the Grain and Warehouse Committee. Parker, who was perceived as a consensus candidate, won the election on January 2 by a nearly unanimous vote. Only two members, Ernest G. Strand of Two Harbors and Andrew O. Devold of Minneapolis, both Socialists, declined to vote for the Spring Valley man. [2]

On the next day Governor Burnquist delivered his inaugural message to a joint session of the legislature. The program he laid out was ambitious. Among other things, the message recommended submission of a statewide prohibition amendment to the voters in the 1918 election; woman suffrage; more generous appropriations for public health with emphasis on prevention of illness; "earnest attention" to a forthcoming report of a gubernatorial child welfare

Magnus Johnson with his wife Harriet and their children on the family's Meeker County farm, about 1920

commission; several conservation measures; and continuation of an effort begun under previous administrations to streamline state government. The message also noted "considerable criticism" of the existing grain marketing system without, however, suggesting specific corrective measures. Coupled with these recommendations were approving references to what already had been accomplished in such areas as workers' compensation, factory inspection, and regulation of working hours. Unrestrained economic freedom, Burnquist implied, was yielding to the imperatives of social justice. [3]

As the term was understood in 1917, Burnquist's message was decidedly progressive. A *St. Paul Daily News* columnist characterized it as "the most progressive message any governor has handed out yet," adding, "It sounded like the Joe Burnquist who used to be in the house." [4] In other words, Burnquist appeared to be returning to his roots. As a young legislator representing a St. Paul district in the 1909 and 1911 sessions, he had gained a reputation as an advanced progressive, a reputation based in part on his vigorous promotion of social

*Governor
Joseph A. A.
Burnquist, 1917*

justice legislation and in part on his militant opposition to the Smith-Eberhart machine.

Despite the euphoria generated by the harmonious launching of the 1917 legislative session, hopes that the session would be exceptionally productive were exaggerated. Structurally both the Senate and House lacked cohesion. The 1913 session had placed the election of members on a nonpartisan basis, thereby liquidating the traditional partisan caucuses. As a result, neither body had a majority caucus capable of exerting leadership in support of a unified program. In 1915 the county option issue had precipitated the organization of a two-caucus arrangement in the House, but in 1917 no single issue enjoyed the same priority. The virtually unanimous election of Parker to the speakership suggests an intention to legislate by consensus.

Unfortunately, Parker and Burnquist lacked the leadership qualities required by a consensus arrangement. Moreover, it is doubtful that even the most inspired leadership would have sufficed in the early months of 1917. Lying beneath the surface of state politics were the ugly tensions described in the last chapter, tensions that politicians on the state level had deftly managed to contain for several years. The diplomatic break with Germany in February 1917 and the subsequent entry of the United States into the war would create a situation wherein they could no longer be contained.

Surprising as it may seem in retrospect, to the general public the possibility of an early break with Germany seemed remote in early January 1917. On January 8 the *St. Paul Pioneer Press* reported on the front page that a dinner had been held in Berlin the previous evening honoring the United States ambassador to Germany, James W. Gerard. According to the story, the event was a veritable love feast graced by the presence of the German vice chancellor, the foreign secretary, and the director of the Deutsche Bank. The Germans lavished compliments on Gerard, who responded by declaring that "never since the beginning of the war have relations between Germany and the United States been so cordial."[5]

A *St. Paul Pioneer Press* editorial on January 7 noted the highly visible farmer presence within the new legislature. Unlike earlier sessions, bills addressing agricultural grievances were taking priority over antiliquor legislation. An upbeat Equity convention held in December had raised morale, encouraging farm groups to organize what promised to be an effective lobby. Within the legislature a group of about fifty Senate and House members established a caucus called the Farmers' Forum. Announcement that NPL headquarters would soon be transferred from Fargo to St. Paul strengthened the impression that agriculture's political influence was growing. When the NPL move was made in mid-February the *St. Paul Daily News* exulted: "St. Paul today becomes the political center of all rural America."[6]

No one could doubt that the Nonpartisan League was becoming a potent force in Minnesota politics. The league-dominated North Dakota legislature was demonstrating to the world that Townley's movement was not a passing fad, but a dynamic crusade fired by zealous determination to achieve its declared objectives. Those who spoke for the Minneapolis-based grain trade expressed deep alarm. A *Commercial West* editorial appearing on February 3 (the same day that President Wilson severed diplomatic relations with Germany) quoted "a prominent citizen of North Dakota" as saying that capital in his state found itself "under the gun" to such an extent that "bankers and prosperous citizens, other than farmers" found it expedient to avoid "unnecessary attention." NPL organizational progress in northern Minnesota, the editorial continued, was bringing the peril dangerously close to the Twin Cities. The editorial issued a call to arms: "Isn't it high time that something be done?"[7]

Although small-town progressives were less alarmist than the editors of *Commercial West,* they too responded to the NPL movement with caution. In reacting to a Townley speech that did not entirely displease him, Gunnar Björnson editorialized: "Personally we should have liked to have heard him come out stronger than he did for cooperation and unity between and among the farmers and the people of the small towns."[8] Björnson's reservation understated a significant reality: the adversarial relationship between the NPL and the state's small-town elites, whose role in the progressive movement had been significant. The league was a movement by, for, and of "producers" — in other words, farmers and wage earners. Bankers, lawyers, and merchants were not numbered among God's chosen people. The services of country editors might be welcomed, but only if their papers sacrificed editorial independence by submitting unconditionally to the Townley line. Worse yet, the league threatened small-town business enterprise with murderous competition. Its program envisaged creation of a network of cooperative enterprises that could succeed only at the expense of existing small-town firms. The impact of this adversarial relationship was already crystal clear in North Dakota. According to historian Edward C. Blackorby, many progressives in that state had been "frightened by the rural radicals into an alliance with the right-wing Stalwarts."[9] The same trend would soon appear in Minnesota.

Until late January, when a nasty rift disrupted harmony within the House agricultural bloc, prospects that the immediate goals of the farm lobby would be realized appeared bright. Although Speaker Parker's appointments to the Grain and Warehouse Committee sparked some dissatisfaction, the naming of Magnus Johnson to the chairmanship was reassuring. No one could doubt that Johnson was both a "real" farmer and an aggressive champion of agriculture's interests. Moreover, twelve of the committee's nineteen members listed farming as their occupation, leaving only one grain trader, one banker, two real estate agents, one merchant, one lawyer, and one manager of a Minneapolis rebate firm. Not all of the farmers on the committee were sympathetic to Equity or to the Nonpartisan League, but several besides Johnson would shortly become NPL activists.[10]

Dissension within the farmers' bloc became evident on January 25 when Austin F. Teigen, an Equity activist from Chippewa County, introduced a resolution calling for the appointment of a special committee to undertake a thorough investigation of agricultural marketing in Minnesota. The resolution charged that the Minneapolis Chamber of Commerce and the Duluth Board of Trade, "because of their rules, regulations, methods, abuse of privilege, violations and evasions of law and usurpation of power, are being generally and bitterly criticized throughout the Northwest." Such rhetoric succinctly capsuled the farmers' bill of complaints against the commercial exchanges. However, the resolution also focused suspicion on Equity, asserting that "the Equity Co-operative Exchange . . . is grossly mismanaged . . . resulting in heavy losses to farmer shippers."[11]

Bringing the Equity Cooperative Exchange within the scope of the proposed investigation was a serious affront to many in the farmers' movement — and all the more so because the language of the resolution bore a striking resemblance to the vitriolic comments of the Minneapolis press. When the resolution reached the House floor, Johnson successfully moved deletion of the paragraphs indicting the Equity exchange.[12] The special committee was then approved by the House, with Teigen named as chairman.

The question of what motivated Teigen to push for this special investigation remained a topic of speculation throughout the session. No doubt he was rankled by his failure to secure membership on the Grain and Warehouse Committee, where he had served during previous sessions. Equity representatives attributed his hostility to his failure to win a post within their organization.[13] In any case, his special committee put on an unimpressive performance. Its sessions were marred by acrimonious exchanges between advocates of the farmers' movement and representatives of the established grain trade and by hostile confrontations between Teigen and Equity leaders. The final report, released in the closing hours of the session, combined an apologia for the inadequacies of the investigation with a few tentative suggestions aimed at improving state regulation of the grain trade and a dismissal of the more heinous charges against the Equity Cooperative Exchange.[14]

Meanwhile the Grain and Warehouse Committee was enjoying only limited success in winning legislative acceptance of its program. Two bills tightening the state grain inspection system became law, as did one prohibiting discrimination between localities in the purchase of grain — a measure designed to protect locally owned country elevators, which included cooperatives, from unequal line elevator competition. On the other hand, several attempts to legislate against trading in futures failed, and so did an effort to initiate a constitutional amendment permitting the state to construct and operate "facilities for storing and handling fuel, food products, grain and other such necessities of life." A bill calling for establishment of an interim commission to investigate the grain trade passed the House but was indefinitely postponed by the Senate. [15]

All in all, the 1917 legislative session yielded more satisfaction to the established grain trade than to the farmers' movement. However, those who spoke for the grain trade were not inclined to let down their guard. It was possible that the internal rift that had reduced the effectiveness of the farm bloc would be healed, and in any case the Nonpartisan League was gaining the allegiance of thousands of farmers. Given NPL potential, one need not be surprised that the league's adversaries stood ready to take full advantage of any NPL vulnerability that might surface. Before the 1917 session adjourned, NPL opposition to United States entry into the Great War created a dangerous vulnerability.

In June 1916 a spontaneous walkout closed most of the iron mines on the Mesabi Range within a week. Despite the organizing skills of leading IWW activists like Carlo Tresca and Elizabeth Gurley Flynn, who arrived to assist the miners in their cause, the strike collapsed by September. In its failure to establish a union to compel employers to improve working conditions, the strike was similar to its 1907 predecessor. There was an important difference, however: a decade before, the miners had stood alone, whereas by 1916 they enjoyed a measure of middle-class sympathy. Citizens in range towns had their own grievances against the mining companies. Independent investigations by organizations committed to social justice also demonstrated that poor working conditions — particularly abuses inherent in the contract wage system — had done more to precipitate the strike than the efforts of "outside agitators" linked to the IWW. Obviously, the IWW had played a role, but only after the strike had erupted. [16]

Miners and their supporters marching during the strike on the Mesabi Range, 1916

These findings reached a respectable reading audience via the columns of the state's liberal and labor press. Some commentators continued to argue that IWW instigation was the factor precipitating the strike, whereas others focused on the plight of the miners. According to the *St. Paul Daily News,* for example, "The state cannot afford to permit . . . conditions which will make it sure that the miners and their families must always be human clods." Although the Minnesota Federation of Labor declined on jurisdictional grounds to assume leadership of the strike, it, too, gave the miners vigorous moral support. In response to federation demands, the Minnesota Department of Labor and Industries conducted an investigation whose findings validated many of the miners' complaints without absolving the IWW from all responsibility for the conduct of the strike. [17]

On December 28, 1916 — less than a week before the 1917 legislative session convened — a strike organized by the Metal Mine Workers' Industrial Union No. 490, an IWW local that had been created the summer before during the miners' strike, severely curtailed production at the Virginia mill of the Virginia and Rainy Lake Lumber Company. Since this company operated the world's largest white pine mill and combined the interests of several giant lumber enterprises (including the Weyerhaeusers), the strike was more than a minor skirmish. It was an affront to the intransigent anti-union stance of the lumber industry, as well as a test of the effectiveness of the IWW in a major strike situation. [18]

Four days later (January 1, 1917) the strike spread to several Virginia and Rainy Lake Company camps and to nine camps of the International Lumber Company, whose mill at International Falls also was crippled when mill workers walked out. The possibility that a lumberjack strike could succeed had been enhanced by the presence in northern Minnesota of job delegates sent there by the Agricultural Workers Organization, the IWW branch headquartered in Minneapolis. The lumberjack walkout was more than a move in support of the mill workers; with the assistance of the AWO job delegates, the jacks confronted management with a set of demands covering both pay and working conditions — demands that were far from unreasonable. [19]

According to historian John E. Haynes, "the first few days of the strike were surprisingly successful. . . . Both companies ceased all logging operations." However, the local press, whose editorial bias was predominantly promanagement, conveyed an opposite impression, an impression echoed by some of the Twin Cities papers. At the same time, press coverage spared no effort in depicting the strike as a terrorist venture that would, in the words of the *Daily Virginian,* stop at "nothing short of arson and murder." Although these lurid stories lacked substantiation and were later disproved, they "served as an effective smoke screen for lumber company officials and co-operating lawmen while they moved to break the strike."

Among the "co-operating lawmen," the sheriffs of St. Louis, Carlton, Beltrami, Itasca, and Koochiching counties, along with municipal authorities in Virginia and Eveleth, were especially conspicuous. In the first days of the strike, the sheriffs swore in hundreds of deputies who, in Haynes's words, "operated under direct orders of lumber company officials" — a logical arrangement "since the companies paid most of the deputies' salaries." Eveleth officials simply "ordered all active IWW members to leave town or face arrest," a strategy that worked. On January 2 the police and fire commission of Virginia "classified all Wobbly militants as 'undesirables' and ordered them to leave town by 4 P.M. the next day or face arrest." Recalcitrants who defied the banishment order were rounded up and charged with vagrancy. "By the middle of January virtually every IWW organizer

SMOKING HIM OUT.

A political cartoon in the Duluth News Tribune, *January 3, 1917, linked the Industrial Workers of the World with striking northern Minnesota lumberjacks.*

or militant [in Virginia] was either in exile or in jail." As might be expected, the strike also was broken. [20]

The impact of the strike on public opinion throughout Minnesota is difficult to gauge. Although many newspapers applauded the IWW expulsion policy, a number of influential journals — notably the *St. Paul Dispatch* — characterized the actions of the Virginia authorities as undemocratic and unconstitutional. At the same time, those who applauded suppression wondered if the IWW was really a spent force. Reports that the sawmills and timber camps were experiencing difficulty in recruiting workers fostered a suspicion that IWW militants were covertly or overtly intimidating laborers wanting to work.[21] An alternative explanation argued that miserable working conditions, particularly in the camps, discouraged men from seeking jobs in timber, especially at a time when other employment was available. The fact that in early 1917 the companies reformed conditions in the camps lends some credibility to this thesis.

The immediate response of state government to the strike was anything but decisive. After receiving complaints from representatives of the logging companies, Governor Burnquist promised to investigate IWW activity. However, his sense of urgency was not extreme. On January 3 he announced, "I will get in touch with the situation and in due time decide what's to be done. . . . I have no reason to believe at present that [the sheriff] is not doing his duty." Perhaps the governor wanted to avoid stirring up the kind of protest that had followed his intervention in the 1916 miners' strike, when labor activists had accused him of favoring management.[22]

A week later Senator Ellis J. Westlake, a Minneapolis conservative, introduced a resolution calling for a joint Senate-House investigation of the IWW and of working conditions in northern Minnesota. Legislators sympathetic to labor, led by Senator Richard Jones of Duluth, countered with a plan for a wide-ranging investigation of working conditions throughout Minnesota, a proposal reflecting a suspicion that a dismal workplace environment rather than IWW instigation was responsible for the current turmoil.[23]

The committee weighing these proposals declined to recommend the kind of investigation sought by Jones. Instead it formulated a bill "forbidding the causing, soliciting or threatening of the commission of crime and providing for the appointment and payment of special deputy sheriffs . . . to prevent or punish criminal violence" (Senate File 152). Action on SF152 was expeditious. On January 17 it was introduced, given its first and second readings, and placed on general orders — a succession of moves requiring suspension of the rules. A week later the Committee on Finance recommended an appropriation of fifty thousand dollars as a compensation fund for the special deputy sheriffs.[24]

On the same day — January 24, and again under a suspension of the rules — the bill was brought to the Senate floor for a vote. Two significant amendments emerged. The first, introduced by William A. Campbell, who represented a Minneapolis labor district, required that the deputies appointed be state residents. The second, introduced by Anton J. Rockne of Zumbrota, the famed watchdog of the Minnesota treasury, placed a top limit of one hundred thousand dollars on the appropriation, with half to be available immediately and the remaining fifty thousand dollars on July 31, 1918. Both amendments passed. On the final vote, only three senators opposed the bill. All three — Rockne, James A. Carley, and John W. Andrews — were southern Minnesota fiscal conservatives predisposed against spending money. Carl J. Buell, a veteran legislative watcher, commented that Rockne and Andrews "took the stand that there was no good reason why those northern counties, enormously rich in natural resources, should call on the rest of the state to help them take care of their local matters . . . [and] Rockne insisted that if the workers were treated fairly, there would be no strike and no trouble."[25] Curiously, several "liberal" senators, including Jones and Campbell, voted for SF152, apparently hoping that its enactment would promote the investigation they desired.

When formal announcement of Senate passage of SF152 reached the House on January 25, friends of the labor movement had become deeply suspicious of the measure: the appropriation for state-paid deputies was perceived, according to Buell, as "an entering wedge for the establishment of a State Constabulary," an institution bitterly opposed by the trade unions. Depending on how the language of the proposed statute was interpreted, the proscribed "crimes" could include such accepted strike tactics as picketing. On January 26 Representative William D. Washburn, Jr., whose district included several Minneapolis working-class precincts, "surprised many people," Buell reported, by introducing a resolution directing the House Committee on Labor and Labor Legislation to conduct a comprehensive investigation of labor conditions in the mines and lumber camps of northern Minnesota. In explaining the motives impelling him to sponsor the resolution, Washburn was quoted in a newspaper as saying: "I do not know anything about the IWW, and I do not want to antagonize them. I want to find out what labor and capital both have to say about conditions in Northern Minnesota, and it is with the idea of finding out the real situation that I offer this resolution."[26]

The 1917 probe that resulted from the Washburn resolution deserves high marks both for fairness and thoroughness. Operating

with a competent staff, the labor committee permitted both the IWW
and representatives of the employers to subpoena and cross-examine
witnesses; moreover, extensive press coverage provided the reading
public with a day-to-day account of the hearings. Before long several
patterns began to emerge. For one thing, IWW representatives focused
on the specific grievances of working people in the forests, sawmills,
and mines; management advocates, on the other hand, preferred to
underscore IWW ideology, stressing particularly the organization's commitment to revolutionary goals. [27]

For another, IWW advocates appeared more practiced in the ways
of civility than their adversaries. On occasion — and particularly in
the opening days of the investigation — attorneys for the timber interests refused to answer questions put to them by the IWW people;
one of the former "became so abusive at one of the hearings, that
he was forced by the Committee to apologize before he would be permitted to continue in his capacity as attorney." By contrast Joseph
Ettor, a leading IWW spokesman, "showed himself to be a keen, shrewd,
good natured and intelligent gentleman." Some contemporary
observers believed that these contrasting patterns were having a significant impact on public opinion. "Little by little, as the investigation proceeded," wrote one prominent publicist, "it began to appear
that the workers were more sinned against than sinning." [28]

While the House IWW investigation was in progress, two bills
similar in intent to SF152 emerged in the Senate. The first, introduced
by George M. Peterson of Duluth on February 8, in effect legitimated
the tactics employed by local authorities in the recent timber workers'
strike. Peterson's bill empowered the sheriff of any county to order
"vagrants or disorderly persons" to leave the county within twenty-
four hours. A person failing to comply with the order could be jailed
for vagrancy and confined until satisfactory proof could be submitted in municipal court that he or she was not a vagrant. A week later
Senator Francis A. Duxbury of Caledonia introduced a bill that virtually outlawed peaceful picketing and forbade the distribution of
notices announcing a strike or boycott. [29]

Significantly, neither bill proceeded very far in the legislative process. On March 14 the Committee on Judiciary, to which the Peterson bill had been referred, reported the measure back to the full Senate
with a recommendation that it be indefinitely postponed, a report
adopted by that body. After receiving its first reading, the Duxbury

bill was referred to the Committee on General Legislation where it slumbered for the remainder of the 1917 session.

Meanwhile, SF152 (the anti-IWW bill passed by the Senate) encountered stiff opposition in the House. It remained in the hands of the House labor committee, where it was subjected to extensive hearings, until the closing days of the legislative session. By the time it was recalled from the committee (April 4), pressure for the enactment of SF152 had abated. According to Buell, its burial was assured when Governor Burnquist stated in an interview that "he was not willing to father responsibility for the appropriation."[30]

The demise of SF152, the short shrift given the Peterson and Duxbury bills, and the apparent impact of the IWW investigation were viewed with satisfaction by commentators sympathetic to trade unionism. In addition, unionism could claim a few positive gains. Early in the session Thomas J. McGrath of St. Paul, a leader of the House labor bloc, introduced a bill affirming the legality of labor organizations, declaring that labor was not a commodity, and limiting the issuance of court injunctions in labor disputes to situations that threatened "irreparable" damage to property for which the law provided no remedy. This was a moderate piece of legislation, similar in language and intent to the provisions of the federal Clayton Act of 1914 relating to organized labor, and, like the Clayton Act, more symbolic than substantive.[31]

Nevertheless, the McGrath bill encountered determined opposition from the more intransigent foes of unionism. Following addition of an amendment affirming the authority of the executive and the courts to act against "criminal syndicalism," the House passed the measure by a vote of seventy-seven to forty-seven. When it reached the Senate that body's judiciary committee recommended indefinite postponement, a recommendation that the Senate declined to adopt. Labor had scored a point, but since the session was in its closing hours, final passage appeared highly unlikely. However, Senator Jones secured a suspension of the rules, clearing the way for a final vote. Despite last-minute lobbying by employer groups and fierce attacks on the measure by such influential senators as George H. Sullivan, the Senate passed the bill by a vote of thirty-six to twenty-five and Governor Burnquist signed it into law.[32]

The record of the 1917 session on labor legislation seemed to indicate that trade-union power was becoming a factor of some importance in state politics. Nor was the session entirely displeasing to other reformers. Enactment of an enlightened children's code suggested that social justice progressivism was still alive and well. Although an ambitious effort to enact a tonnage tax on iron ore failed (the bill passed the House but was defeated in the Senate), the probability that such a measure would prevail in 1919 encouraged its proponents. Defeat of a state woman suffrage amendment was not a true reflection of the strength of the women's movement. Many supporters within the dry movement assigned immediate priority to a state prohibition amendment, which they feared would be imperiled if a woman suffrage amendment also appeared on the ballot in the 1918 general election; moreover, woman suffrage appeared to be making progress on the federal level. All in all, many "left-of-center" publicists professed to be pleased with the legislature's performance. Buell commented: "The legislature of 1917 is generally conceded by all competent observers to have been the best that ever sat in the State of Minnesota — the best in the sense of having the largest percentage of clean, honest, intelligent and independent men, who gave careful study to every question, refused to vote until they understood, and then cast their ballot according to their honest convictions."[33]

Such an assessment was premature. Under the pressures that boiled to the surface as the United States moved toward hostilities with Germany, the legislature in its closing days passed and the governor signed a package of three bills that effectively undermined several of the modest gains that House and Senate reformers believed they had won in the course of the session. Of the three, the one creating the Minnesota Commission of Public Safety was the most far-reaching in its implications.

CHAPTER THREE

A Package of Three Bills

P resident Woodrow Wilson severed diplomatic relations with Germany on February 3, 1917, a few days after that nation resumed unrestricted submarine warfare. This event ended a period of comparative calm in Minnesota regarding issues linked to American foreign policy. Although tensions surrounding the controversy over "hyphenated Americanism" and the proper American response to German "barbarism" did not reach a flash point for several weeks, it was soon evident that Minnesota lacked a consensus on either. [1]

For a time widespread acceptance of the slogan "Stand by the President" obscured deep divisions among Americans on the fateful question of war or peace. What did the slogan mean? To be sure, Wilson had broken diplomatic relations with Germany, but this did not necessarily commit his administration to full-scale war. Some observers favored a limited naval war, focusing on the defense of American cargo ships on the Atlantic Ocean, whereas others advocated a continuing search for a diplomatic solution. So long as Wilson's course remained unclear, persons of conflicting persuasions could "stand by" their president in the belief that their preferred course was the one he would adopt. [2]

A few intrepid individuals flatly rejected this ethos, a stance that provoked a furious reaction from those who accepted or perhaps welcomed the inevitability of war. Shortly after the diplomatic break with Germany, Mayor Van Lear of Minneapolis issued a statement taking sharp issue with the demand that everyone "follow the flag" and "back the president." The flag, Van Lear declared, sometimes had been used to legitimate cruel repression, as in the 1914 labor disturbances at Ludlow, Colorado, where the mission of its bearers had been 'to shoot the helpless women and babies of the striking miners." Nor could Van Lear back a president who, in his opinion, had been unduly provocative in breaking relations with Germany. [3]

*Thomas Van Lear, mayor
of Minneapolis in 1917–18*

The Van Lear statement evoked an extremely hostile reaction from the Minneapolis business community. The *Minneapolis Tribune* challenged the mayor's authority to speak for the city. Van Lear responded by calling a mass meeting in the Minneapolis Auditorium on February 10 to demonstrate that his antiwar position commanded overwhelming popular support. The rally may not have vindicated Van Lear's authority to "speak for Minneapolis" on issues of foreign policy, but it did prove the existence of widespread antiwar sentiment within the city — estimates of the crowd varied from five thousand to what *New Times* called an "immense throng of nearly 25,000." Those who failed to gain admittance held an overflow meeting on a nearby street corner. On the same day — presumably in the afternoon — Socialists held two "well-attended" antiwar meetings, one at the Minneapolis courthouse and the other at Minnehaha Hall in St. Paul. [4]

As might be expected, the February 10 meetings energized those who wanted to stand by the president. On the next day they sponsored a counter rally that also met in the Minneapolis Auditorium. Again the size of the crowd exceeded the auditorium's seating capacity, and the overflow gathered in neighboring churches. After hearing "stirring addresses" by such individuals as Cyrus Northrop, the venerable president emeritus of the University of Minnesota, and Maria L. Sanford, the popular retired university professor, the auditorium crowd shouted approval of the Minneapolis Loyalty League, an organization founded a few days earlier under the auspices of the Minneapolis Civic and Commerce Association. Many of those present also signed a statement pledging support of the president. Loyalty league officials solicited additional signatures, and the statement was forwarded to President Wilson with some thirty-six thousand signatures attached. [5]

Although the competing rallies generated considerable emotion, the gap between the positions they represented was not as wide as it would be a few months later. To be sure, several speakers at the Van Lear meeting argued for "peace at any price," but one speaker equated working for peace in the present crisis with "standing by the president" because peace, a top Wilsonian objective, was not being served by the current agitation for war. The keynote of the other rally, according to historians Franklin F. Holbrook and Livia Appel, "was an appeal to 'stand by President Wilson,' but there was little ungenerous criticism of those opposed to his policies." "We all want peace," declared Northrop, president of the loyalty league, "but peace without dishonor." Coming from a man who was a lifelong peace advocate, this statement did not sound like a strident call to arms. [6]

Before February gave way to March, loyalty leagues proliferated throughout Minnesota; many of them were initiated by local chambers of commerce. The most influential was the St. Paul Patriotic League, the origins of which dated from a meeting sponsored by St. Paul business and civic leaders in late January to protest German deportations of Belgians from their homeland. Although ostensibly not an elitist organization, the St. Paul league reflected the views of the city's top business executives and professional people. Charles W. Farnham, an attorney to whom Governor Burnquist was extraordinarily deferential, was its president, and Ambrose Tighe — later the counsel for the Minnesota Commission of Public Safety — and corporation lawyer Pierce Butler were among its founding members. The league's purpose was "to promote that spirit of true patriotism which calls for the readiness and the courage, in the pending controversy with

Germany, or in any other emergency, to defend American rights, American ideals and American honor."[7]

From the day it was formed the St. Paul Patriotic League became an advocate of a firm, uncompromising policy toward Germany, a role that grew as relations between the United States and the imperial government deteriorated. On February 25 British intelligence provided President Wilson with the text of the famous Zimmermann telegram, in which German foreign secretary Arthur Zimmermann proposed that, in the event of war between Germany and the United States, Mexico form an alliance with Germany with the prospect of recovering lands lost to the United States in 1848. On February 26 a German submarine sank the armed British liner *Laconia,* a disaster that cost two American lives, among others. On the same day the president requested authorization from Congress to arm American merchant ships, a step taken to avert a slump in the American export trade caused by the unwillingness of shippers to hazard the submarine-infested Atlantic without protection.[8]

Within hours an armed ship bill was on the congressional agenda. Following a spirited debate on March 1 in which, wrote historian Arthur S. Link, "members vied with one another in expressions of patriotism and denunciations of Germany," the House of Representatives approved the measure by a vote of 403 to 13 — undoubtedly release of the Zimmermann text on the morning of March 1 contributed to this lopsided margin. In the other chamber four senators conducted a filibuster for the purpose of blocking consideration of the measure until the automatic expiration of the Sixty-fourth Congress at noon on March 4 would kill the bill, a tactic that worked. Shortly after the Senate adjourned, proponents of armed neutrality circulated a statement permitting senators who would have voted for the measure to place themselves on record as favoring it by signing the statement. Eleven senators, including the four who had conducted the filibuster, declined to sign. Unfortunately and unjustly, the seven who had not been participants in the filibuster — including Moses E. Clapp of Minnesota — were perceived as members of the filibustering group, an impression heightened by Wilson's excoriation of the eleven as "a little group of willful men [who had] rendered the great Government of the United States helpless and contemptible." This outburst overstated the administration's difficulties. Within a few days Wilson instituted armed neutrality by executive order, an action clearly within the bounds of presidential authority.

The St. Paul Patriotic League manifested a lively interest in the armed neutrality issue. At a March 3 meeting it passed a resolution characterizing the votes of Minnesota congressmen Charles R. Davis and Charles A. Lindbergh, Sr., against the armed ship bill as "un-American, unjustifiable and cowardly." A week later the league commended Wilson for instituting armed neutrality and congratulated the town of Lansford, Pennsylvania, "for having a citizenry sufficiently patriotic to deny . . . hospitality to Sen. Moses Clapp," who also had opposed the armed ship bill. At the same meeting several speakers deplored the lack of "militant patriotism" in St. Paul. [9]

The league also launched a campaign designed to energize St. Paul patriotism through a massive display of United States flags. On March 7 Farnham asked Governor Burnquist to issue a proclamation "calling upon all public officers to raise flags upon all public buildings and school houses, and making the same suggestion to citizens." Burnquist responded by providing Farnham with a copy of a speech to be delivered on March 8 in which he would "refer to this matter," implying that the speech would obviate the need for a proclamation. "I venture to renew the request," Farnham replied. On March 11 the governor complied by issuing an official proclamation tailored to Farnham's specifications. This action pleased the patriotic league president, but one gap remained: "the masts on the Capitol Building [had] no flags on them." Burnquist hesitated to break with a long-standing custom of displaying a flag on one mast when the legislature was in session and on the other when the supreme court was sitting. However, on March 13 he again complied. By now only one irritant remained: the Capitol flags were lowered earlier in the day than flags in other parts of the city. Unfortunately the limits of gubernatorial authority had been reached: state law specified when flags on state buildings should be raised and lowered. [10]

Some Minnesotans responded to the patriotic league's flag crusade with less deference than the governor. "How patriotic are the patriots?" asked a March 11 letter writer to the *St. Paul Daily News*. The writer claimed to be "one of those who retain enough '1776 patriotism' to know that the American flag is being wallowed in the mire by big business just as it was in the war with Spain." He suggested that members of the league could make their patriotic claims credible by individually assigning their entire fortunes to the government effective "the moment war is declared." [11]

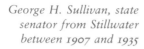

The legislature soon echoed the concerns of the St. Paul Patriotic League. On February 6 Representative Archibald A. Stone of Stevens County introduced a bill requiring boards of education "to provide an appropriate United States flag for and the display thereof at every school in its district." Only one House member, John J. Winter of Stearns County, voted against the bill on final passage, and the Senate adopted it unanimously. More controversial was an amendment attached to a related bill about patriotic exercises in the schools. The amendment, championed by Senator George H. Sullivan, required "teaching the necessity for military preparedness by teaching the history of nations which have been conquered and destroyed by reason of their failure to make sufficient military preparation against aggression." [12]

In the words of legislative observer Carl J. Buell, introduction of this amendment opened the "floodgates of oratory." Sullivan delivered "an impassioned speech" in support of his handiwork. Fellow conservative Francis A. Duxbury opposed the bill, partly because he believed it would, according to Buell, "open the door to some text-book maker to sell millions of books at a big profit"; he urged fellow senators to vote for the amendment in the hope that its enactment would doom the bill on final passage. The amendment lost by a vote of thirty-four to twenty-four, and on final passage the unamended bill prevailed by a vote of forty-eight to nine. The nine nays included an intriguing mix of conservatives and liberals. Duxbury, of course, voted nay; so did Richard Jones, one of the Senate's most outspoken liberals. On the other hand, a number of liberals, including several who had spoken out against the Sullivan amendment, voted for the bill. [13]

Beginning in mid-March a series of events accelerated the trend toward war. On March 15 the American public learned that Russia's czarist regime had collapsed and that a provisional government committed to Western constitutionalism had assumed power. The thesis that the European war was a contest between autocracy and democracy now seemed more credible than heretofore; czarist Russia's status as a major partner in the Allied camp had been an embarrassment to those who wanted to perceive the war as a crusade against absolutism. Three days later, according to historian Arthur S. Link, "Washington was rocked . . . by news that German submarines had just destroyed three American ships" — the *City of Memphis,* the *Illinois,* and the *Vigilancia.* This extremely serious provocation cast doubt on the efficacy of armed neutrality; it stirred the nation's war party into greater stridency than ever; and it evidently encouraged many Americans to accept the inevitability of war. On March 21 Wilson issued a call for Congress to meet on April 2 "to receive a communication concerning grave matters of national policy." [14]

Throughout the country most observers correctly inferred that the president had decided to ask Congress to declare war. Reactions varied, depending on the perspective of the person reacting. The *Minneapolis Journal,* which had consistently pressed for a hard line against Germany, said that by virtue of German submarine policy a state of war already existed; all that remained was for Congress to acknowledge this reality. On Sunday March 25 Maurice D. Edwards, a prominent St. Paul Presbyterian clergyman, counseled his parishioners: "We face today not a threatened war, but a state of war. The time for debate and negotiation is past. The time for action is at hand." Another Protestant clergyman, James Robert Smith of the People's Church, was of the same mind. According to Smith, advising "true Americans to try to keep the peace [with] such an enemy as the imperial autocracy . . . is to offer unspeakable insult."[15]

Editorially the *St. Paul Daily News* "stood by the president" but refrained from demanding that peace advocates abandon their antiwar crusade. Its editorial on March 25 carried the plaintive comment: "In these stirring days of 1917 it has become 'treason' to hope to avoid the horrors of war."[16] The *Daily News* also continued to provide balanced coverage of the now beleaguered peace crusade as well as of the activities of the St. Paul Patriotic League, which was extraordinarily energetic in late March and early April.

Although desperately on the defensive, peace advocates apparently believed that their efforts might still avert descent into the abyss. In late March a St. Paul Peace League organized under the auspices of the city's Woman's Socialist Study Club appeared on the scene. This organization, which expired quietly following the declaration of war, sponsored an enthusiastic antiwar rally on March 31 that attracted a crowd of some three thousand — a crowd described by the *Daily News* as "composed of all classes of citizens, including a large number of working men and women." Initially organizers of the rally had hoped to persuade Senator La Follette to deliver the main address. However, the Wisconsin senator was unwilling to leave Washington at such a crucial time, a situation that left the planners dependent on such local celebrities as James A. Peterson of Minneapolis, an attorney who was active in progressive Republican politics.[17]

On March 30 one thousand citizens of New Ulm assembled in that city's armory to hear speeches by City Attorney Albert Pfaender, Mayor Louis A. Fritsche, and Albert Steinhauser, editor of the *New Ulm Review*. The gathering supported resolutions affirming the allegiance of all present to the United States but denying the existence of any "adequate reason" for American entry into the war. A few days later a number of New Ulmites joined a larger peace delegation for a journey to Washington, D.C., for the purpose of making a last-minute plea for peace. Upon their return home members of the New Ulm contingent reported that they had encountered a hostile reception in the capital, although members of the Minnesota congressional delegation had responded courteously enough to their entreaties.[18]

The intense effort mounted by the peace crusaders evoked a strong reaction from the prowar people. The St. Paul Patriotic League held frequent rallies, culminating in a highly publicized gathering on April 5 presided over by Pierce Butler and featuring addresses by Henry L. Stimson and Frederic R. Coudert, a prominent member of the New York bar, who were on a speaking mission throughout the Midwest on behalf of universal military training. Meanwhile, the principal Twin Cities dailies kept up a constant drumfire in favor of intervention.

In the absence of anything resembling scientific polling, it is difficult to ascertain the orientation of majority opinion in Minnesota on the momentous issue facing the nation in early April 1917. Two years later the Minnesota Commission of Public Safety would affirm: "It is hard . . . to realize the indifference, pacifist sentiment and even opposition to the war which prevailed in some parts of Minnesota two years ago."[19] To some extent this assessment could have been self-serving; the commission may have been claiming credit for overcoming obstacles standing in the way of the state's admittedly impressive contribution to the war effort. On the other hand, it is impossible to ignore the many manifestations of opposition to the war up to the time the fateful decision was taken.

A case in point is the vote against the war resolution on April 6 by four members of Minnesota's ten-man congressional delegation — Charles R. Davis of St. Peter, Carl C. Van Dyke of St. Paul (the only Democrat on the delegation), Harold Knutson of St. Cloud, and Ernest Lundeen of Minneapolis. Davis, Van Dyke, and Knutson, who represented districts with substantial German-American populations, easily won reelection in 1918. Popular wisdom held that Lundeen committed political suicide by voting as he did. It may be true that his antiwar stand contributed to a fourteen-year exile from elective office — he made a comeback by winning a congressional seat in the at-large race of 1932 — but his comparatively narrow defeat in the Republican primary of 1918 required an extraordinary effort on the part of the Republican leadership of Hennepin County.[20]

The St. Paul Patriotic League registered strong objection to Van Dyke's vote against the war resolution. Farnham demanded that the congressman resign and stand for reelection, a process that the league offered to fund. Fortified by a commendation for his vote from the St. Paul Trades and Labor Assembly, Van Dyke responded by requesting permission to offer the services of league members to the nation's armed forces. He pointed out that he had served in a three-thousand-man brigade during the Spanish-American War; given the size of its membership, the patriotic league surely could furnish two brigades of similar size. Farnham's reaction was brief but unmistakably to the point: "Tommyrot." He added that the league's male member-ship was not large enough to fill two brigades and that he, Farnham, would never permit his daughter, who was also a member, to serve in the military.[21]

The specter of profound disunity at a time when passage over the brink seemed inevitable generated a mood of hysteria in some quarters. A Mankato woman who prided herself on descent from "old English settlers" feared that her German-American neighbors would burn down her house "or worse." The preceding Sunday night, April 1, she had attended a local German Lutheran church "to hear some special music" and was "shocked to hear [the pastor] tell that great church-ful of simple, believing people that certain men in this country were willing to bring a 'terrible disaster' upon us for the sake of gold." She feared that "if we loyal Americans here are not well protected, that sometime thirty-eight Germans may hang where once the 38 Indians hung."[22]

Distorted as this impression of German-American attitudes may in retrospect appear, there is no reason to disbelieve the Mankato woman's reconstruction of the pastor's remarks: "greed for gold" on the part of the prowar advocates was *the* stock German-American argument up until the United States entered the war. However, the woman was totally wrong in assuming that her neighbors were on the point of mounting an insurrection. A letter published in the *St. Paul Daily News* on March 3 correctly anticipated the dominant German-American response to the declaration of war:

> The German-Americans, if war should come, will be found ready to do their duty, but down in the bottom of their hearts they will feel that their adopted country has asked them to lay down their lives for a cause in which their life and liberty was [*sic*] not at stake and that they were made martyrs of the greed for gold.[23]

German-American opposition to the war was not the only perceived threat in late March and early April of 1917. At least as frightening was the prospect of IWW-inspired sabotage. While the war resolution was pending in Congress, Twin Cities newspapers were reporting an IWW campaign to discourage enlistment in the armed forces. On April 3, according to the *Daily News,* soldiers and a policeman battled six men wearing IWW buttons near the entrance of a St. Paul enlist-ment center; the six were allegedly seeking to dissuade young men en route to the center from joining the colors.[24] That the outbreak of war would serve as a signal for renewed strike activity in the forests and

The St. Paul Dispatch *poked fun at the rising alarm about German-American loyalty, April 17, 1917.*

mines of northern Minnesota was another pervasive belief. Like the apprehension focusing on the German-American community, anxiety with respect to the disruptive potential of the IWW was exaggerated. However, at a time when the public's emotional boiling point was low, the inflammatory nature of IWW rhetoric was calculated to reinforce hysteria.

Far from containing these growing fears, the actions of leaders within both the public and private sectors tended to elevate the sense of crisis. So did press coverage. "St. Paul is today virtually under military guard," reported the *Daily News* on March 29. Squads from the five St. Paul companies of the Minnesota National Guard's First Infantry Regiment, which had been called into federal service but had not yet been ordered out of the state, were assigned to guard "vital facilities." On April 4 the Minneapolis Civic and Commerce Association announced plans to organize a home guard to replace the National Guard units that presumably would be ordered out of the state. Association spokesmen noted that several Minneapolis plants engaged in the manufacture of munitions were, according to the newspaper, "guarded night and day." After April 6 a number of antiwar diehards, most of them committed Socialists, continued their agitation, but the peace movement lost the bulk of its following once war was declared on Germany. Nevertheless, "patriotic" hysteria continued to mount, a trend aided and abetted by the so-called molders of public opinion. In the first two weeks of April the rumor mills ground out stories of conspiracies (supposedly organized by the IWW) to blow up the Minneapolis milling district, and the Capitol was placed under heavy military guard. "Extraordinary precautions were thrown about the Minnesota state capitol today," reported the *Daily News* on April 12. [25]

The closing weeks of the 1917 legislative session reflected the fevered climate of the period surrounding the declaration of war. From the day that President Wilson issued a call for Congress to meet in special session until adjournment of the Minnesota legislature on April 19, measures relating to the war commanded high priority.

Four closely related concerns preoccupied Senate and House conservatives: suppressing revolutionary IWW agitation; placing aliens under strict surveillance on the assumption that their loyalty could not be trusted; endowing state government with sufficient power to act forcefully against threats to social stability and property; and outlawing speech calculated to discourage enlistment in the armed forces. By the end of March bills focusing on the first three of these concerns were introduced in one or both houses; the fourth was placed on the legislative agenda three days after the declaration of war.

Two significant bills were introduced in the Senate on March 24. Senate File 942, which was sponsored by Senator Leonard H. Nord of International Falls, outlawed the promotion of "criminal syndicalism" — by definition, the teaching and/or advocacy of violence, sabotage, and terror "as a means of accomplishing industrial or political ends." The stringent penalties prescribed for violators were to be visited not only on syndicalist advocates, but also on purveyors of syndicalist literature; members of organizations committed to syndicalist ideology; owners or managers of halls who "knowingly" permitted facilities under their jurisdiction to be used for syndicalist gatherings; and "every person voluntarily participating [in a syndicalist meeting] by his presence."[26]

On March 30 the Committee on General Legislation recommended passage of the Nord bill in amended form. The principal change was addition of a phrase defining "sabotage" as "malicious damage or injury to the property of an employer by an employe." Another revision was a reduction of the number of persons constituting an "unlawful assembly" from ten to five (the final version would read "two or more persons"). The Senate voted approval of the committee report and eventually passed the bill on April 10.

The second bill introduced on March 24 called for an appropriation of $1 million "to be expended by the state in event of war" under the direction of a commission consisting of the governor, the auditor, and the treasurer. The bill's author — Sullivan of Stillwater — moved for immediate passage under a suspension of the rules, but the absence of a quorum precluded this move. Instead the bill was referred to the finance committee.[27] A week later it would be superseded by Senate File 1006, the measure creating the Minnesota Commission of Public Safety. The new bill, also introduced by Sullivan, was considerably more sweeping than its predecessor. SF1006 called for a commission of seven — the governor, the attorney general, and five members to be appointed by the governor — and a fund of $2 million. The powers vested in the commission by the new bill were extensive. The *Minneapolis Journal* correctly interpreted its main thrust by noting that it "would gather the sovereign powers of the State in a few responsible hands for quick and effective use in case of need." A similar bill was introduced in the House on the same day.[28]

Given the wide-ranging implications of the Sullivan bill, it is surprising that introduction of the measure did not evoke a stronger reaction throughout the state. The *St. Paul Daily News* voiced a mixed response. It conceded the usefulness of an agency "able to act promptly for the relief of soldiers' families" but perceived "the provision for sitting in judgment upon public officials and prompting their removal" as being "loaded with trouble." The paper also implied that the bill tended to usurp federal authority to wage war. [29]

Meanwhile, the St. Paul Patriotic League and the Minneapolis Civic and Commerce Association were mobilizing support for the measure. The roster of individuals at joint hearings held on April 3 and 4 by the Senate finance committee included, among others, C. M. Magnuson, vice-president of the Minneapolis Chamber of Commerce; E. C. Loring, president of Pillsbury Flour Mills Company; and F. M. Prince, chairman of the board of directors of the First National and Security Bank, Minneapolis. The *Minneapolis Tribune* noted that "representative business men of Minneapolis and St. Paul crowded the Senate chamber . . . to urge . . . passage of the Sullivan bill." [30]

The hearings built momentum for the Sullivan bill and resulted in several changes, the most important being elimination of a provision calling for alien registration. However, dropping this provision did not dispose of the alien registration question. On March 29 Representative Washburn had introduced a bill requiring the governor to initiate such a registration immediately following a declaration of war. The bill reached the House floor on April 5, shortly after finance committee action dropped alien registration from the Sullivan bill. [31]

The debate that followed the introduction of the Washburn bill was extremely acrimonious — George E. Akerson, political writer for the *Minneapolis Tribune,* characterized it as "one of the most bitter in the history of the Legislature." One supporter argued that the bill provided House members with an opportunity "to show whether we stand by the president in this crisis." Another declared: "Nobody is opposing this bill except aliens, and why should we care for their feelings at a time like this?" A few legislators of recent immigrant origin affirmed their loyalty by coming out in support of the measure. "I am a German to the backbone," proclaimed one, "but I am for this bill." Others regarded the bill as an affront. "I was born in Europe and am a citizen of this country by choice," Magnus Johnson asserted, adding: "I am willing to shoulder a gun to defend the United States, but I am going to vote against this bill and I am not a copperhead." Henrik Shipstead, the future United States senator, saw "no need of . . . frothing at the mouth and challenging the Americanism of any member of this house." [32]

The emotional climate generated by two hours of these heated exchanges persuaded many House members that postponement of further debate was prudent. On motion of Anton V. Anderson of Goodhue County, the bill was "laid over for the day retaining its place on the Calendar." The fifty-nine to fifty-one vote in favor of Anderson's motion did not mean that a majority of House members opposed alien registration. Many friends of the Washburn bill voted for postponement "simply because the House had been worked into such a frenzy by fiery speeches that intelligent and deliberative action had become impossible."[33]

The furor aroused by the idea of alien registration may have heightened the anxiety of safety commission supporters to secure immediate enactment of the Sullivan bill. In an April 6 letter to Burnquist, Charles W. Ames, a future safety commissioner, professed deep disappointment at the failure of either house to pass SF1006 on that day, a Friday. He also conveyed to the governor the suggestion of an unidentified legislator that Burnquist send a special message to the legislature urging action on Monday, April 9. Ames added that release of the text of the message to the press would assure maximum publicity.[34]

Within hours Burnquist composed a message asking the legislature to "pass under suspension of the rules a bill providing for a public safety commission and appropriating money therefor." The message also promised prompt action in appointing the commission and, for good measure, promised cancellation of all gubernatorial speaking engagements not related to the national emergency. The press, too, was cooperative: weekend editions of Twin Cities newspapers gave the governor's message full coverage.[35]

Neither house of the legislature passed the safety commission bill on Monday, but both initiated action on another important administration measure. In the Senate George Sullivan and in the House Albert F. Pratt introduced parallel bills "making it unlawful to interfere with or discourage the enlistment of men in the military or naval forces of the United States or of . . . Minnesota, and providing punishment therefor." The Pratt bill was referred to the Committee on Military Affairs, while Sullivan's version was "placed on the Calendar, with privilege of amending" — a move requiring suspension of the rules.[36]

On April 10 the Senate passed the safety commission bill after adopting several important amendments, including a revised draft of the section defining the fundamental powers of the commission; addition of a section calling for organization of a home guard under the commission's jurisdiction; a refined version of the section endowing the commission with authority to monitor the performance of local officials; a new section authorizing the commission to pay members of the Minnesota National Guard for service rendered from the time of mobilization for duty on the Mexican border (June 1916) until such guardsmen "were actually mustered into the service of the United States"; a new section requiring termination of the commission within "three months after the conclusion of peace" or sooner at the governor's discretion; and a reduction of the commission's appropriation from $2 million to $1 million. Sixty-three senators voted for the bill, and no votes were recorded against it. Three senators were absent, and Frank H. Peterson of Moorhead refused to vote. Before the end of the day notification of passage was transmitted to the House, which some observers anticipated would act on the bill immediately. [37]

An April 11 letter from John F. McGee to Senator Knute Nelson reflects the satisfaction felt by friends of the safety commission proposal in the wake of Senate approval. According to McGee, a Minneapolis attorney who shortly would assume the role of dominant personality on the commission:

> The Senate yesterday, without a dissenting vote, passed the public safety commission bill and I understand that it went through the House last night, and will be signed by the Governor today. Many people here, in banking, grain and milling circles, want me to go on the commission from Minneapolis. Of course, if I would say to the Governor that I would go on and that I wanted to go on, he would appoint me, but I don't propose to do that. . . .
>
> If he does appoint me, I shall serve, because people here think it is my duty to do it. The bill appropriates two million dollars and has teeth in it eighteen inches long. I saw a copy of it in the Governor's office yesterday. There are provisions in it that are unconstitutional and palpably so, so I had Senator [Carlton L.] Wallace inject an amendment into it, providing that if one or more of its provisions be held unconstitutional, it shall not effect [sic] the validity of any other provision in itself not invalid. It is a most drastic bill and when it goes into effect, if the Governor appoints men who have backbone, treason will not be talked on the streets of this city and the street corner orators, who denounce the government, advocate revolution, denounce the army and advise against enlistments, will be looking

through the barbed fences of an interment [sic] camp out on the prairie somewhere. [38]

McGee's report accurately described the Wallace amendment but was not correct in other details. Differences between SF1006 and the safety commission bill evolving in the House precluded immediate House action on the former, and the commission appropriation adopted by the Senate was $1 million. The future commissioner also failed to inform Nelson of Senate passage on April 10 of another measure agreeable to both men: the Nord criminal syndicalist bill.

Opposition in the Senate to the more drastic provisions of the Nord bill was a shade more visible than to the safety commission measure. Frank Peterson introduced an amendment exempting persons present at a "syndicalist" meeting from the penalties of the proposed law. A spirited debate ensued. In opposing the amendment, George Sullivan declared: "It is time to do something for the decent people of the state." "Let's put through measures with teeth in them," proclaimed William S. Dwinnell of Minneapolis. As might be expected, the amendment was soundly defeated: nine senators voted yea and fifty-four nay. Among the nine were William A. Campbell of Minneapolis, Richard Jones of Duluth, and two veteran crusaders for prohibition and woman suffrage, Engebret E. Lobeck and Ole O. Sageng. The unamended bill passed by a vote of sixty-one to one, the negative vote cast by Richard Jones. [39]

On April 12 the House turned its attention to the Senate's public safety commission bill. The impetus for its passage was hastened at about this time when Burnquist, along with the governors of the other states, received a request from the federal government that a state council of defense be established. The uniqueness of the Minnesota agency arose from the fact that its creation was well under way when this communication was received and that its proposed statutory powers were extensive. With little exception the powers of the other state councils would be limited to implementation of federal mobilization policies as issued by the Council of National Defense, which was formed by Congress in 1916 as a part of the preparedness effort. Although supporters of the safety commission bill envisioned an independent course for the Minnesota agency, the federal request gave additional legitimacy to the pending legislation. [40]

House members proposed several amendments to the bill, most of them winning approval. The most significant one specified that "official acts of the said Commission shall be effective only upon approval of the Governor." Another authorized the commission to pay guardsmen who had served on the Mexican border fifty cents "for each day of such service," over and beyond the federal compensation received by these guardsmen. A third amendment provided that the home guard "be discharged from further service at the time of the discontinuance of said commission." The House accepted all three amendments by voice votes. However, a fourth affirming that "conscription shall not be resorted to by said Commission" was soundly defeated. [41]

Following a brief debate the bill passed the House by a vote of 116 to 1, the lone dissenter being Ernest G. Strand, the Swedish-born barber who practiced his trade in Two Harbors. Strand's vote did not pass unnoticed. Several members were heard shouting, "Throw him out," while others counseled, "No, no, keep cool." Andrew Devold, the other Socialist member of the House, did not vote, an abstention that evoked reprimands from Minneapolis Socialists. (Two days later when the Senate-House conference bill came up for passage, Devold voted nay.) Precisely what impelled twelve other representatives to refrain from voting is not clear. Several future critics of the commission — Magnus Johnson, Henrik Shipstead, and Tom McGrath, among others — voted for the bill. [42]

The House next took up the criminal syndicalist measure. As Frank Peterson had done in the Senate two days earlier, Tom McGrath proposed an amendment exempting persons attending syndicalist meetings from the penalties prescribed by the bill. Following the example of the Senate, the House rejected this modification. On the final vote, Strand again was the sole dissenter. [43]

The House passed two other wartime measures on April 12. The first, HF1269, prohibited possession of firearms or explosives by citizens of countries at war with the United States. The second, HF1270, outlawed interference with or discouragement of enlistment in the armed forces. Both passed without a dissenting vote, although twenty-eight members were unrecorded on the first and more than forty on the second. Of the two, HF1270 was undoubtedly the more important. Forbidding enemy aliens to possess firearms appeared to be a prudent precaution that did not unduly infringe the fundamental rights of the persons affected. On the other hand, through loose interpretation of its language, the measure forbidding discouragement of enlistments became an effective weapon against critics of wartime policy. Any such criticism was vulnerable to attack on the theory that it discouraged enlistment, a charge that was used against the Non-partisan League.

Since the criminal syndicalist bill had already been approved by the Senate, it only remained for the governor to sign it into law, which he did the next day. A minor technicality precluded immediate action in the Senate on House files 1269 and 1270: virtually identical bills awaited action there. The problem was resolved on April 13 when the Senate, on motion of George Sullivan, substituted the House versions for their Senate counterparts, thereby clearing the way for final passage (by unanimous vote) on April 18. [44]

House amendments to the safety commission bill posed a more serious problem for the Senate. Sullivan "moved that the Senate do now refuse to concur in the amendments by the House to s.f. 1006" and that a conference committee be constituted to resolve the differences, a motion that prevailed. The most serious sticking point was the House amendment giving the governor veto power over the commission's actions. Evidently Sullivan and his colleagues did not trust Burnquist's steadfastness and wanted to vest ultimate power in men fully committed to a crusade against "treason." [45]

The report submitted to both houses by the conference committee on April 14 proposed elimination of the governor's veto power in favor of a specification that "all official acts of the Commission shall require a majority vote of the entire Commission." Both chambers adopted the report before the end of the day. In the House McGrath moved that it be laid on the table, a move that was defeated. Whether McGrath and the members who voted with him (a group including both Strand and Devold) were seeking to kill the bill or merely delay its passage in order to moderate its more drastic provisions is not clear. In any case, the House passed sf1006 as amended by the conference report by a vote of seventy-five to one, with Devold casting the lone dissenting vote. Strand was not recorded, although he had voted against the bill on April 12. [46]

In the Senate fifty-two members voted for the bill as amended by the conference committee, and none against. Both Jones and Frank Peterson were recorded as voting for the bill. On the following Monday, April 16, Burnquist signed the measure into law, and on the next day he submitted to the Senate his proposed nominees for commission membership. On motion of George Sullivan the Senate confirmed these appointments. [47]

With its remaining life-span limited to less than a week, the legislature was obliged to complete action on a host of measures — including the Washburn alien registration bill. When the bill that had generated such bitter debate was again called up for consideration in the House on April 14, a "wild scene" followed, in the words of the *St. Paul Daily News.* Several supporters of the bill suggested a linkage between opposition to alien registration and the IWW. Henry H. Harrison of Stillwater perceived "an imaginary line running through this house . . . state . . . and . . . country. On one side we find the patriots and on the other side men who are worse than copperheads and traitors to the country." Alfred W. Mueller of New Ulm denied the involvement of German Americans in alleged physical attacks on soldiers, adding that New Ulm was displaying more United States flags than any Minnesota city of comparable size. Washburn read a newspaper story recounting rumors of confrontations between soldiers and antiwar radicals. In response to Washburn, Devold asked: "Is this a story from a Jesse James book or a newspaper?" "It is stern reality," declared Robert Carmichael of Farmington.[48]

Surprisingly, the house was able to dispose of the bill in a manner that quickly broke the tension. An amendment introduced by Martin W. Odland of Fergus Falls, who had spoken against the bill on April 5, called for the institution of alien registration only if the president of the United States requested such action. Since the imperative of the hour was to "stand by the president," and since the Wilson administration was not about to order universal alien registration (as distinguished from registration of enemy aliens), this amendment paved the way for unanimous passage of the bill; even Devold and Strand voted for it. The bill was then transmitted to the Senate where it failed to be called up for final passage. Evidently supporters of alien registration had lost interest in the measure. They may have suspected that it was not on the agenda of the national administration. More important, the newly created public safety commission was endowed with sufficient power to order alien registration on its own authority, a step that it would take ten months later.[49]

Only two bills directly related to the war remained pending: HF1269, the measure forbidding possession of firearms and explosives by enemy aliens, and HF1270, the one prohibiting interference with enlistment in the armed forces; both had passed the House on April 12. The Senate added its approval on April 18, and two days later Burnquist signed them into law.[50]

Analysts of the 1917 legislature failed to grasp the full significance of the three most important wartime measures passed in the closing days of the session. Although ostensibly aimed at the IWW, the criminal syndicalist act could be interpreted as a ban on traditional trade-union tactics. Whether intended by its original sponsors or not, the law prohibiting interference with or discouragement of enlistment in the armed forces would become a weapon in the campaign to destroy the Nonpartisan League.

The significance of the safety commission bill was even more far-reaching. Senate refusal to countenance a gubernatorial veto of the commission's actions in effect delegated the state's sovereign powers to an agency whose appointed members could dominate its proceedings. Theoretically commission actions were subject to judicial scrutiny — a limitation that worried commission members — but few judges were of a mind to invite the recriminations that would follow judicial interdiction of a commission decision. All in all one finds it easy to agree with the statement by William Watts Folwell, a historian not given to hyperbole: "If a large hostile army had already been landed at Duluth and was about to march on the capital of the state, a more liberal dictatorship could hardly have been conceded to the commission."[51]

By implication Folwell raises a question that he does not undertake to answer: Why did the legislature of 1917 see fit to place the state under a virtual dictatorship for the duration of the war? To assert that the representatives of the people were responding to pressures generated by unreasoning fear may be correct so far as it goes. However, the question of what inspired the fear still remains. Certainly, no one fancied that a German invasion fleet was crossing the Atlantic. On the other hand, the presence of an "enemy within" did not appear entirely implausible. Up to April 6, Minnesota opinion was deeply polarized on the issue of peace or war. Throughout the entire period of American neutrality those who claimed to speak for the state's German Americans — the largest ethnic group in Minnesota — had stridently assailed interventionists as warmongers motivated by a "greed for gold"; and one could not anticipate the turnabout in German-American attitudes following the declaration of war. Other groups, too, had militantly opposed going to war: Scandinavian Americans, especially the Swedish contingent; large sectors of the labor movement; the radical wing of the farmers' movement; and many

Minnesotans who took their lead from Senator La Follette. Given the conventional belief that in time of war the people must rally to the flag, the specter of disunity raised by this polarization was a frightening one.

Restraint on the part of public officials and the press might have provided the people of Minnesota with a more balanced perspective, one that could have cooled the ugly passions that erupted in late March and early April. Unfortunately, restraint was a rare commodity in the spring of 1917. On April 14 the *St. Paul Daily News* charged that "certain newspapers of St. Paul and Minneapolis today printed with alarming headlines a mass of untrue and inflammatory reports regarding conditions in Minneapolis." According to the *Daily News,* this was "the culmination of 10 days of inflammatory lying," an assertion based on interviews with officers and men on military duty in the Twin Cities. [52]

The more lurid of these false disclosures included reports that three wounded guardsmen were being treated at the Fort Snelling hospital; that three would-be plotters and murderers also were hospitalized; that six other plotters had been court-martialed and "disposed of in a way not made public"; and that a conspiracy to blow up the Washburn-Crosby mill had been frustrated. Another story reported that an "assassin" with a suitcase filled with dynamite had been placed under arrest. The truth was that an employee of the Minneapolis waterworks department had been detained by the authorities long enough to confirm his claim that he was carrying explosives to be used in the excavation of a new water main.

"The real facts," concluded the *Daily News,* "are that a few shots have been fired at guardsmen by irresponsible or vicious characters, tramps around the railroad yards in Minneapolis, that guardsmen have returned this fire and also have, in a few instances, fired upon men whom they found skulking about. . . . [I]n some instances shots have been fired at imaginary dangers."

Obviously these "inflammatory lies," coupled with a highly visible military presence on the Capitol grounds, had a powerful impact on the deliberations leading to the passage of the criminal syndicalist and safety commission bills as well as HF1270. The linkage between the hysterical climate of the moment and the disposition of senators and representatives to pass drastic legislation is suggested by the lead paragraph of an April 10 story in the *Minneapolis Journal:*

At the same time [that] the state senate was unanimously passing the bill creating a state commission of public safety and a home guard of unlimited size to handle Minnesota's internal war problems, Adjutant General F. B. Wood today called out two additional batteries of the First field artillery, Minnesota national guard, to protect food supplies in the Twin cities, or wherever they may be needed in the state. [53]

Whether the circulation of scare stories telling of conspiracies to paralyze the economic structure of the state was spontaneous rumor-mongering getting out of hand or a deliberate ploy designed to build pressure for the emergency measures pending in the legislature cannot be determined. The motives impelling Twin Cities business leaders to push hard for the passage of the wartime measures, however, are more clear. Although these leaders strongly supported United States intervention on the side of the Allies, they nevertheless feared that the destabilizing impact of the war would release forces inimical to their interests, and there can be little doubt that the rhetoric of some prowar progressives heightened their anxiety. "Why should not the war serve as a pretext to foist innovations upon the country?" queried the *New Republic*. During the first month of the war Walter Lippmann confidently predicted:

> We who have gone to war to insure democracy in the world will have raised an aspiration here that will not end with the overthrow of Prussian autocracy. We shall turn with fresh interests to our own tyrannies — to our Colorado mines, our autocratic steel industries, our sweatshops, and our slums. [54]

A perception that trade-union advances — aided and abetted by the policies of the Wilson administration — were imperiling maintenance of the open shop in their city haunted Minneapolis employers. The reaction of Minneapolis corporate executives to the 1916 law establishing an eight-hour day with no reduction in pay for interstate railroad employees indicates an almost obsessive fear of growing union power. John Washburn of the Washburn-Crosby Company could not "conceive [the] equity or justice of proposed eight hour bill." George M. Gillette, an executive of the Minneapolis Steel and Machinery Company, believed that "our Democracy could not survive many such measures." [55] *Commercial West* warned: "Unless the labor unions sober up and use some reason in their demands, this country will be forced into adopting an autocratic form of government that can control by military power the industrial situation." The same editorial in effect characterized the conservative Railroad Brotherhoods as the enemy within:

> When the feeling was tense in this country over the meddling of foreign agents in American industries, President Wilson stated that the greatest danger to this country was from within and not with foreign nations. If he had used the same sort of logic in this railway controversy, he could have safely stated that an organization of workers that deliberately plans to wreck the business and cripple the industrial life of this country [is] no better than a threatened invasion by a foreign power, from which the nation [should] defend itself at all hazards. [56]

The results of the November 1916 election were especially disconcerting to business leaders. Given President Wilson's recent "swing to the left" and the friendliness of his administration to the Samuel Gompers wing of the labor movement, his reelection was a keen disappointment. Charles Evans Hughes, the Republican presidential candidate, carried Minnesota, but his margin of victory was paper-thin; Wilson triumphed handily in the state's labor precincts. Worse yet, the voters of Minneapolis elected a Socialist mayor, an outcome that made John McGee "sick." [57] If anything, the situation in North Dakota, whose citizens had long regarded the Minneapolis-based grain trade as a colonialist oppressor, was even more alarming. Here the Nonpartisan League had won a sweeping victory on a platform that directly threatened the interests of the Twin Cities industrial complex.

Developments in the early weeks of 1917 were no more reassuring. The NPL invasion of rural Minnesota and the January 1917 timber strike were both seen as formidable dangers to the interests of the Twin Cities business elite. Another disturbing reality was the growing power of the farm and labor blocs within the legislature, particularly within the House of Representatives. Although internal dissension somewhat reduced the effectiveness of the farm group in the 1917 session, organized labor had achieved several modest gains.

Confronted with this multiplicity of threats to their vital interests, Twin Cities business leaders readily accepted the policy of concentrating "the sovereign powers of the state in a few responsible hands for quick and effective use in case of need," as the *Minneapolis Journal* had expressed it. Undoubtedly, a genuine fear of pro-Germanism was also a factor motivating sponsors of the safety commission bill. But demonizing everything German may have had a purpose unrelated to national security concerns. Independent of any threat they may have posed to the safety of the United States, Kaiser Wilhelm and the Prussian autocracy were convenient scapegoats — and the thesis that eliminating them from the face of the earth was a high and holy mission commanded easy acceptance, given the fevered climate of the time. It followed that a cloud of suspicion hung heavily over those Minnesota citizens who presumed to question the need for such an agency as the safety commission or such laws as the criminal syndicalist act, as well as those who articulated the slightest doubt about the wisdom of going to war. Identifying support of the safety commission bill with patriotic obligation discouraged opposition to its passage and enhanced the credibility of the commission's authority once it was in operation.

CHAPTER FOUR

The Original Commission

Three days before signing the safety commission bill into law, Governor Burnquist issued a proclamation setting aside April 19 — the anniversary of the battle of Lexington in 1775 — for special patriotic observances. "No day can be a more fitting one on which the American people should come together for . . . holding patriotic meetings . . . [and] coming to a full realization . . . that we, to-day, are involved in the greatest conflict of history." He asked that "as many as can possibly do so join the national guard immediately" and that "all of our people . . . proceed at once in co-operation with a state public safety commission to use every means possible to de-fend our common country, protect the lives of our citizens and . . . safeguard our homes and our families." [1]

Civic leaders throughout Minnesota responded to the governor's proclamation by organizing flamboyant patriotic festivals. The Min-neapolis celebration "was ushered in at midnight with New Year–like screeches of horns and whistles," prompting the *Minneapolis Tribune* to remark: "Paul Revere would have found 'the village' already aroused if he had staged his famous ride in Minneapolis last night." The day began with a series of programs in the city's schools, followed by a "monster convocation" on the University of Minnesota campus where students and others applauded President George E. Vincent's fervent endorsement of "Americanism." Throughout the afternoon patriotic tunes emanating from the courthouse chimes helped counter the gloom induced by intermittent rain showers. [2]

The high point of the Minneapolis commemoration was an eve-ning parade that drew eight thousand marchers. Undoubtedly this spec-tacle stimulated the patriotism of both those who marched and those who observed along the parade route. Thousands of others were able to participate vicariously by reading the Twin Cities newspapers. The

Bemidji sending off its naval militia — one of the first Minnesota units to be mobilized — on April 7, 1917

Tribune's portrayal of the arrival of the procession at Parade Stadium was particularly exuberant:

> Dusk had settled over The Parade, leaving it in darkness except for the lights that shone from buildings around it, when the wide sweep began to take life from the influx of marching ranks. The dull gleam of rifles became visible and then the regimental colors of the First infantry, as on them played the rays of a searchlight. Soon followed the University cadets in their blue-gray uniforms, and as The Parade swarmed with the mass of marchers, flaunting banners, carrying arms or waving little flags, all became a maze of indistinct color and motion except the composite emblem of world democracy — a group of the flags of the Allies. Carried by a group of girls, the national colors of the Allies fluttered above the waving throng. Far above these symbols of foreign lands — the tri-color of France, the British Union Jack, the emblems of Russia, Japan, Belgium, Ireland and the rest — floated the Stars and Stripes from The Parade flagstaff, with a searchlight picking it out of the dusk.[3]

"St. Paul," the *Tribune* magnanimously reported, "did its part with a monster parade earlier in the day." The St. Paul parade included in its line of march representatives of eleven Allied nations: Russia, England, France, Italy, Rumania, Montenegro, Serbia, Cuba, Japan, Belgium, and Portugal. Schools, stores, and businesses closed their doors to allow widespread citizen participation in the day's events. Visually, both along the parade route and throughout the city, the Stars and Stripes dominated the landscape. In preparing for the day's

Marchers carrying the American flag during an evening parade through downtown Minneapolis, April 19, 1917

events the St. Paul Patriotic League had laid up a stock of eight thousand small flags, primarily for distribution to "unattached citizens" marching in the parade. Through the length and breadth of St. Paul the "American emblem was universal, flying from office buildings, from homes, from autos, from horses' bridles."[4]

Publicists in both cities pronounced the April 19 commemoration of Paul Revere and the heroes of Lexington an unqualified success. Military recruiters reported a healthy upsurge of enlistments, whereas others focused on more intangible benefits. While the celebration was in progress, the *St. Paul Dispatch* affirmed that "the people of St. Paul are engaged in an expression of idealism which has not been equaled in the history of the city." "Minneapolis . . . is showing that its citizens are awake to the national crisis," proclaimed the *Journal*.

Presumably the troublesome legacy created by the Van Lear peace rally of February 10 had been overcome.[5]

The degree to which the April 19 extravaganza enhanced the stature of the Minnesota Commission of Public Safety is impossible to determine. The Burnquist proclamation initiating the celebration had urged Minnesotans to cooperate with "a state public safety commission" that was not yet in existence on the date the proclamation was issued. Doubtless the governor wanted to link the success of the state's war effort with the actions that the commission would soon begin to take. As he had promised to do while the MCPS bill was pending, Burnquist announced his commission appointments hours after signing the bill and the Senate promptly confirmed them. Under the terms of the law, two of the seven members served ex officio: the governor himself and Lyndon A. Smith, the incumbent attorney general. The five appointees were John Lind and John F. McGee of Minneapolis, Charles W. Ames of St. Paul, Charles H. March of Litchfield, and Anton C. Weiss of Duluth. Not all of these men would serve for the duration of the commission's short life. Ames and Lind left in early December 1917, although Ames continued to serve on special assignment. Henry W. Libby of Winona succeeded Ames, and Thomas E. Cashman of Owatonna replaced Lind. The gap created by the death of Smith in March 1918 was filled by Clifford L. Hilton, the new attorney general.

As the state's highest elected official and designated chairman of the MCPS, Burnquist, it would seem, should have emerged as the commission's dominant personality. This he failed to do. Perhaps Burnquist's career peaked too soon: at thirty-eight, his age in 1917, the governor was insufficiently seasoned to cope with the powerful influence of colleagues many years his senior. Moreover, as the son of Swedish immigrant parents he lacked the prestigious family background that enhanced the stature of some of the businessmen and politicians with whom he dealt.[6]

Joseph Alfred Arner Burnquist was born in Dayton, Iowa, on July 21, 1879. After attending Carleton Academy in Northfield, Minnesota, he gained admission to Carleton College, graduating from that institution in 1902. For the next two years he pursued graduate work at Columbia University, where he earned a master's degree. In 1905 he completed his legal studies at the University of Minnesota, passed the bar examination, and established a law practice in St. Paul. Three years later the voters of the thirty-third legislative district elected him to represent them in the Minnesota House of Representatives.

In 1908 the thirty-third district embraced St. Paul's first and second wards, an ethnically mixed, working-class area in northeastern St. Paul within which the legendary "Swede Hollow" neighborhood was located. To judge by the voting behavior of their citizens, the first and second wards were left-of-center in political orientation; in the 1918 race for governor they would decisively reject Burnquist in favor of candidates endorsed by the Nonpartisan League in both the primary and general elections. [7]

As a state legislator, however, Burnquist enjoyed a high approval rating among his constituents; he won reelection in 1910 without opposition. Two factors contributed to his popularity. First, the many Swedish-American voters in the district demonstrated a strong tendency to support candidates of their nationality. Second, Burnquist was a committed progressive. Throughout his two-term legislative career he embraced such causes as compulsory employer's liability insurance, woman suffrage, the eight-hour workday, the direct primary, and county option.

While serving in the legislature, Burnquist also participated in the war against political bossism. In the 1911 session he made a bid for the speakership against Howard H. Dunn, a veteran politician who enjoyed the backing of the powerful Republican machine presided over by Edward E. Smith of Minneapolis. Burnquist's small circle of supporters could not match the power of the Smith organization, but defeat in the speakership contest did not diminish the young legislator's reputation. On the contrary, at a time when voter enthusiasm for progressivism was rising, it advanced his availability for higher office. [8]

The statewide primary enacted by the 1912 special session opened a door of opportunity for Burnquist. On the basis of his record as a Republican insurgent, the young legislator filed for lieutenant governor. His victory in the primary was not particularly impressive: he polled 74,107 votes to 64,946 for his opponent, David M. Neill, a sixty-year-old Red Wing businessman who was well known on his home turf but not statewide. Given the distribution of the vote, one suspects that opponents of county option may have organized a covert operation against Burnquist. [9] The lieutenant governorship was not a major power center in state government, but prerogatives of the office included the appointment of senate committees, a crucial factor in the ongoing battle over county option.

Burnquist's margin of victory in the fall election was more convincing than in the primary. He polled 147,776 votes to 88,534 for his Democratic opponent, a total that exceeded the Eberhart vote by about 18,000. One factor in this success was the broad base of support rallying to Burnquist following his primary victory. Notwithstanding his refusal to support President Taft for reelection, he enjoyed the advantages conferred by the Republican label; in addition he was endorsed by the Minnesota Bull Moose organization and by the Minnesota Progressive Republican League, a La Follette–oriented group, several of whose members backed Woodrow Wilson in the presidential race. [10]

As lieutenant governor, Burnquist was not in a position to generate many headlines in the daily papers. He also responded cautiously to the perilous situation created by the escalating conflict between Governor Eberhart and his "standpat" supporters on the one hand and Republican progressives on the other, although his sympathies clearly were with the latter. He resisted any temptation that personal ambition may have spawned to enter the gubernatorial race in 1914, choosing instead to seek another term as lieutenant governor. Meanwhile, Republican progressives mounted a successful campaign to block Eberhart's renomination. Their nominee, however — William E. Lee — was unable to reunite a factional Republican party, a failure that opened the way for the election of Democrat Winfield Scott Hammond.

Burnquist avoided entanglement with the Eberhart-Lee contest, but his renomination bid ran into complications from another source. His primary opponent, Elias Steenerson of Polk County, was a veteran of the farmers' movement who enjoyed widespread and favorable name recognition, particularly in the grain-growing areas of western and northwestern Minnesota. With little effort, Steenerson managed to poll nearly seventy-eight thousand votes to Burnquist's eighty-nine thousand. This outcome was a harbinger of things to come. While Burnquist was not yet perceived as a politician with close links to the Minneapolis grain trade, he was after all a Twin Citian who had presided over a Senate that in 1913 gave short shrift to the complaints of grain growers against the Minneapolis Chamber of Commerce. Steenerson, on the other hand, symbolized a generation-long battle to bring the organized grain trade under effective government control. [11]

The November election registered a happier outcome for Burn-quist: while Lee lost to Hammond by more than twelve thousand votes, Burnquist prevailed over his Democratic challenger by a margin of nearly fifty thousand. If this enhanced Burnquist's availability for higher honors, his role in the successful battle to enact county option — the featured attraction of the 1915 legislative session — solidified his standing within the dry community. Shortly after the election Burnquist met with leading legislative sponsors of county option and officials of the Anti-Saloon League to map the strategy to be pursued in the upcoming session, and when the legislature convened he used his appointive power to "pack" the Senate temperance committee with enthusiastic drys. This helpfulness was not the only factor working for county option's success, but it facilitated early passage of the bill in the Senate. Although resistance to passage was more formidable in the House, the bill succeeded there and was signed into law by Governor Hammond. [12]

The unexpected death of Governor Hammond at the age of fifty-two in December 1915 evoked a sorrowful reaction throughout Minnesota. Nevertheless, Republican progressives could derive some solace from the thought that Burnquist's elevation to the governorship achieved the broad goals that had motivated their 1914 revolt against Eberhart. Gunnar Björnson of Minneota greeted his accession to the state's highest office with enthusiasm, and Charles A. Lindbergh, Sr., abandoned plans to run for governor because Burnquist's principles and goals were "in accord with my own." [13]

Burnquist met these expectations by initiating action on a problem that had long distressed social justice advocates: Minnesota's chaotic and antiquated child welfare laws. For several years private social welfare organizations had agitated for reform of these laws, only to be rebuffed by successive legislatures. In August 1916 the governor moved to break the deadlock by appointing a semi-official body, the Minnesota Child Welfare Commission, to formulate recommendations for codification and reform. The work of the commission resulted in a series of bills that passed the legislature and were signed into law by the governor. One authority characterized the 1917 Children's Code as "perhaps the greatest achievement in the history of Minnesota's social legislation." For this Burnquist could claim considerable credit. Ironically, however, during this time the governor was alienating a significant constituency within the Minnesota progressive movement: organized labor and those social justice reformers who focused their concern on the working conditions in the mines of northern Minnesota. [14]

In responding to the spontaneous strike that erupted on the Mesabi Range in July 1916, Burnquist followed a policy that in every important respect appeared to favor management. Critics charged that he not only tolerated but actually encouraged the questionable practice of deputizing mine guards as police officers. A Burnquist suggestion to St. Louis County authorities that arrested persons be tried in Duluth rather than in range towns was motivated, critics charged, by gubernatorial preference for "Steel Trust" justice. Nine years earlier when an equally bitter strike had interrupted mining operations, Governor Johnson had helped defuse potential violence by visiting the strike area and establishing personal contact with the miners. Burnquist did not choose to honor this precedent. Instead he sent Gustaf Lindquist, a close associate who later would serve as his secretary, on a range inspection tour. Lindquist allegedly refused to meet representatives of the strikers while accepting lavish entertainment from management. [15]

If these complaints had come only from IWW sources they might have lacked credibility; however, they were taken up by labor and liberal newspapers that eschewed all association with the IWW and were validated by independent investigations. The governor came under heavy fire at the 1916 convention of the Minnesota Federation of Labor, which met in July while the strike was still in progress. A resolution calling for Burnquist's impeachment was vociferously supported on the convention floor, but it was sidetracked in favor of a request to the governor that he order the Minnesota Department of Labor and Industries to investigate the strike. [16]

Organized labor was somewhat placated by the state report, which pointed up the need for substantial improvement in range working conditions, and apparently the governor's reelection campaign suffered only minimal damage. [17] Burnquist may also have learned a lesson: when timber workers struck in January 1917, he responded to management demands for gubernatorial intervention with more caution than during the miners' strike.

Nevertheless, the amicable relationship between Burnquist and organized labor that had prevailed earlier evaded restoration. For the remainder of his tenure as governor, Burnquist seemed unable to escape the captivity to anti-union business elements that had ensnared him during the 1916 range strike. From time to time — as when he signed the McGrath anti-injunction bill — he apparently made an effort to assert his independence, but such efforts were few and far between. One might assume that his chairmanship of the powerful safety commission created an opportunity to exercise strong leadership. Ironically, it had an opposite effect. Even if Burnquist had managed to establish himself as the commission's dominant personality — which he did not — the legislature's refusal, at the behest of the Senate judiciary committee, to grant him the power of veto over commission decisions in effect placed his authority as governor at the disposal of a commission majority.

Attorney General Lyndon A. Smith also did not play a role on the MCPS commensurate with his status as an elected state official. He was not designated to serve as the commission's legal counsel; that responsibility was assigned to Ambrose Tighe, a St. Paul attorney. Given Smith's impressive background this appears curious; perhaps poor health limited his capacity for work (he died in March 1918).[18]

Smith, the son of a Congregational clergyman, was born in New Hampshire in 1854. From an educational standpoint his early years were privileged. After attending two first-class preparatory schools he was admitted to Dartmouth College, graduating from that institution at the head of his class in 1880. Four years later he earned a law degree at Georgetown University, migrated westward, and established a law practice in Montevideo, a small western Minnesota town still in the pioneer stage of development. He soon achieved prominence both within the legal profession and Republican politics, serving several terms as Chippewa county attorney and as lieutenant governor from 1899 to 1903. In 1909 Governor Johnson appointed him assistant attorney general, and when the incumbent attorney general resigned in 1911 Governor Eberhart appointed Smith to fill the vacancy.

Smith was elected to the post in his own right in 1912 and reelected twice. Although not conspicuously involved in the standpat-insurgent wrangle within the Republican party during the Taft years, Smith was perceived as a progressive; like Burnquist he was endorsed by the Minnesota Bull Moose organization in the 1912 campaign. He also enjoyed the respect of professional peers who admired his profound devotion to the law, the depth of his scholarship, and the painstaking approach with which he tackled the problems coming to him for resolution.

John Lind was the best known of the appointed members of the MCPS, and his personal history generated considerable popular

John Lind, governor in 1899–1901, shown here in 1921

admiration. Born in the impoverished province of Småland, Sweden, on March 25, 1854, he migrated to Minnesota along with his family in 1868, settling first in Goodhue County and moving shortly thereafter to Sibley County, where his parents acquired a farm in 1872. By this time young Lind had qualified for a teaching certificate; following a brief stint as a rural elementary teacher he established himself in New Ulm, where he studied law and acquired an excellent command of German. He attended the University of Minnesota in 1875–76 and gained admission to the bar in 1877.[19]

From then on, Lind's rise to prominence was rapid. In the early years of his law practice he served as superintendent of schools in Brown County, an elective position. During the Garfield-Arthur presidency (1881–85) he was receiver for the federal land office in Tracy, an appointment indicating that he was achieving status within the Republican party. In 1886 he won election to Congress from the second district, an area embracing twenty counties in southwestern Minnesota. He won reelection in 1888 and again in 1890, when he was the only Minnesota Republican congressman to survive the anti-Republican landslide of that year.

As a congressman Lind faithfully represented the interests of his district without departing significantly from the Republican mainstream — for example, he voted for the highly protectionist and extremely unpopular McKinley tariff bill. However, when free silver became a dominant national issue in 1896, he rejected the hard money stance of the GOP, embracing instead the free silver gospel and the presidential candidacy of William Jennings Bryan. This bolt established Lind's availability for the governorship on a so-called Fusion slate backed by a coalition of silver Republicans, Bryan Democrats, and Populists. The remarkable thing about Lind's showing in the 1896 election is not that he lost but that he nearly won, an outcome attributable not to the free silver enthusiasm of Minnesota voters but to the unpopularity of the incumbent Republican state administration and to Lind's personal popularity. [20]

Two years later Lind again was the Fusionist candidate for governor, and this time he won the first non-Republican gubernatorial victory since 1857. In contrast to 1896, the "money question" was not a dominant concern in 1898. Lind may have gained some support by opposing "imperialism" (U.S. annexation of the Philippines), but his victory was partly a testimonial to his personal and ethnic appeal and partly the outcome of internal dissension within the Republican party. Although the program outlined in his inaugural message would serve as a blueprint for the future, his one-term governorship was not impressive in terms of concrete legislative achievement; a legislature dominated by top-heavy GOP majorities in both houses was disinclined to facilitate the success of a Fusionist state administration. Lind did not win reelection in 1900. As in 1896, the vote was close, but a combination of McKinley prosperity and Republican unity within Minnesota returned the statehouse to Republican control.

When his term expired Lind transferred his residence from New Ulm to Minneapolis, where he lived until his death in 1930. In this new setting he entered into a law partnership with Andreas Ueland and Waldron M. Jerome. Henceforth, the ex-governor's energies focused more on the practice of law than on politics, although he made a successful bid for the fifth district (Hennepin County) congressional seat in 1902. He declined to seek reelection in 1904, and thereafter he became known as a politician adept at dodging nominations for public office. [21]

On the other hand, his influence continued to be a factor in state politics. He spoke out frequently and bluntly on the issues of the day from the standpoint of a mainstream progressive committed to such causes as conservation, more effective trust regulation, and social justice legislation. His affiliation with the Democratic party was loose enough to permit him to support progressive Republicans: in 1910, for example, he heartily endorsed the reelection of u.s. Senator Moses E. Clapp, a member of the small band of midwestern Republican senators who opposed the policies of the Taft administration.

The advent of Woodrow Wilson revitalized Lind's commitment to Democratic politics. His influence helped persuade the Minnesota delegation to the Democratic national convention of 1912 to support Wilson, and in the fall Lind campaigned for the New Jersey governor. After taking office Wilson offered Lind a number of federal appointments; these he declined, but in August 1913 he consented to go to Mexico — a country enmeshed in revolutionary turmoil — as the president's "personal representative." Wilson distrusted the American diplomatic establishment, suspecting that it was covertly backing General Victoriano Huerta, the unsavory dictator who had seized power following the assassination of Francisco Madero and a leader whose government Wilson refused to recognize. [22]

Although Lind's Mexican mission was not an unqualified success, it focused national attention on his comings and goings; moreover, the aura of mystery surrounding the mission sharpened public curiosity. What was this tall, spare, taciturn Swedish American with no diplomatic experience, no particular expertise in Latin American affairs, and no fluency in the Spanish language up to? The answer was not immediately forthcoming, and the extent to which Lind shaped the administration's Mexican policy remains moot. Lind's relationship with Wilson remained cordial even after the president terminated the appointment in August 1914. The administration continued to seek Lind's counsel on its Mexican policy, and in the presidential campaign of 1916 Lind defended the administration's course in Mexico.

Meanwhile, issues growing out of the relationship of the United States to the European war were becoming a major factor in u.s. and Minnesota politics. Early in the conflict, Lind perceived the war as a bloody struggle for commercial supremacy in which Wall Street might have a stake but which did not imperil the vital interests of the United States. At the same time he remained loyal to Wilson, professing to believe that the president's course was better calculated to preserve American neutrality than the one advocated by eastern seaboard Republicans. German resumption of unrestricted submarine warfare in early 1917 persuaded Lind to change his mind. He now was convinced that the war involved more than commercial supremacy, that Germany indeed had declared war on humanity, and that American intervention on the side of the Allies was imperative. [23]

"For a time," wrote historian George M. Stephenson, "Lind was much interested in the work of the Commission of Public Safety." Although the ex-governor did not precisely define what he hoped the commission would accomplish, he obviously aspired to use his influence to build a strong consensus in support of Wilson's wartime policies. He also confided to Ambrose Tighe that the commission afforded "the machinery to do big things which will count after the war." Exactly what these "big things" were is not entirely clear, but conceivably Lind was referring to the MCPS's potential as a regulatory agency that could help realize unfulfilled progressive goals. [24]

If the prowar consensus that Lind hoped the MCPS would help build was broader than that envisioned by some of his commission colleagues, there were a number of groups whose participation he did not welcome. His relationship with the Gompers wing of the American labor movement was cordial, but as a commission member Lind would work relentlessly for the suppression of the IWW. He also was impatient with what he regarded as the excesses of "hyphenism." He firmly supported the proposition that English should be the sole medium of instruction in the schools of Minnesota, a stance that displeased some of his fellow Scandinavians, and explicit pro-German speech offended him deeply. [25] On the other hand — and unlike some of his MCPS colleagues — he was not in the habit of attaching the pro-German label to individuals simply because they embraced programs that, by contemporary standards, were considered radical.

John McGee's concept of the role of the MCPS differed markedly from Lind's. Instead of seeking consensus in support of the war, McGee saw the commission as an opportunity to suppress not only out-and-out pro-Germans but also trade unionists (whether moderate or radical), members of the Nonpartisan League, Socialists, pacifists, and all who entertained the slightest doubt with respect to the wisdom of America going to war. Nor did he doubt the inerrancy of his own judgments and perceptions. In communicating with a federal official in 1918, he confidently proclaimed: "I have no doubt whatever that

John F. McGee,
1918

I am right and knowing that I am right there is no power on earth
that can budge me one inch from following the path of duty as I
see it."[26]

John McGee was born in Amboy, Illinois, on January 1, 1861, and
reared in an Irish immigrant home. His father, Hugh McGee, who
had arrived in the United States in 1850, was a railroad mechanic who,
it was said, retired "in comfortable circumstances." Whatever level
of affluence this might imply, young McGee's formal education terminated with graduation from Amboy High School in his twentieth
year. Even before graduating from high school McGee began the study
of law in the office of an Amboy attorney, and on November 10,
1882 — two months short of his twenty-second birthday — he gained
admission to the Illinois bar.[27]

In April 1883 McGee migrated west, settling in Devils Lake, Dakota
Territory, where he joined a law firm headed by the local prosecuting
attorney. His practice included assisting his senior partner in the
disposition of criminal cases, an activity that may have sharpened
McGee's prosecutorial talents but offered insufficient scope for his
ambition. In 1887 he moved to Minneapolis where he entered into
a partnership with A. H. Noyes. Following termination of this

arrangement in 1889, McGee established an independent practice specializing in corporation law. Within a few years he was serving an impressive array of clients, including the Chicago and Great Western Railroad and several line elevator companies. In October 1897 Governor David M. Clough appointed McGee to fill a fourth judicial district court vacancy, and the next year McGee was elected to a full six-year term. However, he chose not to serve out his term, resigning in November 1902 to reenter the practice of law, this time in partnership with William A. Lancaster.

Although he displayed an intense interest in public policy issues — mostly from a perspective compatible with the interests of his clients — McGee was not a highly visible participant in organizational politics. Early on he classified himself as an "independent Republican," a label not entirely consistent with the highly partisan stance reflected in his correspondence with Senator Knute Nelson. If Republicanism was an untypical affiliation for an Irish American, so was McGee's avoidance of involvement in Irish-American causes. Until the United States entered the war, most Irish Americans were strong noninterventionists, thanks in large part to their antipathy to Great Britain at a time when their homeland was taking up arms against British rule. McGee, on the other hand, fervently supported the Allied cause, excoriated those Minnesota congressmen who voted for the McLemore resolution, and displayed no visible interest in nor sympathy for the Irish independence movement.[28] His memberships included the prestigious Minneapolis Club — admission to which signaled acceptance by the city's elite — and the Minneapolis Civic and Commerce Association.

If Lind and McGee could be considered "outsiders" by virtue of ethnic background, Charles Wilberforce Ames had at least a tenuous connection with the prestigious New England Ames clan. His father, Charles Gordon Ames, was a foundling who at the age of three was adopted by Thomas and Lucy Foster Ames, farmer folk living near Canterbury, New Hampshire. Charles Gordon's childhood setting offered only limited educational opportunity, but at the age of fourteen he embraced the Free Will Baptist persuasion and ultimately became a clergyman.[29]

In 1851 Charles Gordon Ames moved to St. Anthony, where he started a congregation and made his presence known as a vigorous antislavery and temperance advocate. Most important, he participated in the founding of the Minnesota Republican party and assumed the

Charles W. Ames, about 1920

editorship of the *Minnesota Republican,* a short-lived journal that communicated the new party's message to the voters of Minnesota Territory. His son, Charles Wilberforce Ames, the future safety commissioner, was born in Minneapolis on June 30, 1855. By now Charles Gordon was not only heavily involved in political activity, but also was becoming disillusioned with the Free Will Baptist connection: the denomination's theological frame of reference could not accommodate the young clergyman's expanding intellectual horizons. In 1856 he resigned from the ministry and appeared poised for a successful career in Minnesota politics. However, he chose to return to New England in 1859 where he soon resumed his ministerial career under Unitarian auspices.

Thanks to the mobility and relative poverty of his family, Charles Wilberforce Ames was exposed to a variety of experiences and influences during his formative years. His early education included enrollment in Albany (New York) Academy, a private institution for boys, and in several public schools in California. At the age of fourteen (1869) he became a printer's apprentice on the staff of the *San Jose Mercury* (California), a connection he severed in 1871 to join a surveying party employed by the Mississippi and Lake Superior (later the St. Paul and Duluth) Railroad. He completed high school in Minneapolis, and while working for the Pennsylvania Railroad enrolled at Cornell University where he earned a degree in literature in 1878. For the next two years he assisted his father on the editorial staff of the *Christian Register* (a Unitarian periodical), and in 1882, following a brief term of service with the George H. Ellis Publishing Company of Boston, he joined the West Publishing Company of St. Paul. [30]

The West connection proved to be Charles W. Ames's permanent niche; he remained with the firm until his death in 1921. He rose steadily in the West hierarchy, serving successively as secretary, general manager, and finally president of the company. Under his leadership West prospered, becoming one of the leading publishers of law books in the country. At various times he served on the boards of the First National Bank of St. Paul, the Northwestern Trust Company of the same city, and the American Law Book Company of New York. He played a leadership role within the influential St. Paul Association of Public and Business Affairs.

Ames also achieved prominence as a major patron of arts and culture. Along with Dr. Arthur Sweeney and Lucius C. Ordway, he presided over the founding of the St. Paul Institute, which in the course of time spawned several of the capital city's important cultural enterprises. Other institutions on which Ames left his mark included the St. Paul Public Library; the St. Paul Academy, of whose board he was the first president; and the Loomis School for Girls, which he helped found. He also continued a family tradition by maintaining an active Unitarian affiliation.

Shortly after the outbreak of World War I Ames embraced the Allied cause with a fervor reminiscent of his father's commitment to antislavery. By 1915 he was engaged in the organization of relief activities on behalf of Belgian and French war refugees. In 1916 he journeyed to France for the purpose of overseeing the distribution of the relief supplies that had been collected at his initiative, and out of his own funds he purchased a motortruck to facilitate this distribution. At the close of the war the French government decorated him in recognition of his contributions to the country's war relief. [31]

Given Ames's zealous commitment to the Allies, it is not surprising that he was as impatient with manifestations of "disloyalty" as McGee. The Ames personal style was considerably less strident and correspondingly more amiable than McGee's, but the determination to uproot all traces of "pro-Germanism" was equally strong. The two men also shared another sentiment: antipathy to trade unionism. However, this identity of views did not assure a harmonious relationship between the two commissioners.

Popular perceptions of the two outstate commissioners — Charles Hoyt March and Anton Charles Weiss — were not as sharply etched as those associated with the three Twin Cities men, and their respective roles on the MCPS would not significantly enhance their prominence. March, who was born in Cedar Mills (Meeker County) in 1870, had as a young man qualified for the bar in 1893 by "reading law"; from then until 1929 he practiced law in Litchfield in partnership with his brother, Nelson D. March. During the Spanish-American War Charles achieved military status as organizer and colonel of the Fourth Regiment of the Minnesota National Guard. The term of service was brief, but the title was retained; after 1898 the Litchfield attorney was often addressed as Colonel March. [32]

Meanwhile the March law practice was expanding beyond the confines of small-town litigation; its clientele included the Great Northern Railroad. Charles March also assumed the role of a gentleman farmer, overseeing the tillage of some one thousand acres. Politics was another sphere attracting March's participation. The voters of Litchfield elected him mayor of the city four times, and he was active in the organizational affairs of the Minnesota Republican party.

Weiss was born in Sheboygan, Wisconsin, in 1862 and educated in the public schools of that city. While still in his teens he joined the staff of the *St. Paul Pioneer Press* as an apprentice; notwithstanding his limited formal education, he carved out a successful niche for himself there. In 1884 he moved to Duluth as *Pioneer Press* correspondent in that city. He held this position until 1891 when he acquired a financial interest in the *Duluth Herald,* and in a few years his interest became the dominant one. Meanwhile, he had established himself as one of Duluth's solid citizens, serving on the board of aldermen from 1888 to 1890 and gaining admission to the city's prestigious clubs. He also won respect within the journalistic community; from 1910 until 1921 he was a member of the board of directors of the Associated Press. [33]

Politically Weiss was affiliated with the Democratic party. Although not as "liberal" as Lind, he aligned himself at times with the ex-governor in opposition to the party's conservative wing. In 1912 he and Lind, together with several other prominent Democrats, defeated

Ambrose Tighe, counsel for
the Minnesota Commission
of Public Safety, about 1920

a conservative attempt to send an uninstructed delegation to the Democratic national convention in Baltimore instead of one pledged to Woodrow Wilson. Weiss went to Baltimore as chairman of the state's delegation and participated in strategy meetings convened by leaders of the Wilson effort. Given the narrow margin of victory by which Wilson won the nomination, the support mobilized by Lind and Weiss was not inconsequential. [34]

Ambrose Tighe was technically not a member of the safety commission, but his role as counsel was crucial even before his appointment was formalized on June 30, 1917. He is credited with authorship of the original draft of the MCPS bill, and early on he submitted memorandums to the commissioners clarifying the more ambiguous provisions in the statute. From Tighe's standpoint, this must have been an agreeable task. His prose reflects a personal fascination with the intricacies of constitutional law and the complexities of constitutional history.

Tighe was born in Brooklyn, New York, in 1859. At the age of sixteen he entered Yale University, graduating with a baccalaureate degree in 1879. For the next four years he remained at Yale, combining the study of law with a tutorship in Roman history and law. At the conclusion of his stay in New Haven he published a scholarly volume on the Roman constitution.[35]

In 1885 Tighe moved to St. Paul and began the practice of law, his main pursuit for the remainder of his life. Along with his law practice he engaged in several business ventures and, to a lesser extent, in Republican politics. His most ambitious political foray was a 1912 bid for the fourth congressional district Republican nomination, a race in which Tighe, running as a progressive sympathetic to Theodore Roosevelt's program but not affiliated with the Bull Moose party, challenged Frederick C. Stevens, the incumbent. Notwithstanding the strong progressive tide sweeping over Minnesota, Tighe lost to Stevens by a wide margin.[36]

Throughout his career Tighe maintained his early interest in constitutional questions. The trend of his thinking is clearly reflected in a paper he delivered before the Minnesota Academy of Social Sciences in December 1912. Entitled "The Police Power and Economic Welfare," the paper argues that the recent tendency of the courts to restrict the police power of states on the grounds that specific regulatory measures violated a constitutionally protected "freedom of contract" was an unwarranted departure from long-established Anglo-Saxon constitutional tradition. This tradition, according to Tighe, sanctioned comprehensive regulation of the economy as necessary and proper. Moreover, he added, the courts were not invariably negating all legislation restricting freedom of contract, but were occasionally invoking the principle that "superior to constitutional limitations on freedom of contract is public welfare."[37]

Tighe concluded his presentation with a quotation from Theodore Roosevelt's famous Osawatomie, Kansas, speech acknowledging the right of enterprising individuals to amass large fortunes but insisting that such fortunes must be "honorably obtained and well used." To the ex-president — and presumably to Tighe — this imperative required "a policy of a far more active governmental interference with social and economic conditions in this country than we have yet had, but I think we have got to face the fact that such an increase in governmental control is now necessary."

Thus, Tighe assumed his responsibilities as legal counsel for the safety commission equipped with a constitutional ideology that logically could sanction the broad delegation of power authorized by the safety commission statute. Eventually some progressives —

including Tighe — would question the commission's prudence in exercising its prerogatives. For the time being, however, many of them professed to believe that Imperial Germany, backed by hosts of well-wishers within North America, posed a mortal danger to the very existence of the United States. In the past, progressives had celebrated the trend toward increased use of government to solve social problems; this view led them easily to the belief that a nation's right of self-preservation transcended constitutional limitations on governmental power.

In a world governed by logic, conservatives who hitherto had eloquently championed limited government concepts might have entertained doubts about the constitutional propriety of the safety commission statute. If so, such doubts were never articulated. To believe that logical consistency shapes thought is perhaps utopian, and all the more so at a time when a society is in the grip of a hysteria of the dimensions equal to the one dominating the climate of American opinion in 1917.

Public response to the initial makeup of the safety commission was relatively low-keyed. McGee, who soon would emerge as the MCPS's most controversial member, was not as well known as he shortly would be, and Lind's presence on the commission carried a reassuring promise that its authority would be exercised responsibly. Moreover, at a time when the security of the republic appeared to be hanging in the balance, most people refrained from criticizing public officials. If standing by President Wilson at a time of grave national danger was appropriate, so was standing by Governor Burnquist.

A few exceptions to this pattern of reaction developed. Sigurd B. Qvale, a prominent Willmar businessman, wrote to Burnquist decrying the absence of agricultural representation on the MCPS. The governor replied, "No farmer could be found by me who was in a position to give up his work at this time of the year." Frequent commission meetings could be anticipated over the coming months, and since the commissioners were barred by law from receiving compensation it was "desirable to have men who are living in or near the Twin Cities and who can come to the meetings without great expense or loss of time." Burnquist also noted that he had appointed a commission to oversee food production and that this body included "a large number of . . . farmers."[38]

The protests emanating from organized labor were sharper than the one communicated by Qvale. The MFL report on the 1917 legislative session noted that labor representatives had attempted to influence the makeup of the commission: "We laid the matter before the governor's secretary . . . and he assured us that the matter would be laid before Governor Burnquist. Labor was, however, entirely ignored in the makeup of the commission, so labor will get its orders without consultation from a commission that, with a possible exception, represents organized capital from start to finish."[39]

Other trade-union advocates echoed the MFL complaint. At a meeting of the Minneapolis Trades and Labor Assembly held shortly after announcement of the MCPS appointments, it was intimated that Burnquist's failure to accord labor its due would encourage Minnesota trade unions to bypass the safety commission in favor of direct cooperation with the Council of National Defense, of which Samuel Gompers was a member. In the following weeks, the *Labor World* repeatedly sounded the same theme. An editorial appearing on June 30 conceded that the "integrity" of Burnquist's five appointees "will not be questioned." On the other hand, "while Governor Burnquist had plenty of opportunity to place at least one labor representative on this commission he saw fit to ignore labor entirely." By contrast, the national administration was appointing labor representatives "on all boards and commissions having to do with determining what sacrifices are to be made by the wealth producers of the land."[40]

Obviously, self-interest was a significant factor promoting this less than amiable reaction to the original MCPS membership, but the trade unionists made a valid point. If there was any justification for vesting the sovereign power of the state in the hands of a small group of appointed individuals, then most assuredly the major interests within Minnesota deserved representation within the group. Other commentators, perhaps without meaning to do so, also implied that the commission was less than representative. In addressing the 1918 convention of the Minnesota State Bar Association, Tighe parenthetically noted that "the commission, as originally constituted, included among its seven members five lawyers and a law book publisher."[41] The impression of imbalance is strengthened by the fact that two of the three appointed lawyer-commissioners were corporation attorneys. If Burnquist was determined to appoint lawyers, the naming of, say, James Manahan, counsel for the Equity movement, would have established a semblance of balance.

Given the corporate affiliations of the commissioners, outsiders may have received an impression of commission solidarity; however, this impression was not entirely correct. Ames confided later that his seven-month tenure on the MCPS was not the happiest phase of his career, although he had enthusiastically supported creation of the commission. For one thing, the selection of March as MCPS vice-chairman had deprived Ames of an honor that he coveted. For another, he "was distressed at the theory of organization which prevailed, because it seemed to me that by it we missed a great opportunity for business efficiency." He conceded that his own tendency to be "self-assertive" was part of the problem; in any case, "after four or five months I began to see that I was a misfit on the Commission." [42]

Midway in his tenure as MCPS counsel, Ambrose Tighe voiced similar complaints. He disclosed that at the first commission meeting Ames had proposed setting up the commission as a board of directors, a plan that Tighe endorsed. However, the commissioners rejected this proposal in favor of assigning the MCPS's multiple functions to individual commissioners. [43]

The tension embittering the relationship between Lind and McGee was a more fundamental threat to harmony within the commission. As fellow members of the Minneapolis bar, Lind and McGee knew each other before joining the commission, but not all of their previous encounters had been friendly ones. In November 1915 McGee had written a widely circulated letter characterizing "the . . . conduct of the [Wilson] administration in Mexico" as "almost criminal." Since Lind had helped shape that policy, he naturally resented this attack. [44]

Soon after the safety commission launched its operation, the proper stance of the MCPS toward Mayor Thomas Van Lear and his administration became a bone of contention between Lind and McGee. In a confidential letter to Burnquist dated May 16, Lind reported: "The Mayor continues to co-operate [in averting labor-management strife] and our Chief of Police [Lewis Harthill] is not only loyal, but very efficient." Lind also reported having "succeeded . . . in bringing several prominent members of the Civic and Commerce Association into personal contact and co-operation with the Chief of Police, and they are establishing better relations with the Mayor also." [45]

Two weeks later, McGee wrote to Senator Nelson with a somewhat different perception of Van Lear and his disposition to cooperate. The issue this time was whether the draft registration and exemption boards selected by the mayor were acceptable. According to McGee:

The Mayor, being a Socialist, loaded the thirteen boards up with Socialists and pro-Germans. . . . I had the list investigated by two different persons and got up a counter list and . . . succeeded in having 18 of the 39 men eliminated. Your friend, John Lind, stood up for the Mayor's list from first to last and I had to fight him for about two hours to have the changes made. He stands for Van Lear and Harthill . . . on every proposition. I really think that Lind is a Socialist in his views. [46]

Lind and McGee also disagreed on the dimensions of the pro-German threat within Minnesota. In urging congressional funding of weapons for the state Home Guard, McGee claimed to possess reports that "in centers of population strongly German . . . drilling is going on preparatory to resisting the draft." Lind did not yield to McGee in his perception of the IWW peril, but the danger emanating from German-American neighborhoods was, in Lind's opinion, greatly exaggerated. A personal Lind letter that found its way into the columns of the *New Ulm Review* declared that he, Lind, had "not been much worried that our German friends would shoot up their neighbors or destroy their own property." He was "not lying awake nights to devise schemes to fight the Germans . . . in the U.S." Regrettably, however, the presence on every commission of one or two "bell-ringers" appeared to be inevitable. [47]

Readers of the *New Ulm Review* might have inferred that the "bell-ringer" reference was a barb aimed at McGee. However, until late 1917 when issues related to the street railway strike precipitated an internal MCPS crisis, a public perception that the commissioners were of one mind on all important questions seems to have prevailed. The commission's own propaganda program carefully nourished such an impression. Intimations that Ames and Tighe were becoming increasingly frustrated by the MCPS's lack of "business efficiency" were not permitted to leak into the columns of the press. Some observers may have suspected that McGee and Lind were not working in perfect harmony, but the degree of acrimony separating the two men was shielded from public view.

Meanwhile, the commission was tackling a multiplicity of responsibilities with a show of energy that was not matched by concrete achievement. The first order of business was building the structures required to carry out the MCPS mandate.

Getting Down to Business

T he Minnesota Commission of Public Safety convened in the governor's office in the State Capitol at 10 A.M. on Monday, April 23, six days after the members were appointed, for an informal discussion of the body's powers and duties.[1] Although the minutes yield few clues about the main thrust of the meeting, there was obviously much to discuss. Two problems stood in the forefront of the members' concerns: the constitutional vulnerability of the commission, which raised the possibility that a strict constructionist judge might order the dismantling of all or part of it; and uncertainty about the tools that could most effectively — and legally — compel obedience to its orders.

The authority delegated to the commission by its constituting statute was awesome:

> In the event of war . . . such commission shall have power to do all acts and things non-inconsistent with the constitution or laws of the state of Minnesota or of the United States, which are necessary or proper for the public safety and for the protection of life and public property or private property of a character as in the judgment of the commission requires protection, and shall do and perform all acts and things necessary or proper so that the military, civil and industrial resources of the state may be most efficiently applied toward maintenance of the defense of the state and nation and toward the successful prosecution of such war, and to that end it shall have all necessary power not herein specifically enumerated and in addition thereto the following specific powers.[2]

The first of the five specific powers enumerated in section 3, the statute's core provision, authorized the commission to "purchase, lease, hire or otherwise acquire . . . property of every kind . . . necessary or desirable for use for any of the purposes aforesaid." The second vested the power of eminent domain in the commission. The third required and authorized the commission "to co-operate with the military and other officers and agents of the United States government in all matters pertaining to the duties and functions of such commission."

The fourth clothed the commission with full investigative authority. It empowered the MCPS to

> require any person to appear before it or before any agent or officer of [the] commission for examination . . . under oath as to any information within the knowledge of such person and to require such person to produce for inspection any writings or documents under his control, and to that end the district court of any county in the state shall issue a subpoena upon the request of any of [the commission's] agents or officers, and all said agents and officers shall have power to administer oaths and take testimony and to procure the punishment for contempt of any person refusing to answer or produce writings or documents requested by [the] commission, by any such district court.

The fifth specific power was no doubt the most drastic of all:

> Said commission may inquire into the method of performance of his duty by any public official other than the constitutional officials of this state, and may advise the governor to remove any such official from office, if in the judgment of the commission the public interests demand such removal. Upon being advised to remove any such official by said commission, the governor is hereby authorized summarily to remove such public official.

Less controversial provisions in the MCPS statute conferred on the commission broad discretion "to provide for the comfort of [Minnesotans] in the military service of the United States" (section 4) and to compensate national guardsmen for their 1916 service on the Mexican border (sections 5 and 6). Section 7 cleared the way for creation of one of the commission's most effective enforcement tools by authorizing it "to provide for the enlistment, organization and maintenance of a home guard." Home Guard officers were to be appointed by the governor, who was to "have the same powers in relation to said guard as now conferred upon him by the constitution and laws of the state in relation to the other military and naval forces."

Critics of the commission could derive some reassurance from section 8 of the statute, which ordered termination of the MCPS "within three months after the conclusion of peace and . . . sooner . . . if the governor shall determine and proclaim that the exercise of [its] powers . . . are no longer necessary." However, one disturbing reservation was attached: the governor was accorded the discretion of continuing the commission "for a longer term" if he found it necessary to do so.

Of the remaining sections of the statute, one invites special comment. According to section 10, "The provisions of this act are separable and not dependent, and if any provision, section, or part of either is held unconstitutional, the same shall not affect any other part of this act." John McGee, who had conceded that certain provisions in the MCPS statute were "palpably" unconstitutional, claimed credit for inclusion of this section in the final bill. Other sponsors and supporters of the MCPS shared his anxiety about the legal standing of the commission. Counsel Ambrose Tighe confronted it directly in a speech to the Minnesota State Bar Association on August 15, 1918.[3]

Tighe confessed that the United States Supreme Court had established a precedent in an 1866 case, Ex Parte Milligan, that "arbitrary arrests of civilians, under executive orders or the orders of military officers, are illegal except in times of actual warfare and even then are illegal except in districts where there are contemporary hostilities . . . and where the civil courts are not open and in operation." Subsequent court decisions had relaxed these restrictions on arbitrary governmental action in times of crisis, but crippling limitations were still in force. According to Tighe, the Milligan case "seems to say that the government is powerless, by way of summary anticipatory action under such circumstances [a threat to the life of the state], and that its recourse is limited to the slow process of courts of law and the enforcement of existing statutes."

In Tighe's view, this limitation was extremely unfortunate. Modern wars were not fought by armies alone. "The Civil War . . . was fought also by the farmers . . . and by the factory hands . . . who produced the food the soldiers ate, the clothes they wore, and the arms with which they did battle." When plagued by agitators seeking to promote discontent among farmers and workers, "must the government submit to the demoralization of the industrial branch of its military service; . . . must it follow the painful course of indictments, demurrers, trials and appeals, while the enemy, hampered by none of these things, presse[s] joyously on it?" Tighe did not think so. He argued that:

> in time of war the government of every state has inherent power to
> do all acts and things necessary or proper to defeat the enemy

and . . . it is performing its full duty to the constitution when it exercises every form of activity to preserve the state, on the preservation of which the existence of the constitution itself depends. . . . This is the legal basis of the safety commission act, if it has any legal basis.[4]

The safety commission act, Tighe continued, assumed "the admission of two facts." The first one was that the state constitution, unlike the federal one, was not "a grant of power, but a statement of limitations on power which, but for it, would be boundless." The state retained "every conceivable power" except those that had been taken from it by its own or the federal constitution. "The state has the right to live, and when its life is in danger no one can invoke the provisions of a paper constitution to thwart its work for self defence."

The second "fact" was the need to maintain the industrial front as well as the military one:

It is as essential to winning the war, for example, that the street cars which carry workers to the munition factories in St. Paul and Minneapolis should operate uninterruptedly as it is that our marines should fight in France, and it is as proper a function of a war board to see that they do . . . as it is for the secretary of war to see that the marines get across the ocean.[5]

Tighe compared the role of the safety commission to that of a health board, an analogy that evidently had influenced the thinking of its architects. An 1883 Minnesota law had provided that when an infectious disease threatened the health of a community, the local health board could and should "do and provide all such acts, matters and things as may be necessary for mitigating or preventing the spread of any such disease." When the St. Paul health department ordered the vaccination of all children and barred those not receiving vaccination from the public schools, some parents complained that exclusion from public schools infringed on a fundamental right. In the words of the 1902 district court ruling, however, since "the regulations compelling vaccination are . . . solely for the public good, the rights conferred thereby are primary and superior to the rights of any pupil to attend the public schools."

Tighe believed the analogy between the authority of a health board to combat an epidemic and the powers conferred on the MCPS to be a sound one: "If a health board can be lawfully empowered to exercise arbitrary power in times of epidemic, in the interest of the public health, it would seem as though a safety commission, in times of war, could be given like authority, that the life of the state may be saved."[6]

The address also called attention to a problem that had "puzzled some lawyers a great deal": the appropriate method of enforcing the commission's orders. The original statute provided that defiance of a commission order constituted a felony. This provision was stricken from the bill before final passage, leaving the commissioners in doubt as to how their edicts were to be enforced. Was the commission entirely dependent on moral suasion, reinforced by pressures generated by the patriotic climate of the time?

An opinion emanating from the attorney general's office on April 30, 1917, noted that the courts were "ordinarily the law's agent for law enforcement," but that "they are not under the constitution a necessary factor." Statutes could "provide other machinery, if the legislature believes it will be more effective, and in the present instance has done so." The broad powers possessed by the commission enabled it not only to issue orders but also to enforce them "summarily." Since one could expect that the MCPS would refrain from action "not . . . sustained by the best popular opinion," broad compliance with its orders could be anticipated. On the other hand, if compelling "obedience by the direct apprehension and incarceration of malefactors" appeared desirable, "the machinery to this end . . . [is] at hand."[7]

The five lawyers and one law book publisher on the commission "did not think much of this view," Tighe said. It appeared "to eliminate the courts, and lawyers and law book publishers are apt to think that the earth cannot revolve on its axis except with the assistance of the judges." Consequently, the earlier orders issued by the MCPS would rely on ordinances enacted by municipal councils for legal validation. "The theory . . . was that ordinances so enacted could prescribe penalties, even if the commission's orders could not, and that municipal councils could legislate under the commission's direction, even if the commission itself had not been empowered . . . to do so." After a federal court decision of July 16, 1917, held that the commission possessed the authority to issue orders having the force of law, the MCPS "gradually abandoned the municipal ordinance device and proceeded by direct order"; on April 30, 1918, it would go the whole way by defining violation of a safety commission order as a misdemeanor punishable by not more than three months in the county jail or by a fine not to exceed one hundred dollars. [8]

John S. Pardee, the commission's first secretary

Time did not permit the commissioners to probe very deeply into the legal puzzles confronting them at their first meeting. Moreover, other concerns competed for attention. Following adjournment of the April 23 session, Lind, McGee, and March toured the Minneapolis Bridge Square and milling district, a strategically important area considered particularly vulnerable to sabotage and disorder. The commission met again the next day, holding a morning session and a more prolonged one in the afternoon. The morning session included the appointment of John S. Pardee, a journalist whose experience included employment on the staffs of Red Wing and Duluth newspapers, as commission secretary. [9]

The role of the secretary in the MCPS operation was a crucial one. He was responsible for interpreting commission decisions to affected parties, and virtually all communications from the general public to the MCPS passed through his office. Moreover, the commissioners were not full-time, salaried officials, but a group of ostensibly public-spirited volunteers who gathered weekly or as needed to monitor the effectiveness of Minnesota's contribution to the war effort and to counteract threats to the security of the state. The secretary, on the other hand, was presumably in command of the commission's day-to-day processes.

Pardee, who would continue as secretary until September 1917, when he joined the publicity staff of Herbert Hoover's Federal Food Administration, accepted the MCPS assignment in the hope that the commission would function as a promoter of beneficial change rather than an unrelenting defender of the status quo. In writing to Lincoln Steffens on July 5, 1917, he remarked:

> I felicitate you upon your continued flitting from revolution to revolution. My own work is more humdrum. . . . While much of the work is purely routine it does open some very delightful prospects for constructive plans as to rebuilding men out of broken human material and picking up the slack in the loose jointed system of distribution and otherwise influencing the shaping of the new world in which we are to live. [10]

A few weeks later Pardee remained convinced of the revolutionary impact of the war, but he appeared less confident that state and national leaders were equal to the challenge posed by this impact. On July 24 he confided to a Duluth friend that

> somebody will have to make this world over. As it is being made over in Europe — as it has been transformed in Britain — as it has been completely upset in Russia — more or less there must be a new structure in the United States. . . .
>
> The work lies not so much . . . with the rough necks as with the polite people who are in positions of authority and believe that all they have to do is to preserve order where what they must do is to inaugurate [a] new order. [11]

Whether disenchantment with the MCPS or the appeal of broader vistas persuaded Pardee to accept the federal post cannot be determined. While serving the commission he faithfully carried out its mandates, remarking on one occasion when a controversial issue was pending: "It does not matter what my own views are." However, early in his MCPS tenure Pardee asked the commissioners to clarify an issue that later would subject several Nonpartisan League speakers to criminal prosecution. Shortly after the United States declaration of war, a Northern Pacific Railway official had urged railroaders to "stand in their present places rather than enlist in the army," the implication being that railroading was an essential occupation. Could this be interpreted as a violation of the 1917 Minnesota law prohibiting interference with enlistment? "If it is," confessed Pardee, "your Secretary should be disciplined for having unwittingly broken the law on several occasions when he has urged men in the agricultural industry to stay on the farm, and it is even questionable whether in that case all the members of the Commission are not in contempt of law." The outcome of Pardee's inquiry is not clear from commission records. Use of the law against the Nonpartisan League, however, was part of a pattern that suggests selective enforcement. [12]

When the commissioners convened for their April 24 afternoon session, they discussed and adopted a draft of the bylaws that Colonel March had proposed. The bylaws specified that the commission should meet on Monday (later changed to Tuesday) of each week at 10:30 A.M. in the Capitol office assigned to it; that additional meetings could be held on twelve hours notice, and, in special circumstances, without notice; and that a record of every meeting should be kept. Meetings were to be "executive and attendance . . . limited to the members of the Commission and such of its employes as it may from time to time designate and other persons whose presence it may from time to time invite." If this suggests a closed-door policy, the impression is strengthened by a provision that "information as to the proceedings at any meeting may be given to the public only in written form, approved by the chairman or vice-chairman." [13]

Given the contemporary American distaste for secret diplomacy, it is not surprising that the commission's closed-door policy created some unhappiness. MCPS critics suspected that nefarious conspiracies were afoot, journalists reacted negatively, and in time friends of the commission realized that lack of publicity was not to the agency's advantage. However, the commissioners were reluctant to open the door more than a crack. On May 29, by a vote of four to three (McGee, Burnquist, and Smith voting nay), they resolved that "the By-Laws . . . be so far suspended as to permit a responsible representative of the Associated Press and United Press to sit at meetings of the Commission." [14]

The bylaws also added two new offices to the commission's personnel structure: a vice-chairman to be selected from within MCPS

*Nicollet Avenue at First Street South, Minneapolis, about 1915. Bridge Square —
near the Mississippi River at the intersection of Hennepin and Nicollet avenues
— was the center of a district known for its saloons, pool halls, hotels, and employment bureaus.*

ranks, and a secretary — the post to which Pardee had been appointed.
When the MCPS expanded its staff in mid-September, an assistant
secretary was added.

During the afternoon session on April 24, the commissioners also
began to tackle what they considered to be the volatile situation in
the Bridge Square district, which Lind, McGee, and March had toured
the day before. Mayor Van Lear and Minneapolis police chief Lewis
Harthill were present to provide information on "conditions in the
same territory, the 'rough people who do rough work,' the amusement places, the I.W.W. and the crooks."[15]

Following extended discussion the commissioners unanimously
approved Order 1, a sweeping enactment calling for the closure of
all saloons, pool halls, and moving picture theaters in Bridge Square
and the milling district. Implementation of this order might have provoked a legal challenge to MCPS authority; the affected licensees could

have appealed to the courts (as one saloonkeeper would do when the MCPS issued a subsequent order), and the Minneapolis City Council could have refused to cancel the licenses. However, the saloonkeepers, pool hall operators, and owners of moving picture theaters refrained from pressing legal challenges, and the Minneapolis council cooperated by revoking all relevant licenses within the designated area. [16]

The MCPS convened for two more extended sessions on April 25. Again the saloon situation, this time in the neighborhoods surrounding Fort Snelling, was high on the agenda. The commissioners approved Order 2, which prohibited the sale of intoxicating liquor in an area "to the width of two and one-half miles, immediately surrounding and adjoining the Fort Snelling Military Reservation," a ban that was to remain in effect until ratification of a treaty of peace. As in the case of Order 1, implementation depended on municipal authority, this time not only in Minneapolis but also in St. Paul and the village of Mendota, and again there was compliance. [17]

The food problem also was discussed on April 25. A. D. Wilson of the agricultural extension service appeared before the commission to outline the program formulated by the Committee on Food Production and Conservation — more commonly known as the food committee — in fulfilling its mandate. Organization of the food committee antedated creation of the MCPS. In early April, while the safety commission bill was pending, Albert F. Woods, dean of the University of Minnesota Department of Agriculture, recommended to the governor that such a committee be established and placed under the authority of the projected "State Board of Public Safety" and that its membership include representatives from more than two dozen organizations — the State Dairyman's Association, the State Federation of Women's Clubs, and the Minnesota Editorial Association, among others. Burnquist authorized the committee and appointed the individuals nominated by Woods, who held their first meeting at the University Farm on April 14. Although officially subordinate to the MCPS and partially dependent on commission funding, the food committee was essentially autonomous. The same was true of several other agencies formally operating under MCPS auspices. [18]

One more important matter was disposed of on April 25: assignment by the governor of specific responsibilities to the five appointed commissioners. McGee was placed in charge of military affairs; March, agriculture; Lind, labor; Ames, civic affairs; and Weiss, the press. The division of work suggested by this arrangement was exceedingly fuzzy. Several of the areas overlapped: for example, the needs of agriculture included assurance of an adequate supply of farm labor, a challenge within Lind's arena. The monitoring of loyalty appeared to fall within the civic sector. No one was inclined to accuse Ames of dereliction of duty in pursuing sedition, but this did not inhibit some of his colleagues — particularly McGee — from launching their own loyalty campaigns. Further complicating this arrangement was the time the committee spent collectively dealing with issues like vice and alcohol control. [19]

The commissioners did not convene again until May 7 because of the departure of March, McGee, and Ames to Washington as representatives of Minnesota at a national defense conference. However, beginning on May 7 and continuing through the next two months, the commission adhered rigidly to its meeting schedule and also held frequent special sessions. Within this time span — and not-withstanding the inefficiency of its mode of operation — the agency launched a number of important initiatives.

Among other things, it transformed the Home Guard concept into reality; established a corps of peace officers endowed with the power invested in a constable; created a functioning network of county safety commissions; set up a system of recruitment that helped ameliorate a potentially serious labor shortage, particularly on the farms; facilitated the mobilization of women; monitored the first draft registration; broadened the MCPS role as a regulator of the liquor trade; and placed "suspect" sectors of Minnesota society — including the iron ranges, German-American communities, and the radical wing of the labor movement — under surveillance.

No one could deny that this agenda was ambitious; whether it added up to constructive public policy was another question. Critics charged the commissioners with insensitivity toward the constitutional rights of those whose enthusiasm for the war was less than unqualified, and they pointed to the lack of broad community representation — particularly from within the ranks of organized labor — on the commission. In the early weeks of the war these complaints were somewhat muted. They would become considerably louder as the full MCPS program unfolded in the last half of 1917.

Anticipating that units of the Minnesota National Guard currently guarding sensitive facilities (mills, elevators, railroad bridges, and the like) would shortly be called into federal service, the commissioners assigned high priority to the Home Guard question. In response to plans submitted by McGee, the commissioners adopted Order 3 on April 28, which authorized the recruitment of seven Home Guard battalions to be organized on the National Guard model. Adjutant General Walter F. Rhinow, assisted by a staff of ten, was designated as commandant. Since Rhinow already commanded the Minnesota National Guard and soon would become state selective service director, his role was crucial. Authority to commission Home Guard officers was vested in the governor, who obviously would be guided by Rhinow's recommendations. Unless called up for extended duty outside of their home stations — five days or more — both officers and men were to serve without pay. During extended periods of service they were to be compensated at the same rate as National Guard personnel. [20]

The commissioners then faced the delicate problem of how extensive the guard's role should be. Lind in particular desired to restrict its role as a guardian of private property. On May 29 he introduced a resolution affirming, "It is not the purpose . . . to call on the Home Guards for any duty that can be as well performed by civilian officers or private watchmen." The resolution passed. An action taken by the commission two weeks earlier undoubtedly enhanced the willingness of Lind's colleagues to support his resolution. On May 14 the commissioners enacted an order (No. 4) authorizing the MCPS to appoint a "Peace Officer" invested with constabulary power and supplied with metallic badges stamped "Minnesota Public Safety Commission, Peace Officer." The order also provided that "any person, corporation or co-partnership who desires to have property guarded by any such Peace Officer may make application . . . for the appointment of any voter . . . as a Peace Officer, and . . . he shall be assigned to the duty of guarding the property of such applicant." [21]

Setting up the peace officers in business involved fewer problems than equipping the Home Guard. The former required only a commission and a badge — evidently each peace officer was expected to arm himself — whereas the guards needed uniforms, rifles, and ammunition. Given its limited budget, the MCPS was reluctant to commit large sums for these imperatives. It disclaimed all financial responsibility for the procurement of uniforms, a gap essentially filled by the guardists themselves and by citizens of the communities wherein the guard stations were located. [22]

Weapon procurement was a more difficult problem. McGee asked Washington to come to the rescue with three thousand rifles or marine guns if rifles were not available, but he soon discovered that weapons in this quantity were not immediately obtainable. Congressional delay in appropriating funds for home defense apparently was the main stumbling block, and one that McGee believed cast doubt on congressional patriotism. "There are," he proclaimed, "different types of treason and I don't distinguish between active and passive treason." Ultimately the state received five hundred Springfield rifles along with one thousand rounds of ammunition. The deficiency was filled in part by a federal decision to make available to the Home Guard rifles in the possession of the state's military academies. [23]

McGee also discovered seven thousand rounds of Winchester ammunition in Minneapolis, which his colleagues authorized him to purchase. Presumably this cache, or at least a part of it, had been collected for the Minneapolis Civilian Auxiliary, a military force organized by Minneapolis employers to fill the gap created by the refusal of Van Lear and his police chief to permit city police to serve as strikebreakers. In any case, the missions of the Civilian Auxiliary and the Home Guard were in many respects parallel, a reality that would be underscored during the street railway strike in late 1917. In February 1918 officers of the Civilian Auxiliary requested incorporation into the Home Guard, a request to which the MCPS assented. At that time the auxiliary was "an organization composed of mostly business men" with a strength of "about 600" and armed with "about 25 shot guns and about 120 riot sticks." [24]

Securing uniforms and procuring weapons were not the only problems confronting the Home Guard. Its potential manpower pool was also limited. The prevailing ethos required every patriotic, able-bodied young male either to enlist in the federal service or submit joyously to the draft. Moreover, the MCPS imposed a further limitation by declaring that "commissions in the Home Guard be issued only to such persons as have had adequate training in the National Guard or in service of the United States." [25]

MCPS recruitment specifications scrupulously respected the needs of the federal armed forces. Order 3 limited eligibility to "able-bodied men over the age of twenty-six," the assumption being that the obligation to enlist in the army was especially incumbent on men under twenty-six. Following passage of selective service, "able-bodied men between . . . 31 and 52 inclusive" were declared eligible — originally, the selective service law required registration for the draft of all men between the ages of twenty-one and thirty-one. Men under thirty-one might "be enlisted when it is shown that they are probably exempt from service in the Federal Army."[26]

Thanks partly to the efforts of John McGee, the Home Guard soon leaped over the barriers imposed by meager funding and a limited manpower base. On May 22 McGee reported that he was spending all his time in "organizing the Home Guard." Shortly he would have "four splendid companies in Minneapolis" commanded by officers with military experience. He was planning a trip to St. Louis County, where he expected to recruit seven companies of infantry "consisting of 700 men to start with," and he anticipated the organization of four companies in St. Paul. Two days later, on McGee's recommendation, the MCPS voted to raise the number of battalions from seven to ten.[27]

The Home Guard would continue to grow through the remainder of 1917 and into 1918. By April 15, 1918, the force consisted of 7,131 enlisted men and 370 officers organized in ninety-two companies that in turn were grouped in eighteen battalions, or, in the words of a status report, "an aggregate of 7501 men, representing protection to 58 towns." By war's end, the number of battalions had increased to twenty-one, and personnel, both enlisted and commissioned, totaled 8,373. In its final report the MCPS could point to only a few encounters between the Home Guard and the forces of evil — the most notable during the street railway strike in December 1917 — but the report did affirm that "the moral effect of the existence of this peace force has been marked from the day of its organization."[28]

Organizing the counties was another project ranking high on the MCPS agenda. On May 7 the commissioners endorsed the preliminary steps taken by the governor to bring a network of county safety commissioners into being and agreed that the chairmen should be appointed and commissioned by the governor.[29]

Assisted by March, Burnquist initiated a search for suitable candidates for the county directorships. They asked the Minnesota Bankers' Association for recommendations, an offer to which MBA officials responded enthusiastically. In a form letter to members, George H. Richards, MBA secretary, commented: "The Commission has complimented this Association by asking it to suggest the names of the men best suited for the work."[30] Burnquist and March may have also sought the counsel of other business groups, but it is not evident that they solicited recommendations from either the American Society of Equity or the Minnesota Federation of Labor.

In any case, the banking fraternity could not complain of under-representation on the county directors' roster. A few random examples make the point. Tollef Jacobson, Douglas County director, had served as president of the Farmers National Bank of Alexandria and the First National Bank of Brandon and for many years had engaged in the mortgage loan business. William H. Putnam, head of the Goodhue County commission, was a prominent Red Wing banker. John Dwan, Lake County chairman, is better known for his association with Minnesota Mining and Manufacturing, but he was also an incorporator and long-time officer of the Commercial State Bank of Two Harbors. William I. Prince, St. Louis County chairman, was a founder of Duluth's City National Bank. John W. Boock, Sibley County director, was cashier of the Citizens State Bank of Gibbon.[31]

Fred B. Snyder and Donald R. Cotton, chiefs of the Hennepin and Ramsey county commissions, had significant banking connections. In addition to being an organizer of the Minneapolis Civic and Commerce Association, president of the University of Minnesota Board of Regents, and well-known Republican politician, Snyder was a director of the First National Bank of Minneapolis. Cotton was manager of sales for the Illinois Steel Company offices in St. Paul. Before the United States entered the war he had served on the executive committee of the St. Paul branch of the National Security League, and during America's participation in the conflict he would hold leadership positions in several agencies linked to the federal War Industries Board. Pardee professed respect for the influence Snyder and Cotton exercised within the top echelons of the Twin Cities business community. In discussing the problem of financing county activities, the MCPS secretary remarked: "In Ramsey and Hennepin I guess the directors simply go to the St. Paul and Minneapolis commercial bodies and lie down on them" — a tactic that Pardee believed effective.[32]

Although the directors tended to be bankers and businessmen, county safety commission members were drawn from a wider pool. In rural Minnesota the township committees that were set up by many county committees were typically headed by farmers, and occasionally the name of a person subsequently associated with the Nonpartisan League appeared on the township rosters. Herman Schmechel of the Renville County township organization, for example, was elected to the state Senate in 1918 on the NPL-endorsed ticket; he served in the legislature for twenty years. David H. Evans, the NPL-endorsed candidate in the gubernatorial campaign of 1918, served on the Lyon County marketing committee; Henrik Shipstead of Glenwood was a member of the Pope County general committee; and Victor E. Lawson, editor and publisher of the liberal *Willmar Tribune*, served on the Kandiyohi County Loyalty League. Union representation was invisible within Snyder's Hennepin organization, but George W. Lawson, secretary of the Minnesota Federation of Labor, held membership on the Ramsey County commission's advisory council, and George L. Siegel, a prominent St. Paul labor lawyer, was a precinct representative. The presence of these individuals within the county network, however, was not substantial enough to influence MCPS policy to any significant degree. [33]

A bewildering variety of organizational schemes emerged within the county safety commissions, largely because the MCPS left a wide area of discretion to the county director. He could either appoint his subordinates or invoke the authority of a mass meeting, which, in any event, he was instructed to convene. Most counties created an executive committee and others in such areas as labor, marketing, finance, publicity, and, sometimes, Red Cross. In Ramsey and Hennepin counties, ward and precinct committees were established. [34]

The county directors were not completely comfortable with the vague mandate assigned to them by the parent commission. In a May 23 memorandum Pardee sought to answer "a number of inquiries" addressed to him by various county directors. The most crucial question asked was, "What authority is conferred upon the County Director?" Pardee's reply may not have been completely reassuring: "The extent of his authority will be determined from time to time." Another dominant concern was the farm labor problem. Each county, Pardee wrote, was expected to "take care of its own problem as far as possible and . . . the State will undertake to supply suitable persons to make up whatever shortage may be found."

Ensuring an adequate supply of farm labor had been a focus of MCPS concern from the start. The commissioners proclaimed on April 28 that the MCPS "in concert with the Minnesota Food Committee . . . is preparing such measures as will enable the farmers to meet the demands upon them." On May 5 a conference of "the commercial organizations of the Northwest" assembled in St. Paul to explore all aspects of the problem and communicate its findings to the

MCPS. On May 10 the commission selected a special committee consisting of March, Ames, and Lind for the purpose of "bringing together the several factors in the farm labor problem."[35]

The three commissioners carried out their mandate expeditiously. Lind invited the superintendent of the Milwaukee Public Employment Office — regarded as a model of its kind — to appear before the MCPS on May 21 to enlighten the commissioners with respect to the Milwaukee experiment. After hearing the superintendent's report, the commission directed the special committee to "investigate whether the state labor bureau can be reorganized to handle state labor problems."[36]

Three days later the special committee submitted a report that, instead of proposing a reorganization of the state labor bureau, recommended the establishment in Minneapolis of a free public employment office — more commonly known as the Free Employment Bureau — to be operated under MCPS supervision. Don D. Lescohier, chief statistician of the Minnesota Department of Labor and Industries, was appointed superintendent of the new agency, and the commission asked the University of Minnesota agricultural extension service and the Minneapolis Civic and Commerce Association for assistance in setting up and operating the employment bureau. The MCPS also allocated Lescohier's office a revolving fund of one thousand dollars.

To provide Lescohier and the county directors with essential information, all farmers in the state were required to fill out questionnaires supplying information on their own labor needs and on how they proposed to dispose of surplus perishables. The MCPS office mailed the questionnaire forms to the county directors, who in turn distributed them to the township chairmen who were responsible for placing a questionnaire in the hands of every farmer within the township. The assistance of the town clerk, the local postmaster, and the rural mail carrier was also solicited.[37]

Since the proclamation ordering the census was not issued until June 1, the goal of completing it by July 1 was highly unrealistic. That returns from sixty-four counties, representing about 80 percent of the state's farmers, had been received and tabulated by July 30 was an impressive achievement and one for which the staff of the agricultural extension service could claim considerable credit. Its personnel assumed responsibility for tabulating the forms as they came in, a formidable task given the state of tabulation technology in 1917.[38]

Meanwhile the MCPS and Lescohier were perfecting a process for allocating farm labor to areas where it was needed. Each farmer requiring help was urged to begin by canvassing the immediate neighborhood. If no hands were available, the farmer was then to apply through the county organization. Requests for labor not available within the county were to be transmitted to Lescohier's office, which would endeavor to fill them and even to advance the railroad fare required to transport the laborer to his assigned destination.[39]

The county directors met in St. Paul on June 13 to become familiar with farm labor recruitment as well as with their other responsibilities — above all the mobilization of public opinion in support of the war. Eighty-four of the state's eighty-six counties were represented, in most cases by their directors. If this showed that the task of organizing the grass roots was well advanced, Pardee's report showed that the gathering's total impact transcended the sum of its parts. "That was one of the most important meetings . . . held in Minnesota," exulted the MCPS secretary. One director had benefited not only from "some measure of instruction" concerning his responsibilities but had also gained "a sense of comradeship and a new feeling that out of this war we would find firmer beliefs in the fatherhood of God and the brotherhood of man." The Beltrami County director left the meeting with a determination of "going through his county, if necessary, with a pack sack and a pair of snow shoes."[40]

Although such typical wartime hyperbole deserves to be heavily discounted, the farm labor recruitment program — a dominant but not the sole responsibility of the county organizations — was perhaps the most successful initiative launched by the safety commission. No critical agricultural labor shortage developed either in 1917 or 1918, and officials of the Council of National Defense, who beginning in early 1918 became increasingly critical of the commission's overall operation, exempted the farm labor program from criticism.[41] The program was also one of the least controversial MCPS activities. Anxiety to harvest bountiful crops was a factor operating independently of the issues raised by other aspects of MCPS policy.

In addition to excluding liquor and entertainment from the Minneapolis Bridge Square district, limiting servicemen's access to intoxicants, mobilizing the Home Guard, authorizing the commissioning of peace officers, setting up a network of county safety commissions, and establishing a system of farm labor recruitment, the Minnesota

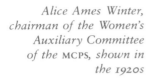

*Alice Ames Winter,
chairman of the Women's
Auxiliary Committee
of the* MCPS, *shown in
the 1920s*

Commission of Public Safety focused its attention on another important concern during the first two months of its existence: the duty
of providing the women of Minnesota with an opportunity to participate in the war effort. In responding to this concern, the MCPS
started out with the advantage of an extraordinarily energetic leader.

Alice Ames Winter was a nationally known participant in the
women's movement. Although born in Albany, New York (1865), she
could claim Minnesota roots by virtue of the fact that her father,
Charles Gordon Ames, began his active career as clergyman and politician in the state. After receiving both a bachelor's and a master's degree
from Wellesley College, Alice Ames taught school in Boston for two
years. In 1892 she married Thomas G. Winter, a Minneapolis grain
dealer who in 1917 would be appointed superintendent of the safety
commission's intelligence bureau. [42]

Following her marriage Alice Winter emerged as an advocate
and practitioner of the precept that women could successfully com-
bine homemaking and career interests. While rearing two children
she found time to write novels "around the edge" of her maternal

responsibilities. Later she served as president of the Minneapolis Woman's Club — which she helped to found — and chairman of the literature department of the General Federation of Women's Clubs. [43]

As manager of the women's sector of the Minnesota war effort, Alice Winter operated under the authority of a dual appointment: chairman of the Council of National Defense Minnesota Woman's Committee and chairman of the Minnesota Commission of Public Safety Women's Auxiliary. The logic of this arrangement is apparent. Given Alice Winter's prominence within the national women's movement, her federal appointment was not a surprise. As a member in good standing of the Twin Cities elite, half-sister of Commissioner Charles W. Ames and spouse of Thomas G. Winter, she was also closely linked to the MCPS power structure. [44]

Nevertheless, the possibility of tension between her two mandates concerned Alice Winter. In proposing a letterhead that reflected the double appointment, she worried about the commission's receptivity to her design. She argued that the federal appointment was too important to be ignored: through it "we are to get a lot of our best help through the Council of Defense . . . the organ used by Mr. Hoover, Miss [Julia] Lathrop of the Children's Bureau, the national Labor Commissions, etc. for disseminating their directions to women." Moreover, "I shall have to explain . . . that I represent the national body in this state, or [people] will wonder why Minnesota is the only state in the Union to be without [a Council of National Defense women's branch]." [45]

Winter's apprehensions with respect to the letterhead proved to be groundless. Ames was an effective liaison person between her office and the MCPS, and the other commissioners were apparently not anxious to engage in controversy with Winter. Following brief discussion the commissioners approved her organizational plans; provided her with a secretary, typewriter, and office supplies; and confirmed her committee appointments. The communication from Pardee informing Winter of MCPS confirmation of her executive committee suggests a pro forma proceeding. "At your convenience," wrote Pardee, "will you kindly furnish me with the names of the women whose appointment the Commission has confirmed as the list which Mr. Ames had has escaped me." [46]

Alice Winter soon developed an ambitious agenda including food conservation in all its aspects, "social hygiene," Liberty loan and Red Cross promotion, recruitment of women for war work, protection of children, and, above all, "Americanization." Moreover, except in a formal sense, MCPS supervision of this myriad of activities was minimal. To Winter the connection with the Council of National Defense must have appeared considerably more important than the link to the MCPS, particularly after Ames left the commission in December 1917.

Unlike the mobilization of women, regulation of the liquor trade was a responsibility that the MCPS was unable to delegate to a strong-minded individual. Moreover, the commissioners regarded it as a troublesome responsibility. Prohibition sentiment was rising throughout the state, but the liquor trade — buttressed by the support of groups whose values did not interdict "social drinking" — was a powerful interest resisting further restraints. Desiring to avoid entanglement with either extreme of the "wet-dry" continuum, the safety commission sought to limit its intervention to measures needed to assure effective enforcement of existing liquor laws except where "military necessity" compelled additional restrictions. In theory this was unexceptionable; in reality, less so. [47]

Existing liquor regulation was based on a maze of statutes passed at different times and subject to varying interpretations. In addition, some sheriffs and county attorneys — particularly those accountable to wet constituencies — assigned low priority to liquor law enforcement. Throughout its existence, the MCPS was besieged with complaints charging local officials with blatant toleration of "blind-pigging" (bootlegging) or defiance of closing hours. "Military necessity" also was an imprecise concept. Convinced drys argued that it dictated total prohibition; their adversaries contended that a "bone-dry" resolution of the liquor problem would not only impair citizen morale but would also have a detrimental economic impact.

Of the eight safety commission orders issued from April 24 through June 5, five related to liquor. Two of these have been noted: the Bridge Square order and the one excluding liquor licenses from the Fort Snelling area. Fearing that alcohol-induced revelry might interfere with the selective service registration scheduled for June 5, the commission on May 29 issued Order 6, which required closure of all saloons on that day. [48]

On June 5 the MCPS adopted two more orders dealing with liquor. Order 8 decreed that "nowhere within Saint Louis County . . . except . . . Duluth, shall intoxicating liquor . . . be sold or in any manner disposed of except in duly licensed saloons and in drug stores as now regulated by statute." Order 7, which generated more controversy than any of its predecessors, ordered all saloons to remain closed from 10 P.M. to 8 A.M. and declared saloons off limits to women and girls. Within cities of fifty thousand or more inhabitants, "all cafes and restaurants, whether designated as roof gardens, chop-suey houses or otherwise" serving intoxicating liquors were required to close at 10 P.M. and no women or girls were "permitted at any time to drink intoxicating liquor therein." In addition, "dancing and cabaret performances in any saloon or place where intoxicating liquor is sold, served or drank" were prohibited. Finally, the order instructed municipalities to enact ordinances putting its provisions into effect. [49]

In formulating Order 7 — particularly the provisions barring women from liquor establishments — the commissioners ostensibly were responding to an entreaty from Secretary of War Newton D. Baker. Anticipating that the draft would soon place thousands of young men in the army, Baker worried about the temptations that would assail those "who have not yet become accustomed to contact with either the saloon or the prostitute." He asked the various state councils of defense to take up this problem. [50]

Reaction to Order 7 ranged from strong approval through confusion to equally strong disapproval. Charles C. Bovey, a prominent Minneapolis business leader, was exultant. "Believe me," he wrote Burnquist, "when I say that nothing you have done thus far in your administration is more convincing of your good qualities than this act." Other communications from Minneapolis business people were equally laudatory. [51]

Organized labor reacted less amiably. Dan W. Stevens, president of the Minneapolis Trades and Labor Assembly, sent Baker a telegram calling attention to the absence of labor representation on the safety commission. He also characterized No. 7 as "a drastic order" that deprived "several hundred cooks, waiters, musicians and bartenders" of their livelihoods. He asked the Council of National Defense to "dispatch a committee here . . . to adjust this matter." As one might expect, the council declined to intervene: regulation of saloon hours clearly lay outside of federal jurisdiction. [52]

Undoubtedly Thomas Van Lear shared Stevens's unhappiness with Order 7, but the mayor immediately placed his administration in compliance with its provisions. However, he declined to endorse the instruction ordering municipal authorities to enact the order's provisions into law, preferring to let enforcement rest upon the authority of the safety commission. After securing an opinion from the city attorney affirming the legality of the order, the city council passed such an ordinance on June 15, thus placing itself at odds with the mayor. Van Lear vetoed the ordinance, but the council repassed it over his veto by a vote of eighteen to four. The veto message advanced three arguments: Order 7 was being enforced without benefit of a supporting ordinance; the proposed ordinance was "an emanation from a body other than your own and not an exposition of your independent legislative judgment [and this] has failed to commend itself to me"; and the issue of Order 7's constitutionality was in the courts, and awaiting judicial determination could do no harm. [53]

The court action alluded to by Van Lear was a suit brought in federal district court by Phil Cook, a Minneapolis saloon owner, petitioning for an injunction that would bar the MCPS and the City of Minneapolis from enforcing Order 7. Cook's attorney contended that his client's property rights were being impaired by a decree not within the scope of the MCPS's constitutional jurisdiction. The presiding judge, Wilbur F. Booth, found in favor of the commission, ruling that the order was a matter of administrative detail clearly within MCPS competence. Although the Booth decision did not immunize the safety commission from constitutional challenge — there would be two more cases before the MCPS expired — friends of the commission regarded it as a vindication of MCPS authority. [54]

Confusion rather than constitutional anxiety marked the reaction of St. Paul City Hall to Order 7. Above all, the precise nature of a "cabaret performance" perplexed city officials. After giving these officials a hearing on June 7, the commissioners approved a motion proposed by McGee that said the term was

> intended to include all performances in licensed saloons, cafes, restaurants, and similar places in which intoxicating liquors are sold, served, or drank, in which female performers take part, whether they remain on the stage or platform or leave the stage to pass through or mingle with the audience. [55]

Finding a discrepancy between the definition of "cabaret performance" in Webster's New International Dictionary and the committee's motion, O. H. O'Neill, the city's corporation counsel, suggested that if Order 7 was subjected to litigation, the courts might "accept the definition contained in the dictionaries." Pardee sought to reassure O'Neill by resorting to an analogy:

You remember the gentleman who came home quite early and upon being questioned told his wife it was eleven thirty, whereupon the clock struck three. As she upbraided him, he replied, "Madam, are you willing to take the word of a one dollar clock against that of your dear husband?"

If the court is called upon to make a decision . . . it will decide that the Minnesota Commission of Public Safety knows what it means better than the man who wrote Webster's Dictionary.[56]

Although Order 7 was spared further court challenges, confusion with respect to its application to women persisted. In September, shortly after Henry W. Libby replaced Pardee as secretary, the St. Cloud city attorney inquired whether the order barred Salvation Army women from entering saloons on their collection rounds. Following consultation with the attorney general's office, Libby replied: "All women are barred from entering saloons and no exception can be made in the case of the Salvation Army." On December 1 a Little Falls attorney wanted to know if a wife was prohibited from tending bar in her husband's establishment. Libby responded: "Order No. 7 . . . makes no exception in the case of a saloon-keeper's wife tending bar."[57]

By reinforcing a general impression that the MCPS was capable of imposing effective discipline on an unruly liquor trade, Order 7 encouraged a flood of complaints against this trade. The commissioners were not pleased. On June 19 they issued a statement that reflected their frustration:

> The Commission, at its session today, found itself overwhelmed with complaints from different sections of the State, rural and municipal, in regard to violations of the liquor laws. Scores of blind pigs were reported and the Commission [was] urged to inaugurate drastic action to stop the evil. . . .
>
> The Commission, with its many other important duties . . . cannot fritter away its time in prosecuting violations of the license laws in this State.
>
> . . . If [manufacturers and dealers] continue to encourage and sustain blind pigging there is no recourse left to the Commission but to issue an order prohibiting the manufacture and sale of liquor in the State or to urge the Governor to call an extra session . . . to pass a bone-dry law.[58]

This angry statement may have encouraged brewers and other participants in the liquor trade to be more law observing, but it failed to stem a continuing flow of complaints with respect to liquor violations. Nevertheless, the commission found time to attend to "its many other important duties," particularly the campaign against "disloyalty." Throughout May and June this concern by no means had been neglected, and by the end of the latter month the machinery required to prosecute the campaign was in place.

CHAPTER SIX

Rooting Out Disloyalty

The image of the Minnesota Commission of Public Safety as instigator of an intolerant loyalty crusade persisted for many years after the agency wound up its affairs. To a considerable extent this reputation is deserved; one searches in vain for evidence that civil libertarian scruples inhibited the commission's crusade against "sedition." On the other hand, the MCPS operated within a context wherein outside pressures provided much of the instigation, and individual commissioners reacted variously to these pressures. Lind discounted rumors that loyalty to the kaiser would impel German-American farmers to destroy their crops, while reports of "seditious meetings being held in a blacksmith shop in . . . Onamia" agitated McGee.[1] Lind accepted at face value Mayor Van Lear's promise to cooperate with the commission; McGee pressed for MCPS action to remove the mayor from office.

All the commissioners, however, regarded disloyalty as a threat requiring attention. A loyalty crusade was viewed — consciously or otherwise — as serving the short-term goals of powerful Minnesota interests. Employers desiring to discredit organized labor could gain a point by alleging lack of trade-union solidarity in support of the war. Representatives of the grain trade could denounce as unpatriotic the Nonpartisan League charge that the nation was waging a "rich man's war." Proponents of "100 percent Americanism" could impugn the loyalty of "hyphenists" who stubbornly persisted in defending the maintenance of "un-American" subcultures, particularly those with links to enemy nations. Given the strong representation of these interests on the commission, preoccupation of the commissioners with "loyalty" is not surprising.

Well before the safety commission was established, Burnquist began receiving complaints from individuals calling attention to manifestations of disloyalty in their communities, most of them involving disrespect for the American flag. According to the mayor of North Branch, the local postmaster was not displaying the flag in front of the post office, an act of omission raising an interesting question: "Does the [postmaster] because he is a German Democrat have the say whether or not the flag should wave over our postoffice?" A resident of Melrose alleged that the town's clerk was unwilling to fly the flag, adding: "The germans here are very bitter. Only yesterday a grocer told me they said they would kill him if he put up a flag."²

On April 11 the Traverse county attorney informed Burnquist that shortly before the declaration of war a local boiler inspector, upon entering a post office where the flag was on display, remarked to the postmaster: "What's that rag up for?" The postmaster "called him down," whereupon the boiler inspector "tried . . . to make out that he was joking." The county attorney rejected this explanation. Recently he had recommended the boiler inspector for an unspecified appointment. Now he wished to withdraw all that he had said in the inspector's favor. Burnquist promised to "take up this matter immediately."³

After the safety commission set up shop, it became the recipient of such complaints. It also served as a forum within which various aspects of the "loyalty" question were discussed. Superintendent of Public Instruction Carl G. Schulz advised the commissioners on May 10 "that a teacher's certificate might be cancelled for [seditious] utterances, on the ground of conduct unbecoming a teacher." A few days later a Roman Catholic priest from St. Bonifacius appeared before the commission to deliver a grim report of "conditions in his neighborhood — the anti-English and pro-German point of view prevailing among ninety-nine percent of the people"; *Der Wanderer,* an independent Roman Catholic weekly published in St. Paul, was described as "a very mischievous influence." The commissioners asked Burnquist "to call in a suitable agent to investigate further the conditions described at St. Bonifacius."⁴

On May 21 the commissioners discussed the foreign-language press and the propriety of using German as a medium of instruction in the state's parochial schools — two issues that would continue to be a focus of MCPS concern. They learned that Solon J. Buck of the Minnesota Historical Society "had undertaken to have read and indexed, the state press as to war matters." University of Minnesota Professor Guy Stanton Ford "had arranged to have the Scandinavian papers read and . . . C. M. Andrist had undertaken to read the German papers.

Extracts from *Der Wanderer* were submitted." Ames had interviewed Archbishop John Ireland "on the use of the German language as a vehicle of instruction." The minutes noted that Ireland deemed it "inadvisable to take positive action at this time," meaning that he recommended against an immediate ban.

Although Congress did not assign a specific role to state councils of defense in connection with the draft registration scheduled for June 5, the Minnesota safety commissioners assumed responsibility for scrutinizing the registration boards appointed by county commissioners in the rural areas and by mayors in the larger cities. Ames proposed a resolution — which his colleagues adopted — excluding from registration or exemption boards any person "opposed to the execution of the law providing for registration and conscription." The roster submitted by Van Lear profoundly displeased McGee, and following a spirited verbal confrontation between McGee and Lind, who defended the Minneapolis mayor's list, the commission ordered several replacements. [5]

The commission also undertook to monitor the registration process. On May 24 it set up a special committee consisting of the governor and two commissioners appointed by him that was charged with the responsibility of selecting an attorney to sit with each registration board during its sessions. The special committee quickly fulfilled its mandate. On May 29 it presented to the MCPS a list of attorneys who had promised to oversee the proceedings of local registration boards.

By late May, the imminence of draft registration impelled the commissioners to expedite action on the secret service front. Already a number of individual operatives had been selected for special missions. On May 7 the commission authorized Lind to appoint three agents for service on the iron ranges, and McGee's frequent reports of subversive activities raise a suspicion that he maintained an informal espionage network of his own. [6] The commissioners believed that the possibility of draft resistance, however, required a more coordinated intelligence system. Just how serious a problem opposition to the draft would be was arguable within the commission itself. McGee claimed to have information indicating that armed resistance was almost certain. Burnquist, whose views seldom diverged from McGee's, was more optimistic. In response to a telegram from the *New York World* inquiring whether he expected full compliance with the June 5 registration, the governor responded: "Expect very few failures to register and look for no disorder." [7]

Nevertheless, the commissioners approved a May 21 motion introduced by McGee that resolved

> to establish a secret service system to be directed by a superintendent, to consist of such employees as may be authorized from time to time, and that all operations be conducted through that department and reported to the Chairman of the Commission, and that Mr. Ames be requested to submit a plan.

The recommendation Ames submitted on May 29 proposed a "temporary arrangement" with O. R. Hatfield, Twin Cities agent of Pinkerton's National Detective Agency, who "would undertake such inquiry as the Commission might direct." His immediate assignment was to "begin inquiry as to conditions at Glencoe, St. Bonifacius, Young America, New Ulm, Sleepy Eye, certain districts in Sibley County, certain districts in Stearns and Morrison Counties, Brainerd, the Cuyuna Range, Mankato; the raising of a pro-german fund in Minneapolis, general conditions in Minneapolis and St. Paul and possibly . . . Winona." Hatfield was to "report to the Governor."[8]

A half dozen Pinkertons soon fanned out over Minnesota in search of subversion. They submitted daily reports to Hatfield, who transmitted them not directly to the governor but to Thomas G. Winter, who maintained close contact with the MCPS from his office in Minneapolis. Winter's connection with the commission, at first unofficial, acquired legitimacy on June 30 when the MCPS named him superintendent of its intelligence bureau. Practically speaking, this appointment enabled Winter to supervise agents who reported directly to him instead of Hatfield. At the same time, the Pinkerton connection was maintained through the summer.[9]

Most of the agents, whether Pinkertons or Winterites, operated undercover. One exception was Burton J. Randolph, secretary of the Bemidji Rifle Club, an affiliate of the National Rifle Association. Impressed by Randolph's performance on a temporary assignment, Winter suggested that the operative submit his "file of papers" to McGee in the hope that the commissioner would approve a permanent appointment, which he did. Randolph reported back to Winter that the interview with McGee had gone well. However, there was one qualification not alluded to "in that file of papers": "I have been on services where I have been compelled to shoot and I am chain lightning with a pistol. I do not intend or wish to pose as a killer . . . but think you realize that before this mess is over a fast and experienced gunman will be a valuable asset to your organization."[10]

*Thomas G. Winter,
the commission's director
of intelligence, shown
about 1921*

Randolph's job performance continued to impress Winter. Nevertheless, the intelligence chief consented to a Randolph transfer from the MCPS to the Twin City Rapid Transit Company in October 1917 — at a time when TCRTC was arming for a confrontation with a recently organized transit workers' union. In recommending Randolph to a streetcar official, Winter noted that the operative was "unprepossessing [*sic*] and needs a bath, but I find him unusually loyal [and] intelligent," adding that he was particularly skilled in persuading unwilling witnesses to testify in court. "For mixing with the lower classes," Winter concluded, "Randolph is O. K."[11]

The identities of the other agents were closely guarded. In late July Hatfield cautioned Pardee, "For the present, it is better that the names of the agents and the fact that this agency is conducting such investigations should not be open to scrutiny." To tighten security further, Hatfield asked that bills for Pinkerton services be paid through a third party rather than directly to Pinkerton.[12]

These precautions notwithstanding, leakage became a problem. On July 28 the *St. Paul Daily News* carried a front-page story accurately portraying the MCPS intelligence endeavor. The headline read: "HIST! — ALSO SHSH! P. S. SLEUTH ON JOB." Two subheadlines followed: "The Goblins 'll Get You if You Don't Watch Out" and "Private Detectives Tried But Now State Safers Have Their Own Nick Carter." The story went on to note that T. G. Winter, a brother-in-law of C. W. Ames, was the safety commission's "chief detective" and that Winter's spouse headed the commission's women's auxiliary. [13]

The publication of this story distressed Winter, all the more so because it accurately disclosed details that the MCPS wanted kept under wraps. Was it possible, he wondered, that the inner sanctum of the MCPS harbored a spy? Pardee, whose circle of friends included a *Daily News* editor, agreed "that leaks in this office might cause serious consequences," but he did "not know how to get at that — would it be the best way to have somebody investigate this office unknown to us?" Pardee added a postscript: "No carbon made of this letter." Worry about leaks apparently faded, possibly because the high level of "pro-loyalist" excitement generated by events in New Ulm on July 25 intimidated potential "leakers." [14]

Meanwhile, operatives in the field were uncovering few serious threats to the security of the republic. In response to an alarming report from a hotel proprietor in Wykoff about resistance to the draft, Hatfield dispatched an agent identified as "CMR" to the Fillmore County village. CMR's findings raise the question of whether his Wykoff mission was worth its expense. He discovered that the hotel proprietor was "inclined to enlarge on matters a great deal, as he uses liquor to excess." Moreover, the agent found no indication of any campaign to block registration, no evidence of an IWW presence, no Socialist visibility, and certainly no signs of an imminent armed uprising.

At the same time, CMR found a prevalence of pro-German sentiment, particularly among older German Americans. He believed that the circulation of German-language newspapers nourished this sentiment. "There would be fewer arguments and less statements made by the Germans," he offered, "if they were unable to get these papers." He added that German Americans in Wykoff felt "that the American papers lie to the public for the purpose of getting them to enlist and fight against Germany." [15]

St. Paul draft board processing men under the Selective Service Act on Registration Day, June 5, 1917

Reporting from Glencoe, operative "vss" delivered essentially the same message. A handwritten note on the report summarized its contents: "Pure German, but will behave. But some persuasive work might be done there." Although no organized resistance to the draft existed, Glencoites were not enthusiastic for the war. But so far as could be determined, all men of draft age registered. The same was true in New Ulm, a city that a few weeks later would be perceived as a symbol of opposition to the draft. "Registration day, Tuesday, June 5, passed quietly in Brown county," reported the *Brown County Journal*. While on assignment in Mankato, "wGs" received a report that "a considerable number of IWW men had arrived in town," ostensibly to disrupt registration. The police chief disclosed that the group was "merely four 'bums' or hoboes who had been driven out of town."[16]

Reports from operatives working in the Twin Cities were equally reassuring. On June 1 "DjG" investigated rumors of organized draft resistance in north Minneapolis. He found "no great excitement about the registration or any indication of an organized effort to prevent same." A day earlier "CH," who was fluent in both German and

Swedish, spent several hours visiting saloons patronized by German Americans. He discovered that "all the Germans are very careful what they say and there does not seem to be any effort on their part to evade or prevent registration." The following day he visited saloons in the Arlington Hills district of St. Paul to determine if the Swedish Americans patronizing these establishments were being influenced by the campaign being waged against registration by *Allarm,* a radical Swedish-language paper edited by Carl Ahlteen. He reported that he "could not learn of any socialist literature being circulated in St. Paul."

> I found that the general feeling is that they do not like the idea of going back to Europe and fighting, but would do so if necessary, and I could not find any indication that there is any organized effort to avoid or prevent registration. I watched closely for anyone agitating among the men, but saw nothing suspicious in this respect. [17]

Although MCPS sleuths discovered pockets of draft resistance in northern Minnesota, compliance even in that section of the state conformed more nearly to Burnquist's expectation than to McGee's. An operative working in Beltrami County reported that 650 young men had registered in Bemidji, "a good showing." The local game warden said that only a few men of draft age had refused to register and that these were being held on federal charges. "All the local pro-Germans . . . ," added the operative, "who were quite active before the . . . war, have now quieted down . . . and [the game warden] has not heard anyone agitating or discussing conscription in any way." [18]

The situation on the Cuyuna Range was less reassuring. In the Crosby area, a substantial number of Finnish-American draft-age men failed to register. The arrest of fifty Crosby nonregistrants is not a reliable measure of resistance there, since many draft evaders managed to elude apprehension by fleeing to the woods or to the protection of sympathetic friends and relatives in remote areas. Others found their way to Canada across a minimally guarded border. Hence, it is not surprising that draft evasion estimates varied considerably. According to the *Minneapolis Daily News,* some three hundred men on the iron ranges had failed to register; Alfred Jaques, United States attorney for Minnesota, placed the number at two thousand. [19]

Judgments with respect to the nonregistrants' motives also varied widely. Mining and timber executives tended to blame a nefarious combination of "outside agitation" and bootleg liquor for Finnish recalcitrance. While not unsympathetic to this perspective, the safety commissioners declined to accept such an explanation at face value. In a communication dispatched to the U.S. attorney general, the MCPS noted the arrest in Minnesota of about "two hundred and fifty foreigners, mostly Finns," on charges of noncompliance with draft registration. According to the commission, "a few" had willfully refused to register and "a few" belonged to the IWW, which opposed conscription. However, "the great mass . . . are persons recently arrived in the United States, wholly unfamiliar with our language[,] living with their own class and without any opportunity to become acquainted with public sentiment in general, or with the legislation or activities of the American people." The communication blamed "local authorities" for failure to provide these people with information about the draft law. Since the nation urgently needed the labor of miners, the MCPS recommended that "those . . . who did not wilfully violate the law be permitted to register and . . . discharged from arrest." The "wilful" should "be disposed of in accordance with the law."[20]

Whether in response to this recommendation or on the basis of other counsels, selective service officials permitted penitent delinquents to register late; some range employers encouraged compliance by requiring workers to show their draft cards as a condition of employment. Meanwhile, the reports of MCPS field operatives were shedding additional light on the nonregistration problem. IWW incitement, it seems, was not a major factor: without abandoning their principled opposition to conscription as a policy, IWW leaders studiously avoided overt advocacy of noncompliance with draft registration. DJG, who visited Crosby early in June, discovered that many Finns and "Austrians" were IWW members. Even so, agitation against conscription was not visible. On the theory that women were more truthful than men, DJG interviewed the wives of several Crosby miners. From them he learned "that the conscription question was never considered very seriously by the I.W.W." On the other hand, nearly all the persons contacted by DJG "were opposed to conscription to some extent, but not radically."[21]

The operative's reports implied that Finnish-American misunderstanding of the draft law was responsible for the failure of many young Finnish Americans to register. Some equated draft registration with immediate enlistment in the armed forces; others were led to believe that Finnish-American registrants would be conscripted into the Russian army, a horrible prospect even after the collapse of czarism in

March 1917. Still others were under the impression that the draft law did not obligate aliens to register.[22]

Despite this lack of organized opposition to conscription, the safety commission declined to relax its vigilance. Sullen acceptance of the war fell far short of the unreserved commitment that the commission professed to be seeking. The situation in the mines and forests of northern Minnesota was particularly worrisome. Wartime need dictated a maximization of ore and timber production, which in turn required a stable labor force. A tight labor market opened hopeful vistas for union organizers, a challenge employers could meet either by accepting "good-faith" bargaining or by resorting to intimidation, preferably with the assistance of government. Some employers clearly preferred the latter option. In reporting on a brief work stoppage on the Cuyuna Range in the second week of June, operative DJG branded as unreasonable a management demand that Burnquist remove the Crow Wing County sheriff because that official had refused to request troops to quell an alleged disturbance. DJG wrote that management wanted "to scare the strikers back to work and to impress upon their minds that the government now was taking a hand in the IWW movements. . . . According to their ideas the men must work in the mines whether they want to or not."[23]

A week later MCPS attention shifted to an embattled relationship between Edward W. Backus and his employees at the Minnesota and Ontario Paper Company in International Falls. On June 18 William S. Jones, business manager of the *Minneapolis Journal,* called Burnquist's attention to "serious mill trouble [in the Backus mill], due to the activities of the I.W.W. sympathizers, who are apparently working under the influence of booze obtained from innumerable blind pigs which seem to exist in the town." Jones explained his interest in the matter by citing the *Journal*'s dependence on newsprint from the mill. Formally no strike had been called and the question of wages was not an issue, but "idlers and bums not connected with the mill threaten and intimidate the men who actually want to work."[24]

Backus delivered essentially the same message to McGee, who brought the matter up at the June 19 MCPS session. The commissioners approved a McGee motion calling upon the governor to name a three-man committee to investigate the International Falls situation. Burnquist immediately announced the appointment of Thomas D. O'Brien, the highly respected St. Paul attorney and civic leader; state Senator

Edward P. Peterson of Meeker County, an attorney and official of the
First National Bank of Litchfield; and E. George Hall of the Minnesota Federation of Labor. One might think that from a conservative
standpoint, these appointments should have been unexceptionable.
Nevertheless, George M. Gillette, a pillar of the Minneapolis open-
shop movement, objected to the absence of "business" representation on the committee. [25]

Meanwhile a Pinkerton operative who had arrived in International
Falls on June 17 was uncovering perspectives sharply at odds with
the Jones-Backus version. There was no strike, he reported, nor
was one contemplated. However, the Backus mill was working way
below capacity, not because of booze or IWW intimidation, but because the company was finding it difficult to retain key personnel.
A week earlier management had dismissed the paper mill superintendent, replacing him with a subordinate who quit after one day.
Other top-level employees also left their jobs, idling all but one
machine. [26]

Interviews with mill employees disclosed that an effort to unionize
the mill underlay the unpleasant relationship between Backus and
his work force. A year earlier the papermakers had formed a union
and requested a collective bargaining arrangement with management.
The company responded by dismissing employees linked to the union.
Following a union protest, management had partially retreated from
the wholesale dismissal practice but had continued a policy of selective firing, which explained dismissal of the plant superintendent. At
a secret meeting the union had come to the defense of the superintendent by encouraging key personnel to leave their jobs — a tactic that
effectively reduced mill production.

The Pinkerton operative also investigated the booze and IWW allegations made by Backus and Jones. With respect to liquor violations
he reported innumerable rumors and some visible drunkenness, but
he failed to find enough evidence to convict alleged violators. He had
learned from an informant that there still were "some I.W.W's here,"
but they were "not causing any trouble at this time" and were not
expected to do so in the future. [27]

Available sources do not illuminate the arrangements that restored
full production in the Backus mill. Although the union failed to gain
recognition, the company may have moderated its selective dismissal
policy. In any case, by June 22 a new superintendent was on the job
and production was approaching full capacity.

Twenty officials from the iron ranges — city attorneys, mayors, sheriffs, and police chiefs — gathered in St. Paul on June 20 for a special' meeting with the safety commission. In opening the session Lind explained the commission's activities "relating to the industrial situation and outlined the extent of its information." He underscored the commission's desire "to cooperate with the local authorities . . . to the end that recourse to military measures might be avoided."[28]

The discussion that followed focused on labor conditions, "agitation by unpatriotic elements," and liquor law enforcement. The potentially constructive role of distillers and brewers in combating the blind pig evil was emphasized: "As fast as abuses are brought to their attention there is a good prospect of regulating this evil." At the same time, identification of blind pigs was conceded to be a troublesome problem: "A quantity of liquor that would indicate a blind pig under some circumstances would under other circumstances signify ordinary hospitality."[29]

The guidance provided by the commissioners to their guests with respect to "agitation by unpatriotic elements" was somewhat more specific than that relating to liquor law enforcement. Both hosts and guests "agreed that unlawful assemblies should be prevented." The commissioners then went into executive session, at the conclusion of which they informed the range officials that a model ordinance "providing methods for restraining those who advocate opposition to the government or hindrance to the conduct of the war" would shortly be submitted to municipalities throughout the state for adoption. They also announced that Finnish, Croatian, Slovenian, Bulgarian, and Italian versions of the 1917 syndicalist law were being prepared for distribution throughout northeastern Minnesota.

Whatever else might be said about the model vagrancy ordinance that the commission approved on June 26, few would argue that it contributed positively to the country's free speech tradition. Section 1 incorporated the key provision of the state's syndicalist law:

> Any person . . . who by word of mouth or in writing advocates or teaches . . . or is about to advocate or teach . . . or habitually advocates or teaches, or is engaged in whole or in part in the occupation, whether for gain or gratuitously, of advocating, advising or teaching the duty, necessity or propriety of crime or of violence as a means of accomplishing industrial or political ends, shall be guilty of vagrancy.

Section 2 interdicted "advocating, advising or teaching the violation or disregard of any duty or obligation imposed by any statute of this State, or of the United States." Defiance of this interdiction also constituted "vagrancy." Section 3 extended the vagrancy concept to include "advocating, teaching or advising that citizens of this State shall not or ought not aid or assist the United States in prosecuting or carrying on war with the public enemies of the United States." "A citizen of this State" was "defined to be any person within the confines of the State." Section 4 left prescription of penalties to the municipality enacting the ordinance. [30]

The significance of the model vagrancy ordinance as a factor in the loyalty campaign is difficult to assess. Although more than 150 municipalities had adopted it by August 1917, persons suspected of "unlawful" speech or writing were more often charged with violation of state or federal law than with transgressing local ordinances. In fact, given the stringency of the federal and state statutes, the rationale for the model ordinance is difficult to fathom. It undoubtedly had an intimidating effect by reinforcing the climate that inhibited discussion of public policy issues. Critics of wartime policy were obliged to keep a wary eye not only on federal and state law, but also on the ordinances within the localities wherein they were speaking or writing. [31]

On June 26 Pinkerton agent Hatfield submitted to Thomas G. Winter a number of recommendations relating to the MCPS intelligence effort. "I believe," wrote Hatfield, "that the most important things to watch at this time are the non-partisan League; the Socialists and the I.W.W." He further suggested "that every effort be made . . . to stamp out the circulars or different pamphlets printed by the I.W.W. organization," and he listed a number of radical newspapers that in his opinion deserved to be closed down. He thought a "censure" should be imposed on all non-English papers and that the commission should consider eliminating the IWW from Minneapolis. [32]

Of these recommendations, the monitoring of Socialist and IWW activities had been an early MCPS priority, and by mid-July the commission had also placed the Nonpartisan League, then conducting an ambitious organizational drive in western Minnesota, under surveillance. A report by operative "GWS" covering a Nonpartisan League rally in Boyd on July 13 throws interesting light on a developing hostility between the MCPS brand of "loyalty" and the message of the league. [33]

Operative GWS identified the main speaker at the Boyd event as "a Mr. Titeen of Chippewa County." Very likely, this was a case of mistaken identification. Ferdinand Teigen, son of state Representative Austin F. Teigen of Montevideo, may have been the star performer. Nevertheless, the report on the content of the address has the ring of authenticity; the rhetoric, as presented by GWS, bears a striking similarity to that employed by other NPL speakers in mid-1917, rhetoric that from a "loyalist" standpoint was considerably more provocative than the line adopted by the NPL a few months later.

According to GWS, the address opened with a description of "the aims and aspirations" of the Nonpartisan League. The speaker then "branched into a tirade against the big business interests of this country and told how they were robbing the farmers . . . more and more each year." Following "nearly an hour of such talk," the orator focused his wrath on the Burnquist administration and the safety commission: "And now you have a body of men called the Minnesota Public Safety Commission who even dictate to you how you shall enjoy yourself and how you shall spend your money that you have toiled so hard for," GWS quoted "Titeen" as saying.

The speaker's lengthy discourse on the war omitted even a qualified endorsement of Wilsonian war aims, an omission that NPL lecturers would later correct. "Titeen" summed up this portion of his speech by declaring:

> After being robbed for years you are now asked to raise bumper crops; give your sons as cannon fodder and give what little money you have ever received for your products to the purchase of "Liberty Bonds" in order that your sons may be transported away from you and fight for a cause that they would not even give you a chance to vote for or against, and yet you are told this is a war for Democracy and freedom. What do you think about this matter and what are you going to do about it when the next election comes around?

The scene following the conclusion of the address anticipated countless similar occurrences during the state campaign of 1918. According to GWS:

> At the close of his address [the speaker] invited all the farmers who believed in what he said to join the Non-Partisan League and a few of them went forward to talk with him about the matter. While the men were talking with him about 35 or 40 young men headed by a big husky fellow, marched into the hall and made a rush for Titeen; the husky leader of the gang grabbed Titeen by the neck and forced

him to kiss the American flag. Titeen's face was chalky-white during this performance and he spoke so low that I could not hear what he said to the men. The mob had broken several chairs and were jumping over the seats in the hall in order to get at Titeen, and some of the "hotter heads" among them were rapidly starting agitation to "beat up" Titeen, and the police officer of the town had disappeared, so I attempted to talk to the leader of the mob, urging him to let Titeen alone after he had kissed the flag.

At first my talk did not meet with the approval of the mob, and I was forced to state that I was not in any way connected with the Non-Partisan League, and after considerable talk relative to "getting" Titeen they finally dispersed and went home.

Socialist publicists tended to approach war-related issues with more caution than did the Boyd speaker, probably because they were more aware of being watched by the MCPS or federal agents. Immediately after Pinkerton accepted its safety commission assignment, Hatfield placed virtually every prominent Twin Cities radical — and some labor leaders who could hardly be characterized as radical — under daily surveillance. [34]

Surviving reports on the comings and goings of these persons throw some light on their life-styles — one learns, for example, that Carl Ahlteen, the radical Swedish-language editor, shopped carefully for watermelons — but reveal no plots to subvert the republic. The operatives sometimes found themselves pursuing shadows, as when "CH" arrived in Minnehaha Park on June 24 to monitor a Swedish Socialist picnic:

> There were no socialists at Minnehaha Falls and I searched the woods in the vicinity of the park, but found no posters or any other indications that a Swedish picnic of any description was being held.
>
> I went to the central part of Minneapolis . . . with the view of locating any other socialist picnic that might be held today, but failed to locate anyone who knew of such a picnic, up to 7:45 P M, at which time I returned to St. Paul.

MCPS surveillance of Socialist activity was not limited to the Twin Cities. While on an investigative mission in Staples in mid-June, operative DJG learned from a Northern Pacific ticket agent that a William E. Reynolds was touring northern Minnesota under the auspices of the Socialist League of the Northwest, an organization directed by Abe L. Sugarman, a prominent leader of the Minnesota Socialist party. For the next week DJG followed Reynolds through the Red River valley. To evade detection he refrained from attending the organizer's smaller meetings, relying instead on information gleaned from persons who had been in attendance. At Erskine, DJG learned, Reynolds had addressed an audience of about thirty-five people. His message concentrated on "the usual socialistic theme of labor versus capital." He "told his audience that he had a great many things of real significance to tell regarding the present war, but owing to the espionage methods now in use . . . he did not dare to discuss these most important subjects as he wished." Reynolds communicated essentially the same message in Crookston, Climax, Halstad, and Bemidji. He arrived in Duluth on the morning of June 24 to assume the editorship of the *Labor Leader,* a small radical paper.[35]

DJG prolonged his stay in Duluth to observe a trial of eighteen IWW advocates — including Elizabeth Gurley Flynn — who had been arrested under the city's emergency vagrancy ordinance. "They were," DJG reported, "arrested as vagrants, alleged to have no lawful occupation and suspected of agitating against the Government." Flynn was eventually released upon her promise to leave town, and others were given sentences of varying lengths.[36]

In the course of reporting on the Reynolds tour, DJG also recorded his impressions with respect to the climate of opinion in the communities visited by the Socialist activist. Several informants had told him that Erskine harbored "Scandinavian socialists . . . [with] Pro-German leanings, but that . . . these people are very careful in discussing the matter." In Crookston he learned that "a number of Scandinavian socialists are greatly opposed to the war, but there are no radical agitators here, especially since this country entered the war." He discovered "that a number of socialists live at Climax and vicinity, most of whom are Norwegians," but since the declaration of war conscription had not been discussed. A banker in the Climax area informed him that all of the young men subject to the draft had registered.[37]

Radical organizations were not the only groups whose loyalty came under MCPS scrutiny in the summer of 1917. The Lutheran church, particularly the German sector, also found itself under suspicion. After learning of an impeachment of Lutheran loyalty by the Nebraska Council of Defense, Hatfield suggested on July 12 that perhaps the MCPS should take a cue from its Nebraska counterpart. "Judging from reports of our operatives," Hatfield added, "there is reason to feel that in . . . Lutheran communities we are not getting the full cooperation of the church." A few days later Hatfield called attention to an

impending merger of four German Lutheran synods, a development
that "may not mean anything, but it would be well to watch it and
endeavor to get further information concerning it." In the Pinkerton
director's opinion, "All publications should be watched closely, as it
is claimed that they are using . . . their religious positions and offices
to turn Americans to German sympathy."[38]

Although the Wisconsin Synod of the Lutheran church would later
come under heavy safety commission pressure in the aftermath of
the New Ulm "antidraft" rally, the MCPS did not, for the time being,
act on Hatfield's recommendation. Confrontation in support of
patriotism was an honorable stance, but alienating a large segment
of Minnesota's population was not a tactic calculated to build enthusiasm for either the war or the MCPS. Perhaps this is what Pardee
had in mind on July 19 when he counseled Winter: "As to warning
the Lutherans. Let's not do any public scolding if it can be avoided, —
private admonition seems to be accomplishing results though it may
not be as swiftly as we could wish."[39]

The commissioners responded with more alacrity to complaints
against individuals. McGee called attention on June 7 to an article
by James A. Peterson in the *Northern Review*, a periodical published
by John N. Lenker, in which Peterson charged that the United States
was sacrificing its youth in the service of British imperial interests.
The commissioners apparently instructed Hatfield to launch an investigation of the two men. Peterson, a practicing lawyer in Minneapolis who earlier had served both as Hennepin county attorney
and as a state legislator, was a fervent supporter of Senator La Follette
and a strident critic of Senator Knute Nelson. He had contested
Nelson's senatorial renomination in 1912 and would do so again in
1918. Like La Follette, he had vigorously opposed American entry
into the war, and following its declaration he persistently argued that
far from being a war for democracy and freedom, the conflict was
being waged to preserve the imperial interests of Great Britain and
France. The Pinkerton operative who interviewed him on June 18
formed the opinion that "Peterson is very radical and would bear
watching." In the course of the interview Peterson asked the operative
how he "liked his article," promised "to write another, better than
the first, and remarked: 'The people are coming over to our side; they
don't want war.'"[40]

The same operative gained a more benign impression of the *Northern Review* publisher. Lenker was a Lutheran clergyman who in the

prewar period had committed considerable column space in his magazine to the advocacy of "trilingual education" — that is, public school instruction in not only English but also Scandinavian and German. Although identification with this cause allied Lenker with "hyphenism," he was considerably less militant than Peterson on issues relating to the war. He assured the operative that he was "for America," admired both Great Britain and Germany with a bias "towards Germany to a certain extent," but not to the point where he hoped Germany would win the war. He confessed that publishing Peterson's article had been a mistake and desired to learn from "some Government agent" what he, Lenker, might and might not write.

On the same day that McGee presented the Peterson-Lenker information to his commission colleagues, Knute Nelson mailed to McGee a recent issue of the *Park Region Echo* of Alexandria containing a Peterson piece critical of the war. In a covering letter the old senator left no doubt as to what he thought of his fellow Norwegians, Carl Wold, editor of the *Park Region Echo,* and Peterson. "We have at Alexandria," wrote Nelson,

> one Republican newspaper and one Democratic paper, both straight and loyal. The Park Region Echo is a socialistic and prohibition paper. The editor . . . is a Norwegian, his wife is an American and she is the smartest and most vicious of the two. If there is any way you can jack up the paper and Mr. Peterson I wish you would try and squelch both the paper and Peterson. [41]

Although the commission did not immediately initiate decisive action to "squelch" either Wold or Peterson, the activities of both men continued to be monitored. The MCPS repeatedly but vainly pleaded with federal authorities to move against Wold's paper, and in the spring of 1918 he was tried and convicted in state court on charges of discouraging enlistment. Wold died before serving his sentence, a circumstance that cast him in a Nonpartisan League martyr's role. In the spring of 1918 Peterson was tried and convicted on charges of transgressing the parallel federal statute. Like Wold, Peterson was spared imprisonment, not by dying, but through a series of appeals that were ultimately rewarded in 1920 when the United States Supreme Court quashed his conviction. The penitent Lenker, it seems, faded from the scene, at least so far as the safety commission was concerned. [42]

If the safety commissioners derived some satisfaction from their part in exposing the alleged disloyalty of Wold and Peterson, they also played a peripheral role in the controversial academic freedom case involving Professor William A. Schaper of the University of Minnesota political science department. Previous to American entry into the European conflict, Schaper had been a sharp critic of interventionist foreign policies. After April 6 he refrained from advocating nonsupport of the war effort, but he did not conceal a conviction that the decision for war had been a mistake. How much concern Schaper's stance aroused in the spring of 1917 is not entirely clear. However, the professor's alleged lack of patriotic zeal eventually came to the attention of the vigilant McGee.

The minutes of the safety commission's July 11 meeting note that "McGee reported facts that had come to his attention relating to the attitude of some of the University staff, which was referred back to him." Interpreting this as a mandate to pursue the matter further, McGee apparently communicated his "facts" to key university regents, thereby setting in motion the process leading to Schaper's dismissal by the board of regents. It should be emphasized that direct responsibility for the dismissal rests on the board of regents, not on the safety commission, although most of the commissioners undoubtedly reacted favorably to the regents' action. [43]

Three months after launching their campaign to stamp out disloyalty and ignite the fires of patriotism, the safety commissioners were not confident that their efforts added up to a smashing success. A July 18 Hatfield letter addressed to Pardee summed up the prevailing consensus within the MCPS circle. According to Hatfield, the climate of opinion throughout the state was marked by "a pronounced lack of patriotic spirit and a general apathy as to the war, although . . . no manifest disloyalty." Mild comfort could be derived from the reported absence of "manifest disloyalty," but even this slight reassurance would be dissipated by the commissioners' interpretation of what happened in New Ulm on July 25, 1917. [44]

CHAPTER SEVEN

July 25 and Its Aftermath

As the afternoon of July 25, 1917, gave way to evening, hundreds of automobiles streamed into New Ulm. By dusk a crowd estimated at more than eight thousand people had gathered in the city. The evening schedule opened with a parade of two thousand marchers, many of them draft-age men. Enlivened by two brass bands performing in the best New Ulm tradition, the parade — led by Brown County Auditor Louis G. Vogel — proceeded from downtown to Turner Park. Dr. Louis A. Fritsche, New Ulm's popular mayor, opened the program by denying intent "to cause any disaffection of the draft law." The chief purpose of the gathering was to formulate a request to "congress and the government . . . not [to] force those drafted to fight in Europe against their will."[1]

Albert Pfaender, New Ulm city attorney, former state legislator, and son of a city founder, delivered the main address. He began by affirming the unreserved loyalty of German Americans to the United States; their performance in both the Civil War and the Spanish-American conflict had established this beyond all doubt. They also were prepared to do their duty in the present war, but along with millions of other Americans they were haunted by a troublesome doubt: did the decision for war conform to the majority will of the nation? Obviously, Pfaender did not believe so; to guard against similar perversions of the democratic process in the future, he advocated a constitutional amendment requiring a popular referendum before war could be declared.[2]

Meanwhile, did the Constitution of the United States empower the federal government to conscript men for overseas military duty? Pfaender was persuaded that it did not. He conceded that drafting men "for the purpose of repelling invasions" was clearly within constitutional bounds, but a German incursion into U.S. territory was not even a remote possibility. According to Pfaender, the constitutional

133

Louis A. Fritsche, mayor of New Ulm, about 1915

issue could be resolved by congressional amendment of the draft law. He counseled men of draft age to register and to accept induction when ordered to do so, but at the same time he urged his large audience to work for legislation to limit overseas service to volunteers. While he was speaking, petitions to that effect circulated through the audience.

Adolph Ackermann, president of Dr. Martin Luther College, a Wisconsin Synod institution located in New Ulm, and Albert Steinhauser, editor of the liberal *New Ulm Review* and its German-language counterpart, the *New Ulm Post,* also addressed the rally. The participation of these two men — Ackermann the staunch theological conservative and Steinhauser the avowed liberal — points up the extent to which the rally united New Ulm's often warring factions. In addressing the crowd, Ackermann struck an Anglophobic note: "If we are fighting for this country's rights, why did we not declare war against Great Britain, which first violated our rights?" He also argued that priority should be assigned to domestic concerns: "There

Albert Pfaender, New Ulm city attorney

Adolph Ackermann, president of Dr. Martin Luther College, New Ulm

is plenty to do in our own country, without sticking our noses into other people's business, without fighting battles for Wall street or John Bull." Steinhauser focused his indignation on the provision authorizing the postmaster to deny mailing privileges to publications adjudged to be "subversive." "There is," Steinhauser complained, "no appeal to a higher court from the decision of a postmaster, consequently the postmaster can make himself an autocrat as they are not found even in Russia."[3]

Earlier on the same day, Bemidji had been the scene of an event considerably more violent than the New Ulm rally.[4] Pinkerton operative DJG, who had participated in planning the event, described what happened:

> At 2 P M about 150 citizens gathered at the Commercial Club where after a short conference with the Mayor, Chief of Police and other City and County officials, and men prominent in the Citizens League which was formed yesterday, for the purpose of driving the I.W.W. from Bemidji, the Mayor cautioned them to refrain from undue violence in driving these people out. The Mayor and Chief Tipple then lead [*sic*] the citizens, 150 strong, to the I.W.W. headquarters where about 25 of its members were found, including Secretary Dunning, who was released yesterday on $1,000 bonds.
>
> After the I.W.W. members were all lined up, the office fixtures, literature and everything found therein was moved to the street, loaded on a truck and hauled to police headquarters where all the I.W.W. property taken in the raid is being held, and everything was removed from the hall. Mayor Vandersluis removed every I. W. W. sign from the front of the building and the window signs which could not be removed were painted over with black paint, and a U.S. flag was then placed above the entrance.
>
> The I.W.W's were then marched to the Great Northern Ry. station where after tickets . . . were provided for them by the Mayor, they were ordered to board the 3:17 P M train and warned never to return to Bemidji. During this procedure there were no demonstrations of violence of any kind on part of the I.W.W. or citizens, and the entire program was carried out in a quiet manner, and as the I.W.W. lined up to board the cars they were forced to march bare-headed under a large American flag and the incident was cheered by about 1500 people who had gathered to witness the occasion.

The posse's next undertaking was a visit to the "business places" of three "radical Jewish socialists and I.W.W. sympathizers" who "were warned to refrain from further . . . i.w.w. talk. . . . [They] were told their fate would be the same as that of the i.w.w's in case they were heard to sympathize with them again." As a guarantee of patriotic behavior in the future, the posse forced the three "to nail up a flag which was furnished them and salute same, which they did, to the amusement of the enthusiastic crowd." This done, the "patriots" proceeded to the office of attorney W. N. Weber, who was known to be "a radical socialist and i.w.w. sympathizer and counsel." Weber responded to the mayor's admonitions by calling the latter "a liar and several other vile names, and as Weber was making a motion as if to strike the Mayor, the latter gave Weber a good beating and . . . ordered two officers to arrest Weber." The attorney was released from custody at 6 P.M. after admitting that he had acted foolishly. He then "drove to his home with a badly disfigured face."

That evening DJG contacted Hatfield to advise the Pinkerton director of the day's "happenings." Hatfield instructed the operative "to examine carefully all i. w. w. literature and matters found in the i. w. w. hall by the police and citizens, and forward . . . anything . . . of interest." In the presence of a lumber company attorney and a confidant of the lumberman, DJG packed up "several . . . books and papers which . . . might be of interest and shipped them by express to . . . St. Paul." A few months later these materials would serve as evidence in the Chicago IWW trials.

In the weeks following July 25, considerably more journalistic attention focused on New Ulm than on Bemidji. At first, coverage of the New Ulm rally was devoid of excessive indignation, although virtually no newspaper outside of the Socialist press and the *New Ulm Review* accorded the rally positive notice. The evolution of *Princeton Union* editor Robert C. Dunn's stance is suggestive. On July 26 the Princeton paper commented:

> New Ulm, Brown county, where English is hardly ever spoken, is, figuratively speaking, up in arms against the United States government, and may secede from Minnesota and the Union and declare itself a "Free City" of Germany. It would be too bad if we should lose New Ulm, for it is a pretty little city, manufactures a fine grade of beer and some mighty nice people live there.[5]

Three weeks later all traces of Dunn's amiability had vanished. "Is it any wonder," queried the paper, "that there are those who regret the Sioux did not do a better job at New Ulm fifty-five years ago?"

Dunn enjoyed a reputation for hyperbolic utterance, but his extremist rhetoric was not untypical. In late August Daniel W. Lawler, a veteran Democratic politician who had frequently campaigned in New Ulm, characterized the previous month's rally as a "traitors' meeting . . . presided over by a traitor mayor and addressed by a lot of other traitors."[6]

This increasingly strident reaction is attributable in part to a perception that the New Ulm example was contagious. According to the *New Ulm Review* of August 1, the men identified with the rally were being swamped with approving letters and telegrams, along with requests to speak at similar rallies. Indeed, a number of gatherings, alleged to be antidraft rallies, were organized in the weeks following July 25. "Seditious meetings are being held with impunity all over Minnesota," reported the *Princeton Union* on August 9, adding: "The Copperheads are rampant."[7]

The reaction of the MCPS to the July 25 rally — a reaction extensively reported in the state's press — also helped to heighten "loyalist" disdain for New Ulm. At a special meeting on August 1 the commissioners discussed the New Ulm affair at length and resolved "that wherever complaints appeared that officers were not doing their duty, such officers should be cited to appear before the commission." The MCPS thereupon voted to issue citations to Fritsche, Vogel, and Henry J. Berg, Brown County treasurer and a suspected organizer of the rally, ordering the three "to appear . . . before the Commission . . . to be questioned in regard to the recent meeting at New Ulm."[8]

At the commission's request Tighe prepared an opinion "relating to the powers of the Commission to recommend removals." In carrying out his assignment, the special counsel made a studied attempt to respect the constitutional context. The safety commission, Tighe insisted, was obligated to act within the limits established by Article 13, Section 2, of the Minnesota Constitution, which authorized the legislature to "provide for the removal of inferior officers, for malfeasance or nonfeasance in the performance of their duties." The statute implementing the provision established the rule that "an inferior officer cannot be removed for any of these specified reasons except after a hearing, and subject to the right of reviewing in the courts the order for his removal." According to Tighe, passage of the safety commission law had not suspended these constitutional and statutory requirements. As he put it, "If [the safety commission statute] undertakes . . . to confer on the governor the power of arbitrary or capricious action in this regard, I think it is unconstitutional."[9]

On the crucial issue of what level of offense constituted malfeasance or nonfeasance, Tighe avoided an expansive interpretation. Although a few court decisions suggested otherwise, "a Register of Deeds could not be removed because he drank too much provided he did his work as Register satisfactorily." Tighe argued further that even unpatriotic utterance did not in all cases constitute an offense warranting removal from office:

> I think that a public officer who is guilty of treason as a matter of course forfeits his office irrespective of any statute, but disloyal talk is not treason. Whether disloyal talk and agitation, which fall short of indictable acts could be made the basis of removal proceedings, depends on the character of the office occupied. A register of deeds, a treasurer or an auditor could not be removed for such conduct alone. No one of these officers has any general law enforcement functions. . . . With an official like a sheriff, a mayor, a city attorney or a county attorney, the situation is different. . . . They are charged with the preservation of order in their several jurisdictions, and with the responsibility of seeing that all properly enacted statutes, whether national, state or local, are observed and obeyed. For such officers to publicly throw discredit on existing laws is inconsistent with the obligations they have assumed, and exposes them to the charge of malfeasance.

Tighe's opinion laid the basis for MCPS action against New Ulm officialdom, but the press of other business delayed implementation. However, the commissioners consented to an unscheduled appearance by Pfaender, requested by the city attorney himself, on August 14. Pfaender delivered "an informal statement as to the attitude of New Ulm officials." According to a safety commission version, he also proposed that the MCPS could allay its anxiety concerning disloyal utterances at his meetings by assigning commission representatives to attend them and to exercise gentle "restraint, if it seemed . . . that the agitation was exceeding safe limits."[10]

The commissioners regarded Pfaender's proposal as "preposterous." Nevertheless, they attempted an "appeal to his patriotism." His apparent acquiescence to a counterproposal that he and other New Ulm officials sign a pledge promising cooperation with the MCPS suggested to the commissioners that their appeal had not been in vain. Unhappily they had underestimated Pfaender's incorrigibility. Following consultation with New Ulm colleagues he rejected the counterproposal, stating that "he and his associates" were "unwilling to sign any writing." The commissioners found this incomprehensible. "In other words," lamented their version of the episode, "they will not help quell the disturbance they have created." Obviously, the MCPS refused to acknowledge a New Ulmite fear that the counterproposal was mined with booby traps. [11]

The July 25 rally dominated deliberations at the August 21 meeting. McGee moved and the commission approved a request that Tighe "prepare a statement in regard to . . . Pfaender, Fritsche, and Vogel." The body also approved appointment of a commissioner to undertake investigation of the New Ulm rally. Finally, the commissioners adopted a Tighe letter directed to the governor "relating to the New Ulm episode" and the removal of the officials. The letter amounted to an MCPS recommendation that Burnquist suspend the three men from office. [12]

Burnquist complied with the MCPS recommendation immediately. On August 22 the evening newspapers carried conspicuous headlines announcing the suspension of Fritsche, Pfaender, and Vogel. The papers also carried a statement — essentially an edited version of Tighe's letter to the governor — that was a virtual declaration of war on the promoters of the July 25 rally. It charged them with planning the affair in conspiratorial secrecy, "an indication that the illegal character of the movement was recognized." No published notices were posted, "and the telephone and word of mouth were the chief media of spreading information about the proposed gathering." [13]

This charge is open to reasonable challenge. The campaign to amend the draft law that the rally was designed to advance was not "illegal" but an effort spearheaded by Illinois Congressman F. A. Britten, author of an amendment calling for the exemption of German-American draftees from overseas service. Through June and July German-American publicists waged an aggressive campaign on behalf of the Britten amendment; the *New Ulm Review* was one of its staunch advocates. On June 15 New York newspaper editor George S. Viereck wrote to Burnquist soliciting the governor's position on the controversial amendment. Essentially, the Viereck letter employed the same rhetoric as the New Ulm speakers: "Viereck's Weekly advocates on purely humane grounds that we should spare German Americans the horror of fratricide. It does not ask that they be exempted from universal service, but pleads that they should have the option of serving their country in other ways than at the front." Burnquist responded to Viereck with a profession of sympathy for the German-American plight. While declining to support the controversial Britten proposal, the governor avoided any implication that advocacy of it was improper, illegal, or seditious.[14]

The accusation that conspiratorial secrecy had concealed organization of the rally is as suspect as the allegation that the purpose of the gathering was of an "illegal character." On July 25 the *New Ulm Review* had published an announcement of the rally, informing readers that it was being sponsored by the People's Council of America for Democracy and Peace, a national organization that was advocating a negotiated peace. This is not entirely convincing: a New Ulm branch of the People's Council would not be organized until late August. Nevertheless, the *Review* story clearly stated the purpose of the rally. From a very different perspective, the July 25 issue of the *Minneapolis Journal* also carried a story about the planned rally. According to the *Journal*, federal and state intelligence agencies were on alert.[15]

The MCPS statement's castigation of Fritsche, Pfaender, and Vogel may have convinced some newspaper readers that the three men deserved not only removal from office but also prosecution on felony charges. "It is an appalling situation," proclaimed the statement,

> . . . when a county auditor, who is clerk of the local exemption board, encourages and even leads a procession of drafted malcontents, and when the mayor and city attorney of one of the most prosperous cities of the Minnesota valley openly promotes a pro-German propaganda. . . .
>
> Pfaender . . . was particularly incendiary. Perverting the president's declaration that this country had no quarrel with the German people as such, he demanded to know why, if this was so, our young men should be sent abroad to fight against the German army, as murderers engaged in murder. The other speakers took the same key with varying degrees of violence.
>
> . . . What they said against the war and the legislation in connection with it excited responsive enthusiasm in their audience, and instead of inspiring the drafted men to patriotically do their duty for the cause of God and their country, they were pictured as martyrs dragged to an unjust fate by a tyrannical and cruel government.[16]

New Times, the Minneapolis Socialist weekly, drew an interesting contrast between the commission's response to the New Ulm rally and the July 25 mob action in Bemidji. In the case of New Ulm, the commission was moving against the three officials for sponsoring a meeting clearly entitled to constitutional protection. In Bemidji the MCPS was ignoring what *New Times* charged was a possible violation by local authorities of the 1917 syndicalist law, the core provision of which prohibited advocacy of or resort to violence and the destruction of property for industrial or political ends. [17]

If the *New Times* editor had enjoyed access to contemporary Pinkerton reports, he might have charged safety commission operatives with connivance in planning and executing the Bemidji action. Before leaving Bemidji on July 26, operative DJG received the thanks of the mayor "for the assistance I had rendered . . . in suggesting and helping plan the clean-up of the I.W.W." "I was told," added DJG, "that if someone had not come here to suggest the movement as I did, the ousting would never have been attempted, as it had often been spoken of here, but no action ever taken." Precisely what instructions guided DJG in the execution of his Bemidji mission is not a matter of record, but it is clear that he went to Bemidji at the governor's insistence. On July 19 Burnquist instructed Pardee to request Winter to send two men to the Beltrami County city "at once." Unable to contact Winter immediately, Pardee relayed Burnquist's request to Hatfield, who dispatched DJG to Bemidji with instructions "to report to the Mayor of that City, who will give . . . the details in connection with matters to be investigated." [18]

Destruction by fire of the Shevlin-Carpenter lumber mill in Bemidji on July 21 heightened tension in the city. Three days later the Beltrami county attorney informed Burnquist that evidence of IWW complicity was lacking but that "the general feeling . . . here is that the fire was the result of action on the part of the I.W.Ws." A Shevlin-Carpenter executive informed a gathering of Bemidji business leaders the same day "that his company would not consider rebuilding the burned mill until the I.W.W. was driven from Bemidji." [19]

Whatever the cause of the mill fire and the extent of MCPS complicity in the July 25 deportation, Burnquist and his colleagues were pleased by the elimination of the IWW from Bemidji. The governor thanked a leading participant in the expulsion "for the information and for the work you are doing." However, the Bemidji action was only a single skirmish in a broader war against the IWW. Precisely why this war was waged with such grim intensity has puzzled some investigators. Surviving reports of agents stationed on the iron ranges suggest a waning of IWW effectiveness there. On July 3 Lind informed his fellow commissioners that the labor situation throughout the state was stable, with no strikes being waged and none in prospect. A July 25 letter to the Wisconsin Council of Defense conveyed an equally optimistic assessment. On the Mesabi Range, according to the MCPS, the IWW had "disintegrated themselves through sheer inability to get any popular discontent to stand upon." However, "It is too early to guess what trouble the I.W.W. will attempt to start in the agricultural districts but we propose to be ready for them."[20]

Anticipation of turmoil in the "agricultural districts" may in part explain the commission's compulsion to liquidate the IWW. A Lind assessment dated July 26 discounted the probability of serious disruption on the range but concluded that "in the agricultural regions . . . the situation is very different."

> The municipal organizations are lax. In many sections the farms are large and the population sparse. A great deal of transient labor is employed, and if the I.W.W. agitators are given free rein, if their organization is not disrupted, it means trouble of a character and extending over areas that we cannot control.[21]

Other factors included reports that the commission received from timber and mining firms of rumored strikes or sabotage actions, as well as urgings by "loyalist" Finnish Americans that "agitators" were responsible for the draft resistance problem. Given the commissioners' unshakable conviction that the IWW was committed to setting the existing social order aflame, it is not surprising that such representations made an impression on them.[22]

Whatever the mix of motives, the commission was moving relentlessly against the IWW in late July. At the MCPS session of July 24, Lind "outlined information obtained as to I.W.W. activities" and Tighe "was requested to go to Washington to take up with the Department of Justice certain matters" in the Lind report. Meeting in St. Paul two days later, Lind, Tighe, and two federal officials concluded that sufficient data were available "to proceed effectively against the head [IWW] organization in Chicago, the agricultural organization here, and to extend the drive as much farther as is deemed expedient." Following the conference Lind composed an appeal to Attorney General Thomas W. Gregory urgently requesting federal action, and Tighe departed for Washington on his mission.[23]

Washington officialdom was not immediately receptive to the safety commission suit, with Gregory doubting that the action requested fell within federal jurisdiction.[24] Officials in the Department of Labor wondered if a sustained effort to improve working conditions in the mines might provide surer guarantees of labor peace than suppression of the ɪww. On July 31 Lind received a wire from Secretary of Labor William B. Wilson informing the ex-governor that Wobbly leader William D. Haywood had threatened a strike by Minnesota and Michigan miners. "May I not urge you," added Wilson,

> to use your influence to induce the mine operators to so arrange the wages and conditions of employment that there will be no basis for agitation, at the same time [that] it should be pointed out to the miners that this [the ɪww] is not a movement to improve their condition but solely intended to coerce the United States Government by interfering with the preparations for defense. [25]

Lind's reply reflected his inflexible determination to eliminate the ɪww. In his opinion, the Haywood message was "pure bluff." Moreover, the MCPS labor committee that Lind headed had

> anticipated your suggestions by months of patient labor to bring about better relations between the mine operators and their employes. . . . In this work we have been continually hampered by the ɪww agitators but we have the latter well under control in the mining region. In fact we have better control than Mr. Haywood. . . . The agricultural situation is more menacing. . . . Many of the agitators infesting this state are aliens. They are guilty of conduct justifying deportation under new immigration act. . . . Deportation of a few would have a most wholesome effect on all aliens. Jail sentences have no terror. [26]

Lind's influence with the national administration undoubtedly helped overcome Gregory's initial reluctance to move against the ɪww. Other pressures also were mounted. Burnquist threatened to lay the issue before President Wilson unless the attorney general granted Tighe a positive response. While this threat was pending, Tighe arranged to have Senators Nelson and Kellogg join him in a final effort to persuade Gregory to institute proceedings against the ɪww. As matters turned out, this proved to be unnecessary. On July 31, the day of the scheduled Kellogg-Nelson-Tighe demarche, Gregory capitulated. [27]

Tighe was jubilant. After conferring with Gregory he wired Burnquist that "everything" was "satisfactorily arranged." O. E. Pagan, a Department of Justice criminal law expert, would shortly leave for Chicago to examine ɪww papers there in the possession of the Bureau of Investigation. While in Chicago, Pagan would confer with Lind and would remain "long enough to make thorough examination" of ɪww materials and to determine if prosecution was warranted. [28]

Duluth headquarters of the Industrial Workers of the World, boarded up after a raid by National Guard soldiers on August 18, 1917

On August 14 Lind informed his commission colleagues "that the objects of Mr. Tighe's recent visit to Washington had been accomplished and that conclusive results would soon appear." The ex-governor spoke prophetically. On September 5 federal agents raided IWW headquarters in thirty-three American cities, arresting hundreds of IWW officers and publicists and seizing records that would serve as evidence in the mass trial in Chicago in the spring of 1918. In the following weeks Department of Justice agents continued to raid IWW offices throughout the country in search of further evidence. In some instances mobs not visibly linked to the Department of Justice organized their own raids. On August 18, some two weeks before the initial federal raids, a mob demolished IWW headquarters in Duluth. According to a Duluth newspaper, about one hundred members of the Third Regiment of the Minnesota National Guard "participated" in the attack. [29]

Minneapolis, Duluth, and the principal iron range municipalities were among the cities visited by federal agents on September 5. A corps of operatives forced its way into the three Minneapolis IWW headquarters, arrested the Wobblies on the scene, and seized available records. At about the same time, "Duluth, Superior and Iron Range cities saw like raids." Following completion of this phase of the operation, secret service agents worked late into the night, scanning the material collected in a search for evidence pertinent to the forthcoming Chicago trials. [30]

Minnesota newspapers generally approved of the September 5 action. The *St. Paul Dispatch* was happy that a crippling blow had been aimed at the dreaded organization but wondered why federal authorities had waited so long; the *Minneapolis Journal* complained that the "slow-moving processes of civil justice [are] becoming irksome to the loyal public." [31] But the *Fergus Falls Free Press,* edited by Martin W. Odland, a state legislator who was affiliated with the Nonpartisan League, articulated a somewhat different reservation:

> Let the government get at the truth in regard to the I.W.W.s and at the same time let it get at the truth as to how the mining and lumber companies treat their employees.
>
> The investigation of the I.W.W.s conducted by the Minnesota house of representatives last winter . . . showed that these corporations . . . have treated their employees like dogs, feeding them half rotten food and housing them in camps full of filth and vermin and hiring roughnecks from Bridge Square, Minneapolis, to lord it over them with shotguns. [32]

The extent to which the safety commission could claim responsibility for initiating the federal assault on the IWW is debatable. Tighe's Washington mission and Lind's fervent entreaties to Gregory and William B. Wilson may suggest a significant MCPS role, but the national administration was being pressured by many groups and individuals demanding immediate liquidation of the IWW. It is, in fact, difficult to imagine how President Wilson could have resisted these pressures in the long run, notwithstanding the presence within his administration of individuals who argued for restraint. By July and August of 1917, anti-IWW hysteria had risen to maniacal heights. One measure of this was the easy acceptance by many prominent Americans of vigilante justice as a weapon against the organization. For example, the *New York Times* of August 4 characterized the recent lynching of Frank Little, an IWW activist, as "deplorable and detestable," but it softened the impact of this judgment by charging that "the I.W.W. agitators are in effect, and perhaps in fact, agents of Germany. The

Federal Authorities should make short work of these treasonable con-
spirators against the United States."[33]

Although the safety commissioners believed that the September 5
raids significantly reduced the IWW danger, they remained alert to
any further threat. An example is a hearing convened by the Minneapolis Board of Education in the fall of 1917 to consider demands
for the dismissal of O. J. Arness, a Minneapolis high school teacher
who was an active IWW member. The board divided into three ap-
proximately equal factions. On the one extreme was a group demanding summary dismissal, and on the other a team of two labor-oriented
members who staunchly argued for retention. A "centrist" faction,
led by Professor David F. Swenson of the University of Minnesota
philosophy department, hesitated to vote for termination solely on
the grounds of IWW membership but believed that commitment to
violence as a means of achieving industrial or political ends (an illegal position under the 1917 syndicalist law) provided sufficient cause
for dismissal. At his interrogation Arness refused to eschew political
and industrial violence, a stance that sealed his fate. Only Mae Snow,
one of two women members of the board, and Lynn Thompson, a
Socialist, voted against his termination.[34]

On September 25 McGee called the case to the attention of the
safety commission. Following McGee's report, Ames introduced a
resolution asking Tighe to investigate the possibility of removing Snow
and Thompson from the school board because they had "voted to
retain the services of a high school teacher . . . who is an active
member of the I.W.W." and requesting Burnquist "to suspend from office
the two said officers pending investigation."[35]

The resolution failed to win unanimous support. Weiss moved that
it be tabled, a proposition supported by Smith. However, McGee,
March, Ames, and Burnquist voted against the Weiss motion, thus
defeating it. In the end the commissioners referred the original motion to Tighe "with request that he ascertain what action could be
taken by local authorities." Apparently this marked the end of the
safety commission effort against Snow and Thompson. The significance of the effort derives not from its abandonment, but from
the fact that it was considered.

In late August a new anxiety arose to plague the safety commission: the People's Council of America for Democracy and Peace was
scheduled to convene in Minneapolis on September 1. The People's

Council was "a loose organization" embracing almost "every shade of political opinion . . . except prowar opinion," wrote historians H. C. Peterson and Gilbert C. Fite. Louis P. Lochner, its founder, was a fervent pacifist who had been a member of Henry Ford's ill-fated 1915 peace expedition. Other prominent leaders included former Senator John D. Works of California — described by Theodore Roosevelt as "perfectly unreasonable about peace" — and Florence Kelley, the well-known social worker. The organization also claimed the allegiance of David Starr Jordan, the famous naturalist and president of Stanford University, "but he had little to do with it."[36]

The strident criticism of wartime measures — and at times of the war per se — by People's Council representatives inevitably aroused a hostile patriotic reaction. "Under the hammer blows of the fervent nationalists," asserted Peterson and Fite, "the more conservative elements gradually dropped out and the People's Council fell into the hands of radicals." By September the process of radicalization was well advanced. Scott Nearing, the radical crusader, was now chairman of the executive committee, Lochner was executive secretary, and Morris Hillquit, a prominent Socialist leader, was a member of the executive committee.

By late 1917 the People's Council was working to promote a negotiated peace, dramatizing its goal with the slogan "Peace by Negotiation — Now." The most important plank in its fourfold program called for a peace "without annexations and indemnities" as demanded by European leftists — and strikingly similar to the main theme articulated by President Wilson in his "Peace without Victory" address of January 1917. A second plank recommended establishment of an "international organization for the maintenance of world peace," an anticipation of Wilson's postwar program. A third demanded repeal of the conscription law, and a fourth called for the maintenance and extension of democracy within the United States. The preservation of free speech in wartime was particularly emphasized.[37]

The People's Council failed to attract a mass following within Minnesota, despite the support of such newspapers as *New Times* and the *New Ulm Review*. However, a few reformers — including James A. Peterson and Sylvanus A. Stockwell, a veteran state legislator who had been identified with virtually every important reform movement since the 1890s — assumed important roles within the organization. Although the Nonpartisan League avoided open support of the council, Arthur Le Sueur, manager of the league's Minnesota branch, served on the organizing committee. Whether Mayor Van Lear held formal membership is unclear, but his friendliness to the organization led its leaders to consider Minneapolis as a possible site for its first national convention. Van Lear responded positively to the suggestion by assuring the group of the hospitality of the city and pledging it the protection of his police force.[38]

Reactions to the mayor's action were not universally favorable. The *St. Paul Dispatch* recommended that the safety commission ban the scheduled meeting and hinted that Van Lear should be removed from office. The newspaper questioned the consistency of suspending "the mayor of a small town" and leaving "undisturbed the mayor of a large city if the basic cause of complaint is the same."[39] Meanwhile, convention planners were confronted with obstacles more formidable than adverse editorial comment. They were denied access to auditoriums and halls, leading to a decision to hold the convention and accompanying mass meetings in two large tents that they proposed to erect on property owned by Stockwell near Minnehaha Park.

On August 21 the safety commissioners "informally discussed" the proposed conference, and pressures against the scheduled gathering mounted in the following week. Hennepin County Sheriff Otto S. Langum appeared before the MCPS on August 28 at the latter's request and "set forth that in his opinion the holding of the proposed meeting . . . would result in grave disorder." A delegation representing the Minneapolis Civic and Commerce Association "submitted a written communication to the Governor asking that the proposed meeting . . . be not held." In response to these testimonials, McGee introduced a motion noting "that . . . [a] breach of peace will result if this meeting is held." Given this probability "and in view of the known character of the meeting," the motion recommended that the governor "issue an order prohibiting the proposed meeting." The commissioners approved of the motion, but not unanimously: Lind voted in the negative.[40]

Burnquist immediately issued a proclamation prohibiting the meeting on the grounds that if held it would prejudice public order and render aid and comfort to the enemy. Reaction to this proclamation was predictable. With the exception of the *St. Paul Daily News*, the Twin Cities press strongly approved; the radical press, however, deplored the governor's action. *New Times* proclaimed: "KAISER BURNQUIST SUSPENDS U.S. AND MINNESOTA CONSTITUTIONS." Less stridently, representatives of the prowar faction of organized labor, who were seeking to counter People's Council influence within the trade unions, also professed disappointment, preferring to "argue it out" with People's Council enthusiasts "on a basis of reason and not of bayonets."[41]

The Burnquist ban was issued only three days before the convention's scheduled meeting time, which found many prospective participants already on their way to Minneapolis. Convention leaders sought to salvage their plans by moving the meeting to Fargo, North Dakota. As a member of the Nonpartisan League, Governor Lynn Frazier may not have been unsympathetic to the conventioneers' plight, but city officials "quickly squelched" the Fargo option. Following hasty deliberations the leaders decided to convene in Chicago.[42]

On September 1 the People's Council actually assembled in Chicago. Some three hours after proceedings began, "the police appeared and brought the gathering to a sudden halt." At this point, Mayor William H. Thompson intervened, promising protection if the People's Council wanted to meet the next day. Unfortunately for the People's Council, the authority of Mayor Thompson could not prevail against the bayonets wielded by the national guardsmen dispatched to Chicago by Governor Frank O. Lowden, an action taken after the governor received a warning from the Chicago Chamber of Commerce that such meetings were "antagonistic to our national purposes in the present world crisis."

Before Lowden's troops were able to disperse its gathering, the People's Council adopted a manifesto calling for "progressive disarmament of all nations, repeal of the Selective Draft Law by the United States Congress, a concrete statement by the Administration of its war aims, and peace without conquest, annexation, or indemnities." To persons of a later generation this program may appear to have been within the bounds of legitimate discourse even in wartime. Nevertheless, according to Peterson and Fite, "the People's Council found that free speech had become drastically circumscribed and the organization was, for all practical purposes, driven out of existence."[43]

Preoccupation with the IWW and the People's Council by no means crowded other concerns off the safety commission agenda. Perceiving that enthusiasm for the draft was less than passionate, the commissioners planned a publicity campaign designed to persuade recalcitrant Minnesotans — particularly German Americans — that

Parade of Brown County draftees, New Ulm, September 21, 1917

patriotism demanded acceptance of conscription. At the same time surveillance of communities wherein pro-German sentiment allegedly persisted was continued and to some degree intensified. [44]

A high point in the publicity campaign was the designation of September 4 as "Dedication Day," a day when warm salutations would be extended to draftees whose departure for training camps was imminent. Governor Burnquist honored New Ulmites with his presence at a "monster loyalty meeting," and he spared no words in depicting the demonic wickedness of the country most of them claimed as their European homeland. Julius A. Coller, a Shakopee businessman and former state legislator, emotionally proclaimed his conversion from pro-Germanism to full-bodied Americanism. "I am of German blood," declared Coller, adding that "prior to 1917 I yielded to no man . . . in the . . . hope . . . that the German eagles should emerge supreme in the conflict across the sea. But the call of blood, strong though it may be, sinks into insignificance when there comes the call of my own, my native land." [45]

Another feature of the New Ulm festivities was a banquet held in honor of those young men who recently had received their draft notices. The draftees, along with the other banquet guests, were asked to subscribe to a loyalty pledge, which they did "by a rising vote."

Part of the pledge was an explicit disavowal of the message delivered on July 25. It read:

> We earnestly believe that any criticism of the Conscription Law under which we have been drafted into the Army of the Nation, or any act or utterance designed to hinder its operation, is a menace to us who are about to assist in fighting the Nation's battles; and we therefore call upon all citizens to be constantly loyal in thought, word and action.

At its meeting on September 4 the safety commission received "verbal reports on a large number of Dedication Day meetings . . . indicating that the civic festival . . . had given splendid results." Some communities anticipated the day by holding earlier rallies. On Sunday, August 26, a crowd estimated at about six thousand persons assembled in Canby to be favored by a flood of oratory from such luminaries as Congressman Andrew J. Volstead, Gunnar Björnson of the *Minneota Mascot,* Jacob F. Jacobson, a prominent progressive Republican leader, and Theodore Christianson of Dawson, the future governor. Christianson defined the sense of the meeting by proclaiming: "Trimmer and traitor begin and end with the same letters and from now on will be treated with the same consideration."[46]

Following a pattern common at other rallies, the Canby orators focused their wrath on New Ulm in general and on Pfaender in particular. According to the correspondent who relayed the account of the rally to the MCPS, one speaker warned: "If any of the Kaiser's spies are here . . . I want them to report . . . that altho the German war lord may own a considerable part of New Ulm, he doesn't have a look-in in Canby." Another remarked, "All the king's horses & all the king's men could not put Pfaender's reputation together again."

The MCPS intelligence apparatus continued to focus a wary eye on the city of New Ulm. Following the August 22 suspension of Fritsche, Pfaender, and Vogel, Hatfield dispatched operative WGS to New Ulm to assess local reaction. The operative's findings were inconclusive. From saloon conversations on which he eavesdropped he gained the impression that the suspensions were frequently discussed, but he had "heard no one express any disloyal feeling." A traveling salesman with whom WGS dined reported that a fellow salesman had "refused to come here for fear that some day the entire town may be interned." The salesman added that he knew "several . . . who seem to feel that way about this town." On August 24, his final day in New Ulm, WGS reported:

> The entire town seemed exceptionally quiet and I was surprised by the manner in which all the men I tried to interview concerning the displacing of the officials, evaded the subject. . . . I left New Ulm fully convinced that this is a bad time to get any information there, more especially so since the removal from office of Fritsche, Pfaender and Vogel. [47]

During the previous weekend WGS had made an equally unsuccessful effort to uncover incriminating evidence against Adolph Ackermann, president of Dr. Martin Luther College, whose stance on war-related issues had aroused MCPS suspicions. On Sunday August 19 the Wisconsin Synod sponsored a festival commemorating the 400th anniversary of the Lutheran Reformation, an observance held at Trinity German Lutheran Church in St. Paul. Acting under Pinkerton instructions, WGS attended the three services on the day's program, with orders to report the delivery of any seditious utterances. Unless Lutheran history and tradition fascinated WGS, the day must have been unrewarding from a personal standpoint. At the 10 A.M. service, "Nothing but religion was mentioned." In the afternoon "Ackerman [*sic*] confined all his speech to the history of the Lutheran Church and the Synod." At the 8 P.M. service "there was nothing spoken that was not of a religious nature."

The benign character of Ackermann's August 19 performance failed to convince Winter that the college president was innocent of sedition. On Monday the intelligence chief ordered continued investigation of the college president "with the expectation that enough evidence might be found to take action against him." This time investigative responsibility was assigned to a Winter operative identified as No. 83, who shadowed Ackermann from 8 A.M. when he left the residence of his St. Paul host until 8:45 P.M. when he departed from St. Paul to New Ulm by train. Again, nothing remotely suspicious was uncovered by the industrious operative. In the afternoon Ackermann attended a showing of the popular cinema feature "The Battle of the Somme." In the evening he went to a baseball game in Lexington Park, but he was obliged to leave at the beginning of the eighth inning to catch his train for New Ulm. [48]

The continuing harassment of New Ulm citizens linked to the July 25 rally, coupled with the virtual excommunication of New Ulm by the state's "patriotic" press, did not work to the advantage of Fritsche,

Pfaender, and Vogel as they awaited the hearings that would determine whether their suspensions from office would be lifted or made
permanent. In mid-September Fritsche and Pfaender attempted to extricate themselves from their situation by offering their resignations
to the New Ulm city council. Upon learning of this development,
the MCPS instructed the council not to accept the resignations, an order
with which it complied. Obviously the safety commission was determined to pursue the case against the two officials to the bitter end. [49]

On September 26 Tighe and other officials met in the Brown County Courthouse to begin the hearing required by Minnesota law before
the governor could permanently remove a local official; after several
days of testimony in New Ulm, the hearing was completed at the
Capitol in St. Paul. Evidence was gathered by special investigators
from twenty-four witnesses. The three accused men affirmed their
complete loyalty to the United States and denied any intent to launch
a seditious movement. Vogel asserted that he had consented to lead
the parade in the belief that its purpose was to honor the participating
draftees and that the goal of the program was to explain the draft
law to them. [50]

Pfaender and Fritsche delivered parallel testimony, although
Pfaender conveyed the impression of being a shade more penitent than
the mayor. Both men explained that the draft was exceedingly unpopular in Brown County, that draft-age men had desired such a
meeting, and that the objective of the rally was to explain the legal
aspects of conscription to these men and to quiet their agitation.
Pfaender conceded his previous doubts with respect to the constitutionality of the draft, but he promised that he now would advise potential draftees to comply with the selective service law to the letter. With
reference to the rally, he still believed that its local effect was
beneficial — insofar as it communicated information about the draft
law — but that its statewide impact was unfortunate, given the angry
reaction it had aroused. He testified further that if he had sensed the
statewide reaction in advance, he would not have participated in the
meeting. Fritsche was less apologetic, pointing out that "Mr. Pfaender
said we were to explain the draft law and that it must be obeyed. But
it was agreed [that] a petition would be circulated asking congress
to amend the laws so that drafted men would not be sent abroad to
fight."

In early December Burnquist granted the accused officials a final
hearing at which they reiterated their earlier defenses. The governor

then ordered the removal of Fritsche and Pfaender from their offices and assented to the reinstatement of Vogel, whose participation had been limited to leading the parade. This ruling was consistent with Tighe's August 13 memorandum, which had pointed out that a county auditor was not vested with responsibility for law enforcement. At its core, the case against the other two officials rested on the charge that they had violated their law enforcement obligations by encouraging disrespect for the draft law. The governor's accompanying statement charged Fritsche and Pfaender with "malfeasance" — one of the two constitutionally permissible grounds for removal of local officeholders. The two men, Burnquist charged, had sponsored a meeting that was "unpatriotic and un-American." The press had reported the meeting

> as an anti-draft meeting and as being in effect pro-German and disloyal to America, and did tend to create among the drafted men who attended it a feeling that the draft law . . . was unjust and illegal . . . [and that the] intended effect of the holding of the meeting was to interfere with the plan of the United States government in the raising of its army and in the prosecution of the war. [51]

Two weeks before Burnquist ordered the ouster of Fritsche and Pfaender, the safety commission had initiated action against Ackermann. On November 20 the commission instructed Tighe to "mail a copy of testimony taken at Brown County hearing to the trustees of Martin Luther College at New Ulm and ask their approval or disapproval of the stand of Professor A. Ackerman as given by him therein." On November 21 Tighe mailed the transcript to the Martin Luther board and asked its "opinion as to the propriety of Dr. Ackerman's conduct . . . [and] as to whether his position represents the position of the college . . . and as to what, if any, action you may be proposing to take." Tighe's communication closed with a warning that the MCPS would "not tolerate the continued operation" of any educational institution within which the "teachings and instructors . . . are not unquestioningly loyal." [52]

A prolonged exchange between representatives of the Martin Luther board and Tighe followed. For a number of reasons — the need for every member of the board to peruse the transcript, the pressures of ministerial duties during the Christmas holidays — the board delayed action on Ackermann's fate. On January 9, 1918, Tighe requested the board to "fix a limit beyond which you will not expect the Commission to withhold action." A week later the board chairman replied that a committee set up to investigate would "report not later than February 20, 1918."[53]

By now Tighe's patience was exhausted. He replied that the February 20 deadline was "not satisfactory" and informed the chairman that he intended to report the status of the Ackermann case to the MCPS on February 5; if the board acted in the meantime he would include "what you write" in the report. "The Commission prefers that the elimination of pro-German teachings and teachers from the state's religious and educational institutions should be made by those directly in control of such institutions, but it will not hesitate to act itself . . . where those in control fail to."[54]

At this point the board bowed to the authority of the safety commission. The board chairman immediately informed Tighe that the Ackermann investigating committee of the board would meet on January 29 and promised that he would report the same day. On January 30 the board chairman provided Tighe with the answer the safety commission had awaited: "Complying with the request of the Committee and board Prof. Ackermann has tendered his resignation, same to take effect immediately."[55]

While a few financial claims related to the New Ulm investigation remained to be adjudicated, capitulation of the Dr. Martin Luther College board to commission pressure formally terminated direct MCPS involvement with the July 25 rally.[56] However, images of the rally continued to have a significant impact. For the duration of the war, sponsors of the allegedly unpatriotic meeting remained hated symbols of disloyalty — although, after the war, both Fritsche and Pfaender would enjoy rehabilitation. The MCPS also stepped up the intensity of its loyalty crusade, assigning a more important role to sheriffs and other local officials; strengthening its publicity apparatus; and encouraging the organization of such private groups as the Stars and Stripes League.

Meanwhile the Nonpartisan League, which the commission had viewed with deep suspicion from the beginning, emerged as the chief focus of MCPS concern and would remain so until the state election of 1918.

CHAPTER EIGHT

The Nonpartisan League under Fire

By the late summer of 1917, the New Ulm incident — joined with other indications that Minnesota patriotism was considerably less robust than it should be — persuaded the safety commission to turn its attention to the problem posed by "seditious" meetings. Unfortunately, the MCPS lacked the resources needed to monitor every suspicious gathering in the state. One promising approach open to the commission was to use local officials — particularly the state's eighty-six sheriffs — in the crusade against sedition. On August 15 the commission sponsored a convention of sheriffs "to consider the organization of . . . automobile squads, the enforcement of laws and other matters connected with public safety."[1]

Attorney General Smith opened the session, which seventy-five sheriffs attended, by explaining "the law governing unlawful assembly, the sedition act, and the federal espionage law." In the area of unlawful assembly, the sheriff was responsible for determining "whether breach of the peace or other disorder [was] probable and [for taking] measures in his discretion to prevent it." In cases of violation of a federal law, the sheriff was to arrest the offenders and turn them "over to the United States Marshal as quickly as possible." The attorney general conceded "the right of citizens to discuss political questions," but he admonished the lawmen to "watch closely where seditious utterances are likely to be made and [to] be prompt to act." "The sheriff," Smith continued,

> should take note of any utterances that discourage enlistment or ser-
> vice in the army. . . . Whoever counsels resistance to foreign ser-
> vice is advising a man to desert, which under court-martial is
> punishable by death. Court-martial does not reach the man who gives
> this advice but he may find himself answering to the law punishing
> incitement to treason.[2]

The sheriffs also learned about "automobile posses" that were being organized in cooperation with the state's automobile dealers. The sheriff and safety commission director of each county were responsible for meeting with automobile dealers within their jurisdictions to acquaint them with the plan for the Minnesota Motor Reserve and to solicit their cooperation. Motor reservists would then be enrolled at an organizational meeting, which would also determine such details as the number of automobiles in each squad and the location of squad headquarters.[3]

The extent to which the Motor Reserve plan was implemented is unclear. In May 1918 the reserve was reorganized along military lines into a Motor Corps attached to the Home Guard. At the close of the war the Motor Corps Division had a strength of 143 officers and 2,440 men organized in a brigade of ten battalions. This corps had a minimal role in the suppression of disorder, conceivably because there was little disorder to suppress. On the other hand, its humanitarian role during the Tyler tornado of August 1918 and the Cloquet–Moose Lake fires of October of the same year was significant. On both occasions units of the Motor Corps delivered life-sustaining commodities to victims of the calamities.[4]

The August 15 assembly also featured a rousing loyalty speech by Darius F. Reese, a veteran Republican politician, to heighten the patriotic zeal of the sheriffs. A give-and-take discussion period provided opportunity for an exchange of views on how to deal with unpatriotic gatherings. The Wright County sheriff "gave an account of a meeting at Hanover which was taken in hand by . . . a squad of soldiers and which ended in the singing of patriotic songs after a few dissenters had been thrown out." The sheriff of Redwood County blocked an antidraft meeting with a simple order: "He just naturally gave out that it must not be allowed." Commissioner Ames pointed out that the vagrancy ordinance authorized "summary action" against persons violating the syndicalism and sedition laws. In response to a question concerning "forbidden printed matter," Attorney General Smith said that possession of such material was not a violation of the law but that the sheriff should try to get evidence of the intent to circulate. "It will be found ninety-nine times out of a hundred, if diligence is used, that the person who has a carpet sack full of this literature is not lugging it around for ballast." Before adjourning, the sheriffs unanimously pledged their full obedience to the government, and promised to "do all we can to carry out not only the duties laid upon us by law, but everything . . . that is asked of us by the Government of the United States."[5]

The cooperative stance of the sheriffs assured the safety commission that subversive agitators would encounter difficulty in attempting to undermine Minnesota's contribution to the war effort. The commissioners also welcomed the assistance of such volunteer groups as the American Protective League, an organization with which Donald R. Cotton, director of the Ramsey County Safety Commission, was affiliated. Another useful relationship was forged with the Stars and Stripes League, a society founded in August 1917 by a group of prominent Minneapolis citizens who professed to be "sickened at heart by the spasmodic manifestations of disloyalty and sedition . . . in different parts of the state." The new league's motto succinctly defined its central goal: "Put every man on record."[6]

The leadership of the Stars and Stripes League guaranteed it a cordial MCPS reception. Samuel R. Van Sant, Minnesota's venerable ex-governor whose penchant for evangelical patriotic oratory was legendary, served as the league's president. Einar Hoidale, a Minneapolis attorney and future Democratic congressman, and Joseph Chapman, the well-known Minneapolis banker, were officers. Less than a week after the league's birth, Ames called the organization to the attention of his MCPS colleagues, stressing in particular "its function in obtaining loyalty pledges from local officials." On August 22 Pardee transmitted a circular letter to the county directors containing essentially the same message and requesting the county safety commissions to cooperate with league sponsors.[7]

Mobilizing sheriffs and encouraging private efforts to "put every man on record" were essentially coercive measures. Commissioner Weiss, who was publicity chairman, and his subordinate William C. Handy, the first director of the commission's publicity department, were searching for more positive ways to communicate the MCPS message to Minnesota citizens. Handy suggested in mid-June that a primary goal should be to create a favorable impression of the agency by using every available means of communication: newspapers, schools, the cinema, chambers of commerce, women's organizations, posters and street banners, and, above all, public meetings. One can imagine that the opportunity of establishing contact with Minnesota's scattered population would have been considerably easier a decade later, thanks to the emergence by that time of radio as a major medium of communication.[8]

Whether at MCPS instigation or in response to other pressures generated within a nation mobilizing for war, the organizations alluded to by Handy joined the crusade to save the world for democracy with apparent enthusiasm. Needless to say, this delighted the safety commission. Deeming the Dedication Days held in reaction to the New Ulm rally to be an outstanding success, the commission also strongly agreed with Handy on the importance of public meetings featuring patriotic oratory. In an August 23 memorandum to county directors, Pardee asked each of them to appoint a speaking campaign committee wherever one did not yet exist. In addition he called attention to the recent organization of a St. Paul–based speakers' bureau known as the Loyalty Lyceum, "an independent, volunteer body, working in full accord with the purposes and plans of the Commission of Public Safety." A month later the commission formally "adopted" the lyceum, an arrangement entailing assumption of financial responsibility for its operation. [9]

Reaching the state's large foreign-born population through its own media was a special problem. On August 1 the safety commission exacted a promise of cooperation from Frederick Bergmeier of the St. Paul *Volkszeitung* and Joseph Matt of *Der Wanderer*. [10] Evidently both pledges were honored to the satisfaction of the commission, even though Bergmeier was interned by federal authorities on the grounds that he was an enemy alien. However, the *Volkszeitung* continued publication under the management of Clara Bergmeier, Frederick Bergmeier's sister-in-law.

In mid-August the commission appointed Nicolay A. Grevstad, a capable journalist who was fluent in several languages, as its "assistant publicity director in charge of the foreign press." Although this title may suggest a broader responsibility, Grevstad's primary mandate was overseeing the Scandinavian-language press, a journalistic network with an extensive circulation throughout the Upper Midwest. Grevstad owed his appointment to the influence of Senator Knute Nelson, who deplored what he considered to be a strong pro-German tilt on the part of Norwegian- and Swedish-language editors. [11]

Grevstad launched an energetic campaign designed to reorient the Scandinavian press fraternity. He supplied its newspapers with a mass of written material, including translations of MCPS releases, Norwegian and Swedish versions of patriotic addresses by Governor Burnquist and other prominent Scandinavian-American politicians, and articles from his own pen. He also lectured Lutheran clergymen on their patriotic obligations, solicited "loyalty pledges" from such organizations as the Norwegian-Danish Press Association, and on occasion

"WARNING" — *Minnesota's syndicalism law was translated into Croatian and four other languages.*

attempted to correct "errors" appearing in Scandinavian-language newspapers. This burst of activity impressed Nelson. Three weeks after the appointment was made, the senator commented to Grevstad: "I have already seen the effects of [your appointment] in articles in our newspapers."[12]

Primary responsibility for evangelizing the foreign-born residents of the iron ranges was assumed by Commissioner Weiss. His initial effort was the circulation of printed cards carrying translations of the syndicalism law in Finnish, Croatian, Slovenian, Italian, and Bulgarian — one set of cards for each language. Shifting from coercion to persuasion, the commission later authorized the printing of 27,500 leaflets carrying the patriotic piece *Why We Are at War* — 10,000 each in the Finnish and Croatian languages, 5,000 in Italian, and 2,500 in Bulgarian.[13]

WHY WE ARE AT WAR

PUBLISHED BY THE ORDER OF MINNESOTA COMMISSION OF PUBLIC SAFETY

Our government did not declare war on Germany. It declared that a state of war existed, because Germany was already committing acts of war on us.

Germany was sinking American ships and drowning American citizens, and declared her intention of so continuing to do.
Germany was paying agents to burn and destroy American factories.
Germany was trying to incite Mexico and Japan to fight us.
Germany was filling our country—even our government offices —with spies and hostile agitators who "set criminal intrigues everywhere afoot."

IF WE ARE BEATEN, WHAT HAVE WE A RIGHT TO EXPECT?

What Germany has already inflicted on conquered peoples:
Towns laid waste; homes desolated.
Men driven into slavery.
Women driven into slavery, worse than slavery.
Huge indemnities that shall cripple all industries.
The loss of personal freedom.

In Germany the people exist for the sake of the military class.
In America the army exists for the sake of the people.

The Kaiser declared:
"Nothing more henceforth may be settled in world without the intervention of Germany and the German Emperor."
Wilson says:
"We must make the world safe for democracy."

THAT IS WHAT THIS WAR MEANS

EVERY ONE MUST MAKE EVERY NEEDED SACRIFICE. EVERY ONE MUST GIVE ALL NEEDED HELP

Posters explaining the war's aims were widely distributed by the Minnesota Commission of Public Safety.

On the assumption that the Finns posed a particularly tough challenge, Weiss enlisted the assistance of Oscar J. Larson of Duluth, a Finnish-American attorney and Republican politician. Larson's activities included overseeing distribution of leaflets, composing and distributing inspirational essays of his own, and promoting patriotic rallies. Apparently influenced by Larson's assessment, Weiss moved toward a less alarmist view of Finnish turbulence than earlier. On August 3 he assured his commission colleagues that there was "no hurry" in launching a special effort on the ranges, adding that

if we can get along by having a certain amount of volunteer missionary work done amongst the "Reds" . . . without spending any money, the State of Minnesota will be that much the gainer and we will not have to establish a precedent that really ought to be unnecessary. A few deportations I think would be more effective than a coat of calcimine.

Viewing the publicity scene from a broader perspective, Handy was equally optimistic. By late August he was persuaded that "the work of the Publicity Department had been so simplified and . . . so largely taken over by voluntary associations that his own services . . . were no longer needed." On September 1 he resigned and was replaced by Charles W. Henke, former editor of the *Dassel Anchor*.[14]

Despite this progress, the commissioners declined to accept the view that voluntary associations alone were capable of carrying the publicity burden. At their August 7 meeting they explored the question of "whether the Commission should begin issuing a weekly bulletin." They eventually approved a plan submitted by Henke, who may have harbored more enthusiasm for the project than his predecessor. *Minnesota in the War,* the weekly bulletin that would serve as the voice of the MCPS for the duration of the war, first rolled off the presses on September 8, 1917, with a run of four thousand copies. By early 1918 its circulation and its size would double.[15]

Several other significant changes in the operation and structure of the safety commission coincided with the establishment of *Minnesota in the War*. Henke's replacement of Handy was more than a routine succession. It involved a new title — assistant secretary in charge of publicity — and an expanded role including not only editorship of the bulletin but also management of the speakers' bureau, which had been augmented by absorption of the Loyalty Lyceum. Under Henke the publicity program was extended to include massive distribution of pamphlets with such titles as *Perils of Prussianism* and posters captioned "How Can I Help My Country," "Why You Must Help," and "What You Can Do." Some of these pieces emanated from George E. Creel's Committee on Public Information, which President Wilson had established to educate the public on the war effort; others were MCPS originals.[16]

When Pardee resigned in September 1917 to accept a post with the Federal Food Administration, he was replaced by Henry W. Libby of Winona, who brought to the secretaryship a style that contrasted sharply with Pardee's. Libby was a machinist, a trade unionist (a status he would shortly lose when the Winona labor movement expelled him from its ranks because of his association with the MCPS), and a practicing Republican who had served one term in the Minnesota House of Representatives. He conscientiously replied to every query addressed to his office, and he adhered closely to the mandates laid on him by the commission. Pardee occasionally enlivened his correspondence with flashes of self-deprecating humor, a luxury that Libby never permitted himself. One suspects that the most comprehensive job search imaginable could not have located a more faithful MCPS employee than Henry W. Libby. [17]

Another change that the commission made in September was termination of the Pinkerton connection "for the present." The rationale for this decision is not entirely clear. Possibly the commissioners felt that the cost of Pinkerton services placed an undue strain on a limited MCPS budget and that Thomas G. Winter had expanded his operation sufficiently to fill the gap. Moreover, influential MCPS allies in northern Minnesota were suggesting that the Pinkerton connection was counterproductive. In requesting the dispatch of three operatives to the Bemidji area, Elmer E. McDonald of the Crookston Lumber Company declared that these operatives "should not be taken from the Pinkerton Detective Agency or perhaps any detective agency. . . . [T]he mere fact that a detective agency is in any manner connected with the case gives the defense something to shout about and prejudices the case in the minds of some." [18]

With the sheriffs mobilized, the Stars and Stripes League in process of putting "every man on record," an expanded publicity apparatus, and an intelligence operation more tightly under its control, the safety commission stood ready to confront the Nonpartisan League. By the late summer of 1917 the league was the commission's most feared and hated adversary. Frank A. Day, the prescient editor of the *Martin County Sentinel,* had predicted in February that the "little Non-Partisan league cloud, now no larger than a man's hand, is quite likely to envelop the heavens." Day added, "If we were in the republican household, we would send in an S.O.S. order for lightning rods." The advancing year appeared to vindicate Day's prophecy. By mid-August Fred B. Snyder was warning Knute Nelson that "unless something is done to counteract this movement I fear that our State offices and the control of the Legislature will pass into the hands of that organization." [19]

What to do was the problem. In March individuals associated with the grain trade created an organization known as the Minnesota Nonpartisan League (as distinguished from the Minnesota Farmers' Nonpartisan League) that sponsored a "program" deceptively similar to that of the authentic NPL. Exposure of the transparency of this scheme soon backfired on its sponsors: "In July [1917]," according to historian

Robert L. Morlan, "the . . . project, which had flopped miserably, quietly ceased to exist."[20]

Attacking the patriotism of the Nonpartisan League was a more promising approach; on this front the organization appeared vulnerable, although undeservedly so. Before adjourning in early March 1917 the NPL-dominated North Dakota House of Representatives passed a resolution calling on Congress, in the event of war, to place property under the same control as that imposed on lives. "If a portion of [the property] is used up during the war," declared league official Henry G. Teigan to a correspondent, "let that part remaining be returned to the owner without any compensation for what has been used up or destroyed." Ostensibly this proposal was advanced in the hope that it would chill the growing enthusiasm for war. If such a law were enacted, explained Teigan, "The capitalists . . . could see [in the clamor for war] a danger rather than an advantage." Although the North Dakota proposal did little to impede the descent into war, the conscription of property on the same terms as manpower remained a core provision in the NPL program. At the same time, wrote Morlan, league support for the war "was not enthusiastic and it was highly critical of certain government policies at both the national and state levels."[21]

Any support of the war effort, however, failed to please erstwhile admirers of the league within the Socialist party. In early June a Socialist activist confessed to Henry Teigan that she was completely disillusioned by the prowar attitude of NPL leaders — especially the editor of the *Fargo Courier,* who was even promoting Liberty bonds.[22] Teigan replied to her complaint with a spirited if apologetic defense of the league's position:

> Of course, I feel that it is a mistake for anyone to openly oppose the war even if he should feel that way. There must be some solidarity on the part of a nation or it has little chance to survive. The thing to do, as it appears to me, is just what the Nonpartisan League is now doing; namely, to conscript wealth as well as human beings. By so doing, the men of wealth are placed on a par, or nearly so, with the working class.[23]

Teigan's reply left his correspondent unappeased. She particularly objected to his invocation of the word "solidarity." The NPL secretary responded with an argument that was essentially pragmatic:

> I did not mean . . . that we should all support a war whether right or wrong merely on the ground that our country was involved.

. . . There is no more detestable toast than that of Stephen Decatur . . . my country right or wrong.

The thing that I had in mind was this: in attempting to set our country right . . . it is not wise to go at it in a manner by which we separate ourselves from the rest of society. If we take a position so strong on the face of it that we alienate all those who might otherwise be with us, we are destroying the possibilities that might be ours if we proceeded along more tactful lines. [24]

Joseph Gilbert, another league official, prepared a comprehensive statement defining the organization's position on the war that was endorsed by local NPL mass meetings and circulated throughout the country. The first resolution acknowledged "that a crisis now confronts us in which it becomes necessary that we all stand unreservedly pledged to safeguard, defend and preserve our country." To emphasize the unequivocal force of this pledge, the resolution proclaimed "that we stand for our country, right or wrong, as against foreign governments with whom we are actually engaged in war." However, "still we hold that when we believe our country wrong, we should endeavor to set her right." [25]

Several resolutions looked toward a proper and just postwar settlement. "Bitter experience has proved that any exactions, whether of land or revenue, serve only to deepen resentments and hatreds which inevitably incite to future war." To safeguard future peace, the U.S. government and its European allies should

> make immediate public declaration of terms of peace, without annexations of territories, indemnities, contributions, or interference with the right of any nation to live and manage its own internal affairs, thus being in harmony with and supporting the new democracy of Russia in her declaration of these fundamental principles.

One of the other resolutions called for "the abolition of secret diplomacy." Another demanded "that gambling in the necessaries of life be made a felony, and that the federal government control the food supply of the nation, and establish prices for producer and consumer." Still another reiterated a core NPL belief: "To conscript men and exempt the bloodstained wealth coined from the sufferings of humanity is repugnant to the spirit of America and contrary to the ideals of democracy." Another resolution declared "freedom of speech to be the bulwark of human liberty," adding that "a declaration of war does not repeal the Constitution of the United States." The final resolution in effect proclaimed the NPL program to be the key to a tolerable postwar future. It declared:

> At the close of this war sound international standards must be established on the basis of a true democracy. Private monopolies must be supplanted by public administration of credit, finance, and natural resources. The rule of jobbers and speculators must be overthrown if we are to produce a real democracy; otherwise this war will have been fought in vain.

A superficial reading of this document might raise the question: Why all the professed anxiety with respect to Nonpartisan League loyalty? One might, in fact, conclude that it articulated Wilsonian idealism. In January 1917 the president had called for "peace without victory." A year later his Fourteen Points would include, among other things, "open covenants of peace, openly arrived at" and territorial settlements honoring the principle of national self-determination. [26] On the other hand, the NPL demand for the overturning of "private monopolies" was not on the national administration's agenda, although there is no evidence that administration officials regarded such a demand as unpatriotic or "un-American."

From the standpoint of the Twin Cities business community, the demand obviously was both; like nearly everyone else — including NPL partisans — members of this community tended to equate their special interests with the weal of the nation. Baldly avowing this, however, might appear excessively self-serving and not entirely convincing. More points could be won by "proving" that the NPL's patriotic pretensions were false and hypocritical, that league orators were in reality "pandering to a treasonable sentiment." [27] Hence, it is not surprising that the NPL resolutions on the war failed to dissuade the safety commissioners from placing the organization under as strict surveillance as their limited resources permitted.

The commissioners were particularly interested in Arthur Townley's speeches and the possibility of seditious nuances in his utterances. They failed to discover anything indictable — such as incitement to draft evasion — but may have been entitled to feel that the league president was half-hearted in his support for the war. At Williston, North Dakota, shortly after the declaration of war, Townley affirmed the willingness of farmers to produce more food but demanded as a quid pro quo the adoption of measures guaranteeing that the crops grown "reach those who need them, and . . . are not given over to the

tender mercies of food exploiters." Later in the same address he proposed another "deal" between the government and the farmers:

> Let's make this proposition to the Government: We are willing to serve
> our country with our lives, the greatest gift we can offer. Take the
> money from the rich, and let them save their lives. Then, when we
> return minus arms and legs, let's beg the Government to permit us
> to have what little is left of us, and, at the same time, let us request
> the Government to treat the rich likewise — Leave them enjoy that
> part of their wealth which is left over, after all the cost of the war
> has been paid. [28]

A Townley speech delivered in Glencoe on June 21 charged that
"autocracy" was as baneful within the United States as abroad. According to a stenographic report communicated to Burnquist, Townley
declared:

> On registration Day about three weeks ago millions of boys pledged
> their lives in defense of our country. . . . I don't believe they go
> to war with the idea of destroying any people . . . but to destroy
> an autocracy that threatens the world. . . . But it is our first duty
> to crush the gamblers of that autocracy in this u. s., the food gamblers
> of the world. I have not much patience with the patriotism of the
> people who would build an autocracy to crush the German autocracy
> and build an autocracy worse than the one over there. [29]

This line of argument left the league open to several complaints.
For one thing, league publicists were accused of arraying class against
class at a time when national unity was absolutely imperative. For
another, NPL adversaries charged, Townley's insistence that the war
should be financed solely from exactions on the rich discouraged purchase of Liberty bonds by the less affluent. North Dakota's poor performance in the First Liberty Loan campaign left league advocates
sensitive to the latter complaint, and their promotion of both Liberty bonds and the Red Cross became more conspicuous as 1917
advanced.

In the summer of 1917 Townley and his associates also kept a wary
eye on the evolution of federal food policy. They enthusiastically endorsed the national administration's call for maximum food production, and in addition they demanded government control of the
marketing system. The appointment by food administrator Hoover
of a price-fixing commission in August appeared to be a step in the
right direction. However, when this commission established a

ceiling of $2.20 a bushel for No. 1 Northern wheat at a time when the market price was $3.06, league publicists found themselves in an embarrassing position — they, after all, had been among the staunchest advocates of price control. At first they accused the federal government of "commandeering the crop." Later they accepted the $2.20 ceiling "on the . . . assumption that other groups were to be treated similarly." Again the league felt betrayed. The Federal Food Administration declined to establish ceilings of processed agricultural products, relying instead on the "patriotic cooperation" of millers and other middlemen. [30]

Shortly after the government established the ceiling, the league held a massive Producers and Consumers Convention in Fargo on September 17 and in St. Paul on the three succeeding days. One objective of the gathering was to build pressure to correct the imbalance in federal food policy. Another was to promote agreement between farmers and organized labor on basic food policy: farmers wanted the highest prices possible for their commodities, whereas consumers — whose interests labor presumably represented — were intensely worried about the rising cost of living. This conflict produced tension between two groups that Townley desired to unite politically.

"The Fargo gathering . . . was merely a warm-up for the St. Paul meetings," wrote Morlan. An impressive array of speakers addressed the latter sessions: Senators William E. Borah of Idaho and Asle J. Gronna of North Dakota, Congresswoman Jeannette Rankin of Montana, the mayors of Minneapolis and St. Paul, representatives of the Federal Trade Commission and the U.S. Department of Agriculture, the president of the Equity Cooperative Exchange, and leaders of organized labor. All the speakers "proclaimed the support of the common man for the war effort and developed at length the general themes of the convention" — the urgent need for comprehensive federal regulation of marketing and the obligation of the affluent to assume their share in financing the war. On September 20 the convention approved a series of resolutions pledging support of the government and of the war effort, endorsing the league's war finance and marketing program, and calling for cooperation between organized farmers and organized workers. The manifesto closed with a statement more notable for "fervor than originality," according to Morlan. It proclaimed: "We pledge our lives, our fortunes, and our sacred honor to our country and our flag in this, OUR WAR." [31]

The final event scheduled for the convention was an address by Senator Robert La Follette of Wisconsin, then known for his bitter-end opposition to American entry into the war. The NPL leaders were mildly apprehensive with respect to what the irrepressible Wisconsin senator planned to say; in deference to the climate of the moment, they had sought to interdict any discussion of the rights and wrongs of American participation in the war. When James Manahan, the NPL counsel, and William Lemke, a member of Townley's directorate, arrived in La Follette's hotel room — where he had closeted himself for thirty-four hours completing a text of his address — to accompany him to the St. Paul Auditorium, the senator showed them a copy of his handiwork, a speech defending the maintenance of free speech in wartime. Fearing that the topic was unduly provocative, the two league leaders persuaded La Follette to speak extemporaneously on the subject of financing the war. This undoubtedly was a tactical blunder. The free speech theme may have been provocative, but it was riskier to turn La Follette loose without the discipline of a written script. [32]

As La Follette, Manahan, and Lemke approached the St. Paul Auditorium, they encountered an emotionally charged throng eagerly anticipating the senator's arrival. The auditorium was filled to capacity, and an overflow crowd at least as large as the one occupying the auditorium was gathered outside. The vast assemblage included a few critics of La Follette, but the wild enthusiasm of the senator's fans discouraged inclinations to protest his presence. While delivering his address La Follette was frequently interrupted by spontaneous manifestations of approval and only occasionally by heckling.

The senator opened his speech with a few excerpts from his famous discourse on representative government. As he approached his central topic — financing the war — he digressed briefly to explain why he had voted against the war resolution. "Germany," he asserted, "had interfered with the right of American citizens to travel on the high seas" — here he paused for dramatic effect — "on ships loaded with munitions for Great Britain." This, he suggested, was an insubstantial reason for going to war: "The comparatively small privilege of the right of an American citizen to ride on a munition-loaded ship, flying a foreign flag, is too small to involve this Government in the loss of millions and millions of lives."

At this point a voice from the gallery shouted: "Yellow!" Angered by the interruption, La Follette responded: "Any man who says that

in an audience where he can conceal his identity is yellow himself."
The senator's partisans rose to their feet looking for the heckler.
"Throw him out," a number shouted. For a moment panic threatened, but La Follette's commanding voice soon quieted the clamor,
whereupon he completed his explanation of why he had opposed going
to war:

> I don't mean to say that we hadn't suffered grievances; we had — at
> the hands of Germany. Serious grievances! We had cause for com-
> plaint. They had interfered with the right of American citizens to
> travel upon the high seas — on ships loaded with munitions for Great
> Britain. . . . We had a right, a technical right . . . to ride on those
> vessels. I was not in favor of the riding on them, because it seemed
> to me that the consequences resulting from any destruction of life
> that might occur would be so awful.

Again a few hecklers threw down the gauntlet. One persisted in
badgering the senator about the *Lusitania*. In reply, La Follette contended that Secretary of State William Jennings Bryan had warned
President Wilson before the great liner sailed that it was carrying six
million rounds of ammunition. He further argued that persons who
booked passage on the *Lusitania* in the knowledge that the vessel carried ammunition were in violation of a federal statute forbidding travel
"upon a railroad train or . . . a vessel which carries dangerous explosives." Following a brief recapitulation of his remarks concerning
the war, La Follette proceeded to discuss war finance, a discussion
consuming considerably more time than his comments on the folly
of u.s. entry into the war.

There can be no doubt that La Follette's September 20 speech to
the Producers and Consumers Convention proved to be more news-
worthy than either the senator or his NPL sponsors had anticipated.
However, coverage of the event was scarcely a model of journalistic
balance. An Associated Press dispatch that soon dominated the front
pages of the nation's leading newspapers quoted La Follette as having said: "We had no grievance against Germany." Perhaps the senator
and his supporters made too much of this admittedly gross misquota-
tion: a correct rendition of the senator's remarks would have left the
impression that the grievance prompting American entry was too insubstantial to qualify as a genuine grievance. More impressive were
complaints that news reports failed to note that the speech contained
much more than a defense of La Follette's vote against the war resolution. So were complaints against the Twin Cities press for its failure

to focus attention on the proceedings of the four-day convention. Morlan reported that the league was obliged "to buy advertising space in the St. Paul papers in order to get the resolutions of the convention before the public."[33]

The same basic complaint can be directed at the small-town newspapers, few of which printed accounts of the convention beyond the La Follette speech. One of the more judicious comments appeared in the *Minneota Mascot* on September 28. Editor Gunnar Björnson cautioned the league to exercise more care in dealing with issues relating to the war. "The Townley meeting in St. Paul," wrote Björnson,

> was an unfortunate thing. Not that we desire to charge the promoters of that affair with disloyalty, but the fact remains that there were things said at that meeting that were disloyal and while Mr. Townley may not be personally to blame for these things yet he is getting the blame for them, because it was his meeting and he stood in a way sponsor for what was said and done.
>
> . . . We have felt friendly toward the league and feel so still. But it seems to us that the members should lose no time in checking any and every display of disloyalty on the part of those who speak at meetings that are . . . calculated to represent the league.[34]

The public safety commission responded quickly to the September 20 episode. On September 25 the commissioners summoned Townley to appear before them "for examination as to any information within his knowledge as to the attitude and relation and conduct of the Non-Partisan League on matters relating to the prosecution of the war." Townley promptly complied with the summons, appearing before the commission that same day in the company of James Manahan, the NPL's legal counsel. After "being sworn [he] was examined at length by Mr. Tighe and members of the Commission."[35]

The interrogation opened with a series of questions concerning the Nonpartisan League as an organization. What benefits could members expect from affiliation with it? Who controlled the purse? How adequate were the organization's guarantees of financial accountability? Conclusive answers to those questions were not forthcoming and perhaps were not expected: the interrogators had other fish to fry. The focus soon shifted to the Producers and Consumers Convention. Townley testified that its purpose was to direct attention to the high cost of living, and he stated that if consumer prices were brought under control, NPL farmers would accept without complaint the $2.20 ceiling on wheat. [36]

Although the commissioners also professed to be concerned about the high cost of living — at the moment they were seeking to control the price of bread — they were less interested in Townley's effort to seek accommodation between producers and consumers on issues relating to food policy. Predictably, the interrogation quickly turned to the September 20 incident. Townley insisted that he had negotiated a prior understanding with La Follette that the wisdom of American participation in the war would not be questioned in his address, that this issue was off limits as a convention topic. The league president also insisted that he had interceded with the senator when the latter breached this understanding.

This explanation failed to reassure Townley's interrogators: they suggested that La Follette should have been ejected from the platform, presumably by physical force. They also continued to press Townley for his opinion on the content of the senator's remarks. "Is there any doubt in your mind that what Senator LaFollette said was seditious and disloyal?" he was asked. Townley replied: "No, there is no doubt in my mind." [37]

The commissioners also explored possible NPL complicity in the New Ulm rally on July 25. Ames asked Townley how many members the league had in Brown County, to which Townley replied: "Fairly well organized — one-half to two-thirds." Ames then asserted:

It has been reported that your organizers in . . . Southern . . . Minnesota joined very cordially in the pro-German propaganda which was going on, and I have been informed that you have some one thousand to fifteen hundred members in Brown County and that they were secured largely before the celebrated New Ulm propaganda. . . . What is the attitude of your organizers down there?

Townley responded that he sent letters to the organizers once in a while telling them that "their business is only organizing the farmers . . . and to stop the discussion of the war, and that anything they do outside of this program is contrary to direction and without authority." [38]

At the conclusion of Townley's testimony, Ames introduced and the commission approved a lengthy resolution beginning with a condemnation of the "disloyal and seditious nature" of La Follette's speech.

The utterances of Senator La Follette . . . made under protection of a guaranty by the President of the Non-Partisan League that no disloyal expressions would be permitted . . . have already served to create treasonable sentiments in the State of Minnesota, and being spread through the public press can have no other effect than to weaken the support of the Government in carrying on the war. [39]

The next paragraph took the form of a petition calling for the expulsion of La Follette from the u.s. Senate because he was "a teacher of disloyalty and sedition giving aid and comfort to our enemies, and hindering the Government in the conduct of the war." Copies of this petition were forwarded to the president of the Senate and to Senators Kellogg and Nelson. Determined to leave no possibility unexplored, the commissioners also addressed an appeal to the federal judiciary for an investigation to determine whether La Follette "and others at the recent Non-Partisan Convention" had violated federal law.

The Ames resolution left the Nonpartisan League in a more ambiguous position than the one it assigned to La Follette. Although the league was not flatly charged with being a disloyal organization, the possibility that it was warranted investigation. On September 26 the commission directed Libby "to request of A. C. Townley transcripts of the speeches and reports in full covering the meetings recently held in Saint Paul under the auspices of the Non-Partisan League exclusive of . . . [the] La Follette meeting." A week later the commission took note of "numerous complaints . . . against an organization known as 'The Non-Partisan League'"—complaints "alleging that said organization is disloyal and guilty of disseminating sedition and disloyal propaganda." The commissioners concluded that an organization so suspect deserved a thorough investigation by an agent clothed with full subpoena powers. He was instructed to investigate not only the league but also all its branches and collateral organizations, including "among other things . . . the constitution of such organizations, their method of operation, their financial methods, their purposes, their various activities, and the effect thereof." The commission delegated this awesome responsibility to Ames. [40]

The various initiatives launched by the MCPS on September 25–26 turned out to be unproductive. Kellogg introduced a Senate resolution calling for La Follette's expulsion from that body; it remained pending until early 1919 when it was dropped. (At that point the Republican leadership needed the senator's assistance in blocking the Wilsonian peace program.) Federal authorities also declined to prosecute La Follette; instead of moving against the Nonpartisan League, moreover, the national administration courted the support of Townley and his associates for its war policies. Ames proceeded with his investigations but failed to uncover evidence warranting legal interdiction of the league. The reports reaching Ames, whether from MCPS operatives or private individuals, indicated that Townley's rhetoric was explicitly loyal, down to appeals for support of the Red Cross and the Liberty loan drives. [41]

Nevertheless, Ames remained unconvinced. In a report directed to the MCPS on February 25, 1918 — some weeks after his membership on the commission had been terminated — he flatly stated:

> My own conclusion is that the Nonpartisan League is essentially disloyal; that it is in effect a conspiracy on the part of an ambitious man with his unscrupulous associates to secure . . . great wealth and political power to be used in a revolutionary campaign and incidentally to embarrass the Government in the conduct of the war; that their recent protestations of loyalty are pure camouflage.

Aside from citing a *St. Paul Pioneer Press* story of February 9 alluding to a content analysis by the Nebraska State Council of Defense of a series of NPL resolutions, Ames offered no evidence in support of his allegations. However, he attached great importance to this "masterly analysis," which to him demonstrated "beyond question that the loyalty of the League is a sham and that its war sympathies" were "rather with Germany than with America and [the] Allies." [42]

Ames's failure to develop a foolproof case against the Nonpartisan League was only a minor setback for enemies of the Townley movement. An escalating antileague war raged on several fronts, some of them under direct safety commission management and others directed by the state's business and industrial elite and heartily supported by the leading Twin Cities newspapers.

The sheriffs were the shock troops on the most important MCPS front. In response to a request made by Burnquist on October 10, Attorney General Smith composed a memorandum "relative to the duties of sheriffs and peace officers in respect to public meetings" that was shortly transmitted to local law enforcement officials and county safety commission directors. Although Smith gave lip service to the obligation of sheriffs to respect the constitutional guarantees safeguarding free speech, the lawmen were accorded wide discretion in determining when the exercise of speech might result in a "breach of the peace."

> The duty of the sheriff is a delicate one but not uncertain in its character. He must preserve the peace. That which disturbs the peace

must be prevented, but the exercise of legitimate freedom of speech is not a disturbance of the peace and any attempt to prevent by force the exercise of freedom of speech is a violation of law. Between these two things a sheriff must decide. . . . He should be, in such matters, "wise as a serpent and harmless as a dove" and act unaffected by fear or favor of any man. . . .

I may add that any meeting, the tendency of which is to create or promote disloyalty to the United States in time of war, should not be tolerated. [43]

On October 7 a group of businessmen, politicians, editors, educators, and a few labor leaders assembled in St. Paul "for the opening of a campaign to combat the traitorous and seditious influences . . . which have centered very largely in the Nonpartisan league." Organizers of this conference had intended it to be a secret gathering, but the *Duluth News Tribune* of October 8 gave it full coverage. Some participants were said to have resented this as a breach of confidence, but no serious questions with respect to the story's accuracy were raised. In the days that followed, several leading newspapers reprinted portions of the story. [44]

According to the *News Tribune,* a comparison of "notes" by conference participants produced a remarkable consensus with respect to the Nonpartisan League. Among other things, the conferees agreed:

That the league contains hundreds of members who openly insult the flag and get away with it.

That the league is so strong in some counties that those who are loyal have to . . . express under cover their belief in the United States government. . . .

Speeches were made which showed that sedition in some places is thriving and that to be known as loyal is almost as dangerous as it was for a man in the south to be known as Union after the ordinance of secession was adopted at Montgomery.

In short, the Nonpartisan League was "actually a pro-German organization and is doing more than any influence to make it appear that Minnesota is not loyal to the government." Equally if not more important, rising NPL fortunes threatened the existing economic order. League-sponsored boycotts were endangering the business life of some towns, and "the commercial life of Minnesota" would be "attacked by legislation" if the league obtained "a large voice" in the legislature. This frightening prospect threatened some sectors of economic life more than others: "the mining interests of northern Minnesota will have a special drive made against them."

The conferees then discussed countermeasures. One participant suggested "shooting such men" as La Follette and Townley. Undoubtedly this suggestion appealed to some, but the conference settled on a more practical move: the organization of a gigantic Twin Cities loyalty rally. This rally was not to be just another patriotic gathering. In the words of the *News Tribune:*

> The idea is to have . . . the most stupendous expression of loyalty possible. To arrange such a program that every loyal man and women [*sic*] in Minnesota will want to attend . . . and to make it so effective that it will stand as a final, crushing, cleansing answer to the polluting Nonpartisan league gathering in this city.

The sponsors of the projected loyalty convention, scheduled for mid-November, hoped for the appearance of either President Wilson or a cabinet officer, an appearance that would identify the national administration with the crusade against NPL "disloyalty." Unhappily for the sponsors, this plan went awry. A few weeks later Joseph Chapman, a leading planner, disclosed that the administration was unwilling to furnish a high-level official as a speaker unless the participation of Townley and the Nonpartisan League also was solicited. According to Chapman, "promoters of the meeting, of course, refused to agree to this arrangement." [45]

However, CPI Director George Creel did send two lower-level officials to the rally: Carl Vrooman, assistant secretary of agriculture and an outspoken friend of the NPL, and Monteville Flower, a California farmer. Neither man delivered a message consistent with the goals of the planners. On the contrary, according to Morlan, "Both delivered scathing attacks on profiteering and stressed the need for extending democracy at home as well as abroad." Flower argued that government direction of the economy was setting useful precedents for peacetime. "We are . . . in the process of the re-definition of government. . . . We are surmounting political mountains we thought we could never ascend." [46]

If the tone of the Vrooman and Flower addresses suggested an unwillingness by the national administration to climb aboard the anti-NPL bandwagon, a well-publicized Townley journey to Washington early in December strengthened this impression. While in the capital the league president met with President Wilson, Hoover, and Creel, who had arranged the Townley itinerary. Reports that these conferences had produced a meeting of minds between Townley on the one hand and Wilson and Hoover on the other did not please the league's adversaries in Minnesota, nor did they enhance Creel's reputation. On April 8, 1918, Senator Nelson called Creel's attention to intimations of "an alliance . . . of some kind" between Creel's committee and the NPL. The CPI director's reply denied the alliance intimation but affirmed the amicable outcome of the conferences. "As you must understand," wrote Creel,

> the business of this Committee is to try to put the people . . . thoroughly and enthusiastically behind this war. Last summer it came to my attention that the Nonpartisan league was not in harmony with the national purpose, and when Mr. Townley came to Washington, I insisted that he call upon me. I sent him also to Mr. Hoover, and . . . the President. The whole point of these interviews was to bring home to him that this was not a "rich man's war," that it was a war of self-defense. . . .
>
> I can say truthfully that, since that time, the Nonpartisan league has done nothing, so far as my knowledge goes, that could not be approved by every patriotic citizen. [47]

Within Minnesota, the public safety commission continued to adhere to the guideline established by the attorney general on October 11 — that is, delegating the authority to ban or to permit NPL meetings to the local sheriff. A letter from Libby to A. D. Stewart, director of the Redwood County Safety Commission, was a studied effort to dissociate the MCPS from the proscription of NPL meetings:

> The governor and the Public Safety Commission have on several occasions advised county sheriffs and peace officers that it was the duty of such officers to prohibit and prevent the holding of any meetings of a seditious nature, or the holding of any public meeting that in the judgment of the sheriff and peace officer might result in disorder and possibly blood shed. . . .
>
> . . . [T]he Commission has issued no instruction that Non-Partisan League meetings shall not be held and instead the matter [has been] left as stated above. [48]

The caution reflected in Libby's letter was perhaps motivated by a realization that league lawyers might mount a formidable legal challenge if such involvement could be proven. In any case, the secretary understated MCPS complicity in the war against the NPL. Shortly after the La Follette speech, A. D. Wilson of the food committee provided the MCPS with the NPL speaking itinerary for the next few weeks. Libby immediately mailed copies of this itinerary to county directors where NPL events were scheduled, along with a request that the directors arrange to have a stenographer at league meetings "to take down . . . any seditious" utterances. [49]

Burnquist responded to complaints with respect to scheduled NPL meetings by reminding the local sheriff of his responsibilities. For example, on January 5 the mayor of Wells informed the governor of league plans to hold a rally in the Faribault County town. According to the mayor, NPL meetings "already held in Faribault County have been of such a disgusting character that the feelings of all decent people have been aroused to a point of indignation." He predicted that "if the meeting now advertised . . . is allowed to be held, disorder inevitably will result." Upon receiving the mayor's communication the governor phoned the sheriff, who anticipated no disorder but promised to be on the alert. In replying to the mayor, Burnquist stated: "If the Sheriff finds insufficient cause to prevent the holding of this meeting, it is his duty to arrest anyone guilty of any seditious utterances." [50]

The governor and his fellow commissioners demonstrated considerably less concern about protecting "legitimate" speech. In February 1918 the Butterfield Commercial Club, declaring the Nonpartisan League to be dominated by "Pacifists, Socialists, Pro-Germans and other reprehensible elements," resolved that the NPL should be prohibited from holding any meetings in Butterfield for "the duration of the war." One might assume that upon being informed of this step, Burnquist should have reminded the commercial club of the dictum laid down in Smith's October 11 opinion that "any attempt to prevent by force the exercise of freedom of speech" was "a violation of law." Instead the governor responded: "While the right of free speech must be given the fullest respect and loyal and lawful meetings should be given full protection, . . . everything possible must be done to prevent and punish all seditious utterances." [51]

In the late winter of 1917–18, by which time mob action against the league had become epidemic, NPL leaders addressed appeals to the governor for action against local officials who were failing to protect the exercise of free speech and assembly. At first the possibility of influencing him seemed favorable. On February 19 he received a delegation headed by Magnus Johnson and another NPL leader that presented a letter detailing the "outrages" perpetrated on the league by mobs with the apparent connivance of sheriffs and county attorneys. Characteristically, Burnquist responded to the group courteously enough, but McGee was reported to have later told Johnson: "I came into the Governor's office when you were reading that [the letter of complaint], and if I had known what you were reading and had had a club, I would have knocked your brains out."[52]

The hopes generated by Burnquist's amiability were short-lived. The February 19 letter had requested the removal of several local officials for illegal persecution of the league. On March 2 the attorney general ruled that the charges against these officials were insufficient to warrant removal, and Burnquist dismissed NPL complaints as inspired by "troublemakers." Meanwhile, on February 26 the executive committee of the Minnesota branch of the Nonpartisan League had addressed a number of questions to Burnquist, the most important one being: "Is the National Nonpartisan League to be regarded by the executive and peace officers of the State as an outlaw?" According to Morlan, Burnquist replied that "insofar as the League complied with the laws of the state and nation it was not an outlaw." A month later the safety commission delivered a more emphatic answer to NPL complaints. A statement in *Minnesota in the War* proclaimed:

> It is hard to conceive of a more contemptible coward than the near traitor and seditionist who makes every effort . . . to discourage patriotism of the militant sort. . . . When the patience of the loyalists is thus tried to the breaking point, and drastic action is taken by the citizens themselves, he is the first to emit a squeal of mortal terror, and rush to the protection of the very law that he has openly scorned and defied.
>   . . . [T]he ever increasing number of cases daily noted where it [mob law] is used on pro-Germans . . . should at least indicate to the near-traitor that he is surely and certainly bringing the day of reckoning nearer every hour that he persists upon his despicable course. The time to "get right" is NOW, and in a manner that will leave no doubt of sincerity. Noses are sure to be counted in every community.[53]

Perhaps popular wisdom has exaggerated the effectiveness of the safety commission's undeclared war on the Nonpartisan League. To be sure, the exercise of free speech and assembly was a casualty of this war: Morlan concluded that "by March of 1918 nineteen Minnesota counties had completely barred all meetings of the League. . . . [N]o fewer than forty scheduled meetings had been prevented by local officials, and no one kept track of the number interfered with by self-appointed guardians of the public welfare."[54] Nevertheless, the league survived. It is true that the immediate goal of the undeclared war — defeating the NPL in the 1918 election — was achieved, but the coalition assembled by Townley and his associates emerged in the 1920s as the state's second party. To a considerable extent, bitter memories of the excesses of the loyalty crusade enhanced the strength of this coalition.

The success of the antileague campaign — such as it was — owed much to the support of Main Street in nonmetropolitan Minnesota. The mobilization of this important sector of the state's power structure could not, however, be taken for granted. Many small-town businessmen responded positively to the rhetoric against big business that the league inherited from prewar progressivism, and they were not immediately persuaded that the hostility of the Minneapolis elite to the Nonpartisan League was totally justified.

The Glenwood Commercial Club is a case in point. Early in 1917 the club held a debate to educate its members about the Equity movement and the Nonpartisan League. According to a club leader, "The business men of the small towns feel that they are not well enough informed, regarding the general aims, or the ultimate results that will follow the possible success of these movements, to be in position to either uphold or condem [*sic*]." The impact of the debate is not on record, but it is clear that as 1917 advanced the inclination of Main Street to condemn the Nonpartisan League overwhelmed any tendency to uphold it. The loyalty issue alone was not responsible for this trend. Even if the nation had not entered the war, and even if the strident attack on the league by the Twin Cities newspapers had never been launched, small-town interests would have discovered reasons to fear the Townley movement. The NPL advanced beyond mere political agitation to a widely publicized promotion of a cooperative network that promised to supply farmers at cut-rate prices with goods and services heretofore provided by Main Street merchants. Moreover, when Townley organizers moved into a community they generally bypassed established merchants, bankers, and newspaper editors. In response to the first manifestation of hostility from these groups, the Townleyites organized boycotts designed to point up "producer" economic power. [55]

The reaction of E. E. Sterling, Elysian town clerk and a pronounced anti-Townleyite, to a July 4, 1918, address delivered by a league orator at a picnic sponsored jointly by Equity and the NPL strikingly articulates most of these small-town concerns. To begin with, Sterling was astonished by the strong support for the national administration and the war effort professed by the speaker. "I was," Sterling continued,

"at a loss to account for that until I realized that the Equity and the
N. P. League advocate government price fixing and control of
everything. Then, with the farmer in political control he [the farmer]
would be the whole push." The speaker

> told a story about a newspaper failing to do what some farmer
> organization wished with the result that 600 farmers stopped their
> paper and remarked: "The only way to get those fellows who interfere
> is through their pocketbook." . . .
>
> The gist of it all was that the politicians and business men are
> afraid to allow the farmers to organize and are doing what they can
> to prevent, making it more imperative that they should.
>
> Looks like [the NPL is making] preparation to sell stock to start
> stores, newspapers and banks. . . . The farmers ought to be pro-
> tected from the results of their own short sightedness until the war
> is over at least. . . . [T]he policy of the Safety Commission should
> be one of strong repression of any further activities of [the league].
>
> The speaker defended socialism saying that it is the proper doc-
> trine for farmers. He defined it as being the getting together for mutual
> protection and benefit.
>
> He also said there were no farmers on the Safety Commission,
> that lots of the farm papers are farming the farmers, that farmers
> are not spreading German propaganda and that if the farmers were
> as disloyal as the business men are Germany would have won long
> ago.[56]

Obviously the deep hostility of the small-town business community
to the Townley movement cannot be attributed primarily to the
machinations of the safety commission. Even if the safety commission had never come into being, Townley's confrontational style and
a perception that his program demanded "all power to the producers"
would have evoked strong negative reactions from small-town elites.
At the same time the loyalty issue provided a moral justification for
actions that mocked the goal of saving the world for democracy.

While Main Street became a bastion of support for the safety commission, the stance of the trade unions was increasingly hostile. From
the beginning, those who spoke for organized labor had objected to
the failure of Burnquist to accord the unions representation on the
commission. The MCPS response to the streetcar strike of late 1917
solidified labor opposition to the commission and inadvertently promoted the forging of a farmer-labor alliance.

CHAPTER NINE

The Button War

A merican entry into World War I confronted the country's trade unions with both opportunity and peril. On the one hand, the material needs of the war machine and the inroads of military service on the labor pool tilted the job market in favor of the supply side. On the other, organized labor was a house divided on the issue of the war itself. Its left wing had maintained a resolutely neutral stance through the period of American neutrality, and the American Socialist party, which enjoyed a growing influence within the labor movement, flatly refused to support the war after its declaration.

Several factors tended to counteract the antiwar sentiment that persisted within labor's ranks. For one thing, many rank and file workers welcomed the increased job opportunities created by the war. To be sure, the rising cost of living spawned bitter complaint, but the upward pressure on wages generated by potential labor shortages tended to offset the price inflation. For another, the resolute prowar stand taken by AFL President Samuel Gompers strengthened prowar proclivities among workers, most of whom were as responsive to the call of patriotism as other citizens. For still another, the Wilson administration appeared to be friendly to organized labor: unions were accorded representation on agencies established to manage the war effort, and the evolving policies of the administration were congenial to labor's moderate wing.

In Minnesota, however, the potential for labor strife was clearly present. The business community and its reliable ally, the safety commission, stood ready to resist the national administration's espousal of labor policies that threatened their interests. Many of those who claimed to speak for labor — including Thomas Van Lear — professed to support the war, but some unionists with ties to the Socialist party declined to do so and even counseled resistance to the draft. From a rhetorical standpoint, moreover, the pronouncements of Van Lear did not appear consistently "patriotic"; from time to time he complained that the heavy export of democracy overseas was depleting that precious commodity at home. Nevertheless, he scrupulously carried out the mandates of the safety commission while remaining critical of what he regarded as commission excesses. If this ambivalent stance fell short of what the superpatriotic mood of the times demanded, John Lind, the commissioner most intimately in contact with the mayor, established excellent rapport both with Van Lear and Lewis Harthill, the Minneapolis police chief.

The relatively conservative leaders of the Minnesota Federation of Labor also cooperated with the MCPS, although Burnquist's failure to accord the labor movement representation on the commission continued to rankle them. MFL Secretary Lawson was a member of the advisory council of the Ramsey County Safety Commission and, according to Pardee, "almost a member of the Commission" by virtue of serving on a food investigating committee presided over by Commissioner March.[1]

Acrimony among unionists on issues relating to the war became painfully evident at the MFL convention that convened in Faribault in July 1917, a convention characterized by historian David Paul Nord as "one of the liveliest in the history of labor in Minnesota."[2] Hostilities broke out when the executive council presented a flamboyantly worded report, the key paragraph of which was calculated to eliminate all doubt with respect to trade-union loyalty:

> Hail, Columbia, happy land! Grand and glorious nation! the last great charity of a beneficient [*sic*] Creator to the human race! We hear your call and with alacrity and joyful hearts we respond to it! The Minnesota State Federation of Labor . . . speaking for the organized workers of this whole commonwealth, pledges to you and your chosen officials, in the supreme crises which is now upon you and them, the support of those workers in full loyalty, without reservation or abatement; in all the service they can render, without subtraction or evasion; in every sacrifice your necessity may require, even to the last extremity of their resources![3]

Another paragraph professed supreme confidence in the leadership of President Wilson.

> Hail, Woodrow Wilson, peerless leader of Columbia's hosts. Matchless expounder of her high principles and pure purposes! The organized workers of Minnesota are firmly with you in the present

strenuous situation. . . . You have stood by their interests and have sought to promote their welfare, and they will stand by you.

Presentation of this report, which was eventually approved by a vote of 186 to 93, sparked an intensely bitter debate. "Some things were said that should not have been said," Lawson recalled years later.

The minority, whose main strength lay within the Minneapolis delegation, sought to commit the federation to a key plank in the Nonpartisan League program. Its resolution read:

> Whereas the government of the United States has considered it necessary to conscript men for . . . waging war . . . abroad, therefore, be it
>
> Resolved, That we favor conscription of wealth as equally necessary for the successful conduct of war.
>
> We endorse the position taken by . . . the National Nonpartisan League and hold equally with them that to conscript men and exempt the blood stained wealth coined from the sufferings of humanity is impotent to the spirit of America and contrary to the ideals of democracy.

After lengthy debate and removal of the third paragraph, the resolution was adopted. In other words, the convention endorsed a cardinal NPL principle without implying a special relationship with the Townley movement or approval of its overblown rhetoric. [4]

The left-wing minority also charged that the Minnesota Employers Association had conspired with the legislature to create the safety commission in order to destroy the state's labor movement. The dissidents demanded that a special session of the legislature be called for the purpose of abolishing "this unnecessary and menacing Safety Commission" and threatened "a state-wide general strike" if this action was not taken. It also recommended "that no member of organized labor accept any appointment whatever from this State Safety Commission." The measure was defeated by a vote of 228 to 72. A competing motion to commend Burnquist and the safety commission, however, was also defeated by a wide margin. [5]

Spirited discussion also followed the introduction of a resolution that called upon the U.S. government to "clearly state just what are the aims of the Government in this war, and to state the conditions upon which peace will be made." The demand for clarification of war aims may not seem unreasonable, but the motion attacked the national administration at a time when the federation was linking its fortunes to the Wilson regime. Predictably, the resolution was soundly defeated on a voice vote. At this point about forty agitated Socialist delegates walked out, vowing to found a rival federation. Although a few unions subsequently withdrew from the MFL, the emergence of a new central body failed to materialize.[6]

In the late summer of 1917 two prowar organizations purporting to speak for labor appeared on the scene. Labor's Loyal Legion was initiated by William C. Robertson, managing editor of the *Minneapolis Daily News.* Robertson assembled

> a little group of working men and suggested that since those who work for a livelihood were looked upon with suspicion as to their patriotism by quite a number of our citizens, it would be well to form an organization of working people to hold loyalty meetings and in every way co-operate with the government in stamping out sedition.[7]

Whether Labor's Loyal Legion deserved to call itself a society of working people is open to some question. According to Robertson, membership was open to "all classes of men who work for a living" and after six months was "more than half non-union." Nord pointed out that most of its officers were not trade unionists, although "at least some workers" enthusiastically supported the organization. The *Union Labor Bulletin,* a monthly periodical claiming to speak for trade-unionist conservatives, urged all union members to affiliate with it and gave its activities generous coverage. While visiting one of its meetings, a *New Times* reporter overheard a member proclaim: "These people who aren't patriotic — we are going to hang them to lamp posts and drive them out of town." Apparently intimidated, the reporter left the meeting before ascertaining, in Nord's words, "how they could both hang a traitor to a lamp post *and* drive him out of town."[8]

The American Alliance for Labor and Democracy was a national organization founded to counteract pacifism within the labor movement. The trade-union credentials of the Alliance were not open to challenge: Samuel Gompers was one of its sponsors. A national Alliance conference meeting in Minneapolis in early September 1917 recommended government control of all industries within which employers failed to establish a harmonious relationship with their workers and called for direct labor representation on all government boards.[9]

These proposals may have encouraged hopes that a cooperative relationship could be established between the Nonpartisan League and the labor movement. On the other hand, suspicions of NPL loyalty appeared to preclude such cooperation. In the immediate aftermath of the La Follette speech, MFL President E. George Hall was quoted as characterizing the NPL as "a seditious outfit" whose promises to the labor movement could not be kept; according to the *Duluth News Tribune,* moreover, MFL Secretary Lawson was one of the participants in the October meeting called to find ways of counteracting the influence of the Nonpartisan League. [10]

By the spring of 1918 the reluctance of such trade-union moderates as Lawson and Hall to consider coalition arrangements with the Nonpartisan League had diminished considerably. The explanation is simple: The safety commission's response to the streetcar strike that dominated the Twin Cities labor-management scene in the winter of 1917–18 persuaded virtually all sectors of Minnesota trade unionism that the Burnquist administration was seeking to destroy the state's labor movement. Under the circumstances, unionism needed all the support it could muster, and from the beginning of the strike the Nonpartisan League unreservedly backed the carmen's unions.

Foremost among labor's opponents in Minnesota was the Citizens Alliance of Minneapolis, a business group that was determined to uphold the legitimacy of the "closed non-union shop" — that is, a workplace where union members were denied employment. The Citizens Alliance had been founded in 1903 by members of the Minneapolis Commercial Club (predecessor of the Minneapolis Civic and Commerce Association) and operated for several decades as the means by which the business elite suppressed the development of trade unionism in that city. [11]

After war was declared, Citizens Alliance spokespersons were able to argue that maintenance of the "status quo" in labor-management relations was the cornerstone of federal labor policy. In May 1917 Secretary of Labor William B. Wilson had issued a statement declaring that "this is no time to take advantage of emergencies to force recognition of the union." The same statement characterized efforts "to force or bring about a stoppage of our industries in order to force the establishment of standards . . . [not in force] during normal conditions" as "the height of disloyalty." According to Citizens Alliance doctrine, the status quo principle legitimated the closed nonunion shop where it already existed. Organized labor favored a different interpretation. From its standpoint, strikes and work stoppages were to be avoided, but peaceable union advance was not interdicted.

Neither was union membership by individual workers, an issue separate from the question of union recognition. [12]

When employees of the Twin City Rapid Transit Company began to unionize in August 1917, the Citizens Alliance blamed "outside agitators" who were bent on sowing discord within a happy work force. George Lawson, however, who conceded that top MFL leaders had not initiated the campaign, pointed out that the organizers had arrived in the Twin Cities on request. According to Lawson, a delegation of streetcar employees had petitioned TCRTC President Horace B. Lowry for a raise. Lowry replied that no money was available to fund a pay increase, but he held out a hope that one might be forthcoming in January. [13]

Dissatisfied with this response, a group of about thirty-five TCRTC workers gathered in the South Minneapolis home of an employee named Hanson to weigh alternatives. A consensus emerged that a union should be organized, and the group solicited the assistance of Lynn Thompson, a leader of the radical faction of the Minneapolis labor movement. At Thompson's behest, Thomas F. Shine, vice-president of the International Amalgamated Association of Street and Electric Railway Employees, and Edward McMorrow, a general organizer employed by the International, arrived in the Twin Cities to lead the organizational effort. Before long two Amalgamated locals — one in Minneapolis and the other in St. Paul — were in existence. With apparent reluctance Lawson, who spoke authoritatively for the Minnesota Federation of Labor, recognized the legitimacy of the two locals.

Lawson's respectability — underscored by his deep involvement in wartime activities — failed to soften Lowry's disinclination to deal with the carmen's locals. From start to finish the TCRTC president refused to negotiate with Shine, McMorrow, or Lawson. Instead he and his Civic and Commerce Association colleagues prepared to meet force with force in any confrontation that might be in the offing. On September 6 officers of the association's private army, the Minneapolis Civilian Auxiliary, met in the city's athletic club to plan antistrike strategy. They decided to organize their force into four companies of 150 men each, all deputized by the Hennepin County sheriff. [14]

Lowry invited a showdown by discharging employees affiliated with the unions, a process begun on September 22. As a manifestation of generosity, Lowry offered his workers a 10 percent wage increase but resolutely refused to reinstate the discharged unionists. Predictably, the unions rejected this overture, calling instead for a strike to begin at 1 A.M. on Monday, October 6. Not enough carmen responded to disrupt normal streetcar service in Minneapolis, but the potential for violence was high. Throughout the two cities scores — if not hundreds — of union sympathizers gathered in crowds to demonstrate for the cause, and armed units of the auxiliary were deployed near key points in the Minneapolis sector of the TCRTC transportation network.

Thanks to the vigilance of the Civilian Auxiliary, law and order triumphed in Minneapolis. The most serious incident occurred in the evening of October 6 when a crowd of union sympathizers gathered near the northside carbarn for the purpose of persuading carmen still on the job to join the strikers. Confronted by a heavily armed auxiliary unit, the crowd failed to achieve its objective. Its armament, consisting of clubs, bricks, and stones, could not prevail against 66 Krag-Jorgensen rifles and 115 Springfields. Following a brief but tense confrontation with its armed adversaries, the crowd dispersed. [15]

In St. Paul, where no paramilitary force stood ready to intervene, the potential for violence was realized. According to the *Pioneer Press,* "Wild rioting in which the police were unable to control mobs numbering in the thousands marked the end of the first day of the . . . strike." For a time streetcar service was suspended, and an argument among state and local officials on the issue of what force should be called in to contain the violence — the Home Guard or federal troops — delayed resumption. Ultimately units of the National Guard assumed responsibility, and their presence intimidated the rioters sufficiently to permit a return to normal schedules.

On October 9, the fourth day of the strike, the safety commission intervened. During their morning session the commissioners resolved to summon Lowry to appear at 2:30 that afternoon and George Lawson at 3:00. At the appointed hour Lowry appeared, accompanied by a TCRTC attorney and a company official. "Upon their retirement," according to the minutes, Lawson, accompanied by the presidents of the two carmen's locals and Shine and McMorrow, "were heard and the claims of the strikers presented." Before the afternoon session adjourned, a number of resolutions that on the surface appeared evenhanded were approved. One noted that the issue dividing the two parties had "narrowed down primarily to the previous discharge of fifty-seven men and their reemployment." Another noted Lowry's assurance that it was not the policy of the TCRTC to discharge employees on account of membership in any organization and affirmed that "unionism or non-unionism should not, during the war, be involved." A final resolution ordered that

> the strike be called off . . . and that the men go to work immediately and, in that event . . . the Street Railway Company reinstate the men who suspended their work . . . and that the status of each of the fifty-seven discharged men be immediately . . . investigated by this Commission and that those . . . unfairly discharged be reinstated when the Commission shall so order.[16]

Two days later the commission received a compliance report from a TCRTC attorney. Following his departure, Shine, representing the fifty-seven discharged employees, "appeared and stated none of the men had been taken back as yet." On the basis of evidence at hand, the commission ordered that twenty-seven of the discharged workers be reinstated and that the status of the remaining thirty "be considered and disposed of as speedily as possible." On October 12 each of the thirty was given an individual hearing. At the conclusion of this proceeding, seventeen of the thirty were ordered reinstated. The remaining thirteen, it was noted, had either resigned or had been dismissed "for actions."[17]

The commissioners now hoped that the dispute had been resolved. Before adjourning on October 12, they approved a resolution noting that their action with respect to the thirty discharged employees had concluded "the work of the Commission in connection with the recent Street Railway Strike." Representatives of both sides professed satisfaction with the settlement. *Commercial West* lauded the MCPS for "calling off the strike, on the grounds that unionism and non-unionism was not a question to be settled during this war period." On the other side, *New Times* called the settlement a major victory for the carmen. Not only did they win a wage raise, but the reinstatement of discharged union men broke a precedent of many years standing. The *Union Labor Bulletin* hailed the safety commission action as a "signal victory" for the carmen and one that boded well for the future of trade unionism.[18]

If Lowry and his associates sensed the same trend, they remained determined to make the future of trade unionism within the TCRTC as bleak as possible. Union carmen complained of being harassed, intimidated, and in some cases physically assaulted by foremen and procompany workers. Worst of all, the TCRTC organized the Trainmen's Co-operative and Protective Association, a company union operating under what historian William Millikan described as the

*Rival buttons issued by the streetcar unions (left) and the company's employee
organization, 1917*

"constitutionally decreed" presidency of Horace Lowry. The cooperative's membership card declared the competence of TCRTC employees
"to manage their own affairs and represent . . . their own interests
without interference by or affiliation with any other individual or
organization." [19]

To promote esprit de corps within the company union, the TCRTC
provided each member with a blue button to be worn on his cap or
lapel. From the standpoint of the TCRTC, this was a blunder. The
unions responded by creating a yellow button of their own, leading
to a competitive display of insignia popularly known as "the war of
the buttons." The sympathies of streetcar passengers more often than
not favored the "yellows" — notwithstanding the connotations of that
color. According to a TCRTC official, passengers dealing with a blue-
buttoned carman "in some cases would throw their nickel on the floor
and in some instances spit on it before giving it to the conductor or
throwing it on the floor." Meanwhile, the unions were gaining in
membership at the expense of the cooperative. [20]

Despite finding itself on the defensive, the streetcar company intensified its covert war against the carmen's unions. The latter responded by filing an appeal to the MCPS "calling attention to alleged discrimination by the company and other grievances." TCRTC officials
countered "that the claims of the Union employees were not well founded" and presented "evidence in support thereof." The commissioners
responded by appointing a three-man investigatory committee

comprised of Samuel F. Kerfoot, president of Hamline University; Robert Jamison, a prominent Minneapolis attorney; and Norman Fetter, a St. Paul businessman.[21]

Although Kerfoot, Jamison, and Fetter were highly respected within their own circles, organized labor had grounds for suspecting that its interests were not well represented. Kerfoot was not directly affiliated with the business community, but the chairman of Hamline's board of trustees was a Citizens Alliance director. Jamison declined to serve because he held TCRTC stock; he was replaced by Waldron M. Jerome, also a Minneapolis attorney and a former Lind law partner. Fetter was suspected of owning TCRTC stock, an allegation that he denied and which his critics failed to establish.[22]

On November 19 the committee presented a completed report to the MCPS. Two of its findings were not particularly favorable to the company. The first noted that the TCRTC had paid full wages to non-union men for time they had spent soliciting on behalf of the cooperative. The other disclosed that the company had offered a bribe to two union men if they would retract their complaint against the TCRTC. However, the committee did not choose to regard these actions as "discrimination." It also endorsed the principle that "in discretionary cases where evidence was evenly balanced" doubts should be resolved "in favor of the company."[23]

The committee's most important recommendation called for "total disuse and abandonment of buttons or other insignia symbolizing the Union or Non-union organizations." Both sides, the committee insisted, had agreed to this stipulation. Another recommendation specified that all union solicitation "shall cease on the company's property, in . . . stations, and upon the cars," a rule that the streetcar company was to enforce. These recommendations were eminently agreeable both to the MCPS and the TCRTC. Union representatives also had agreed to them, albeit with evident reluctance. The safety commission approved them in full on November 20, and on the same day Lowry issued and posted an order that all buttons be removed, without, however, decreeing this as a condition for continued employment.[24]

At the same meeting McGee presented a statement calculated to define the commission's labor-management policy. To maintain an appearance of balance, the statement opened with a ringing condemnation of "machinations . . . to artificially raise prices to consumers." It threatened suppression of such malpractices "even to the point where the Commission will take over the plants and operate them in the . . . public interest." If this threat suggests a McGee conversion to NPL doctrine, the balance of his statement dispels any such notion. The safety commission, he wrote:

> declares that this is not a convenient time for agitation about abstract principles like Unionism or non-Unionism or the closed shop and the open shop. The great thing now is to have the work done.
> . . . [I]t is ordered that in what are commonly known as open or closed shops, in whatever industry or activity employed, every employer . . . entering the period of the war with a union shop shall not by lockout or other means undertake to alter such conditions for the duration of the war, nor shall any individual or combination of individuals begin to unionize or undertake during the like period, to further unionize or close an open or non-union shop industry or industries. [25]

The MCPS minutes for November 20 leave the status of the McGee manifesto in some doubt. They indicate that a motion to adopt it prevailed but that following adoption Lind moved that the "resolution be laid on the table." Burnquist, March, and Ames, along with Lind, voted for this motion. McGee cast a lone negative vote, and Weiss and Smith were absent. Nevertheless, the manifesto was generally accepted as a definitive statement of MCPS labor policy, as, indeed, subsequent developments would prove it to be. [26]

Although the commissioners hoped that they had resolved the TCRTC labor dispute, a substantial number of union members questioned the authority of their leaders to commit them to a "no-buttons pledge" without a membership referendum. Lind and Libby therefore negotiated an agreement with union leaders calling for a vote at a union meeting scheduled for November 26, the expectation being that the assent of the membership would be secured. Upon learning of this agreement, the company took a fateful step. On November 25 — a day in advance of the scheduled union meeting — it issued an order proclaiming that any employee displaying a button on company property would be immediately dismissed. About eight hundred union members interpreted this order as a company lockout, an interpretation soon accepted by the Twin Cities labor movement as a whole. Lawson believed that the men were locked out "because the proposition they were to submit to the Street Car Co. was so fair that the latter would have had to accept it and thereby in some degree [commit] itself to treating with the Union men. Consequently, in order to prevent this, the company locked the men out deliberately." [27]

On November 27 the safety commission launched a final effort to resolve the issues fueling the bitter confrontation between the TCRTC and the carmen's unions. After eliciting testimony from representatives of both management and the unions, the commissioners, on Lind's motion, adopted Order 16, a three-point decree that was considerably less evenhanded than a first reading might suggest. The first point called on the company "on or before November 29" to reinstate any employees who had been terminated "for any reason growing out of the Commission's recommendations of November 19." The second provided that the employees in question should "return to the company's service within the time hereinbefore stated." The third required these employees and all other employees to "comply with the Commission's recommendations of November 19 . . . which are hereby given the force of orders binding both on the Company and its employes." In other words, abstinence from button display was elevated from a recommendation to an order. [28]

Possibly no one outside of the labor movement anticipated the intensely hostile reaction to what in labor circles became known as the safety commission's "infamous button order." "Before making this ruling," wrote the conservative *Union Labor Bulletin,* "the safety commission was dealing with about one thousand street car employes, but after making the ruling it was dealing with about 50,000 workers throughout the state." [29]

In late November and early December, angry union locals throughout the state convened protest meetings at which unequivocal solidarity with the carmen was loudly proclaimed. Speakers at a gathering in St. Paul's Rice Park on Sunday evening, December 2, included Representative Thomas J. McGrath, St. Paul Commissioner Oscar E. Keller, and NPL counsel James Manahan. McGrath offered an apology for having voted for the safety commission bill, and the other two joined him in excoriating both the streetcar company and the MCPS. [30]

After hearing the speeches the crowd failed to disperse. Instead, it formed itself into an ugly mob that attacked streetcars in the vicinity, inflicted injury on an estimated fifty nonunion car operators, and stopped streetcar service for the evening. When the inability of St. Paul police to control the situation became apparent, company officials appealed to Ramsey County Sheriff John Wagener for protection. Wagener rejected this appeal, whereupon Burnquist dispatched Home Guard units to the scene to restore order. Violence

Streetcar strikers gathering at Rice Park, St. Paul, November 28, 1917

also threatened tranquility in Minneapolis, but here the Civilian Auxiliary prevented an outbreak.[31]

In the wake of the December 2 disorders, Burnquist suspended Sheriff Wagener from office; he would be returned to office in the next election. At the same time Ramsey County officials placed McGrath, Keller, and Manahan under arrest on charges of "inciting riot and sedition." The three were immediately indicted, but the case against them — which, according to ex-Congressman Frederick C. Stevens (a staunch friend of both the TCRTC and the MCPS) was based "in large part" on their having "denounced the Safety Commission [and] the Governor" — was dismissed before coming to trial.[32]

Evidently this brief encounter with the law did not materially damage the fortunes of McGrath, Keller, and Manahan. McGrath won reelection to his House seat in 1918; following the death of Carl C. Van Dyke in May 1919, St. Paul voters elected Keller to Congress; and Manahan maintained both his reputation and law practice.[33] However, while pending, the indictments served a purpose. Stevens, who undertook to coach Senator Nelson on what Woodrow Wilson should be told about the transit controversy, believed it . . . very advisable that the President understand fully that the leaders and inciters to the riot and sedition here are under indictment, that this is based primarily upon their onslaught upon the Safety Commission and the Governor, and that any attempt now to cause the State administration to change its position will only encourage these malefactors and disloyalists in the future. [34]

When Stevens posted this communication on December 22, the threat of federal intervention had hovered over the controversy for more than three weeks. Shortly after MCPS issuance of the button order, the unions had appealed to federal authorities for assistance in settling the dispute. In response, the Department of Labor appointed federal conciliator Robert S. Coleman as arbitrator. This action pleased the unions but deeply distressed both the streetcar company and the MCPS. Lowry wired Acting Secretary of Labor Louis F. Post: "You surely do not intend to suggest arbitration whether the company shall obey or disobey an order made after full hearings by the Minnesota Commission of Public Safety." Burnquist was equally adamant. On December 1 he wired Post that "interference at this time will simply result in an attempt to defy duly constituted authority. . . . I shall use every power at my command to uphold the dignity of the State." [35]

The determination of the labor movement to secure at least a modification of the button order equaled the resolve of the streetcar company and the MCPS to uphold it. Union leaders scheduled a massive labor convention to be held in St. Paul on December 5 and hinted that this assemblage might ask the Minnesota union movement to participate in a general strike for the purpose of forcing repeal of the button order. Upon learning of this threat, Secretary of War Newton D. Baker wired Burnquist on December 4, warning that such a strike would hamper war production as well as rail transportation, requesting suspension of the button order, and suggesting MCPS acceptance of federal assistance in settling the controversy. Burnquist replied in the same vein as he had to Post three days earlier, declaring: "Re-opening of the decision as matters now stand would be a surrender of government by reason of riots and agitation and would be an incentive to further riots and agitation." [36]

Burnquist followed up his curt response to Baker with an action that surprised many, pleased some, and dismayed others: the summary dismissal of Charles W. Ames from the commission and the appointment of Henry Libby in his place — from now on, Libby would serve both as secretary and commissioner. After learning that Ames, who was in Washington on business not related to the MCPS, had conferred with Post, Baker, and others concerning the streetcar controversy, Burnquist dispatched the following telegram to the commissioner:

> I understand you are assuming to represent the State of Minnesota and the Public Safety Commission in matters before the Federal Government affecting the action of the Commission. You have no such authority and, as you know, you have been obnoxious to Union labor and so should not act in matters concerning it without authority. Whenever I desire some one to act for the Commission in Washington I shall designate Ex-Governor Lind for that purpose. [37]

The bewilderment occasioned by the Ames dismissal and the Libby appointment extended to Senators Kellogg and Nelson, who were doing their best to discourage federal intervention. Curiously, Nelson found himself dependent on Joseph P. Tumulty, President Wilson's secretary, for information about the matter. On December 11 Tumulty reported that, according to Post, Ames had been removed "for having acquiesced in the telegram to the Governor from the Secretary of War." However,

> Mr. Post states that this is one version of the cause of Mr. Ames' removal; another is that it was because he assumed to act for the Commission in a conference with the Secretary of War; still another is that he was removed because his presence on the Commission was offensive to organized labor. [38]

One can safely postulate that the basic reason for Ames's dismissal was a fear that his contacts with Post, Baker, and other officials, as well as his alleged acquiescence to the Baker telegram of December 4, compromised the defiant MCPS stand against federal involvement in the transit crisis. That McGee heartily agreed with this stand is another safe assumption. In an early December speech before a local club, the fiery commissioner — according to the report wired to Nelson — "expressed his and his associates determination to defy the requests [for] . . . further federal action." He also "characterized the federal government as 'weak and wobbly'" and made a "contemptuous reference to Wilson as [a] college man." The informant characterized McGee's attitude "as [a] most dangerous one" that would "precipitate [a] most intolerable labor crisis." [39]

McGee, perhaps misled by the strong support for the MCPS from the Twin Cities business community, pronounced on December 5 that "the trouble is practically over now and will not be serious unless interference from Washington should revive it." Instead of improving, however, the situation grew more ominous by the hour. The labor convention that had been meeting in St. Paul issued a call for a general strike to commence at 10 A.M. on December 13.[40]

On the appointed hour of the designated day the strike began, and by noon an estimated ten thousand Twin Cities unionists had left their jobs. Fortunately, no violence erupted, and at 1:30 P.M. MFL President E. George Hall called off the strike. He was persuaded to take this action by a plea from Secretary Baker to revoke the strike call, coupled with a promise that the President's Mediation Commission — a distinguished panel headed by Secretary of Labor William B. Wilson and employing Felix Frankfurter as its counsel — that was then en route back to Washington, D.C., from the West Coast would visit the Twin Cities to confer with all parties to the controversy. Union leaders enthusiastically welcomed this development and willingly signed a pledge to abstain from any further sympathy strikes.

Burnquist's telegram to Baker expressed the opposite view:

> I respectfully submit that if instead of creating an opportunity for further agitation . . . the Federal authorities had issued a statement to the effect that both parties to the controversy ought to abide by the orders of the State tribunal practically all attempts to defy the state government would now be at an end. . . . I however shall be very glad to meet the members of the President's Commission informally with the understanding of course that the matters in dispute . . . have been decided and the decision cannot now be reopened.

Baker's reply was conciliatory, emphasizing that the commission was on its way east and was merely asked "to stop in the Twin Cities in order that their informal observations might be available to us here when they return."[41]

While in the Twin Cities the federal mediators conferred with both the safety commission and Horace Lowry. Neither budged an inch from the adamant positions staked out earlier. Speaking for the MCPS, Burnquist held that "submission of disputed questions to arbitration . . . would practically mean arbitrating the arbitration already concluded."[42] That an arbitration had been concluded assumed Thomas Shine's authority to bind the carmen's unions to the "no button" recommendation without an assenting vote by the union membership, an assumption flatly rejected by the Minnesota labor movement.

Accompanied by employees representing the company union, Lowry met with the mediators on December 19. Two days later the TCRTC president confided to Senator Nelson that he believed the mediators "thoroughly" understood "all of the facts" but that he feared they might return to Washington to recommend that "we reinstate those employes not now in our service" — that is, those who considered themselves locked out by the button order. Such reinstatement would, Lowry declared, "mean absolute disruption of our Company, and it is so serious that no matter who signs the communication from Washington, it will be necessary for us to refuse to comply."[43]

Lowry correctly anticipated the future. In mid-February 1918 the mediation commission recommended reinstatement of the locked-out workers "insofar as possible" and called upon the company to cease recruiting replacements from rural Minnesota, a practice that allegedly was depleting agriculture's labor pool. Lowry vehemently refused to honor this recommendation. He also was spared any pressure from the MCPS to do otherwise. If this appearance of MCPS subservience to Lowry created a measure of unease within the commission, reassurance was forthcoming from Ambrose Tighe, who declared that the MCPS had no power to compel a settlement of the transit crisis. The orders issued in October and November were only "to spare [the contending parties] the discomfiture of appearing to yield to each other and to make it seem as though they were yielding to the Commission's power." He added that it "clearly was not in fact within the Commission's power to compel the railway company to employ certain men against its will."[44]

At this point — mid-March 1918 — union prospects appeared exceedingly bleak. The button-order protesters remained locked out; Lowry persisted in his refusal to accord the AFL unions any vestige of recognition; and the MCPS was disinclined (or powerless, although this was not publicly acknowledged) to implement the recommendations of the President's Mediation Commission. But the unions continued to hope for redress from the national administration, and the clearer focus of Wilson's labor policies in 1918 appeared to offer some basis for such a hope. However, the safety commission remained as determined as ever to resist any federal "intrusion" that strengthened unionism at the expense of the open shop. The consequence was an ongoing adversarial relationship between the MCPS and the federal government that would continue until after the armistice of November 11, 1918.

Although the safety commission claimed to have won a resounding victory over the "outside agitators" who allegedly had precipitated the streetcar strike, the effectiveness of the commission was substantially weakened by late December 1917. The dismissal of Ames deprived St. Paul of representation on the commission. Ames continued as supervisor of investigations of the Nonpartisan League and the status of the German language in Minnesota schools, but this was not the same as holding the title of commissioner. One might doubt that the hostility of organized labor to Ames was a major factor prompting Burnquist to dismiss him; if the governor really had desired to mollify the unions, he could have fired McGee. Nevertheless, Burnquist undoubtedly hoped to gain some credence within labor circles by appointing Libby, a lifelong unionist, as Ames's replacement. If so, the chief executive nourished a vain hope. Following Libby's acceptance of the appointment, his own union — the Winona Lodge of Machinists — "expelled [him] for conduct unbecoming a union man for the position he took in defense of the safety commission in the street car controversy." [45]

The defection and subsequent resignation of Lind from the commission in January 1918 was a more serious blow to its effectiveness. His antipathy to McGee was beyond doubt the major factor in his decision. Notwithstanding the commission's calculated effort to preserve an image of internal harmony, glimpses of an escalating tension between the two commissioners occasionally emerge from available sources. An important issue dividing them was Thomas Van Lear. Lind was convinced of the mayor's loyalty and good faith, whereas McGee was determined to drive him from office. In pursuing this goal McGee utilized every opportunity to heap discredit on Van Lear and his administration.

A case in point is McGee's version of a remark allegedly delivered by Van Lear's police chief, Lewis Harthill, at a conference participated in by McGee, Harthill, and a Fort Snelling officer on ways and means to reduce prostitution in the vicinity of the fort. As reported by McGee at a subsequent MCPS hearing on the vice problem, Harthill allegedly had said that his police officers "knew the prostitutes [in Minneapolis] so well that they could call them all by their first names." Doubting the accuracy of this report and suspecting that "it was only for the purpose of reflecting on the police services," Lind requested Harthill to comment. [46]

Harthill's response raises a suspicion that McGee had distorted the police chief's remarks. As Harthill recalled the incident, he and some military officers had, indeed, conferred with McGee in the latter's office on the subject of prostitute infiltration of the area around the fort. McGee asked Harthill if the police department could send officers out to the fort, particularly on Sundays, to "look over the crowds coming into the Fort and prevent the well known prostitutes from going [there]." Harthill replied that this "could be done," even if technically the fort was not within the Minneapolis city limits. The chief also recalled saying "that undoubtedly there were men on our department who would be able to pick out from the crowds the well known prostitutes around town whom they had known through court trials." However, he categorically denied having said "that the policemen knew the prostitutes in . . . Minneapolis so well that they could call them by their first names, because such a statement would . . . have been an untruth."[47]

On instruction from the ex-governor, Lind's secretary forwarded this exchange of correspondence to Libby, indicating that Lind wanted it to be placed in the MCPS files. A few weeks later the tensions between the two commissioners erupted into an ugly confrontation. The exact date cannot be established with absolute certainty, but very probably the explosion occurred on December 5. The MCPS minutes of that date note Lind's presence; minutes of subsequent meetings do not. There also are indications that on December 5 McGee was reacting strongly to the threat of federal intervention in the streetcar controversy. On the same day he dispatched telegrams to high cabinet officials declaring that "nothing more unfortunate could occur than action by the . . . Government to re-open [the button order issue]."[48]

It is likely that Van Lear's role as a leader in the protest against the button order received more than casual attention when the commissioners met on December 5, and it was a McGee proposal to oust Van Lear and Harthill from office that ignited the explosion. Seven years later Lind recalled that he, Lind, had blocked the proposal, arguing that its adoption would be illegal and would very likely provoke disorder, given Van Lear's popularity. McGee was enraged by this rebuff. According to Lind, "He called me everything vile you can think of before the committee — with the governor in the chair. The latter sat silent and I walked out. I did not return to any meeting. The governor begged me to come back. I told him that I could not and would not with McGee on the board."[49]

An exchange of correspondence between Lind and Burnquist soon after the December 5 meeting throws additional light on the embattled Lind-McGee relationship. On December 7, shortly before departing for Washington, D.C., on business unrelated to the safety commission, Lind informed the governor that he would "not take up or discuss the Lockout situation with any one except by your order." He was taking this precaution to place Burnquist in a "position to discount Judge McGee's probable comments on my [Lind's] action." On arriving in Washington, Lind was asked by President Wilson to meet with Secretary of War Baker and Acting Secretary of Labor Post. Lind agreed to the meeting on condition that he "did not and could not represent the [MCPS] in any degree and . . . would not discuss the [MCPS] action or the Governor's action on any phase of the situation except to answer any questions." After meeting with the two officials, Lind claimed adherence to this promise notwithstanding reports to the contrary. He had neither asked for federal intervention, he said, nor offered any advice to federal officials.[50]

On January 7, 1918, Lind formally submitted his resignation as safety commissioner to the governor. An accompanying letter indicated that the McGee factor was responsible for this step. The key paragraph explained:

> I have enjoyed our common work and should have been glad to continue did I feel that my self-respect could permit. But I cannot, and will not, sit through another session with Judge McGee. The venomous slanders which he has circulated about me in Minneapolis and his taunts and abuse at our meetings have become intolerable. Such service as I may be able to render the public I think I can perform in some capacity which does not demand the sacrifice of my self-respect; hence my action.[51]

Lind's departure from the commission was not immediately communicated to the public, and his absence from the Twin Cities — temporarily it was believed — allayed suspicions that he might have defected. Nor was Burnquist willing to accept the resignation as final. In response to the resignation communication, the governor wrote:

> I wish to say that if there is any way in which you can continue your work on the Commission I would consider it a great favor.
>
> I, of course, very much regret the situation to which you refer and realize the disagreeableness of the whole matter from your

standpoint, but . . . I greatly appreciate the valuable work you have done and the wise advice you have given from time to time. I . . . sincerely hope you will be able to remain a member of the Commission even though you cannot attend all its meetings.

Commissioner March also hoped that Lind's absence was temporary. In a letter dated January 12, March requested a conference with Lind "about . . . a great many . . . matters." He closed his letter with a declaration of confidence: "I appreciate more than I can tell you our relations on the Commission."[52]

A month later Lind received a warm letter from Ambrose Tighe. "I miss you very much at the meetings and a great deal of the joy of life is gone because of your absence," wrote the counsel, adding, "I think you saw how much pleasure I got from my work with you." Tighe went on to paint a less than flattering portrait of the MCPS. "The weekly meetings," he commented, "are largely consumed with the insolvable vice problem and . . . the many impossible and trivial projects . . . presented from without." However, the basic flaw "in the scheme" was "its departure from the principle of constitutional government." Tighe then proceeded to analyze this flaw:

> The ruthlessness of the Commission's procedure shows if further evidence was required, how dangerous it is to vest even good men with arbitrary power. If we are going to have a reign of the proletariat after the war, I sometimes think the Commission is setting a bad example for our future rulers. I am flattered that you think I may have some influence in inducing sanity and discretion, but I cannot see that anything I can do will count for much, now that I haven't the benefit of your cooperation.[53]

Tighe's letter raises several tantalizing puzzles. One is the gap separating this private point of view from the public posture reflected in his opinions and the ruthless pressure that he was exerting on Adolph Ackermann at the very time the letter was written. Lind's belief that Tighe promoted "sanity and discretion" in MCPS procedure is equally fascinating. In comparison with McGee, this may have been true; in formulating his legal rulings respecting MCPS authority, Tighe consistently sought to anchor his conclusions to the state and federal constitutions. However, to a generation schooled in the civil liberties tradition developed in reaction to the mindless World War I loyalty crusade, his reasoning is not always convincing. The reference to a possible "reign of the proletariat after the war" is also of interest, underscoring as it does elitist fears that the war was unleashing revolutionary forces that threatened the existing socioeconomic order.

Burnquist's entreaties and Tighe's professions of good will not-withstanding, Lind persisted in his refusal to rejoin the MCPS. Aside from his implacable antipathy to McGee — which he freely communicated to federal officials — the ex-governor may have been influenced by a belief that Allied victory was not far off and that when that victory was clinched "our local warriors would . . . have no one to fight except organized labor." On March 16, 1918, Burnquist regretfully accepted Lind's resignation. Thomas E. Cashman, Lind's replacement, was a resident of Owatonna, a former state senator, a conservative Democrat, and a businessman with varied interests, including nurseries, farms, and a bank directorship. Cashman's role on the safety commission would be a relatively modest one. [54]

Lind divided the remaining months of the war between his Minneapolis law practice and special assignments in Washington. In January he accepted appointment as commissioner of conciliation on an advisory council to the secretary of labor, an agency established to assist the secretary in the development of a coherent labor administration. This responsibility kept him in Washington until early April 1918; he then returned in September to accept an assignment as umpire on the National War Labor Board, which had been established the previous spring to implement the administration's new labor policy. Although service in Washington entailed financial sacrifice, Lind, according to his biographer, found the assignments there "more agreeable than his service" on the safety commission. [55]

Lind's secession from the MCPS destroyed whatever slim hope remained for a tolerable relationship between the commission and the Hall-Lawson wing of the Minnesota labor movement. Even more important, MCPS intervention in the streetcar strike reunited a labor movement that a few weeks earlier had been bitterly divided on the war issue. "By the end of [1917]," wrote Nord, "the commission had succeeded, with the help of the Street Railway Company, in revitalizing the coalition that had elected Thomas Van Lear in 1916." [56] Moreover, this reunited coalition was now moving toward acceptance of political action in alliance with the Nonpartisan League.

In explaining the origins of the Minnesota Farmer-Labor party, William Mahoney, a significant participant in the party's founding, pointed out that before the streetcar strike, "organized labor in general felt some scruples against aligning itself with the League on account of the taint of disloyalty that the politicians and newspapers had fastened on it." However, the friendliness and assistance forthcoming from the NPL during the strike "made it easy to induce co-operation, although it involved a departure from organized labor's traditional course; it meant the launching of an independent political course." The emerging farmer-labor coalition also was able to exploit a "loyalty" issue of its own: In refusing to accept federal mediation, the MCPS was not "standing by the president," and the streetcar company was endangering food production by recruiting young men from the farms as replacements of the locked-out carmen.[57]

At the end of 1917 the safety commissioners could congratulate themselves for having frustrated attempts to unionize Twin Cities transit workers and for having upheld Minnesota sovereignty against federal intrusion. But obviously these victories exacted a price. The federal government was still holding the streetcar controversy under advisement, and it was uncertain whether the MCPS in the long run could successfully defy evolving federal labor policy. In different ways, the resignation of Lind and the demotion of Ames to special agent left gaps that were difficult to fill and that aroused antagonisms damaging to MCPS credibility. Worst of all, a heretofore divided opposition was now coalescing into a political movement that endangered Burnquist's 1918 reelection prospects and the very survival of the safety commission.

These various factors had a significant impact on the MCPS agenda. Through most of 1918 the commission's chief concern was assuring the reelection of Burnquist, and as the year advanced its publicity apparatus was increasingly placed in the service of this goal. Tentative experiments with economic regulation were abandoned, while the infamous loyalty crusade reached new heights of fanaticism. At the same time, a continuing adversarial relationship with federal wartime agencies — the Committee on Public Information, the War Industries Board, which was in charge of economic mobilization, and the Council of National Defense — frustrated cooperation between the MCPS and the federal government. Given these circumstances, it is not surprising that other agencies, particularly Alice Ames Winter's far-flung organization and the St. Paul branch of the War Industries Board, assumed roles that in other states were carried by state councils of defense.

CHAPTER TEN

Bread, Booze, and Bonds

N otwithstanding its reluctance to confront the organized grain trade, the Minnesota Commission of Public Safety could hardly ignore the bitter complaints in the spring and summer of 1917 about the rising cost of living. Beginning in May the Minneapolis City Council repeatedly appealed to the commission and the federal government for action that would roll back the prices of basic necessities. Alderman Charles F. Dight, the most insistent advocate of governmental intervention, was a principled Socialist who had broken with the antiwar stand of his national party. From his viewpoint the war was morally justifiable in its own right and particularly deserving of Socialist support because its needs dictated the adoption of government ownership and operation of the food processing and distribution sectors of the economy. [1]

In late June the safety commission launched a venture that in effect put the state into the fishing business, a step that Dight probably viewed as a reinforcement of his thesis concerning the impact of the war. For some time the MCPS had explored the feasibility of promoting increased consumption of "rough" fish — carp, dogfish, garfish, sheepshead, suckers, and the like. On June 26 it directed Carlos Avery, game and fish commissioner, to issue licenses to persons designated by the state Board of Control as its agents, authorizing these persons to "catch and capture with seines" rough fish inhabiting the lakes and streams of the state. The fish thus obtained were to be used by state institutions, with any surplus to be marketed by the Board of Control "at a reasonable price taking into consideration . . . the cost of securing such fish." [2]

Some weeks later the MCPS authorized the game and fish commissioner to organize a fishing enterprise under his direct control. The catches collected by fishermen employed by Avery were marketed through designated "state dealers" who were permitted a profit margin of three cents per pound "and no more." According to the MCPS this program permitted consumers to obtain fish at "about 50% of the current market prices for the various kinds of fish."[3]

Although confined to Red Lake "and a couple of other lakes so as not to interfere with . . . licensed fishermen," reported the commission, the experiment with piscatorial socialism also yielded the state a handsome profit. Initially the MCPS awarded Carlos Avery one thousand dollars to cover the cost of equipment and to defray other expenses connected with organizing the enterprise. When the venture was terminated at the close of the war, the Game and Fish Commission returned to the state treasury the original appropriation and in addition had acquired cash and equipment approximating thirty-five thousand dollars in value, a sum representing the "net proceeds from the sale of fish taken from various lakes in the state."

The commercial fishing firms protested the intrusion of government onto their turf, but for the duration of the war they failed to achieve their desired objective. Perhaps Avery's aggressive advocacy of his fishing enterprise was the decisive factor here. On January 8, 1918, he invited the commissioners to a well-publicized carp luncheon at the Capitol Cafe at which he hoped "to present a number of matters for the consideration of the Commission." The commissioners accepted the invitation. Presumably the carp was delectable, for after feasting on it they appropriated nearly five thousand dollars to fund the purchase of needed equipment.[4]

Public response to the fishing venture was highly favorable. At the close of the war a substantial number of legislators urged that it be continued, a recommendation that the 1919 session honored. On the other hand, MCPS critics were not persuaded that the fishing enterprise, by itself, was doing enough to combat the high cost of living. On August 1, 1917, the *St. Paul Daily News* noted a recent pledge by Charles W. Ames promising commission action against gambling in food. The *Daily News* was not overly impressed. John Lind had called for action "weeks ago," but his suggestion had evoked the response, "what can we do?" The paper hoped that Ames's rhetoric presaged "a changing point of view, a larger vision of the war, including food as well as cabarets." In any case, the MCPS was empowered to do something: "With a detective bureau well supplied with Pinkerton operatives, the commission now should be able to locate some food speculators."[5]

The newspaper's skepticism was justified. Ames had declared that the campaign against food speculation would be carried on "by working in harmony with the really big men." It mattered little, according to the *Daily News,* whether the effort was carried through with big or little men so long as the goal was achieved. But it was to be hoped that the MCPS would "not jump to the conclusion that the 'really big men' were those who in times past have been associated with the food gamblers and that . . . the American Society of Equity and the Farmers' Nonpartisan league are so unimportant that their service and assistance is not needed."

The safety commission was, of course, not of a mind to solicit the counsel of either Equity or the Nonpartisan League. But the commissioners had already adopted a few modest measures designed to quiet the growing clamor generated by the high cost of living. On July 3 they resolved to conduct a "thorough investigation" of the price situation as it related to food and fuel. Two weeks later Burnquist named William S. Moscrip, a prominent dairyman, George W. Lawson of the MFL, and Commissioner March to conduct this investigation. The committee worked diligently through the summer and early fall, convening open hearings and examining available data on production costs and profit margins. Ultimately the MCPS rewarded these labors by issuing two orders embodying most of the committee's recommendations, one dealing with milk and the other with bread.[6]

Order 13, adopted on November 2, fixed the maximum price that milk producers could charge Twin Cities wholesale distributors at six cents a quart and the price that distributors could charge consumers at ten cents a quart. Responsibility for setting up enforcement machinery was assigned to the Minneapolis and St. Paul city councils. The investigation leading up to enactment of this order was considerably more than a cursory exercise. Moscrip, a milk producer, was excused from participation on grounds of conflict of interest; the extensive involvement of Ambrose Tighe filled the gap created by this abstention. The committee held three public meetings in the Minneapolis council chamber, each one covering an entire day and one extending until 10 P.M. According to the committee report to the MCPS, "All interested parties who had anything to contribute, or thought they had, . . . were given the fullest opportunity to do so." In addition the committee gained access to the books and records of the Milk Producers' Association and the principal Twin Cities milk distributors.[7]

Bread posed a more formidable challenge than milk. According to a report submitted to the MCPS by the March committee on August 28, the profits accruing to millers were reasonable but the toll being exacted by bakers and distributors was excessive. A thirteen-ounce loaf of bread commanded a wholesale price of eight cents and was being retailed at ten cents, which the committee found to be unwarranted. Three and one-half cents of the ten-cent price was attributable to the delivery cost from baker to grocer and to the profit margin of the grocer. "If a large business could be concentrated in a few points," the report concluded, "and the bread sold for cash without delivery, a large fraction of this 3 ½ ¢ could be saved to the consumer." To test this thesis, the committee recommended that the MCPS set up two experimental cash and carry stores, one in St. Paul and the other in Minneapolis. "Leading bakers" had promised to furnish bread to these stores at six and one-half cents per loaf, bread that could be sold at fifteen cents for two loaves.[8]

Following a delay of more than two months, the safety commission acted on these recommendations. In early November it negotiated an arrangement with the Occident Baking Company of Minneapolis under which Occident furnished the MCPS with "well-baked, wholesome bread" that was "manufactured from Bakers' patent flour" and priced to sell at no more than five and one-half cents per loaf of sixteen ounces. The MCPS retailed this bread at several central stations at thirteen cents for two loaves. The additional one cent per loaf charged the customer "covered all the Commission's marketing expenses except the pay of its superintendent." According to the MCPS, this meant that Minneapolis customers were able to buy thirty-two ounces of bread for thirteen cents instead of twenty-six ounces for twenty cents.[9]

Notwithstanding the apparent success of this experiment, the MCPS chose not to remain in the bread business. Instead it retreated to a policy of regulated private enterprise. On December 4, following negotiations with the baking industry, the commission issued an order (No. 18) applying to all Minneapolis bakers licensed by the Federal Food Administration who produced in excess of five hundred pounds of bread per day and to all bread retailers. The bakers were required to deliver "Standard Bread" to the retailer at a price of "not more than thirteen cents . . . the two-pound loaf." The retailer was obligated to provide the consumer with two-pound loaves "at a price not less than that paid the baker and not to exceed fourteen cents." If the consumer requested wrapping and delivery, the maximum price was fixed at fifteen cents. [10]

The safety commission's bread policy soon encountered unexpected difficulties. The most serious problem was an increase in the price of producing bread. Under rules promulgated by the federal authorities in late 1917, bakers were required to reduce the proportion of wheat flour in a loaf of bread by using 20 percent barley or corn flour. A consequent rise in the price of barley and corn diminished the bakers' profit margins, allegedly to the vanishing point. Conceivably the MCPS could have adjusted its maximum prices to accommodate the increase in production costs, but monitoring day-to-day fluctuations in the grain markets would have demanded more expertise than was readily available to the commission.

The MCPS intervention in the bread market ended on March 9, 1918. According to a memorandum that explained this termination, the commission's price-fixing effort had been confined to the Twin Cities. Since other localities were entitled to the "same attention," continuance of the bread order would have required its extension to the entire state. Such a step was an administrative impossibility, given varying local conditions — "a fair price for commodities in one place might be too big or too small in another." Nevertheless, the memorandum contended, the bread experiment had yielded positive results. It had demonstrated that "ten cents for thirteen ounces of bread in Minneapolis was an unwarranted price. . . . [This is] an important contribution to economic knowledge." Moreover, it had disclosed an available remedy: action by local authorities within their own jurisdictions. Most city charters sanctioned municipal price-fixing, as did a number of court decisions. Meanwhile, the MCPS stood ready "to supply any inquiring municipality with the information . . . which [the commission's] investigations have elicited." [11]

One suspects that this evaluation of the worth of the bread project was a trifle overblown. On the other hand, the implication that managing food prices statewide was beyond the administrative capability of the commission is more convincing. In early 1918 the MCPS bureaucracy consisted of Henry Libby plus a small staff, and a tight budget afforded little room for expansion. Moreover, the defection of Lind and the alienation of George Lawson — a legacy of the streetcar strike — deprived the commission of two effective supporters of the bread policy.

Nevertheless, repeal of Order 18 was not universally applauded. B. F. Ward, who had supervised the bread distribution program in Minneapolis, charged that a leading Minneapolis baking firm had informed Libby of its intention to begin violating the order in advance of its expiration date, an action characterized by Ward as "an insult to the commission." Ward further charged that a national association of bakers had sought "to knock out the Minnesota Order and to prevent the cheap bread propaganda from spreading to other sections of the United States." He hinted that an unidentified member of the safety commission had participated in this effort. Lind, too, regretted abandonment of the bread program. Following a conference with federal officials on the subject of price control, he informed March of his own confidence "that we would have had the cooperation of the Food Administration here [in Washington] in its enforcement." He also disclosed that telegrams to that effect had been sent to members of the Minnesota food committee. [12]

Fuel was another area engaging the attention of the MCPS. In the spring and summer of 1917, prospects that a coal famine would render the upcoming winter a chilly one aroused deep anxiety throughout the Upper Midwest. Beginning in May and continuing through the summer, the commission delivered spirited communications concerning both the price and availability of coal to federal authorities and to Senators Nelson and Kellogg. On July 17 Burnquist appointed McGee as a "special agent . . . to expedite coal shipments" to Minnesota. In carrying out his assignment, McGee journeyed to Washington for conferences with federal officials and to Cleveland, Ohio, where he met with railroad officials to urge them to facilitate the shipment of coal to Lake Erie ports. His appointment as Federal Fuel Administrator for Minnesota on October 8, 1917, presumably strengthened the McGee role as the state's coal czar. [13]

The safety commission's final report assigned high marks to McGee's performance as fuel administrator. Personally McGee did not take issue with this evaluation, but he recognized that his coal stewardship had failed to win universal approval. A McGee apologia issued shortly after the armistice acknowledged that 95 percent of the fuel dealers and consumers in Minnesota blamed him for delays in coal deliveries. He conceded the validity of complaints about delays but disclaimed responsibility for them, declaring that as fuel administrator he possessed authority to allocate coal but lacked the power "to issue an order to a dock company to move coal anywhere."

Authority to do so was vested in a district representative of the Federal
Fuel Administration who was in charge of the movement of all dock
anthracite and bituminous coal in Minnesota. According to McGee,
this official — who happened to be the longtime secretary of the Northwestern Coal Dock Operators' Association — assumed complete jurisdiction over the movement of coal from the docks. For his part, McGee
"was not at liberty to communicate with a dock company much less
to order it to move coal to a dealer or consumer." [14]

Given the improvisation and disarray characterizing federal economic mobilization in World War I, McGee's complaint is not entirely unconvincing. On the other hand, his allotment policy did not
escape all criticism. In September 1918 the manager of the Farmers'
Co-operative Elevator Company in Cottonwood informed Burnquist
that his firm had filled out all applications required for an allotment
of hard coal but had received no response. He had "written Mr. McGee
frequently about this matter, all to no avail." He called attention to
the Cottonwood cooperative's generous response to the Fourth Liberty
Loan, implying that expeditious action on the coal application was
an appropriate quid pro quo. The manager remained convinced that
"we are being discriminated against," a conviction strengthened by
the fact that other dealers in Cottonwood had received their full
allotments. He requested the governor to do something — anything
but referring the matter to McGee, who would not "do anything for
us on a bet." [15]

Although the governor's office replied promptly to the communication, the response was not calculated to enhance confidence in state
government's sensitivity to citizen complaints. A letter signed by Gustaf
Lindquist pointed out that "the only other place we can take up the
matter is with the Fuel Administration at Washington, and . . .
[they] would refer it back to Judge McGee, who is the Federal Fuel
Administrator for Minnesota." Lindquist advised approaching McGee
again and professed to believe that "the matter will have prompt
attention." [16]

Issues linked to liquor posed more difficulties for the safety commission than those related to food and fuel. Twenty-one of its fifty-
nine orders dealt with some aspect of the liquor trade, including dance
halls and poolrooms. [17] However, this breakdown is not a true reflection of the commissioners' priorities. It is attributable rather to the
intense pressures mounted by militant drys on one side and equally

determined wets on the other. The predominant sentiment within the commission was undoubtedly dry, but its members had a healthy respect for the power wielded by the wets. The lobby representing breweries and distilleries was considerably more inclined than persons accused of disloyalty to challenge the safety commission in the courts. The wet coalition also included many unions affiliated with the Minnesota Federation of Labor, as well as small-town elites who presided over wet municipalities.

Arrayed against the liquor lobby and its allies was a coalition of drys that appeared to be gaining in strength month by month. It included such organizations as the Anti-Saloon League, the Woman's Christian Temperance Union, and a multitude of Protestant churches of both liberal and conservative orientation. Additional support emanated from small towns and counties that had excluded saloons within their jurisdictions through either local or county option. Pressures from towns that were dry under local option but were located within so-called wet counties were particularly intense. Other advocates of a hard line against booze included members of the Minneapolis business community whose values had been shaped by their New England backgrounds and mining and timber executives who contended that excessive drinking was impairing the efficiency of their workers.

One such executive, whose firm was located on the Cuyuna Range, placed his views before the safety commission in no uncertain terms. He complained in November 1917 that "a handful of foreigners" whose drunken and disorderly behavior was benignly tolerated by "a half-breed Finlander [the county attorney?] and Swede sheriff" were a menace to the entire area. He considered it "an outrage that this mining range should be domineered by a bunch of foreigners." The situation was critical. As he put it, "We want relief from this whisky business and we want it now."[18]

Following issuance of Orders 7 (the famous cabaret ordinance) and 8 (restricting the sale of liquor in St. Louis County areas adjacent to mines and timber) on June 5, no further orders related to liquor were adopted until September 12. Nevertheless, the flow of complaints continued unabated. Most were "received and filed" with a promise of further action. However, the commissioners felt impelled to respond to the situation in Martin County that came to their attention in midsummer 1917. Martin was the only Minnesota county adjacent to the Iowa border that had not adopted county option. Its

Beer and whiskey cases stacked behind a bar in the village of Trosky, Pipestone County, about 1915

principal city, Fairmont, was dry, but the villages of Ceylon, Triumph, and Welcome boasted thriving saloon businesses. Following the receipt of a myriad of complaints from officials and citizens residing in southern Minnesota and saloon-free Iowa, the commission convened a hearing on July 16. Several prominent southern Minnesota politicians presented statements signed by residents of neighboring towns alleging the "vicious" impact of the Ceylon-Triumph-Welcome oasis in both Martin and adjacent counties. Senator Frank E. Putnam of Blue Earth, appearing on behalf of his Faribault County constituents, argued that the excessive drinking promoted by the saloons in the three towns "interfered with food production . . . was a menace to the military, including men of registration age, and . . . [the saloons were] a rendezvous of the I.W.W." [19]

Pipestone County, within which the tiny village of Trosky (population 250) harbored a prosperous saloon that allegedly employed fifteen bartenders, had also come under scrutiny. The county bordered on South Dakota (like Iowa a dry state) on the west and the dry counties of Murray, Cottonwood, and Watonwan on the east. The saloon's volume of business coupled with its location aroused suspicions that its clientele extended beyond Trosky's hinterland. [20]

On July 24 the commissioners authorized Burnquist to appoint a committee of three to investigate saloon conditions in Martin and

Pipestone counties. After receiving a report from this committee that supported many of the complaints, the commission convened another hearing that featured presentations from advocates on both sides. The deliberations that followed disclosed a divergence of opinion within the commission. A motion by McGee imposing total prohibition on the two counties commanded only his and Burnquist's support. A Lind motion had more success. It called for limiting liquor sales in the two counties to intoxicants consumed "on the premises, in the licensed saloons now existing in said counties." McGee proposed an amendment requiring closure of the Martin-Pipestone saloons between 5 P.M. and 9 A.M. This amendment passed by a vote of four to three, with Lind, Ames, and Weiss voting in the negative. [21]

The amended motion, which passed by a vote of five to two (with Ames and Weiss in the negative), laid the basis for Order 10. It limited transactions in the saloons of the two counties to purchase of drinks to be consumed "upon the premises" between the hours of 9 A.M. and 5 P.M. Violation of the order would "operate in itself, and without any further act . . . to terminate the right" of the violator to remain in business. Sheriffs of the two counties were charged with responsibility for enforcing the order. [22]

The commissioners also took notice of complaints originating in northern Minnesota. By virtue of county option and Indian treaties, the northern region was saloon-free, the one exception being Red Lake County; under existing statutes, however, the shipment of liquor directly to consumers was legal. Koochiching, Beltrami, and Clearwater counties had all adopted county option, although several saloons were operating in Beltrami and Clearwater within the grace period allowed for orderly liquidation of their businesses. In all three counties the complaint was the same: enormous amounts of liquor, enough to demoralize the population to the extent of impairing the war effort, were being shipped in. The commission reached a consensus that the railroads were the key to the problem. If they could be persuaded or compelled to refuse shipments of liquor destined for points within the three counties, the difficulty would be resolved.

After considering the possibility of relying on voluntary compliance, the commission opted for compulsion. On September 18 it issued Order 11, which forbade any "common carrier, or other carrier" to ship liquor in any quantity to Koochiching County. The sheriff and other peace officers were ordered to seize any intoxicants shipped in violation of the order "and forthwith [to] report such seizure to the Commission for . . . further instructions." On October 16 an identical order (No. 12) was applied to Beltrami and Clearwater counties. However, the plight of saloonkeepers operating under the county option grace period persuaded the commissioners to amend the order to permit the saloons an additional thirty days to dispose of existing stocks. During these thirty days, all intoxicants purchased had to be consumed on the premises. [23]

Promulgation of Orders 10 through 12 marked a turning point in the evolution of the MCPS's liquor policy. The precedents established by the three orders were a useful tool, but ones which the commission proceeded to apply selectively. Moreover, the commission resolutely declined to decree a "bone-dry" solution for the state as a whole, notwithstanding frequent entreaties that it do so. According to McGee, such a solution would go beyond the intentions of the legislature when it established the commission. [24] "As matters now stand," the commission declared on February 5, 1918, "the general closing of saloons in this state and nation is a war measure upon which the Federal Government has already acted." In addition,

> the President . . . has now the power to eliminate the liquor traffic throughout all of the states and, if he deems it advisable . . . he will undoubtedly do so. Unless additional causes should develop justifying a course which now appears inconsistent with the present policy of the Federal Government, . . . the Commission does not feel it should act in this matter. It takes this position without regard to its own views which are clearly disclosed by the course it has heretofore followed. [25]

An important component of "the course . . . heretofore followed" was the selective application of the precedent established by Order 10. In late 1917 and through 1918, the MCPS was deluged with demands from dry activists throughout the state urging imposition of the Martin-Pipestone model on their communities. Citizens of Chisago County complained that their tranquility was being shattered by intoxicants procured in Forest Lake, a wet town located in neighboring Washington County. After considering the complaints the commissioners decided that the evidence did not justify taking action similar to that taken in Martin and Pipestone counties, "where the situation had been extraordinary." Residents in the Rochester area delivered similar complaints, supported by petitions carrying scores of signatures. One petition signed by ninety-one people complained bitterly about the hazards posed by drunken drivers. The MCPS sought the counsel of A. C. Gooding, a local banker and member of the Olmsted County Public Safety Committee, who replied equivocally, noting that fatality statistics did not suggest an increase in highway deaths. [26]

Citizens of Hastings, a dry town in a wet county, complained of lax law enforcement. The MCPS sent an agent to the town who, during a one-day inspection, "saw many . . . influential citizens" who denied the alleged abuses. From Elba, in Winona County, came allegations that a saloon in that village was not only violating the provision with respect to hours as laid down in Order 7 but even employed a woman bartender. Libby responded by sending the mayor a copy of Order 7 and expressing the hope that he would enforce the rule against female saloonkeepers. [27]

The safety commissioners were cautious in responding to such complaints, beyond referring the matter to local officials or reminding complainants of their own responsibilities as citizens for law enforcement. In deciding whether to intervene, the commissioners relied heavily on the testimony of "influential citizens" within the communities under dry attack. One cannot escape the conclusion that the MCPS was not eager to court confrontations with the power structures of Main Street, particularly in southern Minnesota. [28]

The commission's experience in dealing with the saloon situation in Blooming Prairie (Steele County) pointed up the wisdom of restraint. Located within a wet county and surrounded by counties that had adopted county option, Blooming Prairie saloons enjoyed a thriving business. Inevitably, dry activists demanded that the MCPS take strong action, ranging from closing down the village's saloon complex to applying the Martin-Pipestone formula. The commission did not respond immediately; perhaps it realized that the village's virtual liquor monopoly within a wide area was an asset prized by many Blooming Prairie citizens. Finally, however, the commissioners yielded to the clamor of the drys; on December 5, 1917, they adopted Order 17, which applied the Martin-Pipestone precedent to Blooming Prairie. Saloons in the village were compelled to remain closed from 5 P.M. until 9 A.M. and to confine their business to intoxicants "drunk upon the premises." An accompanying memorandum noted the argument that the order would have the effect of "making Owatonna the distributing point hereafter, instead of Blooming Prairie." The MCPS promised that if this should indeed happen, the commission could be "depended upon to deal with the case." [29]

Order 17 aroused more protest in Blooming Prairie than its predecessor had in Martin and Pipestone counties. Fourteen residents of the village appeared before the commission early in January with a request that the order be modified, a request that the MCPS denied. Meanwhile, obedience to the commission's ukase came into question. By mid-May the commissioners had learned that three saloons within the village were openly defying the order. They responded by issuing a further order (No. 34) that closed the saloons for the duration of the war.

W. R. Carroll, one of the affected saloonkeepers, reacted to this edict by applying for a state district court injunction restraining the MCPS and Blooming Prairie officials from interfering with his business. Perceiving merit in Carroll's application, Judge Frederick N. Dickson of the second judicial district ordered the safety commission and Steele County officials to appear in his chambers on June 29 to show cause why such a restraining order should not be issued. In reply the commissioners instructed Tighe "not to appear in response to the notice." For his part, Carroll resumed business on the assumption that Dickson had placed him on sound legal footing. Burnquist responded by instructing Adjutant General Rhinow "to investigate the situation in said village and [to] close the saloons that are violating the law and [to] keep the same closed by the use of such of the National Guard as is necessary . . . until the validity of the order involved has been determined by the courts of this State."[30]

Following this move by the governor, Judge Dickson ordered him to appear in court on July 13 to show cause why he should not be held in contempt for defying the June 29 order. Thereupon Burnquist obtained a writ from Andrew Holt, associate justice of the Minnesota Supreme Court, forbidding Dickson to proceed further pending action by the higher court. The supreme court reached a decision on August 9 that, in effect, upheld Burnquist but stopped short of endorsing the constitutionality of the MCPS statute. Instead it focused on the propriety of a district court instituting contempt proceedings against the governor. According to the decision, such a court was not empowered to do so if the governor's acts in question "were done in discharge of official duties requiring the exercise of judgment and discretion imposed upon him as chief executive by the Constitution."[31]

Even though the decision had not placed the MCPS on absolutely secure constitutional grounds, the commission reacted aggressively when reports reached it alleging persistent liquor law violations in Blooming Prairie. On September 24 it promulgated the most stringent order yet issued in the interminable battle against illicit liquor. Order 48 prohibited "the sale or keeping for sale or delivery of intoxicating liquors in . . . Blooming Prairie" for the duration of the war and for three months after ratification of a peace treaty. All existing liquor licenses were "cancelled and revoked." Existing stocks were to be removed "under the supervision . . . of an agent . . . designated . . . by the Governor." Responsibility for serving the order was delegated — not as heretofore to local officials — but to a commission-appointed peace officer who was instructed to serve the order not only on persons having liquor in their possession, but also on the sheriff of Steele County and the "President of said Village." On the same day the safety commissioners imposed a similar fate on Ceylon's saloon enterprises, which had been the subject of persistent complaints since the original order had been issued a year before. [32]

The replacement of local officials by MCPS peace officers reflected an innovation in the commission's enforcement policy. The commission initially relied on local governing entities to enact ordinances embodying the orders of the commission, but from time to time this expectation appeared to be misplaced — particularly so far as liquor ordinances were concerned. To fill the gap the commission on April 30, 1918, enacted Order 33, which specified that "any person, violating . . . any order of the . . . Commission . . . , shall be guilty of a misdemeanor" punishable "by imprisonment in the county jail for not more than three months, or by a fine of not more than One Hundred Dollars." Obviously the role of peace officers who operated directly under MCPS jurisdiction was enhanced after the commission embarked on a policy of directly enforcing its orders. [33]

The liquor challenge in northern Minnesota differed somewhat from that posed by Blooming Prairie and Ceylon. Dry activists continued to complain to the MCPS about the transportation of enormous quantities of intoxicants into the so-called dry counties of that region. The MCPS responded by applying the precedent created by the Koochiching County order, which forbade common carriers from accepting liquor for shipment into counties that had adopted county option. Order 19 (December 11) applied the precedent to Polk County and Order 20 (January 15) to Clay County. By this time the commission was faced with the problem of disposing of the liquor seized by local officials. Order 22 directed sheriffs and other peace officers to destroy — "in the presence of a witness" — the confiscated beer in their possession. "Liquor other than beer" was accorded more respectful treatment. The sheriffs were instructed to pack it for shipment to Rhinow, who in turn was directed to "turn over any such liquor to the United States Government under such arrangement as he may make for the purpose."[34]

Order 24 (January 30, 1918) substantially broadened the Koochiching precedent. It prohibited all common carriers and "any person, firm or corporation" from accepting "intoxicating liquors in any container whatsoever" for transportation into any area wherein "the sale of . . . liquors is . . . prohibited by . . . operation of the County Option law . . . or . . . the provisions of any Indian Treaty." Following implementation of this order, the dry counties of northern Minnesota presumably enjoyed substantial protection from the debilitating impact of strong drink. Unfortunately, the operation of saloons in two villages in Red Lake County — a county not affiliated with the county option fraternity — mocked the goal of making the north an alcohol-free zone. Plummer, according to a Soo Line agent, was annually importing 2,728 gallons of whiskey, brandy, gin, alcohol, and wine and 100,118 gallons of beer. For a village inhabited by fewer than 350 people, this appeared excessive. Over a period of five and one-half months, Red Lake Falls, a village of about 2,500 inhabitants, had received 218 tons of hard liquor and forty-five carloads of beer. That the two villages were serving a market extending way beyond their immediate hinterlands was an inescapable conclusion.

With the legal aspects of MCPS action against the Blooming Prairie saloonkeepers still unresolved, the commissioners proceeded cautiously in dealing with dry demands for drastic steps. They engaged Thomas D. O'Brien to conduct an on-site investigation and to recommend an appropriate course of action. They also convened several hearings at which both wets and drys were afforded an opportunity to present their arguments. After hearing both sides, they weighed the pros and cons of applying the Martin-Pipestone formula versus the imposition of total prohibition on Red Lake County.[35]

On August 13, 1918 — four days after the Minnesota Supreme Court had resolved the Blooming Prairie case — the commissioners elected total prohibition. Order 43 banned "the sale or delivery of intoxicating liquors in the County of Red Lake . . . during the period of the existing war and for a period of three months after . . . ratification of the Treaty of Peace." All existing and outstanding liquor licenses were revoked and all existing stocks of liquor were ordered removed within ten days "to some place" where sale was lawful. Service of the order was assigned to "a Peace Officer of the Commission."

An appended memorandum offered a lengthy justification for the admitted severity of the order. This document emphasized the beneficent impact of the order on the war effort. Sober and industrious workers were urgently required at a time when "the largest crops of wheat and other food stuffs ever known" were being harvested. Testimony at the hearings had presented incontrovertible evidence that demoralization in Red Lake County was "very great." Fortunately, Order 43 offered a corrective: "With the sale of . . . liquors prohibited in Red Lake County, a thirsty resident of that County or of the nearby counties . . . would have to travel from one hundred and eighty-three to three hundred miles to the nearest saloon for relief."[36]

Casual perusal of safety commission orders relating to liquor might leave the impression that implementation of the Eighteenth Amendment — destined to go into effect on January 1, 1920 — was a mere formality. Such an impression would be mistaken. The MCPS declined to act on a substantial number of complaints alleging abuses as serious as those directed against Blooming Prairie, Plummer, and Red Lake Falls. The vast majority of Minnesota saloons operating on April 6, 1917, remained in business for the duration of the war, notwithstanding multiplying federal restrictions on the manufacture of intoxicants. It is, of course, true that Order 1 banned the saloon trade in the Bridge Square area of Minneapolis, that No. 2 established a dry zone around Fort Snelling, and that No. 7 mandated a 10 P.M. closing of all saloons statewide. On the other hand, forty Minnesota counties remained outside of the county option club when national prohibition went into effect. These forty constituted a minority, but they included the large urban and a number of middle-sized counties, Winona and Stearns among them.[37]

The promotion of Liberty bonds was a more agreeable responsibility for the safety commission than containing the high cost of living or limiting the debilitating impact of alcohol. The bread issue created a dilemma for the commission. To restrict profiteering in the basic necessities of life, many argued, was a patriotic imperative that a patriotic safety commission was in duty bound to accommodate. On the other hand, stringent price regulation risked offending the "really big men" whose cooperation Charles Ames courted. Moreover, a popular perception that MCPS authority knew no bounds exaggerated the agency's actual capacity to control food prices. Dealing with the high cost of living was clearly a federal responsibility.

Coping with problems linked to liquor also posed a dilemma. Persuasive arguments contended that commitment of vast quantities of scarce grains to the distilling and brewing of intoxicants — particularly since beer drinking especially was overwhelmingly a German-American activity — verged on disloyalty. Many convinced drys perceived the concept of a patriotic drinker as a contradiction. However, circumstances obligated the MCPS to assume a less extreme view, whatever the opinions of individual commissioners.

Liberty bond promotion was mercifully free of such dilemmas. Willingness by a citizen to invest his or her money in the war effort became an acid test of that citizen's patriotism and loyalty, and the sacrifice required was not onerous. The purchaser of Liberty bonds was not making a donation but investing in an interest-bearing security. If she or he lacked the cash to participate in a particular drive, the local banker was eager to provide a loan to finance the bond purchase. Happily, the risk assumed by bankers within the Liberty loan network was minimal. The instructions communicated to them by Arthur R. Rogers, chairman of the Second Liberty Loan campaign in the Ninth Federal Reserve District, included the following advice with respect to credit purchases:

> For your protection you will probably desire to incorporate in your receipt to the purchaser, a clause which, in event of default in any of the payments for a certain period of time, would authorize and empower your bank to sell the bonds at private or public sale without notice, deduct any loss or charges, and remit balance to purchaser.
>
> It did not seem advisable, from a selling standpoint, to print this provision on the order blank. [38]

The successive Liberty loan campaigns were organized by the U.S. Treasury Department, operating through the Federal Reserve system. The drive within each district was headed by a director who in turn appointed county, municipal, and township committees, many under the leadership of bankers. The cooperation of both public and private agencies invested the campaigns, beginning with the second one, with the aura of a religious crusade. This was particularly true in the Upper Midwest, where failure of the region to meet its allotment in the First Liberty Loan campaign had bred a sense of frustration and fortified a determination to "go over the top" in subsequent drives. [39]

Liberty Loyalty Day Parade during the Second Liberty Loan campaign, St. Paul, October 1917

The safety commission responded enthusiastically to a plea from the Council of National Defense that it, along with councils of defense in the other states, assume an active role in the Second Liberty Loan campaign. At its meeting of September 18, 1917, the MCPS pledged Theodore Wold, governor of the Ninth Federal Reserve District, full cooperation, promising assistance "in the sale of these bonds by every means in its power." It also designated Commissioner Ames to act for the MCPS in the forthcoming campaign. [40]

In late September Chairman Rogers dispatched a circular letter designating the forenoon of October 15 as the time when "every committeeman in the Ninth District shall be on the job prepared to sell Liberty Bonds." But Rogers did not anticipate completion of the task in a single day.

> The committees will continue their work of solicitation until every man or woman, who is able to buy, has either purchased a bond or declined. This office intends to keep a record of every person seen with their reply, for future reference, and when we have finished our campaign, the list with the amount subscribed will be the possession of the proper government officials. [41]

The coercive impact of keeping a record of each bond transaction was enhanced by recording failures to purchase on "blue cards." Thomas E. Cashman, who headed the Second Liberty Loan campaign in Steele County and who would shortly succeed Lind on the safety commission, believed these cards to be "worth their weight in gold."

> When the average man finds that he is going to be reported to his government, giving in detail the amount of property he owns and his reasons for not subscribing, he usually calls up those who are carrying on the campaign and wants further information and then usually comes across. . . .
>
> This Liberty Bond Campaign has done wonders towards making seditious people loyal in this county. [42]

Ames shared with Cashman a belief in the efficacy of the bond campaign as a promoter of loyalty. In conveying instructions to the directors of the county safety commissions, he occasionally delivered a special message to directors of those counties where disloyalty was perceived to be rampant. "We are fully aware of the difficulties under which you labor," he informed the Le Sueur County director. Such difficulties were similar to those "in many other parts of the state." However, "If the Germans know what is good for them they will come across strongly on these government bonds. It is the cheapest way and the quickest way in which they can bring themselves into the ranks of American citizens." [43]

On the same day Ames delivered a similar if less sympathetic message to H. C. Hess, Brown County director. According to Ames:

> Certainly there is no county in the State that is more in need of redemption in the eyes of the world than Brown[;] justly or unjustly, the citizens of your county are considered to be backward in their support of the government.
>
> I am informed by the Federal Reserve Board that only forty-eight thousand of the first Liberty Bonds were sold in Brown County. Now, is your opportunity to show that the newspapers are mistaken in their theories about New Ulm and vicinity. [44]

In replying to Ames when the campaign was virtually completed, Hess was able to report at least partial "redemption." New Ulm and Springfield had exceeded their quotas, while Sleepy Eye had failed to do so. The country districts remained doubtful; not all the returns were in. The local bond committee had mounted an extraordinary effort in New Ulm, where "every wage-earner was solicited." Hess implied that the county's moderately creditable performance was not a response to Ames's surliness. "Should you . . . have any connection with future drives," wrote Hess, "I must ask you to refrain from putting the matter up to us the way you did this time. We subscribed . . . not because we had any good name that needed redeeming, but because it seemed a patriotic duty. Your attitude is likely to arouse resentment." Ames did not respond directly to the Hess complaint. Instead he turned it over to Henke, who informed Hess that "Mr. Ames is out of the city . . . but I shall take special care to call his attention to the last paragraph." [45]

In organizing his promotional campaign, Ames employed the carrot as well as the stick. To stimulate grass-roots enthusiasm he instituted a competition among the counties, the reward being two achievement banners. One was awarded to the county purchasing the "largest percentage of sales in proportion to its allotment." (The allotment was a monetary figure determined by the Federal Reserve Bank based on the county's financial resources.) The second was awarded to the county with the largest number of individual subscribers in proportion to its population. The commission excluded Hennepin, Ramsey, and St. Louis counties from participation in the first competition. When the returns were in, Lake County, with an oversubscription of 371 percent of its quota, gained possession of the first banner. Nobles, wherein one-third of the population subscribed, won the second. [46]

Notwithstanding a notable statewide improvement over Minnesota's performance in the First Liberty Loan drive, the MCPS professed to be disappointed at the response. About two-thirds of the counties — many of them in southern Minnesota — failed to meet their allotments, and some raised only one-half of what was expected of them. "When every allowance is made for variations in wealth," editorialized *Minnesota in the War,* " . . . it must be admitted that in many counties the citizens of Minnesota are not yet awake to their patriotic obligations, and to the necessity of individual and personal effort to support the Government in the great crisis of our national life." [47]

When the third bond campaign was organized in the spring of 1918, the Ninth Federal Reserve District and the MCPS would heighten the pressure in an effort to close the gap disclosed by the outcome of the second. Meanwhile, at least modest satisfaction could be derived by the second's improvement over the first and by the state's overall performance in the second. Along with the other commonwealths in the ninth district, Minnesota oversubscribed its quota by about one-third. One out of seven of its residents was now a bondholder, a proportion equal to that in the nation as a whole. The record of the three largest cities was particularly gratifying. With a quota of $16 million, Minneapolis subscribed more than $22 million; Duluth exceeded its allotment by about $1.5 million, and St. Paul oversubscribed its quota of $12 million by $600,000.[48]

Although the MCPS willingly accepted a share of the credit for the positive side of Minnesota's performance in the Second Liberty Loan, it also acknowledged the contributions of other groups. One such group was the network of women's organizations, operating under the leadership of Alice Ames Winter. By the autumn of 1917 the Winter network had been perfected, and as had been true from the beginning, it was functioning only nominally under the supervision of the safety commission.

Mobilizing Minnesota Women

T he network presided over by Alice Ames Winter was considerably more than an appendage of the Minnesota Commission of Public Safety. Winter derived her authority from a double appointment: she was chairman of both the Council of National Defense Minnesota Woman's Committee and of the MCPS Women's Auxiliary Committee. On her letterhead, Winter listed the national title above the state one.

If the double appointment enhanced Winter's autonomy, other factors contributed to the same end. Physical separation limited contact between Winter and the MCPS. The safety commission operated out of the State Capitol, whereas Winter's base was her home at 2617 Dean Boulevard, in an affluent section of Minneapolis. Financially, too, Winter's dependence on the MCPS was minimal. Following her appointment the commission provided her office with a typewriter, a paid secretary (who took up residence at Winter's home), and office supplies. From time to time Winter or the secretary filed requests for stamps, funds for printing, and travel reimbursement, requests that the commission usually but not invariably honored. Since the vast Winter network was staffed by volunteers, its needs placed no undue strains on a slender MCPS budget.

Another factor reinforcing Winter's autonomy was her complete commitment to the tasks at hand. Although MCPS duties exacted a toll on the time and energy of the commissioners, all of them had other responsibilities — service on the commission ostensibly was a part-time activity. By contrast, Winter devoted most of her waking hours to the manifold projects linked to her double chairmanship. Occasionally intimations of a heavy workload emanated from her office. In late July 1917 her secretary, Katherine Parsons, was obliged for health reasons "to stop all work for some months," according to Winter. Parson's successor, Aimee Fisher — one-time secretary of the

Alice Ames Winter in her Minneapolis home, about 1925

Minnesota Suffrage Association — remained on board for the duration of the war, but her correspondence at times dropped hints
of weariness. "Mrs Winter is now taking a week in bed to take
care of her back," Fisher reported on September 20, 1917, adding:
"It is not easy but it ought to help her." Months later Fisher apolo-
gized for her own inability to remain abreast of a large volume of
correspondence. [1]

Still another factor strengthening Winter's autonomous role was
her satisfactory relationship with federal officials. The parent commission found itself at continuous odds both with the labor policies
of the Wilson administration and with George Creel's friendly stance
toward the Nonpartisan League. Winter may not have approved of
federal labor policy, and on occasion she voiced virulent hostility
toward the Nonpartisan League; trade-union issues, however, were
not on her program, nor did her organization participate directly in
the state campaign of 1918. She was concerned with food conservation, the protection of children, and, of course, Americanization —
concerns commanding high priority within the Wilson administration.

One also suspects that the Winter organization more nearly conformed to Council of National Defense norms than did the safety

commission structure. The safety commission would come under severe criticism from council officials in 1918 for not according all sectors of the state's population equitable representation within its network. Winter's structure was not a model of inclusiveness either — one searches her rosters in vain for such activists as Maud C. Stockwell and Fanny F. Brin — but its membership base was considerably broader than that of the commission. Ideologically the Winter group emitted more than a faint whiff of middle-class social justice progressivism.

At the top of the Winter establishment was an executive committee of seventeen members that met weekly in the early months of the war and biweekly thereafter. Many of its members headed one of the sixteen standing committees that addressed such areas as Americanization, food conservation, patriotic education, publicity, women in industry, and, inevitably, Liberty loan. In compliance with a mandate from the Council of National Defense calling upon every state to organize statewide women's societies into a women's state council of defense, Winter also established a "war council" that, when completed, consisted of fifty-eight members. This body met monthly. Given its size and diversity — for example, groups both opposing and supporting suffrage were represented within its ranks — one suspects that the council was less significant than other components of the Winter network. [2]

Most members of the executive and standing committees, as well as of the war council, resided in the Twin Cities. An organization was established as well within each of the state's ten congressional districts, headed by a chairman and vice-chairman who divided responsibility for the district. Each of Minnesota's eighty-six counties was also provided with a chairman, and these county leaders were closely supervised by Winter and the executive committee. A weekly letter from her office to the congressional district and county chairmen served as the principal channel of communication between Winter and her subordinates. The MCPS publication *Minnesota in the War* also carried news about women's activities. [3]

Constructing the county chairman network generated potential tensions between Winter and the safety commission's male sector. In late June 1917 Winter said that she was "having a hard time to get our county chairmen listed." She added that "in some cases the men who are county chairman have appointed a woman's Committee without consulting us and have appointed a woman who is not the same as our appointee." In such cases, she continued, "we have tried to withdraw our name, so that there would be no friction." Winter's complaint drew an emphatic response from the safety commission. Pardee wrote to the county directors instructing them to "cooperate with the women's organization in every way that may be helpful." Specifically, he ordered that new appointments "will come from Mrs. Winter, not from this office. Recommendations that may be offered by the county director will be carefully considered, but the appointment itself will be made by Mrs. Winter." [4]

Perfecting grass-roots structures — on the township level in rural Minnesota, on a village basis in the small towns, and within the wards in the larger cities — was the final step in Winter's organizational effort. As might be expected, this process took some time. Undoubtedly, a women's conference representing most of the state's counties that convened in the Twin Cities in early July gave it considerable impetus. In mid-November, Winter reported that 1,016 local chairmen had been appointed. [5]

Although the Nonpartisan League and organized labor were not represented within the women's network, several members of the executive committee were well-known equal suffrage and social justice advocates. Agnes Peterson, who headed the committee on women in industry, was superintendent of the Bureau of Women and Children within the Minnesota Bureau of Labor, Industries and Commerce. She also had filled leadership roles within the Minnesota Federation of Women's Clubs and participated actively in the campaign to strengthen child labor laws. Mary Frances Harriman Severance, whose post as first vice-chairman of the executive committee placed her second in command under Winter, had participated in the activities of the Ramsey County child welfare and child labor committees and served as a director of the Minnesota Woman Suffrage Association. [6]

Anna H. Phelan, chairman of the speakers' bureau, also possessed an impressive set of credentials. A graduate of the University of Wisconsin where she earned a doctoral degree in 1908, Phelan had been a member of the University of Minnesota English department for several years, her specialty being creative writing. Her activities outside of the classroom included a two-year stint on the state's minimum wage board, advisorship of the College Equal Suffrage Club, and chairmanship of a committee on laws affecting working women. Her ideological inclinations are suggested by a book she published in 1927 entitled *The Social Philosophy of William Morris.* [7]

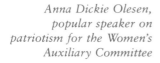

Anna Dickie Olesen,
popular speaker on
patriotism for the Women's
Auxiliary Committee

Outside of the Twin Cities, several of the congressional district and county committees were headed by the spouses of prominent local men, women whose visibility in their own right was not striking. An exception was Anna Dickie Olesen, state vice-president of the Federation of Women's Clubs, who was vice-chairman of the eighth congressional district organization. [8] Early in the war Winter called the safety commission's attention to Olesen's potentialities:

> In Cloquet there is a woman who, I think, might be of real value to the Safety Commission. For some years she has been singularly successful among groups of foreign women, getting them to classes to study English, child welfare, and American ways. She seems to have the power to reach them. She is a very good speaker and a vivid little person. . . . [H]er name is Mrs. Peter Olesen. [9]

Well before completing mobilization of its troops, the women's executive committee launched a number of programs calculated to assist the war effort. "July begins to show results," reported Winter,

Posters from the Federal Food Administration were used in Minnesota to preach the virtue of food conservation.

and the most impressive results were in the area of food conservation. Next to the military draft, the food conservation crusade inspired by Herbert Hoover undoubtedly had a more direct impact on U.S. society than any other facet of wartime policy. As historian Robert H. Ferrell pointed out, "Fathers and mothers denied children a spoonful of sugar on their cereal 'because Mr. Hoover would not like it.'" Social pressures as powerful as legal sanctions obliged homemakers to observe meatless and wheatless days. Farm journals carried slogans issued by Hoover's office admonishing readers: "Don't let your horse be more patriotic than you are — eat a dish of oatmeal!" [10]

In Minnesota, jurisdiction over the food conservation drive was assumed by a committee headed by Alice Winter and including A. D. Wilson, state food administrator; C. G. Schulz, superintendent of public instruction; Fred B. Snyder in his capacity as a University of Minnesota regent; and Annabel C. Coe, president of the Minnesota Federation of Women's Clubs, who also served on Winter's executive committee. On the county level, a committee consisting of the chairman of the women's committee, the superintendent of schools, and the county safety commission director supervised activity. Township and ward committees operated on the neighborhood level.[11]

In July this network received a mass of printed material from Winter's office. The biggest single item was a batch of 275,000 Hoover pledge cards, the signing of which was a commitment to honor the guidelines formulated by the Federal Food Administration — guidelines based on what Ferrell called "a gospel of the clean dinner plate" and epitomized by the advice, "Eat plenty, wisely and without waste." The pledge cards were mailed to a corps of some three thousand canvassers whose responsibilities included not only distributing the cards, but also persuading lukewarm homemakers to take the Hoover pledge. The various local women's committees also established classes in food preservation, dispatched women skilled in the arts of food conservation to farm kitchens, circulated recipes that economized scarce commodities, and organized patriotic meetings featuring talks, moving pictures, and slides. In addition, exhibits demonstrating the techniques of food conservation were prepared for display at county fairs, many of which were held in the late summer.[12]

Within a few weeks Winter received progress reports and signed pledge cards from forty-eight county chairmen. This was not a true measure of the response, however: many chairmen had sent the pledge cards and accompanying reports directly to the food administration. Those reaching Winter communicated a variety of messages, some of them going beyond food conservation. The Anoka County committee was "hampered by lack of funds." Nevertheless, it had managed to distribute patriotic pamphlets printed in the Swedish and German languages. In Cottonwood County "the large foreign speaking element was reached through their churches. They were reluctant to sign." The Dodge County committee requested "a lecturer on morals." Its Hennepin counterpart reported focusing attention on the culinary and cultural needs of the troops at Fort Snelling and the sentinels guarding the bridges. The Kandiyohi committee commented on the impact of Maria Sanford and Anna Dickie Olesen, both of whom had delivered patriotic addresses in the Willmar area. The Hoover campaign in Lincoln County had been slowed by "great interest in Red Cross and also because of canning season." One of the Ramsey County committee projects was distributing a poster "everywhere" admonishing women not to "let a fighting man carry your parcels. Save the man-power for essential service." The Wadena County committee had sponsored a physician's address to recently drafted men "on moral problems."[13]

Several county directors expressed anxiety about the loyalty of their fellow citizens. The Redwood County director felt "certain that someone had been working against the Hoover pledge before the canvass, also against the Red Cross." The Rice County director reported overt opposition to the Hoover cards, adding, "The percentage of purposeful sedition is low but the percentage of ignorance, intolerance and distrust is high." Jackson County, according to its director, was "pro-German." The Scott County director reported that "Shakopee has pro-German elements" and that "signers [of the Hoover pledge] were reluctant at first."

Among the grass-roots concerns reaching Alice Winter as 1917 advanced, none alarmed her more than reports of disloyalty within several Minnesota counties. Early in August she pushed the panic button by informing the safety commission that one of "our women" had disclosed that within her county "we have about 25% of loyalty and 75% of disloyalty." Within Pennington, Norman, McLeod, Blue Earth, and Mahnomen counties, hostility had reached the point of "pulling down the flag." Socialists were "carrying on active propaganda" and winning some converts. "Downright ignorance" was part of the problem; eighteen teachers in Big Stone County had never heard of Herbert Hoover. Ominously, "the ugly elements [were] taking advantage of the ignorance and giving it instruction."[14]

Although Winter's reaction to these reports was intense, she did not believe that repression was the answer. Instead the situation required a massive effort. The presence of large colonies of Finns, Slavs, and Wobblies in northern Minnesota and of Germans in the southern counties meant that "Americanization work and patriotic propaganda were the fundamental work and those on which all others depend."[15]

Winter believed that an effective Americanization program had to be multifaceted. In the urban centers, welfare workers serving foreign-born clients needed the assistance of people familiar with the clients' languages and able to interpret foreign-born rights in the areas of police protection, sanitation, and education. Special celebrations for "newly-made citizens" should be routine. Above all, committees of representative citizens in each area should encourage recent immigrants to adopt English as their language of communication and to apply for naturalization. By the autumn of 1917, such a committee was functioning in Minneapolis under a threefold mandate: to secure voluntary teachers of English, to solicit the cooperation of employers in the development of Americanization programs, and to disseminate publicity on behalf of these programs. Primary responsibility for reaching rural women was assigned to the Young Women's Auxiliary, a standing committee headed by Elisabeth Congdon of Duluth.

Americanization was not, of course, reserved exclusively for immigrants. A prevailing view in 1917–18 held that all Minnesotans needed to nurture a more militant patriotism. Most important was the necessity of evangelizing the upcoming generation, the thousands of children enrolled in the state's public and private schools. Happily, the women's executive committee was strategically placed in relation to the educational system. Annie Shelland, a supervisor within the Minnesota Department of Education, was chairman of the committee on patriotic education, and the county superintendents of schools were ex-officio members of the women's county committees.

The program developed by Shelland and her colleagues was not startlingly innovative. It included the singing of patriotic songs and rendering the pledge of allegiance to the flag at the beginning of each school day, classroom instruction in democracy and on the present war, the staging of pageants and plays, arithmetic exercises based on statistical data relating to Liberty bonds and food conservation, and poster and essay contests stressing loyalty and patriotism. The announcement of one such contest cautioned that the entries "should emphasize the idea of patriotism rather than war."[16]

If this caveat suggests a less than enthusiastic embrace of militarism even for a holy cause, there is additional evidence that the war's negative potential worried the Winter circle. Winter's circular letter to her county chairmen in August 1917 articulated this worry rather eloquently: "You can destroy property and . . . laws and these things can be restored, but when you destroy life or health you injure the

Children playing war games, Boyd, about 1917. In contrast to the atmosphere of militarism that pervaded Minnesota during the war, Alice Winter's group sought to emphasize patriotism and child welfare.

race permanently. The protection of women in industry and child welfare . . . is vital to the well-being of our country."[17]

The obligation of recruiting women for industry without impairing their motherhood role confronted Winter and her colleagues with what they regarded as a serious dilemma. "Wherever any women are working outside their homes, you have the beginning of a problem," Winter advised her county chairmen in April 1918. Nevertheless, her office responded to federal directives relating to the mobilization of women with apparent enthusiasm.[18]

In the late summer of 1917, the women's committee distributed five thousand copies of a brochure listing places where women could secure training that would equip them for a variety of occupations, including many hitherto regarded as inappropriate for women. Her office also cooperated with a Council of National Defense project that called for the voluntary registration of women available for war-related work. At her suggestion — a suggestion conveyed to the MCPS by Ames — Burnquist issued a proclamation informing "the people of Minnesota" that the federal council desired the "voluntary enrollment or registration of all women who are able and willing to assist the government in any manner in the present emergency." The proclamation also informed Minnesotans that "Mrs. T. G. Winter" was in charge of the project in Minnesota and that her organization reached "into almost every community in the state."[19]

On balance the Winter organization focused more concern on child conservation than on efforts to lure women into the workplace. Women whose family responsibilities did not include the care and nurture of small children were given every encouragement to go out to work and even to accept jobs not conventionally filled by women. But mothers of small children were placed in a different category. The final report of Agnes Peterson's committee on women in industry, a report covering the months from June 1917 through January 1919 and based on data from seventy-nine counties, noted with alarm that 8 percent of the female workforce consisted of mothers with children under the age of sixteen. Peterson's committee regarded this as "dangerous both for the health of the mother and for the future of the children." It recommended that "every effort . . . be made to provide support for the family through County Allowances and Home Service of the Red Cross and any social agency in order that the mother may stay at home and care for her children."[20]

"Social hygiene," another concern that commanded the attention of the women's committee, also preoccupied other participants in the war effort. "Venereal disease, dread malady of armies of the past," wrote Ferrell, "worried [General John J.] Pershing almost as much as battlefield casualties." Nor was the experience of America's allies reassuring. Venereal disease "reportedly afflicted one-fourth of the men of a British division." It was estimated that if the Americans failed to take corrective action, their afflicted soldiers "might have filled twenty base hospitals, 20,000 beds."[21]

When this problem was laid before French Premier Georges Clemenceau, he offered to place official houses of prostitution at the disposal of the American armed forces. Pershing forwarded the premier's letter spelling out the offer to Raymond Fosdick, the War Department's special assistant for troop morale, who in turn passed it on to Secretary of War Baker. After reading the letter twice, Baker expostulated: "For God's sake, Raymond, don't show this to the president or he'll stop the war." Wilson's anticipated rejection of Clemenceau's solution evidently tipped the balance in favor of a "get tough" policy, meaning the imposition of stiff punishment on men unfortunate enough to contract venereal disease. Moreover, the policy worked. "By draconian measures," the colonel on Pershing's staff in charge of venereal disease control "reduced the [American Expeditionary Forces] rate to less than that of Americans at home."

Unfortunately, the draconian measures that worked in areas under military occupation did not provide suitable models for encampments near metropolitan centers where prostitution flourished. For decades, authorities in Minneapolis and St. Paul had wrestled with the vice problem without determining whether tough repression or benign containment was the more promising approach to its management. State laws relating to prostitution and venereal disease were no more helpful. Several statutes outlawed prostitution, but there were no laws dealing with the reporting or treatment of venereal disease.[22]

The women's network assigned high priority to the problems associated with prostitution. Rather than formulating a comprehensive vice control program, however, it focused on moral suasion. In the early months of the war, several women's organizations concentrated their efforts on getting a pamphlet containing Lord Kitchener's famous address to his troops in India — an address extolling the physical and moral rewards of sexual restraint — into the hands of every Minnesota serviceman.[23]

Meanwhile, initiatives undertaken by other groups generated two closely related proposals: the appointment of a social hygiene commission representing the various agencies concerned with prostitution and venereal disease and the creation of a venereal disease division within the State Board of Health. After a delay of some weeks because of a jurisdictional dispute between the health board on the one hand and the university medical school, state medical societies, and public health organizations on the other, the safety commission on November 20 passed a motion authorizing formation of a social hygiene commission of fifty-two members appointed by the governor. Sponsors of the hygiene commission initially hoped to secure MCPS funding, but the commissioners declined to honor their request for an appropriation of about fifty thousand dollars; instead the MCPS recommended that the health board pick up the tab.[24]

Thanks largely to Henry M. Bracken, secretary and executive director of the State Board of Health, the Minnesota Social Hygiene Commission made a significant and permanent contribution to public policy in the venereal disease area. To be sure, financial stringency remained a problem, but the volunteer spirit was strong, Bracken knew where to secure outside assistance, and the health board had access to emergency funding to help fill the gap until the 1919 legislature could come to the rescue. Operating through committees on the control of venereal diseases, law enforcement, education, social service, and protective work, the hygiene commission formulated recommendations that eventually acquired the force of law. The most important recommendation — the creation of a division of venereal diseases — was adopted by the State Board of Health on January 8, 1918. Under the capable leadership of Dr. Harry G. Irvine, the new division initiated a program that not only significantly reduced venereal disease within the military but also brought the problem under more effective control within the civilian sector of Minnesota society.

Although Winter's network retained and expanded its credibility through 1918, the opposite was true of the safety commission. Following its intervention in the streetcar strike, the effectiveness of the MCPS as a mobilization agency diminished. To be sure, it retained an immense capacity to intimidate vulnerable persons — as Minnesota aliens learned when the MCPS ordered their registration in February 1918. However, other organizations were obliged to assume responsibility in areas where persuasion based on rational appeals to self-interest and patriotism was needed to move men and women to action.

Winter's organization not only continued but expanded its roles in child welfare, food conservation, and Americanization. A factor contributing to this expansion was the essential compatibility between the Winter programs and those sponsored by such agencies as the U.S. Children's Bureau. When that agency launched the "Year of the Child" by calling for a campaign to save children's lives, Winter responded enthusiastically. After all, this was basically an extension of a program that she and her colleagues had already initiated. [25]

Winter dispatched a modest appeal to the MCPS for assistance in the campaign. Specifically she asked that it provide her office with "one paid stenographer, a typewriter, and . . . postage." She justified this request, to which the MCPS assented, by pointing out that the death rate for men in the trenches was 2 percent (according to her information), whereas the death rate for Minnesota babies under one year was 7 percent — and Minnesota, according to Winter, was the "best state in the union in this respect." It followed that it was "safer to be a fighting man at the front than to be a young baby." [26]

The program developed by Winter and implemented by a corps of volunteers was ambitious. Central administrative authority was vested in a children's year committee, the membership of which was

Red Cross unit at Welcome Hall Community Center, St. Paul, about 1918

drawn from the largest women's organizations in the state, and child welfare boards coordinated volunteer efforts within each county. The goals of the program included the promotion of public nursing work, establishment of baby clinics, instruction of prospective mothers in prenatal care, and the promotion of healthy sanitation practices. The program also envisaged the recruitment of doctors and nurses in every community as "Home Health Volunteers." In addition Winter sought the cooperation of such agencies as the State Board of Health, the State Board of Control, the Minnesota Public Health Association, and the State Department of Public Instruction.

This cooperation was forthcoming; Bracken, the health board director, unreservedly backed the program. With his help it got off to a promising start in the spring of 1918. Before long, welfare boards were functioning in seventy-four of the state's counties and Bracken had set up a division of child conservation within the State Board of Health. Thanks in part to the publicity originating in Winter's office, a strong child welfare constituency also was emerging. Soon after word went out that the child conservation division was being established, community after community requested assistance in setting up child welfare clinics. According to historian Philip D. Jordan, "So many requests for assistance came [to the division director] that he deplored his lack of facilities to care for them."[27]

Unfortunately, two adverse factors stopped the child conservation program in its tracks. First of all, Burnquist and the MCPS declined to provide financial assistance. On June 27, after according the chairman of Winter's children's year committee and Bracken a hearing, the MCPS passed a "sense of the Commission" motion declaring "that the matter of an appropriation to carry on Child Welfare work is a matter for the Legislature to consider."[28] Four days later Bracken dispatched an urgent plea to Burnquist imploring the governor to draw on his contingency fund. Again the director was rebuffed. Evidently Burnquist had retreated somewhat from his strong social justice stance of the previous year when his backing had helped assure adoption of the 1917 children's code.

Perhaps the funding problem could have been overcome had not the second adverse factor — the dreadful 1918 influenza epidemic — intervened. Many private groups indicated a willingness to render financial assistance to a project that had won such strong acclaim. On the other hand, the flu epidemic that invaded Minnesota in mid-September and continued its deadly assault into early 1919 created a more formidable obstacle. Jordan wrote that while the epidemic raged it clearly was "unwise to continue public clinics for children." Moreover, combating the epidemic stretched the state's medical resources to the limit, leaving a dearth of personnel for other tasks.[29]

Nor was flu the only devastating blow to strike Minnesota in the autumn of 1918. Well before the epidemic crested, a disastrous fire wrought havoc in the Cloquet area of northern Minnesota, leaving countless persons homeless, including many who had contracted influenza. An influx of refugees into neighboring towns and cities, particularly Duluth, imposed a heavy burden on these population centers. While coping with the two disasters, the people of Minnesota learned that the November 11 armistice had ended the blood-letting phase of the war, and their understandable inclination to celebrate complicated the challenge of controlling the epidemic and providing assistance for the victims of the fire.[30]

A Winter report issued in December 1918 reflects more concern with the impact of the flu epidemic and the Cloquet fire than with the implications of the armistice. The flu disaster, the report noted, had forced cancellation of virtually all public meetings. All organizational work had been halted. Various projects linked to the children's year were temporarily suspended. The network of organizations under Winter's jurisdiction had diverted its energies to providing relief for the victims of the two disasters. In Minneapolis a demonstration kitchen had provided ten gallons of soup per day for ten days to ill soldiers quartered at Fort Snelling. In St. Paul volunteers had served 141 families with soup and other food items for more than a week at the height of the epidemic. In Duluth the local women's committee was providing relief for fire victims, and in other communities fund drives on their behalf had elicited generous responses. [31]

Nevertheless, Winter was unwilling to admit that the program on which she had lavished so much attention had suffered decisive defeat. On November 30 she proclaimed to her county chairmen that the children's year "must be carried to its completion, and . . . County nurses, baby clinics, and wider recreation facilities should be permanent factors." This aspiration was somewhat unrealistic. Jordan concluded that the flu epidemic "really put an end to the [state] health department's first formal effort to create and keep going a division devoted to child care." Still, all was not lost, thanks in part to Winter's inspirational efforts. By 1921 the Minnesota legislature would finally begin to recognize the child conservation imperative, and in the meantime local governments and private agencies to a degree filled the gap. [32]

The Americanization campaign sponsored by the Winter organization escaped the setbacks suffered by child conservation. Moreover, its relative importance increased with the passing months. In the beginning, Hoover pledge card canvassers were expected to deliver brief patriotic homilies along with the cards. By the end of the war, Americanization had evolved into a crusade with a life of its own, a crusade that continued long after other wartime activities had been terminated. Shortly after the armistice, Winter enthusiastically proclaimed that many people were "coming to a full realization that the Americanization problem is at the very *basis* of our future national welfare." [33]

Unfortunately, Winter never precisely defined the goal of her Americanization program. Presumably it was a process designed to convert a "hyphenate" resident of the United States into a "true American," but what traits characterized such an American? In the absence of precise definition, one is obliged to rely on inferences derived from the ongoing program. First of all, a true American was not entitled to doubt the redemptive role of the United States in the world. Manifestations of doubt concerning the prudence or wisdom of American participation in the Great War immediately raised a warning flag. Such a manifestation might be overt, as in suggesting that the United States entered the war at the behest of organized wealth, or covert, as in refusing to buy Liberty bonds or declining to make a contribution to the Red Cross. Any display of support for the Nonpartisan League, particularly during the state campaign of 1918, was an almost certain display of disloyalty.

Reports from a number of her county chairmen, coupled with her own observations, reinforced Winter's belief that "true" Americanism was tragically deficient in many Minnesota communities. One informant reported widespread pro-German sentiment in Inver Grove, Eagan, and West St. Paul. The church presence was a helpful counterforce, but only in a limited way. "Catholics," she wrote to Winter, "can be reached through the archbishop's authority but these people are well organized Lutherans," and Lutheranism, of course, originated in Germany. As an antidote she asked for "a large number" of copies of the leaflet *Why We Are at War with Germany* in German translation. [34]

A tour through Isanti County in April 1918, when that year's primary contest was heating up, unnerved Winter. The "pro-Germans . . . up there . . . are fierce!" she reported. She requested the MCPS to provide her with "some material in German," together with "any printed matter . . . that would hit the Non Partisans below the belt." Libby complied with her request for material in German and indicated that he would also make available to her a scurrilous anti-NPL polemic written by C. D. Bacon, a well-known North Dakota opponent of the league. [35]

In mid-June 1918, Winter wrote to the safety commission that she was satisfied with all aspects of her program except one: "systematic propaganda in Patriotism in the smaller places." She indicated an ability to recruit "a group of fine and patriotic women who are willing to give their services." She wondered if the MCPS "could . . . go so far as to help them to travelling expenses." The safety commission agreed that "splendid service would be rendered by these speakers" but proposed that "the local safety commission or other societies . . . could take care of the traveling expenses." Notwithstanding lack of MCPS funding, the speaking campaign went forward. [36]

The written and spoken word was not the only medium employed by the Winter organization in its Americanization campaign. Song was also an important tool. Many communities organized patriotic choruses, leading Winter to encourage further "sing-alongs." In her April 1918 letter to her county chairmen, she suggested a Waseca practice as a model: "One lovely thing — Waseca has initiated a town habit of singing 'America' in every household every evening at 7:30. As you walk along the street you hear it. I wish every town in Minnesota would do likewise and make ours a 'Singing America State.'"[37]

Along with being unreservedly committed to America's redemptive mission in the world, Winter's true American had to be an English speaker. The special English classes taught by volunteers for the benefit of recent immigrants took care of part of this imperative. Unfortunately, a commission investigation had found that an estimated ten thousand Minnesota children attended schools wherein other languages — mostly German — served as a medium of instruction. In the closing weeks of the war and continuing after the armistice, Winter returned again and again to Americanization, with particular emphasis on the seminal importance of English. In October her circular letter announced the printing of a small booklet entitled *Practical Methods of Doing Americanization Work,* and in late December her office distributed a pamphlet called *America! One Nation Made from Many Peoples — English Our Common Language.*[38]

Noblesse oblige permeated the latter publication. Americanization was a process proceeding from the top down rather than the bottom up: "The work of creating a United People must fall most heavily on those who have been here longest. They must forge the link that binds the new-comer to the national spirit." However, in carrying out their sacred obligation to the newly arrived, old-stock Americans should eschew coercive intimidation. Immigrants should be befriended, and respect for their homeland cultures should be nourished. On the other hand, the goal of converting the nation's new residents into English speakers should be relentlessly pursued. A Winter circular issued soon after the armistice advanced an even more impassioned argument for the assignment of highest priority to Americanization. "We ought . . . to demand of our next legislature," wrote Winter, "that ENGLISH SHALL BE THE MEDIUM OF INSTRUCTION IN EVERY SCHOOL IN MINNESOTA. It should never again be possible that there should be 190 schools in the state where German is the sole language." The letter also stressed Americanization in the broader sense. "Before the impetus of war is lost," declared Winter, "we must be sure that we have set in motion forces that will Americanize every foreigner in our midst. EVERY COUNTY SHOULD HAVE A PERMANENT AMERICANIZATION COMMITTEE."[39]

When this letter was composed, the organization of a network of Americanization committees was already well under way. By mid-October 1918, Winter's colleagues had established such committees in fifty-six counties. The MCPS also became involved in a formal way when it agreed on October 8 to provide staff assistance for an Americanization organization being set up by Carol Aronovici, a social worker affiliated with the Wilder Foundation. The Aronovici enterprise, which coordinated its efforts with those of the Winter network, soon acquired visibility. Hester Pollock, Aronovici's field secretary, appeared before the MCPS on December 31 to present "a verbal report on the work of the Americanization Committee to date." Evidently her report pleased the commissioners, who appropriated one hundred dollars to cover the traveling expenses Pollock had already incurred. The MCPS was not inclined to make an unlimited commitment, however, possibly because its termination was being contemplated. On January 14, 1919, the commissioners adopted a motion affirming an understanding "that financial aid in connection with Americanization work be discontinued on and after March 1st, 1919."[40]

Coordination of the two efforts was part of a larger challenge. Secretary of the Interior Franklin K. Lane, who headed the field division of the Council of National Defense, wired a message to the MCPS on October 12, 1918, "urging immediate amalgamation [of the] state council and state womans division." Alice Winter responded negatively to the Lane recommendation, which was part of an ongoing federal effort to coordinate war-related activities. She suggested instead that a field committee, consisting of two safety commission members and two members of the women's committee, be appointed "to confer on Field work" until the 1919 legislature convened. She further stipulated that "until changes are made by the legislature, the present Woman's committee [should] remain intact." She also asked the MCPS to instruct the county directors to work with the county women's committees to establish similar field committees within their bailiwicks. On October 29 the MCPS acted favorably on Winter's recommendation that the women's committee retain its separate status. To what extent the other recommendations were implemented is not clear. In any case, close cooperation between Winter and the Aronovici enterprise was achieved. [41]

Winter's reluctance to approve an immediate merger of the women's committee and the MCPS may have been prompted by a desire to retain a measure of independence until the committee had formulated its policy recommendations for the 1919 legislative session. Perhaps she and her colleagues lacked confidence in the enthusiasm of the commissioners for these recommendations, which included demands for tighter regulation of workplaces employing women and several other protections for working women: limitation of the workday to eight hours and the workweek to forty-eight, one day's rest in seven, and a ban on employment between the hours of 10 P.M. and 6 A.M. The program was to be statewide in application, but in extraordinary circumstances exemptions from its provisions could be secured by permit from the state labor bureau. The legislative committee also called for English to be established as the sole medium of instruction in Minnesota schools, both public and private. [42]

Before presenting this program to the legislature, the women's committee secured the endorsement of its major provisions by several other organizations, including the Minnesota Federation of Women's Clubs, the Minnesota Federation of Fraternal Women, the Minnesota Federation of Labor, the Woman's Occupational Bureau, and the Young Women's Christian Association. Notwithstanding this impressive manifestation of support, the 1919 legislative session would be so preoccupied with concerns relating to the "foreign" threat to American institutions that the program received scant attention. However, the recommendation respecting the use of English in the schools was adopted. [43]

Within the context of Minnesota's political tradition, the behavior of the Winter organization was less aberrant than that of the MCPS. At a time when the social justice goals of the progressive era were in peril, the women's network helped to prevent their complete subversion by an intolerant chauvinism threatening to run amuck. Although the projects linked to the Year of the Child failed to be implemented in 1918–19, they attracted a constituency that boded well for their success in the future. Their inclusion on the wartime agenda preserved a fragile thread of continuity between the progressive era and the postwar period.

The causes embraced by the women's network, however, were in no sense radical. Basically they were the same as those that had been supported by affluent, upper-class progressives since early in the century and before. One searches in vain for advocacy of pay equalization between men and women engaged in the same work, a proposition enjoying the support of the National War Labor Board and the Minnesota Federation of Labor in 1918. Support of minimum wage legislation also is conspicuous by its absence. In short, the Winter program posed no threat to the groups whose interests were being so zealously guarded by the safety commission. Winter's hostility to the Nonpartisan League, along with the lack of trade-union representation within her organization, reinforce the point.

Although Winter's Americanization program was well intentioned, it fell short of achieving its goals. Minnesota was dangerously polarized in the World War I period, and efforts to heal the breach were entirely appropriate. However, an Americanization program based on pluralism — in other words, one recognizing the virtues of cultural diversity and reposing confidence in the capacity of the state's political system to manage conflicts — might have enjoyed more success than the attempt to remake the state's large non-Anglo population in an old-stock American image. Whether a program recognizing the claims of pluralism could have promoted reconciliation given the frenzied atmosphere of the period cannot be ascertained. On the other hand, the World War I loyalty campaign and its postwar successor created a bitter legacy that was not overcome for many years.

The extent to which the Winter effort altered the status of Minnesota women also is unascertainable. The food conservation and Americanization campaigns promoted more interaction among the state's women than ever before, but it is uncertain how much they enhanced a sense of unity and community. Cultural exchange does not invariably enhance amity, particularly when one party to the exchange assumes a guardian role. Although Winter counseled respect for immigrant cultures, it is doubtful that women of German ancestry responded kindly to intimations that German civilization was depraved. Persons of other nationalities were spared this humiliation, but implicit assumptions of American superiority were calculated to evoke hostile reactions.

Whether or not the women's committee opened many doors of female opportunity likewise is questionable. Winter and Agnes Peterson cooperated faithfully with federal efforts to recruit women for industry and other war-related activity, but they deplored and discouraged the entry of mothers with small children into the work force. Nor was service within the network politically advantageous. Among the women who later achieved a measure of political prominence, only Anna Dickie Olesen occupied a position of importance within the Winter organization.

Thus, when measured against announced objectives, the impact of the women's mobilization effort was relatively modest. Given the scanty resources made available to it, this was perhaps predictable. Winter could, however, point to a record of faithful cooperation with federal mobilization officials, a claim that could not be advanced by the safety commission. Throughout 1918 its policies — particularly in the labor relations realm — remained sharply at odds with those of the federal government.

Defending the Status Quo Ante

B y the end of 1917, conflicts between the Minnesota Commission of Public Safety and representatives of federal organizations dealing with the home front had become impossible to ignore. On December 11 the MCPS adopted a motion calling upon all "voluntary patriotic organizations and committees" in Minnesota to accept the state safety commission as the coordinating agency for "all voluntary patriotic work within the state"; the motion informed county directors that their organizations were the only "legal and recognized authority of the National Government in the county, through their connection with this Commission."[1] Both of these actions were ostensibly inspired by a recent Council of National Defense declaration urging a more effective coordination of patriotic activity.

One suspects, however, that other factors also encouraged the safety commissioners to assert their authority. All was not sweetness and light at a mass meeting of representatives of the volunteer organizations held in late December for the purpose of implementing the December 11 motion. Burnquist had declined to preside, a responsibility assumed by Libby. The assembly adopted a motion introduced by Donald R. Cotton of St. Paul, who attended as director of the Ramsey County Public Safety Commission, that called for the appointment of a committee of five charged with the coordination task. This action was promising, but publicity director Charles Henke was left with a "hazy feeling" with respect to what the MCPS expected of the organizations. "Personally," Henke informed March, "I feel that the only way to handle this proposition is to take the bull by the horns and make a demand on all of these organizations to work in and under the supervision of the Commission, through the Advisory Committee. . . . They would understand a demand and misunderstand an invitation."[2]

The safety commission set up the advisory committee and named Cotton as its chairman. Shortly his committee presented the MCPS with a plan proposing establishment of a bureau of public information responsible for "coordination of existing speaking forces of the State." Henke, whose role in getting the new bureau on track was central, reported to a friend that achieving the coordination goal was "rather ticklish business," but that he hoped it would "go through without friction in any direction."[3]

Indeed, within Minnesota the "speaking forces" worked together with a fair degree of visible amity, but relations with the federal propaganda effort were anything but amiable. In early February the safety commission flatly rejected a proposal advanced by the state councils section of the Council of National Defense that a patriotic "war conference" and mass meeting, jointly sponsored by the MCPS and the state councils section, be convened in St. Paul. A telegram of reply dispatched in Libby's name declared that Minnesota's propaganda effort would operate independently of the federal government: "Minnesota Commission feels war conference . . . not adviseable [*sic*] at this time. Prefers routing prominent speakers individually through . . . our speakers bureau. County units are very active in conducting speaking campaigns and doing effective work."[4]

Libby's assurances notwithstanding, federal officialdom was becoming increasingly unimpressed with the MCPS operation. The basic flaw in its structure, according to John H. Winterbotham, a Chicago-based official in the state councils section, was its failure to encompass all elements within the Minnesota community. The basic responsibility of a state council of defense, Winterbotham contended in a letter to Cotton, was

> to utilize to the straining point, every facility which your State affords which is either now in existence or can be brought into existence to put Minnesota as a solid unit behind the war. This cannot be done by a few men sitting in a room once a week with one or two men to carry out their instructions.

Winterbotham added that a change in MCPS personnel could be avoided if the incumbent commissioners were persuaded to appoint an advisory committee "of not less than 20 or 25 members" whose duty would be reorganization of the state "on active lines." The fundamental necessity was creation of a committee network that would invite the participation of every sector of Minnesota's population, a goal compatible with Alice Winter's approach.[5]

In his effort to reform the MCPS, Winterbotham managed to recruit a valuable Twin Cities ally. Cotton was a prestigious member of the state's business community and a longtime advocate of an interventionist U.S. foreign policy. In addition to his work as a county director for the public safety commission, he headed the St. Paul branch of the War Industries Board, an agency that increasingly helped fill the gap left by the ineffective economic mobilization role of the MCPS.[6]

In its early stages the Winterbotham-Cotton campaign demonstrated some promise of success. Burnquist appeared favorably disposed. A series of conferences between him and Cotton produced an elaborate organizational chart embodying the major recommendations advanced by Winterbotham. Unfortunately the governor's ability to implement the proposed reforms did not match his amiability. In response to a Winterbotham inquiry on April 25 with respect to the status of the proposed reforms, Cotton replied: "I am sorry to say that I have been away so much that it has been impossible for me to follow it. I am afraid nothing will be done until I can again push on the Governor." Six weeks later Winterbotham wondered if MCPS reorganization was "a dead proposition." Cotton replied that while he did "not consider it entirely a dead proposition, it certainly has had a long sleep." Burnquist, Cotton added, had "been very busy the last month, making loyalty speeches," meaning that he was campaigning for renomination against the challenge posed by Charles A. Lindbergh and the Nonpartisan League.[7]

The influential Minneapolis Civic and Commerce Association reacted negatively to the reorganization plan. Following a conference with Howard Strong, an association official, Winterbotham confided to Cotton: "I do not think that Mr. Strong wants to get it in his mind that the plan . . . is going to be jumped into and put through without any trouble." One can assume that the Minneapolis employers' group viewed the plan as being too inclusive, proposing as it did trade-union representation within the MCPS network. Cotton's approach was to prefer co-option to exclusion. Sensing that the embattled labor-management situation in Minnesota was impeding the quest of Minnesota firms for war contracts, he and his associates within the St. Paul branch of the War Industries Board successfully negotiated a truce with George Lawson that included a Lawson promise to support the war contract procurement process. Following a two-hour conference with Lawson while the negotiations were pending, a Cotton associate remarked: "You can talk with Lawson. He is not Red by any means."[8]

This amiability did not extend to Townley and the Nonpartisan League. Cotton was probably inhibited from assuming a more hostile stance toward the safety commission because he perceived it as a bulwark against NPL radicalism. From Cotton's standpoint the existing safety commission left much to be desired, but one appointed by a Nonpartisan League administration would be intolerable. A month before the 1918 state election, Cotton commented to Winterbotham: "I can conceive of no worse thing happening to . . . Minnesota . . . than to have Mr. Evans [the NPL endorsee for governor] elected, as he is the choice of Mr. Townley and his associates, and even to you I refuse to ask [my secretary] to write my opinion of the whole outfit."[9]

MCPS reorganization remained in limbo until the armistice rendered it irrelevant. Meanwhile, the safety commission rejected a parallel recommendation calling for restructuring on the grass-roots level. State councils official Elliot D. Smith complained that county safety commissions in Minnesota were based on political units and as such were not "community councils" in the true sense of the word. Notwithstanding this and similar urgent pleas, the MCPS defended existing arrangements. "Minnesota is already pretty well organized," asserted a safety commission field agent, adding that "the Minnesota Commission of Public Safety does not see the necessity of any further organization along this line."[10]

While the safety commission was stonewalling federally sponsored reorganization pressures, a more serious conflict between it and the national administration was brewing. Disturbed by the debilitating impact of industrial disputes on war production, the federal government in the spring of 1918 was moving toward adoption of a new set of labor policy guidelines. On March 29 a War Labor Conference Board, headed by William Howard Taft and Frank P. Walsh and including five AFL and an equal number of employer representatives, promulgated a statement of principles that received the full backing of the Wilson administration when a presidential proclamation was issued on April 8.[11]

Taken as a whole, the April 8 proclamation pleased labor more than management. To be sure, workers engaged in war production were directed to forgo strikes, but in return they were accorded a guaranteed right to unionize and to bargain collectively, a right that could not be "denied, abridged or interfered with by the employers in any manner whatsoever." Employers, too, were granted the right to bargain collectively, but the discharge of workers for union membership or "for legitimate trade-union activities" was explicitly forbidden. Union shops, where they existed, were to continue. Shops employing both union and nonunion workers were legitimate, but this did not preclude the organization of a closed shop. Women engaged in "men's work" were to receive the same pay as men. Workers were forbidden to coerce fellow laborers to affiliate with a union. All workers were declared entitled to a living wage, by definition a wage that would "insure the subsistence of the worker and his family in health and reasonable comfort." Responsibility for putting these guidelines into effect was vested in a National War Labor Board, which was created from the membership of the conference board.

On paper the April 8 proclamation appeared to offer substantial protection to organized labor. However, the guidelines enunciated were neither self-enforcing nor free of ambiguities. Such terms as "legitimate trade-union activities" could be variously interpreted. Much depended on how the new NWLB understood its mandate. Theoretically the board was finely balanced between labor and management, each represented by five members, and apparently the balance was reinforced by the respective orientations of Walsh and Taft, the joint chairmen. Walsh, an industrial relations careerist, was correctly perceived as friendly to labor. Most observers expected that Taft, a major symbol of Republican conservatism, would weigh in on the side of management. [12]

Before many weeks had passed, Taft mocked these expectations. One of his first ventures as NWLB chairman was an extended journey through the South where he presided over hearings involving labor-management disputes in munitions and textile mills. Before the chairman departed, W. Jett Lauck, NWLB secretary and a well-known liberal, attempted to brief his chief on what he might expect to find in the southland. Taft doubted the authenticity of Lauck's report. "Don't fill me with labor propaganda," he said, adding, "I know you're a Socialist." Lauck retorted that personally he was a "conservative" who simply was seeking to provide Taft with "the facts."

Several weeks later, according to biographer Henry F. Pringle, Taft returned from Dixie "tired and discouraged." Upon meeting Lauck he asked: "Why didn't you tell me about the conditions down there?" Lauck protested that he had tried to, whereupon Taft responded: "You didn't tell me anything. Why, I had no idea! How can people live on such wages!" The NWLB chairman followed up this verbal outburst with an order, approved by the board, doubling and in some cases tripling "the wages in question." From then on a delighted Walsh and an equally exhilarated Lauck "insisted that Taft was the most radical member of the National War Labor Board."[13]

The transformation of Taft's perspective may have been unexpected, but it is not inexplicable. Distinguished as his previous career had been, it had kept him, noted Pringle, "fairly remote from actual contact with the problems of the workingman." His responsibilities on the War Labor Board established such contact, and what he observed tapped a vein of Taftian compassion that at times overwhelmed his legendary judicial balance.

The new turn taken by administration labor policy exacerbated a dilemma for the MCPS and its allies within the Minneapolis Citizens Alliance. On the one hand, now more than ever, federal authorities were explicitly encouraging unionization, a course diametrically opposed to the "status quo ante" position of the alliance and the MCPS. (The phrase referred to the view that both labor and management should maintain the status quo that prevailed before the United States entered the war, with neither side seeking to advance its interests during the national emergency.) On the other hand, frontal assault on the administration appeared imprudent. After all, "standing by the president" had been the standard battle cry of the MCPS loyalty campaign from the time of its inception, and federal labor policy was identified not only with the incumbent president but also with a highly respected former president.

In the privacy of their own circle and to friendly public officials, Citizens Alliance leaders felt freer to vent their hostility to the administration's labor program. In early July, Harlow H. Chamberlain, president of the Boyd Transfer and Storage Company, delivered to Senator Nelson a critique of past and present federal labor policy and in the process shed considerable light on the role of the alliance. Chamberlain identified himself as

> a member and Director of a local organization known as the Citizens Alliance, which, before the war stood for the maintenance of the open shop and is now backing up the principle of the status quo ante with respect to the labor unions. This organization embraces many of the

leading banks, and other business concerns, and for several years past has taken a hand in the adjustment of all important labor disputes in this city. Thus it has acted in behalf of the street railway company in all negotiations with respect to the so-called strike of the street car employees, which was really no strike, but merely an attempt on the part of outsiders to force unionism upon a non-union organization, the employees of which were bitterly opposed to the idea. . . .

Our experience with respect to the street car matter gave the Directors and Officers of the Citizens Alliance an insight into the policy of the Administration. . . . We found that the so-called Federal Mediation Commission was merely a strongly pro-union body . . . which was making a business of forcing the closed shop on to every business institution, where labor troubles occurred, and they were very careful to see that such troubles occurred about as fast as they could settle the various cases by their peculiar methods of adjustment. . . . [T]hey were much pained and grieved when they found that they had come up against a stone wall in this case, for here we had the backing of the majority of the State Safety Commission in our stand for the status quo ante, and in any event we would have backed the street car company to the limit, in resisting the subversive policy of the Federal Administration. [14]

Unfortunately, from Chamberlain's standpoint, the safety commission's war against the federal government's "subversive" labor policy remained to be won. However, Chamberlain had

no doubt that the Governor and the majority of the other members of the Commission have the moral courage to stand by their guns in this matter. . . . In our minds the Administration's policy . . . constitutes a grave menace to the industrial and social life of the Nation and it is high time that effective action should be taken to check the Bolsheviki tendencies of the Democratic Administration, which seeks to build up the power of irresponsible labor agitators to a point where they would have dictatorial powers with respect to industrial and economic matters.

Chamberlain closed his letter with a request that Nelson "hold in confidence, the part which the Citizens Alliance" had taken in the streetcar strike, "as it is our policy to avoid any unnecessary publicity with respect to such matters."

The streetcar strike remained unresolved at the time federal authorities were moving toward formulation of the policy that would be embodied in President Wilson's April 8 proclamation. The President's Mediation Commission had issued a finding in mid-February recommending reinstatement as far as possible of the transit employees whom the company allegedly had "locked out" during the button war. Not unexpectedly, the TCRTC defiantly rejected this solution, contending that displacement of the carmen hired to replace the union members was manifestly impossible. This response created a dilemma for the safety commission. Should it exercise its theoretically vast power to compel management acceptance of the proposed settlement? To do so would run counter to the inclinations of a majority of the commissioners, and it would also be a humiliating reversal of the "resolute" stand taken early in the strike. On the other hand, members of the business community were pressing for reconciliation in the belief that the state's dismal labor-management climate was robbing them of their share of war contracts. [15]

Presumably, Tighe's opinion of March 13 that the safety commission lacked the power to compel either the company or the union to accept the proposed settlement temporarily alleviated the problem. As the Wilson administration moved more actively to resolve labor disputes, however, the safety commission felt compelled to formulate a policy of its own before the federal government preempted the field.

On March 30 Burnquist reactivated the moribund State Board of Arbitration, which began immediately to develop guidelines for labor peace that would be agreed to by both management and labor. Conferences between the board and representatives of the Minnesota Federation of Labor and the Minnesota Employers Association yielded apparent assent by both parties to a "petition" calling for the adoption of six "basic conditions to cover both employer and employe, organized or unorganized, during the period of the war." On April 16 the safety commission incorporated the petition into Order 30, thereby giving the six conditions the force of law. [16]

Of the six, two were sharply at odds with the presidential proclamation of April 8. Number 2 stated that "employes shall not ask for recognition of a union . . . not . . . recognized before the war"; number 4 affirmed that "employers and employes agree in good faith to maintain the existing status, in every phase of employment, of a union, non-union or open shop" — the famous status quo ante principle. The remaining four were relatively noncontroversial. Number 1 piously eschewed any dispute capable of disrupting war production. Organized labor presumably could derive some satisfaction from number 3: it committed employers not to "try to break . . . a union which had been recognized before the war" either "by a lockout or other means." Number 5 provided that "differences with respect to wages or hours . . . shall be referred to the State Board of Arbitration" in accordance with Minnesota's arbitration statutes. Number 6 affirmed that "during the period of the war, there shall be neither strike nor lockout under any circumstances."

Securing Lawson's signature to this policy statement was a major coup, and one that the MCPS and its allies would exploit to the limit in the immediate future. For his part, Lawson claimed that he had been victimized by a triple deception. First of all, he contended, the MFL accepted the petition only on the condition that the streetcar controversy be settled by the state arbitration board before Order 30 became operative. Second, he maintained that the conferees had agreed that the order should remain secret until the streetcar issues had been arbitrated. Third, and most important, he charged that the document he had agreed to sign had been altered before being incorporated into the order. According to Lawson, condition 4 as originally assented to by the MFL council forbade discrimination against workers "on account of membership or non-membership in any labor organization." As finally promulgated, it unequivocally endorsed the status quo ante principle. George M. Gillette, acting on behalf of the Minnesota Employers Association, was allegedly responsible for the alteration. [17]

Herbert R. Brougham and Raymond G. Swing, two examiners dispatched by the War Labor Board to the Twin Cities to investigate the myriad of complaints emanating from the area, found substance in Lawson's charges. The secrecy promise had been breached on April 15 — one day before the MCPS promulgated Order 30 — when the *Minneapolis Tribune* published the text of the petition. With respect to the Lawson stipulation calling for prior settlement of the streetcar controversy, the two examiners found that it, too, had turned into a fiasco. Upon learning of the stipulation, Burnquist had resisted the suggestion that he pressure the streetcar company to accept arbitration. Such an action, the governor contended, would subject the streetcar company to discriminatory treatment, since a number of other companies embroiled in labor disputes were not being pressured to accept arbitration. However, the governor implied that he would support arbitration *after* the six agreed-on conditions were operative.

Lawson tentatively accepted this modification of his original stipulation, but he insisted that his acceptance required ratification by the MFL council. At the same time he unwisely appended his signature to the petition, trusting that the agreement to await ratification by the MFL council before submission of the petition to the MCPS would be honored. This proved to be a mistake. The governor delivered the document to the safety commission immediately, and that body incorporated its text into Order 30. [18]

Understandably, MFL leaders did not respond kindly to what they regarded as a breach of faith on the part of the governor. Nevertheless, they accepted the arbitration option. On June 8 Thomas J. McGrath, counsel for the carmen, presented the unions' appeal to the arbitration board. Among other things this appeal called for immediate reinstatement of the "locked out" carmen and recommended that the board move to end TCRTC discrimination "as between union and non-union employees." [19]

Lowry firmly declined to accept the jurisdiction of the board. According to his June 10 response, the arbitration portion of Order 30 did not apply since a proper petition for arbitration had not been submitted. He then proceeded to argue his side of the controversy. To discharge the men hired since November 1917 would be grossly unfair. The financial state of his company precluded wage raises. Finally, the men leading the union effort had "lent themselves to lawlessness" and hence deserved no consideration. [20]

The State Board of Arbitration convened a further hearing on the controversy on June 12. This time TCRTC attorneys did appear, but they "refused to make any proposal or to enter into a discussion of the merits of the controversy." Nevertheless, the board made an award not unlike the one issued by the President's Mediation Commission in mid-February. It affirmed that the men desiring reemployment should make application within twenty days and that the company should rehire "desirable men" as vacancies occurred. If disputes should arise, the names of the men involved were to be submitted to the board, and it would adjudicate the merits of the controversy. [21]

Predictably, Lowry refused to be bound by the award. "I see no reason to change our position . . . as expressed in my letter of June 10th," he informed the arbitration board. The union response was more ambiguous. At a meeting of the Minneapolis carmen's union on June 18, a motion to reject the award was laid on the table "and never acted on." However, a resolution to refer the controversy to the AFL convention then meeting in St. Paul prevailed. To no one's surprise, that body recommended an appeal to the National War Labor Board, a course of action immediately adopted by the carmen. [22]

According to Brougham and Swing, the carmen's appeal to the NWLB raised the possibility that the MCPS might "use its mandatory powers to enforce its own arbitration upon complainants should they appeal to the National Board, and punish those who accept National, in preference to State adjudication." To discourage such defiance of NWLB authority, the examiners met with Burnquist and the other safety commissioners in late July and opened the discussion by pointing to the "discrepancies" between MCPS and NWLB labor policies. Pretending ignorance of any discrepancies, the commissioners asked what they were. In reply the examiners "cited the subject of discrimination against union members and the fact that the State law endorsed the status-quo-ante, whereas the War Board does not regard the closed non-union shop as a condition necessary to maintain, inasmuch as it would deny the right to organize."[23]

In an unimpressive effort to minimize the gap between the two labor policies, the commissioners declared that "by its silence on the question the State law did permit men to join unions if they did not demand recognition of Unions unrecognized before the war." The examiners retorted that "the State law did not prohibit employers from discharging Union men, whereas the right to organize was protected by the national principles." Thus the gap remained as wide as ever. Unable to find a basis for reconciling the irreconcilable, the examiners finally asked what the MCPS would do if the NWLB "acted upon its own principles." A reassuring reply was forthcoming. Brougham and Swing "were told by the Governor and all the members present that the State would . . . concede the precedence of the War Board."

The comfort that the two examiners could derive from this response was diminished somewhat by the garbled account of the conference issued to the press by the MCPS. On July 30 the *Minneapolis Tribune* informed its readers that the commissioners had "convinced representatives of the Federal War Labor Board that the labor policy of the commission [was] entirely harmonious with that of the federal government." Admittedly, the "federal plan" recognized "the right . . . to join a union, while the commission order is silent on the subject." However, according to the *Tribune,* "both preclude enforcement of union recognition."[24]

Incensed at what they regarded as a gross distortion of their position, Brougham and Swing dispatched a telegram to NWLB Secretary Lauck requesting permission to issue a clarifying statement to the press. Such a statement could affirm "that government principles go farther

than the safety commissions" but that, in case of conflict, state
authorities would "concede precedence" to the NWLB. Lauck's response
was prompt and abrupt: "Do not give any statement to the press whatsoever." For whatever reason, the NWLB did not propose to engage
the MCPS in public controversy. At the same time, it promised the aggrieved carmen a hearing to determine whether their complaints warranted NWLB adjudication. [25]

The conflict between Lowry and his locked-out employees was
not the only labor-management dispute investigated by Brougham
and Swing during their July sojourn in Minneapolis. Probing an embattled situation within the Minneapolis Steel and Machinery Company was, in fact, their primary mission. Management resolutely maintained a so-called nonunion closed shop arrangement, dismissing any
employee suspected of collusion with Local 91 of the International
Association of Machinists and refusing to hire any applicant known
to have union affiliation. [26]

Promulgation of the new federal labor policy on April 8 had encouraged Local 91 to press aggressively for wage adjustments and
acknowledgment of a collective bargaining role for the union. The
nearly simultaneous issuance of MCPS Order 30 briefly raised the question of whether relief should be sought from the reactivated state arbitration board or from the NWLB. Wisely, from their standpoint, Local
91 officials chose the NWLB. Following receipt of their appeal, the
War Labor Board dispatched Brougham and Swing to Minneapolis.

The two examiners discovered that George M. Gillette, Minneapolis Steel and Machinery's chief executive officer and a prominent leader within both the Minneapolis Civic and Commerce
Association and the Citizens Alliance, was accessible but not notably
forthcoming. Initially, according to the examiners, he informed them
that his staff "would only give information to the Board if required
to do so." He offered Brougham and Swing a guided tour of his plant
but refused to permit interviews with individuals selected by the examiners. He suggested instead an investigation of the political
backgrounds of Local 91's leadership. [27]

Brougham and Swing acted on this suggestion. From conversations with Thomas E. Campbell, the U.S. Department of Justice agent
stationed in Minnesota, and others they gained an impression that
Gillette's accusations were essentially groundless. "It is true," they
reported,

that . . . Minneapolis has a Socialist Mayor and a Socialist Chief of Police. . . . Harthill, had been the Business Agent of the Machinists' Union prior to his appointment, and Mayor Van Lear had been his predecessor. . . . [T]here is no question of [their] personal antagonism to the Gillette interests. . . . The belief, however, is general in Minneapolis that neither Mr. Van Lear nor Mr. Harthill are disloyal, and there was no evidence to the contrary given your examiners by those who most naturally have it.

Nevertheless, Brougham and Swing predicted that adjudicating the machinists' appeal would be a delicate operation:

Mr. Gillette . . . is looked upon by union men as the bitterest and leading foe of organized labor in the State. . . . [T]here is an element of passion in every controversy between labor and capital in Minnesota and . . . this explains why the street car strike of last winter . . . was so intense . . . and why Order No. 30 is not only a state law but a momentary victory for capital in this war with labor. This is why the National Labor Board is, in this case, by even considering it, giving political aid to the faction of labor, as it happens . . . to the faction of Socialists who dominate the labor group which filed these grievances. [28]

Despite the potential for embarrassment created by the involvement of radical unionists in the controversy, Brougham and Swing believed NWLB intervention to be warranted. For one thing, the labor policy of Minneapolis Steel and Machinery was sharply at variance with federal guidelines. The company was even refusing to meet with employees to discuss grievances, a practice at odds with Order 30. The dismal working climate within the plant was another argument for federal intervention at one level or another. Wage scales were not standard, productivity was lagging, and morale was low. Even management acknowledged that the workplace atmosphere needed significant improvement, but it attributed all plant difficulties to the nefarious influence of "pro-German agitation."

On October 10, 1918, a section of the National War Labor Board headed by Taft and Walsh convened a hearing in Minneapolis to examine a "formidable array of complaints" filed by Minnesota workers against their employers. The two most significant cases involved the Minneapolis Steel and Machinery Company; others were the Twin City Forge and Foundry Company, a Stillwater firm represented by Senator George H. Sullivan, and several grain elevator firms. Safety

Women workers at Minneapolis Steel and Machinery, about 1917. "Equal pay for equal work" was one of the principles endorsed during the war by the National War Labor Board.

commission representatives did not participate in the proceedings, but Tighe and two members of the state arbitration board were present in an observer status. According to Tighe, Walsh and Taft initially had invited state participation, but at the last minute they had called this an error because "the pending controversies were entirely between private parties."[29]

Since the contending sides tended to regard their adversaries as subjects of the prince of darkness, the proceedings of the October 10 meeting were extraordinarily spirited. The labor attorneys, with Arthur Le Sueur in the lead, argued passionately that the employers had grossly violated the guidelines established by the president's April 8 proclamation; they also maintained that the state of Minnesota lacked adequate machinery for the adjustment of labor disputes. According to a summary of the hearing that Tighe drafted, Le Sueur charged that the safety commission had "conspired with the employers of labor for the oppression of workmen and has undertaken to make membership in a union a misdemeanor punishable by fine and imprisonment." "Preposterously untrue," retorted Tighe in the MCPS statement.

The MCPS agreed with management attorneys that industrial unrest in Minnesota was minimal as witnessed by a high level of agricultural and iron ore production. A "great mass of willing workers" was happily doing its part. The complaints before the NWLB were attributable to "a horde of political freebooters [who], after the conquest of a sister state, undertook the rape of Minnesota that they might loot its treasury also." Arthur C. Townley and Arthur Le Sueur were named as the principal culprits. [30]

Taft presided over the proceedings with as much evenhandedness as the tumult permitted. He frequently interrupted counsels on both sides when they departed too far from the central issue at stake: the applicability of NWLB jurisdiction to the complaints that had been filed. Obviously, the challenge that attorneys for management mounted to this jurisdiction concerned him greatly. As the hearing moved toward adjournment, the ex-president pressed the TCRTC attorney for a clear definition of his stance with respect to NWLB authority. "Do we understand correctly," asked Taft, "that you decline to submit to the Board? First your contention is that we have no jurisdiction for the reasons you have advanced, and now subsequent to those being overruled [a possibility] do you decline to submit to the jurisdiction of the War Labor Board?" The attorney replied equivocally. "I have not," he said, "discussed that with either the president [Lowry] or any of my superiors. I have just come into this matter. I didn't expect to submit this at all." To this Taft responded: "I suggest with the concurrence of Mr. Walsh that in the preparation of your brief you state with some degree of definiteness just what your attitude is in that regard." [31]

The brief delivered a few days later on behalf of the managements evaded Taft's question. Instead it launched a renewed attack on the authority of the NWLB, proclaimed the competence of other tribunals to adjudicate labor-management disputes, and contended that the guidelines laid down in the April 8 proclamation did not proscribe the status quo ante principle.

> The Board has no power . . . in the absence of a controversy, and that controversy must be between the employers and those who work for them. A controversy alleged by a union, which has never been recognized . . . is not sufficient. In such case, the union is a stranger to the situation and has no right to be heard. Under the Proclamation

it is the right of the employer, if so advised, to decline to treat with that union; it is [his] right to decline to engage in arbitration with it; it is [his] right to insist that the *status quo* in [his] relations with trade unions shall not be disturbed during the war period. [32]

The brief submitted by the labor attorneys repeatedly emphasized that the complainants were not requesting the War Labor Board "to suspend the open shop during the war." Labor was objecting to "the practice of discharging men who are appointed as committees by the workers to voice their grievances to the employers" — a clear violation of the federal guidelines. [33]

Whether the MCPS delivered a formal response to the October 10 hearing is unclear; as a nonparticipant in the proceedings, it was not required to do so. However, Tighe believed that the attacks made by the labor attorneys on the commission necessitated a response "for the protection of the state's fair name and in the public interest." To help meet this need, the MCPS counsel prepared a draft suggesting what could be covered in such a response. In addition to stressing that Order 30 had been approved by both the Minnesota Federation of Labor and the Minnesota Employers Association, Tighe's draft sought to minimize the divergence between state and federal labor policy. It pointed out that before the war the state's labor-management arena had known three categories of shops: union shops employing only union labor, open shops employing both union and nonunion labor, and nonunion shops employing only nonunion labor. This was the status quo ante that Order 30 was seeking to maintain for the duration of the war. [34]

The Tighe draft then went on to advance an argument that cynically trivialized the central issue in the ongoing controversy between management and labor. Under the provisions of Order 30, Tighe contended,

> no worker was forbidden to join a union. . . . But if he did, he must find work in a union or an open shop and the proprietor of a non-union shop was not required to employ him. It has been said that there were a variance and divergence between the state's program . . . and the federal program. . . . But there was not. The spirit and purpose of the two were the same.

In a decision announced on November 22, 1918 — eleven days after the armistice — the National War Labor Board accepted jurisdiction in all but one of the cases argued on October 10. The one exception was the complaint of the TCRTC employees; however, they were accorded the right to file further appeals. From the standpoint of the safety commission, the most interesting (and undoubtedly most distressing) aspect of the decision was its rejection of the management contention that the complaint filed by machinists' Local 91 was "a case properly within the cognizance of the Minnesota State Board of Arbitration," the jurisdiction of which was derived from the Minnesota Commission of Public Safety. Attorneys for Minneapolis Steel and Machinery had argued that the provision in Order 30 requiring that "differences with respect to wages or hours . . . shall be referred to the State Board of Arbitration" barred NWLB jurisdiction in the case. [35]

In weighing this contention, the decision briefly narrated the history of Order 30, noting that it ostensibly was the product of an agreement between the Minnesota Employers Association and the Minnesota Federation of Labor. The basic guidelines created by the order differed "but little" from those proclaimed by the president on April 8, "except in one important particular." Order 30, the award noted,

> in effect affirm[ed] that where an employer before the war had re-
> fused to employ or continue in his employment, any member of a
> trade union, no employe of his could object to discharge because he
> joined a union or made that a basis of complaint justifying the
> remedial intervention of the Commission or the Board of Arbitra-
> tion. This is not in accord with the rules of the National War Labor
> Board, which provides that there shall be no interference by employers
> with the right of their employees to join labor unions, or to exercise
> legitimate union activity.

Thus, from the standpoint of the NWLB, the "variance" between state and federal labor policy was more significant than Tighe acknowledged. However, the variance was not a major factor influencing the decision of the NWLB in the cases under review. Instead, concurrent jurisdiction — "no anomaly in our country" — was the governing principle. The complaints filed by International Association of Machinists Local 91 and the other unions could be adjudicated by either state or federal authority. No impediment stood in the path of the local's quest for a federal remedy. [36]

If the concurrent jurisdiction principle worked to the advantage of Local 91, it failed to benefit the aggrieved carmen. Lowry's lawyers had argued that adjustment of grievances against Minnesota employers was "properly within the cognizance" of state government and its agencies. They further argued that the dispute between the TCRTC and its workers had been settled by an agreement between Lowry and his company union — the Trainmen's Co-operative and Protective Association.

The NWLB rejected the latter contention out of hand. However, the first one seemed "to have much more substance." A year earlier TCRTC employees had in effect chosen state jurisdiction by appealing to the safety commission. It appeared to the NWLB that the case was "still within the jurisdiction of the machinery of the Public Safety Commission." Moreover, the federal board was "relieved . . . from any conflict as to a denial of rights to organize in a trade union by the street railroad companies in the decision of the Public Safety Commission itself, enjoining the . . . company from discrimination on account of union activities." Hence, the complaint was dismissed. 37

Both the carmen and Minneapolis Steel and Machinery exercised the right of appeal that was granted by the NWLB. Neither was successful. The carmen attempted to extricate themselves from MCPS jurisdiction by filing a set of grievances that their attorneys argued constituted a new case and not the one dismissed by the NWLB on November 22. Specifically, the attorneys charged that the streetcar company's traditional discrimination against union members was still in place — an accusation buttressed by affidavits sworn to by some 250 discharged employees. They also charged that TCRTC wages were not keeping abreast of a rising cost of living. 38

The issue was joined at an NWLB hearing in Minneapolis on January 14, 1919. Lowry's attorney stoutly maintained that the streetcar company had faithfully discharged the obligations laid on it by the safety commission. Representing the carmen, Thomas E. Latimer, a future mayor of Minneapolis, contended that grounds for complaint not explored on October 10 had emerged in August and September, a situation urgently requiring a new hearing. The hearing produced an agreement calling for additional briefs and the possibility of further hearings. Because the carmen proceeded no further, however, this ended the controversy. 39

Minneapolis Steel and Machinery pursued its appeal with more vigor than the carmen, but to little avail. On April 11 the NWLB reaffirmed its claim to jurisdictional competence in the dispute, and on that basis announced a six-point award upholding the union. Point 1 prescribed an increase in pay for both skilled and unskilled Minneapolis Steel and Machinery employees. Point 2 directed the company to maintain a forty-eight-hour workweek, with double pay for

Sundays and holidays. Point 3 ordered the firm to adopt the principle of equal pay for men and women. From the union's standpoint, point 4 was the sweetest triumph of all. It proclaimed:

> The right of workers for this company to organize in trade unions, or to join the same, and to bargain collectively, is affirmed, and discharges for legitimate union activities, interrogation by officials as to union affiliations, espionage by agents or representatives of the company, visits by officials of the company to the neighborhood of the meeting place of the organization for the purpose of observing the men who belong to such unions, to their detriment as employees of the company, and like actions . . . must be deemed an interference with their rights as laid down in the principles of the board.

The two remaining points helped to clarify the intent of the fourth one. Point 5 ordered the reinstatement of employees "wrongfully" discharged (union members), and point 6 required the company to negotiate, not with Local 91, but with committees representing the employees.[40]

Theoretically, the April 11 award was a stunning victory for Minneapolis unionism. In the real world it was of less consequence. While the safety commission was no longer in a position to resist federal labor policy (it had closed up shop in early 1919), other factors inhibited implementation of the award. The national administration was now under considerably less compulsion to enforce its labor policy than earlier. Cessation of hostilities in Europe had diminished the need to maintain war production at maximum levels. An escalating Red Scare, too, fueled by such episodes as the so-called Seattle General Strike, nourished suspicions of a linkage between organized labor and extreme radicalism that inevitably tended to weaken the administration's prolabor orientation.[41] Finally, throughout 1919 President Wilson focused most of his energies on his campaign to secure ratification of the Versailles treaty, a preoccupation diminishing his concern with other issues.

Moreover, even if the administration had been of a mind to enforce the April 11 award, it would have encountered formidable obstacles in so doing. While hostilities raged, the ethos of supporting the president had operated as an enforcement tool in its own right. If worst came to worst, the administration could seek congressional authority to seize and operate a recalcitrant firm, a threat that proved its efficacy in 1918.[42] The election of a Republican Congress in the November 1918 election effectively removed this sanction.

Thus, the high hopes of a resurgent Minneapolis labor movement were dashed in the early months after the war — a not untypical experience for the American labor movement generally. For the next fifteen years the Citizens Alliance would remain the arbiter of labor-management relations in Minnesota's metropolis. For this the safety commission could claim some credit. It had ceased to be a player in the last stages of the struggle, but its assistance in holding the closed nonunion shop fort through 1918 had been significant.

CHAPTER THIRTEEN

Chauvinism at High Tide

N otwithstanding President Wilson's commitment to make the world safe for democracy, democratic liberties within the United States did not fare well in 1918. Several factors caused an intensification of the assault on freedom of speech and expression that had been launched in 1917. Through 1917 the U.S. troop presence in Europe had been minimal; in late September the American Expeditionary Forces in France numbered 61,531 men. By the late spring of 1918, however, troop arrivals escalated into the hundreds of thousands. In May, 245,457 U.S. soldiers set foot on French soil, and the numbers rose in the following months. When the blood-letting ended on November 11, the AEF had expanded to forty-two divisions. Since most of these troops moved straight to the front after arrival, lengthening casualty lists underscored the reality that the nation was at war, and the impact on persons even remotely suspected of pro-German sympathies was devastating.[1]

The Bolshevik overthrow of the Russian provisional government on November 7, 1917, created additional opportunities for the crusaders against disloyalty. The new government moved to negotiate peace with Imperial Germany, a process completed in March 1918 with the Treaty of Brest-Litovsk. Keepers of the patriotic flame could now argue more plausibly than earlier that an unholy alliance linked "ultra-radicalism" with Prussian autocracy. "It is no mere coincidence," pontificated *Commercial West* in mid-July, "that the socialistic propaganda throughout the world coincides with the time when Prussia has been plotting for world domination."[2]

The end of the war on the eastern front released thousands of German troops for redeployment in the West. Utilizing this opportunity to the full, the German high command launched a furious offensive designed to overwhelm Allied defenses in France and end the war on German terms. From March 21 when the offensive began until midsummer when it stalled, the possibility of total German success reinforced the American crusade against pro-Germans, pacifists, and radicals. Postwar Memorial and Armistice Day observances would glorify AEF performance at Château-Thierry — the engagement that turned the tide against Germany — but seldom if ever took note of the ugly hysteria that gripped the nation in the spring and summer of 1918.[3]

In Iowa, Governor William L. Harding issued a proclamation on May 23 restricting oral communication within the state to English, a rule that he applied to all schools, public and private; to conversation in public places, on trains, and over the telephone; and to all public addresses, including sermons in Iowa's churches. Freedom of speech, the governor conceded, was constitutionally grounded but did not include "the right to use a language other than the language of the country — the English language." Montana passed a law imposing a fine and a twenty-year prison sentence on anyone convicted of using "disloyal, profane, scurrilous, contemptuous, or abusive language" when referring to the Constitution, the flag, the American form of government, or the military and its uniforms. A Nebraska law provided a similar sentence for anyone convicted of "disloyal acts or utterances." A Texas law prohibited any "disloyal" or "abusive" language with respect to "the entry or continuance of the United States . . . in the war."[4]

Inspired by this feverish agitation, Congress in early 1918 reexamined existing federal statutes dealing with subversion and found them wanting. After extended debate, both houses passed and the president signed the famous Sedition Act of 1918, which, among other provisions, banned the willful utterance, printing, writing, or publishing of

> any disloyal, profane, scurrilous, or abusive language about the form of government of the United States, or the Constitution of the United States, or the military or naval forces of the United States, or the flag of the United States, or the uniform of the Army or Navy [or any language calculated to bring these institutions] into contempt, scorn, contumely, or disrepute.[5]

The Minnesota Commission of Public Safety adapted more easily to the spirit of the Sedition Act than to the awards of the National War Labor Board. To McGee and his colleagues, crusading against disloyalty was inherently more agreeable than regulating the price of bread or disciplining the liquor trade. Moreover, the so-called loyalty issue was an extremely useful weapon in the commission's campaign against the Nonpartisan League and a helpful ploy in upholding the status quo ante principle in labor relations.

To reinforce its campaign against sedition, the MCPS in early 1918 modified and expanded its antisubversion network. The Pinkerton connection had been terminated in the autumn of 1917, and by 1918 Thomas G. Winter's intelligence bureau was no longer functioning. Several new arrangements filled the gap. In January the commission gave forty members of the American Protective League the status of MCPS peace officers. The APL was "the most omnipresent of the repressive organizations . . . sponsored by the Department of Justice," according to historians Peterson and Fite. In June 1917 it maintained branches in some six hundred cities and claimed a membership of 100,000; a year later its membership had increased to about 250,000, and a suspicion that its intrusive activities endangered civil liberties disturbed, among others, Secretary of the Treasury William G. McAdoo. APL antics also worried President Wilson, who suggested to his attorney general that perhaps the organization's semiofficial status be discontinued. However, "the Attorney General refused to withdraw his support, and Wilson did not press the matter."[6]

Commissioning peace officers for special assignments was another tactic employed by the MCPS in its crusade against subversion. On February 27, 1918, Sheriff Joseph J. Moriarty appeared before the commission with a request that it "authorize some person in Scott County to subpoena witnesses in connection with certain loyalty complaints." The commission responded by appointing Moriarty as its agent. Upon being informed of any "conduct or utterances contravening" existing sedition statutes, Moriarty was to submit to Libby "a brief statement of the facts alleged . . . and on the approval by the Secretary of his so doing," was to launch an investigation. Moriarty was empowered to compel the appearance of the accused

at any convenient place in said County, [and was authorized to] . . . administer oaths, [and] examine any person appearing before him under oath as to any information within his knowledge pertinent to said investigation, and to require him to produce for inspection any writings or documents under his control. . . . At the conclusion of any such investigation the agent shall report to the Commission the proceedings . . . and his conclusions and recommendations.[7]

The Moriarty arrangement established a precedent that shortly would be applied in the alien registration process and against "slackers" refusing to purchase their allotted shares of war bonds. Meanwhile covert operations continued to be part of the MCPS program. Anthony Pleva, an operative employed by Lind in the 1917 IWW investigation, enrolled at commission expense in the Finnish Work People's College in Duluth, an institution that combined business training with indoctrination in the tenets of radicalism. Commissioner Weiss learned enough about the school from Pleva to become convinced that it would be "the breeding and hatching place for a lot of future trouble."[8]

In July the safety commission negotiated an agreement with the Northern Information Bureau, a detective agency specializing in espionage on behalf of status quo ante employers. L. W. Boyce, general manager of the NIB, was appointed as a special MCPS investigator and charged with the responsibility of providing McGee and Libby "with copies of all reports," presumably reports circulated among the NIB's employer clients.[9]

The Boyce reports informed the commission that unity within the radical camp was, at best, fragile. Socialists, Wobblies, and left-wing unionists were able to cooperate in supporting the defendants in the Chicago IWW trials, but in other areas serious tensions were developing. Alexis E. Georgian, editor of the Minneapolis *New Times,* was reluctant to make his office available to the IWW because he feared eviction, but both he and the Wobblies deplored the "defection" of Representative Devold and Mayor Van Lear to the Nonpartisan League. Georgian disbelieved in Socialist cooperation with pragmatic reformers, and IWW doctrine eschewed political action generally. If this apparent disunity was a source of comfort for the MCPS, the degree of rank-and-file support for trade-union cooperation with the Nonpartisan League — a trend also indicated in NIB reports — was less reassuring.[10]

In late October the MCPS sought to terminate the NIB connection.[11] For all their fear of radicalism, the commissioners may not have found Boyce's reports about the imminent outbreak of revolutionary violence to be credible. By late October a mighty Allied offensive presaged an early end to the war, and Burnquist's reelection prospects appeared more promising than earlier. Moreover, there were reasons to doubt the NIB's professional competence. A report covering a union meeting held in Dania Hall in Minneapolis on October 3 failed to identify the speakers. According to Boyce, "When the speakers were introduced, it was by some Swede who talked as though his mouth was full of mush, and our operator could not understand the names of the speakers as they were introduced." The operator was able to report that the speeches focused on the strategy to be followed in the October 10 NWLB hearing and the need for trade-union solidarity in the campaign to defeat Governor Burnquist. The operative closed his report by noting that "a Nigger then gave a hysterical talk about sticking together." [12]

A coalition of groups on the local and county levels was the most valuable component within the safety commission's antisubversion network. The Goodhue, Jackson and Martin county attorneys launched prosecutions against Townley and his associate Joseph Gilbert at the height of the 1918 gubernatorial campaign — prosecutions ultimately culminating in jail sentences. In conformity with its policy of avoiding a direct legal confrontation with the Nonpartisan League, the safety commission assumed a stance of noninvolvement with respect to these prosecutions. However, it is difficult to believe that the initiation of legal proceedings against Townley in the midst of the 1918 state campaign displeased the commissioners. [13]

In areas where anti-NPL sentiment ran strong, sheriffs frequently exercised the power that the safety commission had given them to prevent seditious meetings. The Lindbergh gubernatorial campaign was barred from holding rallies in some nineteen counties, most of them in southern Minnesota. Occasionally the banning of a meeting evoked individual protests (not to speak of formal complaints by NPL leaders). On February 18 a Norman County resident presented his concerns directly to the governor:

> Is it the entantion of the Publick Safty Comision in Minnesota to stop naborhod meetings, such as Farmer clubs and school intertanments from jusing the School houses in the evening?
>
> The Depoty Sherf in Norman County forbids us to hold our farmer club meetings but permits Publick Danses to be held all night in the Publick Haal in Hendrum. [14]

A member of the governor's staff replied:

> Neither the Governor nor the Safety Commission has issued any order against the holding of neighborhood meetings such as you describe. General instructions have been issued to all sheriffs regarding all public meetings, no matter by what organization they are arranged, to give full protection as long as they are loyal, lawful and orderly, but disloyal and seditious meetings, of course, must be stopped. [15]

Automobile caravan of Lindbergh supporters in rural Minnesota, 1918

Considerable power inhered as well in the directors of the county safety commissions, and from time to time the parent commission enhanced this power by giving them the investigative authority created by the Moriarty precedent. Clearly, too, the relationship among the county attorney, the sheriff, the county director, and small-town elites terrified by the prospect of a Townley "dictatorship" was an important factor. Some sheriffs and county attorneys assigned higher priority to frustrating Nonpartisan League appropriation of patriotic symbols than to protecting the right of leaguers to communicate their message. Flag Day, June 14, coincided with the closing of the 1918 state primary election campaign. As a final campaign ploy, the Nonpartisan League organized parades of automobiles that proceeded from town to town bedecked with u.s. flags and Lindbergh banners. Some of the parades reached their destinations — usually a well-attended rally — without incident. Others encountered resistance that local officials either tolerated or abetted. [16]

A victim of an incident near Redwood Falls, where a mob halted the NPL parade and proceeded to strip the automobiles of their banners, complained to Burnquist. The governor's office referred the matter to the Brown county attorney, who placed blame on the victims rather than the attackers, asserting that the leaguers were trouble-makers who "ought to take the consequences like men. In my judgment [the complainant] is not entitled to much consideration. . . . I would advise him to put on the American flag alone, and if he is molested then his case will receive serious consideration."[17]

The Lincoln county attorney appeared to take his obligation to protect the rights of persons within his jurisdiction more seriously than his colleague in Brown. In May this official attempted to act on the complaint of a county resident claiming that, notwithstanding his impeccable record as a Liberty bond purchaser, local mobs had invaded his farm, defaced the buildings with yellow paint, and mistreated his sister.[18] Convinced that the claim was bona fide, the county attorney attempted to build a case against the alleged vigilantes; the barriers blocking prosecution, however, proved to be insurmountable. The complainant confessed his inability to "identify any of the men" in the mob. He also had reneged on a declared intention to enlist after the neighborhood had given a party in his honor. His father had been tardy in the purchase of Liberty bonds. In other words, there was considerable "local prejudice" against the man and his family. The county attorney professed strong disapproval of "these yellow paint escapades," calling them "unlawful." However,

> where there is some apparent justification, you know how difficult it is to get evidence. . . . I am satisfied that I have talked with several who know all about it, but as far as giving me the benefit of anything they know, they are to all intents and purposes deaf, dumb and blind. If the safety commission can and will send an investigator to Tyler, possibly something may be obtained.[19]

The safety commission is unlikely to have dispatched an investigator to Tyler. Its policy in such cases was essentially one of "see no evil." Local officials of proven "loyalty" deserved full trust and confidence. In late July a Butterfield woman complained to Burnquist that a "lynching mob" under the leadership of that town's power structure was threatening "the lives of several people here," including her brother. She reported that houses were being painted yellow, that windows were being broken, and that members of the mob boasted that no jury would convict them. Currently several were under arrest, but if the jury failed to convict them, "the mob has threatened to lynch my brother and several others." Since "the officials of the town" were leading "these rioters," intervention by state authorities was, in the woman's opinion, clearly appropriate.[20]

Gustaf Lindquist, Burnquist's secretary, responded to the Butterfield woman's alarm with minimal urgency.

> You state . . . that the men supposed to be guilty of creating the disturbances are now arrested and that they will be tried by a jury. We take it for granted that a fair jury can be found in your county and that the men will have a fair trial. It is impossible for the Governor to interfere with matters which are pending in the courts.[21]

Several MCPS orders promulgated from January through August 1918 allowed the safety commission to advance the loyalty crusade within its own areas of assumed competence. Orders 23 and 25 instituted a comprehensive process of alien registration, embracing both personal data and alien property holdings. Order 32 prohibited the employment of aliens in the teaching profession on the primary, secondary, and teacher-training levels in both public and private schools. Order 37 required all able-bodied men either to "fight or work." Order 44 expanded and tightened the surveillance of Minnesotans failing to meet their Liberty bond quotas.

Alien registration was not a concept that suddenly emerged early in 1918. Proponents of such a measure in the 1917 legislative session had encountered formidable opposition that obliged them to accept a watered-down substitute, one that required alien registration only at the request of President Wilson. The federal government did order the registration of German male aliens, but not of other noncitizens.

According to John Lord O'Brian of the Department of Justice, the decision to register German males was easily taken. On the other hand, the registration of Austro-Hungarians had been discussed at length, leading to a decision not to do so. "[I]n view of the experience of the department with these people," O'Brian explained in a letter to Senator Kellogg dated April 18, 1918,

> and in view of the representations . . . by a very large number of steel manufacturers and coal operators it was thought inadvisable to provoke discontent . . . by compelling them to register. . . .
> Registration in itself accomplishes very little, except perhaps for the psychological respect of implied restraint in the mind of the person registered. It is a police measure of purely preventive character of value, chiefly because it enables the policing officials to know the whereabouts of an enemy alien and [to] keep an eye on him.

O'Brian assessed the "danger" posed by various alien groups in a predictable order: Germans, Austrians, Hungarians, and "other aliens."

However, he also noted a lack of correlation between seditious activity and nationality; many native-born Americans had, according to him, demonstrated their unreliability while most aliens posed no threat whatsoever. [22]

Since Orders 23 and 25 were promulgated more than two months before this advice was given, it is obvious that O'Brian's views had no impact on the commission's decision. That his counsel would have made any difference is extremely doubtful. The MCPS final report indicates that the safety commissioners regarded alien registration as one of their more constructive achievements. It had "probably done more than any law or measure previously adopted in Minnesota to bring foreign-born civic slackers — to the number of 225,000 — within the full sway of our laws and the American spirit; to make them realize their duties and appreciate their high privileges as Americans." [23]

Order 23, promulgated on January 15, 1918, mandated a registration of all alien-owned real estate within Minnesota. The specific goals of the registration, which was to be handled by the county boards of commissioners, included identifying all real property under alien ownership, determining whether the alien owner resided on the property, identifying corporations having alien stockholders holding property in each county, and providing a legal description of all real property "herein above referred to." The state auditor was instructed to supply the county boards with the names of all aliens on lists available to him, and the boards were to deliver the registration results to the state auditor by March 1. [24]

The commissioners soon discovered that Order 23 could not accomplish all that in their view needed to be done. On February 5 they adopted Order 25, a decree designating February 25 through 27 as "Alien Registration Days." Every alien in the state was instructed to register on one of these days at a location designated by the unit of local government under whose jurisdiction he or she resided.

The data sought in the sworn declarations totaled 35 items. The first 17 covered personal and family history. Number 18 called for the names of relatives participating in the "present war" either for or against the United States and its allies. Nineteen through 21 probed the male registrant's draft status: "Did you register under [the] selective draft, and if so, where? What is your serial number? Did you claim exemption from military service and why?" The next three dealt with the delicate question of naturalization: Had the registrant taken out First Papers? If so, why not Second Papers? If he or she had never

Registration of aliens in the St. Paul Armory, February 1918

applied for naturalization, why not? Numbers 25 through 35 required submission of a complete inventory of property holdings, including land; city lots; securities; property held in trust for minors; and personal property "such as cattle, sheep, horses, autos, farm machinery" and the approximate value of these assets. Finally the registrant was directed to reveal the location of any safe deposit vault under his or her control. To emphasize that it meant business, the safety commission decreed that aliens failing to register on one of these days would be "interned or subjected to other action which the Minnesota Commission of Public Safety will prescribe."

Undoubtedly the commissioners anticipated that their reputation for toughness would ensure almost universal compliance with Order 25. If so, they were mistaken. On February 26, the second scheduled registration day, State Auditor Jacob A. O. Preus reported "that more than two thousand and possibly as many as three thousand aliens" had departed for Wisconsin and Canada, a serious matter given the labor needs of the region. Preus surmised that some of the defectors were actually citizens who had falsely claimed alien status in order to evade the draft. Others were bona fide aliens who had "been engaged in the spreading of propaganda . . . to throttle the output particularly of timber and iron ore" and who now feared disclosure of their true identity. The impact of both groups of derelicts, the MCPS

concluded, had "been such as to substantially aid the enemy and injure our country."[25]

As a countermeasure, the safety commission asked the U.S. Department of Justice "to cause a registration of ALL aliens resident in the
United States," a suggestion that the justice department declined to
follow. A week later the safety commission approved a Preus request
that authorized him "to grant extension of the registration period in
specific cases." It also approved a resolution designating Preus and
two other men as agents of the commission with authority to subpoena anyone having knowledge of "facts pertinent to the registration of alien residents of the State."

While the Preus trio supervised the roundup of suspected evaders,
the registration process uncovered few serious threats to the stability of
the republic. A native of Sweden employed by the state institution
in St. Peter allegedly remarked to his registrar: "I am here [in the United
States] only to make money." Upon learning of the comment, the safety
commission called it "to the attention of the State Board of Control,"
with an implied recommendation that the man be disciplined.[26]
Most aliens responded to the registration requirement more discreetly,
which does not mean that they escaped the pain of wounded self-
respect. A profile of rural noncitizens residing in the Elbow Lake vicinity is suggestive on this point. According to the probate judge of Grant
County:

> This district is populated mainly by Scandinavians. Many of them
> have only limited schooling. . . . They settled in neighborhoods
> where their mother tongue was used in church and by neighbors.
> Hence, they did not learn to read and write English, nor did they
> participate in public affairs as they perhaps would have under other
> circumstances, and they failed to understand the formal steps needed
> to acquire citizenship. At the same time, they always have been re-
> garded as among our best people. They were often the first settlers
> of the frontier; they guarded law and order; they supported schools
> and churches; and in many cases their sons are in the armed
> forces.[27]

Wounded self-esteem was not the only burden placed on Minnesota
aliens by the requirement that they register. The detailed declarations
relating to property ownership raised the specter of confiscation. The
apparent threat was made more real by the emergence in the spring
of 1918 of a campaign calling for dispossessing "disloyal" persons of
their property. In early April a group of Fairmont citizens organized

a "monster rally" that adopted "a resolution . . . requesting a special session of the legislature and [calling] for the enactment of laws confiscating to the war fund the property of all disloyal persons in Minnesota." In the same week, a "huge mass meeting" held under the auspices of the Cottonwood County America First Association adopted a similar resolution. [28]

Fearing that a special session would open a can of worms, Burnquist firmly declined to convene one. He argued that the questions involved were clearly within the competence of Congress and the safety commission. MCPS resistance to the hysterical excesses of the moment was not remarkable, but compared with that manifested by superpatriotic legislators who inflamed the issue, it was impressive. [29]

Nevertheless, alien fears of confiscation were not easily allayed. They were sustained in part by enterprising land speculators who suggested to immigrant farmers that since their land titles were shaky by virtue of the owners' alien status, prudence dictated acceptance of the speculator's ridiculously low bid for the property. There is no clear evidence that this tactic enriched anyone. The Scandinavian-language press, for example, assured its readers that an influential Scandinavian presence in state and local government (including Preus, a Norwegian American) would help protect alien landowners from the prospect that their property rights would be abrogated. [30]

On the other hand, families subjected to alien registration would not — in the short run at least — cherish fond memories of the humiliation and insecurity engendered by the process. The perspective of later generations would be different. In the 1970s and 1980s, descendants of the 1918 registrants discovered that their ancestors' alien registration declarations were an invaluable source in the pursuit of family history.

Order 32, enacted on April 30, 1918, prohibited the employment of aliens in "any public, private, or parochial school or in any normal school in which teachers for these schools are trained." The ban did not include institutions of higher learning, and Superintendent of Public Instruction Schulz — the order's designated enforcement agent — was authorized to grant permits to qualified teachers holding their First Papers "or to a special teacher . . . employed for technical work." [31]

MCPS policy with respect to the "foreign" factor in education was not extreme when assessed within the context of the time. The presence of German language and culture within the state's schools had been a matter of deep concern not only to the safety commissioners but also to Superintendent Schulz and Alice Ames Winter. In the autumn of 1917 the commission launched two investigations, both under the supervision of Schulz. The first probed the extent to which languages other than English served as the vehicles of instruction in both private and public schools. The other evaluated the acceptability, from a "patriotic" standpoint, of the textbooks currently used in German classes throughout the state. [32]

Schulz completed both investigations by early November. The first reported that some two hundred schools utilized "a foreign language in whole or in part as a medium of instruction," meaning that an estimated "10,000 children were being brought up as aliens and foreigners, and are not being properly prepared for American Citizenship." Although Schulz indicated that these findings were "preliminary," the safety commission was sufficiently alarmed to approve the following motion:

> RESOLVED: That school-boards, principals and teachers be recommended and urged, as a patriotic duty, to require the use of the English language as the exclusive medium of instruction in all schools in the State . . . and to discontinue and prohibit the use of all foreign languages in such schools, except as a medium for the study of those languages themselves, or as a medium for religious instruction. [33]

In conducting the second investigation, Schulz recruited a committee of eight educators to examine the character of the German textbooks being used. Following presentation by Schulz of the committee's report on November 6, 1917, the MCPS adopted a resolution requesting the committee

> to reduce the findings of its report to the form of recommendations calling for the elimination from the public school curriculum of Minnesota of all the books which they find objectionable on patriotic grounds as to their contents, and that the committee be requested to prepare a "white list" of unobjectionable books, from which school boards may safely make their selections. [34]

The safety commissioners were not convinced that these two actions should be their final word on the language "problem" in Minnesota schools. For one thing, the conclusion that some ten thousand students were being deprived of instruction in English was based on a partial survey; conceivably, the number could be larger or smaller. For another, the challenge of assuring compliance with the MCPS recommendations remained. Within the public school sector, Schulz's authority carried considerable weight, but no central authority exercised jurisdiction over the parochial system.

Following Ames's dismissal as commissioner in early December 1917, his erstwhile colleagues requested him to continue as an agent in charge of investigating the Nonpartisan League and the German school problem. He accepted the dual appointment. Obviously his abrupt dismissal deeply humiliated him, but a belief that the Nonpartisan League was a clear and present danger to the American war effort impelled him to swallow his wounded pride. His antipathy to use of the German language as a medium of instruction reinforced his willingness to maintain a limited connection with the MCPS. In responding to a complaint concerning a school within which allegedly no English was being taught, he characterized the employment of German as a medium of instruction as "a practice . . . objectionable at all times, [but] intolerable in time of war." [35]

Ames's report, submitted on March 20, noted that the investigation had been hampered by lack of information on the status of English and German in the private schools. It suggested that the county superintendents of schools be instructed to collect data on this question. It also articulated an Ames conviction that compliance with the MCPS recommendations was a matter of "growing importance." The employment of German "as a medium of instruction should be absolutely discontinued in Minnesota," the report argued. [36]

The MCPS failed to promulgate an order embodying this view, but it tacitly accepted a "rule" — a mandate lacking the force of a full-blown MCPS order — proposed by Schulz and specifying that English be used "as the only medium of instruction in all branches of study in elementary schools, public, private, and parochial, except that for purposes of religious instruction or the acquisition of another language, some other medium may be used." [37]

Schulz also delivered to the MCPS the findings of two surveys relating to language instruction. One of them, carried through with the assistance of county superintendents, probed the status of English in the state's parochial schools. Of the 307 schools in the survey, 94 used English exclusively as their medium of instruction. The remaining 213 were bilingual. Of these, German was the second language in 195, French in 10, Dutch in 4, and "Bohemian," Polish, Norwegian, and Danish in one each. None reported using German exclusively. [38]

The other survey measured public school compliance with the recommendation relating to "objectionable" textbooks. Of the 325 high and graded elementary schools responding to the query, 119 reported using "Group A" texts — the "objectionable" ones. Ninety-three had discarded books in that category; 23 had eliminated the offending parts; and three were using Group A books to teach the "evils" of Prussianism. The survey also explored the extent to which public schools were abandoning German instruction. It found that 25 had done so in the 1917–18 school year and that 34 proposed to do so in 1918–19. A report issued by the Minnesota Department of Education in June 1919 suggests that the dropping of German courses was proceeding more rapidly than the survey indicated. Before the war the department received, on average, about 5,000 state board examinations in German for correction; in 1919 the number declined to 340. [39]

Although the safety commission cannot be credited with resisting the assault on foreign-language usage and instruction in 1917 and 1918, its policy in this area was more restrained than that adopted in Iowa, Nebraska, and South Dakota. The commission apparently never considered banning "foreign" speech on the streets of Minnesota towns or over the telephone. It consistently upheld the legitimacy of foreign language instruction, although this was not its highest priority. In responding to a protest against the anti-foreign language crusade, Burnquist defined his own and presumably the commission's stance on the latter issue: "Although I would be opposed to using a foreign language as the exclusive medium of instruction, I would not be opposed to the teaching of foreign languages in our schools as a cultural study." [40]

Given the overall record of the safety commission, its relative restraint in responding to foreign language issues may seem surprising. However, its stance is not inexplicable. The foreign language "lobby" was a significant factor in Minnesota politics, as the proceedings of the 1919 legislative session would demonstrate. Church leaders whose support of the war was unconditional were sensitive to implications that their schools were insufficiently patriotic.

On this point, a protest by Joseph F. Busch, bishop of St. Cloud, against the line being taken by Superintendent Schulz is instructive. In addressing a group of St. Paul business leaders in October 1918, Schulz declared: "There are ten or twelve thousand children in the private schools of St. Paul, and a great percentage of them are not being taught in the English language by teachers imbued with Americanism." After reading an account of Schulz's remarks in the *St. Paul Pioneer Press,* Busch, a churchman widely credited with counteracting pro-German sentiment within the German Catholic community, dispatched an angry letter to the governor. "I am sure," wrote Busch,

> as far as our parochial schools are concerned, all branches are taught in English and possibly that in some the religious instruction may in part be in German and in some schools also an optional course in German besides the usual studies of the public school courses. I think Mr. Schulz should be asked to produce his evidence or to retract his statement. I am told that a general protest is being considered by all those in charge of private or parochial schools against this and other unwarranted acts by Mr. C. G. Schulz.

Evidently the "general protest" alluded to by Busch failed to materialize. Nevertheless, his individual protest demonstrated to the safety commission that caution was advisable when dealing with issues relating to language instruction, particularly in the parochial school system. [41]

Dealing with idlers required less caution than confronting loyal bishops. Since early in the war, the MCPS had regarded the existence of a large body of unemployed "employables" as an abomination. In July 1917 it commissioned Carol Aronovici of the Wilder Foundation (and future chairman of the state's Americanization Committee) to investigate the problem. The Aronovici project had a triple focus: determining the extent of idling; ascertaining its causes; and devising ways and means of recruiting employable idlers either into the military forces or the workplace. [42]

From a St. Paul Police Department study of twenty-five pool halls, Aronovici learned that on a given day 263 patrons of these establishments were "men unemployed during business hours." Of 1,107 applications to United Charities of St. Paul for assistance, 237 came from families whose "male head" was habitually unemployed. The percentage of dependent families in Minneapolis headed by male idlers was even higher. Aronovici estimated that from 8,000 to 10,000 Minnesota men were idlers, "at least one-half" of whom were employable. [43]

Aronovici sought to illuminate the causes of idleness by categorizing the idlers. Some were men unfit for "continuous effort" by virtue of physical or mental disabilities. Others were "incapacitated" by "special disabilities." Still others were cursed "with habits of idleness and drunkenness." Idlers in the age group between 16 and 21 were especially prone to dependence on friends and relatives. Seasonal workers unwilling to shift occupations constituted another group. A final category consisted of men with criminal and "semi-criminal" tendencies.

The Aronovici prescription for overcoming idling indicated a preference for the stick over the carrot. A statewide registration system for all unemployed, a system linked to a central bureau, was to be established. Peace officers should be authorized to demand a registration card from any man "appearing to be unemployed." Those failing to produce a card should be arraigned in a local court. Persons convicted were to be given a mental and physical examination to determine fitness. Those pronounced fit would be assigned suitable jobs under employers obligated to report the employee's absenteeism to the police and ultimately to the MCPS. Those found unfit were to be institutionalized; Aronovici estimated that from one thousand to two thousand of his unemployables were salvageable. He also recommended the establishment of "farm colonies" where the marginally fit could be productively employed. In addition he urged a special effort to locate suitable occupations for the handicapped.

Lacking the bureaucracy required to administer a complex program, the safety commission did not implement the Aronovici plan. However, Order 37 — the "fight or work" edict promulgated on July 4, 1918 — adopted the central concept. Calling attention to the necessity of providing "reinforcements for the Army" and supplying labor on the home front, the order decreed "that every male person residing in Minnesota shall be regularly engaged in some useful occupation." Exemptions were allowed for students enrolled in "recognized" schools or in training for an occupation, children under 16, physically handicapped men, and those "usually employed in some useful occupation and temporarily unemployed owing to differences with his employer common to similar employes with the same employer."[44]

Violation of Order 37 was declared a misdemeanor punishable by imprisonment in the county jail for not more than three months or a fine not exceeding one hundred dollars. Responsibility for enforcement was vested in local officials, who were instructed to report suspected violations to the county attorney for possible prosecution.

Implementation of the order did not proceed smoothly. The term "useful occupation" was not self-defining, an ambiguity disturbing to a number of county prosecutors. Stearns County Attorney Paul Ahles professed to be thoroughly confused. He asked Attorney General Clifford L. Hilton (who had become a safety commissioner following the death of Lyndon Smith in March 1918) to comment on several hypothetical cases. Would "a young man owning two farms but renting them . . . who spends his summers in Stearns County and winters in California" be in violation of the order? Or "a middle aged man, about forty-five years, who is a retired farmer now living in the city and taking life easy[?]" Or "a curb-stone land agent who hangs around to see whether he can't find some sucker out of which [*sic*] he might make a little money[?]"[45]

Hilton referred Ahles's inquiry to Assistant Attorney General Rollin L. Smith, who after conferring with Tighe responded with the following opinion:

> The special attorney for the Minnesota Commission of Public Safety has construed Order No. 37 as being primarily aimed against habitual idlers, and . . . that in the beginning prosecutions thereunder should be limited to people habitually loitering in idleness in streets, roads, depots, pool rooms, saloons or other places. . . . It is my opinion that Order No. 37 was not intended to cover the persons described by you.[46]

Libby, who was now a commissioner as well as MCPS secretary, zealously followed up virtually every complaint of idling with action of one kind or other. At times he would refer the complaint to the prosecutor within whose jurisdiction the alleged idler resided, and if Libby disapproved of the prosecutor's disposition of the case he did not hesitate to make his displeasure known. On other occasions he would contact the accused person by letter, reminding him of the seriousness of his dereliction and vaguely hinting unpleasant consequences if he failed to change his ways. To one unfortunate young man accused of idling, Libby wrote, "I believe it only necessary to call this matter to your attention and you will take steps to comply with the same. However, should this not be the effect I assure you that the Commission is determined that this order shall be enforced and more drastic steps shall be taken."[47]

One potential hazard facing accused idlers was special attention from draft officials. If a suspect appeared eligible for military service, Libby would refer his case to Adjutant General Rhinow, who in turn would delegate responsibility for contacting the accused to Lieutenant

H. W. Pfiffner, a draft inspector. A Pfiffner report on one case illuminates what sometimes happened next:

> Proceeded to [suspect's home] and found that subject was out, but expected back at noon. After lunch returned and found that subject had been in and left again. Proceeded to Payne Ave. where subject was located in one of the saloons. Talked to him about the Federal service in the different branches and the desirability of enlistment — worked on his patriotism, so proceeded to his home where we both talked to his mother as to whether he should enlist or be picked up under order No. 37. He signified his preference which was enlistment.
>
> Proceeded to the United States Recruiting Office located in the Baltimore Bldg. . . . where subject enlisted as a private in the United States Army. [48]

Another Pfiffner report raises doubts that these efforts served the armed forces from a qualitative standpoint. According to the lieutenant, "Subject is a heavy drinker, does not work except occasionally, and is of no good to his family. If subject is able to pass the military examination, I recommend that he be placed in Class 1 and inducted into the service. His wife is anxious to have him serve." [49]

In addition to promoting military recruitment, Order 37 undoubtedly discouraged assertiveness within the state's labor force. Although the order appeared to exempt workers on strike from its penalties, presumably the exemption would not apply in a strike deemed by the MCPS to be illegal. In any case, the commission used the order to discourage "excessive" wage demands. Either on his own initiative or at the direction of the full commission, Libby instructed the city marshal of Comfrey in August 1918 "to prosecute, under Order No. 37, any men refusing five dollars per day wages, or whatever the prevailing wages may be." [50]

The usefulness of the order also appealed to mining and timber executives. In requesting copies of all MCPS orders, John Butler of Butler Brothers informed Libby: "We are especially interested in Ruling #37 to post as a bulletin around our operations on the Mesaba Range." Similarly, Alger, Smith and Company, a Duluth lumber manufacturing firm, indicated that it "would be very pleased to receive one dozen copies to post up in our camps and other places where we have men employed." [51]

An MCPS edict "Providing for Investigation in Connection with Sale of Liberty Bonds" — Order 44 — was designed to boost the Fourth

Liberty Loan campaign, which was launched on September 28, 1918. Consistent with the hardening superpatriotic mood of mid-1918, organizers of the fourth campaign relied more on coercion and less on patriotic exhortation than in preceding drives. Within each county, Liberty loan committees, on which bankers were heavily represented, assigned each resident an allotment that he or she was expected to meet. Theoretically, failure to meet this allotment was not an indictable offense, but the extralegal and in some cases clearly illegal penalties inflicted on bond "slackers" could be at least as painful as a jail sentence. [52]

The specific goal of Order 44 was to build a fire under persons suspected of not being forthcoming in disclosing their assets to the local bond committees. Each county safety commission director was designated an agent of the MCPS for the purpose of investigating such persons. The significance of this investigatory arrangement is difficult to assess. Possibly because the order stipulated that "no publicity shall be given to the evidence elicited," the proceedings of investigations that may have been held are not available. Conceivably, too, formal hearings may in most cases have been unnecessary. Many county directors were members of their local Liberty loan committees and hence able to use the threat of a formal investigation as a means of persuading lukewarm patriots to accept their allotments. In any case, Minnesota's performance in the Fourth Liberty Loan, particularly within areas of NPL strength, far exceeded the quotas established by officials heading the Liberty loan campaign. [53]

However, not all Liberty bond purchasers responded to their patriotic obligations cheerfully. Following announcement of the Fourth Liberty Loan, the governor's office received complaints alleging undue pressure on vulnerable persons. A Viking resident asked Burnquist, "Do a person need to take Liberty loan, when they have not got any money, and not got any income more then he works for, and six in the family. And this winter I shall chop cord wood for a living." Characteristically, a prompt but not altogether sympathetic response was forthcoming from a member of the governor's staff:

> While the law does not compel anyone to buy liberty bonds, it is the duty of all patriotic citizens to do so. At the present time when work is plentiful and wages good, there are very few persons who cannot afford to [buy at least] one small bond. If you tell the local committee of your circumstances, I am sure they will not ask you to buy more than you are able to pay for. [54]

A farmer residing near Staples voiced a complaint similar to the one delivered by the Viking woodchopper and received an almost identical response. The farmer inquired if a person was legally compelled to buy Liberty bonds if the money required had to be borrowed. He added that in his case, additional bond purchases would require him to "sell unmatured young stock and cut down the production of beef and pork and other farm produce," steps not entirely supportive of the war effort. The governor's staff replied that "while the law does not compel anyone to buy liberty bonds, all patriotic citizens should buy as much as they possibly can. Many persons have borrowed money to pay for their bonds or bought them on the installment plan."[55]

With slight variations, the assertion that purchasing Liberty bonds was not legally compulsory but that every patriotic citizen should buy as many as possible, coupled with an admonition to "trust your local bond committee," was part of the standard gubernatorial response to virtually every complaint alleging undue pressure. Anonymous communications purporting to identify "slackers" commanded more serious attention. Upon receiving a report accusing a local brewery employee of not participating in the various Liberty loan drives, of being unsympathetic to the United States, and of driving "his automobile on Sunday," Libby referred the allegation to the county chairman of the loan drive. The chairman in turn "asked the American Protective League to look into the matter."[56]

As the summer of 1918 faded into fall, faint signs of a growing reaction against MCPS tolerance of the hate-filled loyalty crusade began to surface. The prospect of early Allied victory in Europe diminished the putative pro-German threat within Minnesota and the nation. The influenza epidemic and the Cloquet fire failed to distinguish between "bond slackers" and "patriots"; like most disasters, they pointed to cooperation as a condition for survival. The national administration also was issuing declarations deploring mob violence as an abomination violating the integrity of the country's war effort.[57]

Within Minnesota, two incidents — one in August and the other in September — registered a sobering impact.[58] The August episode involved mob action against an elderly Rock County farmer burdened with a double handicap: a German name and affiliation with the Nonpartisan League. Rock County was not exactly a Nonpartisan League stronghold, but by June 1918 Townley organizers had recruited 382 members within the county's borders. To counter this fearsome threat, the Luverne Loyalty Club, an organization ostensibly representing that city's business community, ordered all known NPL members to pledge loyalty to the United States and to renounce the Nonpartisan League. Most leaguers complied; the Rock County NPL roster soon shrank to twelve members, a number of whom suffered "deportation" into Iowa, among them the elderly farmer.

In August the farmer returned to the Luverne area to help his sons with threshing. Upon learning of his return, local loyalists came to the farm on August 19, seized the elderly man, subjected him to a classic tar and feathers treatment, and deported him for a second time — not to Iowa but to South Dakota. Thanks to the national left-wing press, this incident received more publicity than many other equally outrageous episodes.

Notwithstanding his age, the Rock County farmer survived the ordeal inflicted on him by local patriots. A Finnish immigrant residing in the Duluth area was less fortunate. As a noncitizen this individual apparently had pleaded exemption from the draft on the basis of his alien status, a grave offense in the eyes of a Duluth patriotic group calling itself the Knights of Liberty. After being physically mistreated by a mob, the man was discovered hanging from a tree. Whether he was the victim of a lynching or had committed suicide was not immediately ascertainable. In either case, the mob was primarily responsible for his death.

Burnquist took no official notice of the Rock County incident, but the Duluth atrocity, involving as it did the loss of life, impelled him to issue a proclamation offering a reward for "information leading to the arrest and conviction" of the perpetrators. The proclamation also implicitly recognized that mob rule was getting out of hand: "The public welfare demands that persons suspected of disloyalty be given a fair trial and, if guilty, be punished by the lawfully constituted authorities, and that mob violence shall not be tolerated."[59]

Undoubtedly Burnquist hoped that his proclamation would regain the confidence of valued erstwhile supporters who were reacting negatively to the safety commission's failure to restrain mob violence. If so, he was not entirely successful. On October 11 Gunnar Björnson's *Minneota Mascot* carried an editorial that in effect declared the governor's action a tardy first step that needed to be followed up with resolute action:

The governor of the state of Minnesota has come out against mob rule.

After due deliberation he has decided that he does not want any more men tarred and feathered or horsewhipped or deported, beaten up, disgraced or shamefully treated, without due process of law. . . .

The governor has made the discovery that there is a law against dragging a man out of his home and beating him up and subjecting him to all kinds of indignities. . . .

Mobs have been doing, — free and unmolested, — so many Hun stunts in this state that we had almost come to believe that the mob was a new form of law and order enforcement.

The governor and the Safety Commission have been silent . . . so long that we really did not know what to think about it. . . .

But the governor has saved the day — also he has saved the constitution. . . .

We hope now that he will keep this up and make his proclamation extend to every corner of the state. We hope that hereafter there will be no more stealing of banners, no more tearing off of the United States flag from cars that carry a Nonpartisan League banner, no more of the dirty, sneaking yellow paint brigades, no more of this tarring and feathering, no more of the disgraces that have taken place in Rock County, no more deporting of citizens, nor more of the hundred and one different kinds of outrages that have gone unmolested and unnoticed, if not encouraged by state and county officials. [60]

CHAPTER FOURTEEN

The Campaign of 1918

The October 11 Björnson blast, exploding as it did one month before the 1918 state election, was not particularly helpful to Burnquist's reelection effort. Had it been detonated by a Nonpartisan League activist or a labor advocate, the impact would have been inconsequential. But Björnson was a journalist known for rectitude and independence, a respected Republican remembered by many as organizer of the successful 1914 campaign to reclaim the Minnesota Republican party from the clutches of the Eberhart machine. When Burnquist succeeded to the governorship at the end of 1915, Björnson had praised the new governor as a public official whose record demonstrated that "no special interests dictated to him."[1] Until the United States entered the war, the *Minneota Mascot* followed a strong neutralist line, but since April 6 the paper had staunchly supported the president's policies. All in all, according to loyalist conventional wisdom, a journalist-politician of Björnson's stature should have enthusiastically joined the Burnquist Hallelujah Chorus.

On the other hand, Burnquist managers may well have calculated that their candidate's margin of safety was sufficiently wide to tolerate the defection of several Björnsons. For more than a year they had pursued a systematic campaign to impeach the loyalty of the Nonpartisan League, an effort commanding the support not only of the Twin Cities business community but also of small-town elites smarting under the threat of NPL boycotts. Overtly when this was politic and covertly when it was not, the safety commission backed this campaign. Unable to locate a proverbial "smoking gun," it stopped short of branding the NPL as seditious and hence illegal while encouraging local officials to interdict delivery of the NPL message.

A mortal fear of Townleyism rather than enthusiasm for Burnquist inspired the fervent crusade on behalf of his reelection. There were, in fact, several grounds for distrusting the governor. For one thing, his prewar progressivism was at odds with the orientation of many in the MCPS circle. For another, the cordial hearings he occasionally gave dissidents were a source of disquiet — John McGee preferred a more militant approach when confronting persons like Magnus Johnson. For still another, his leadership did not always appear steadfast: his failure to keep his pledge with respect to MCPS reorganization is a case in point, and one that distressed Donald Cotton. [2]

Nevertheless, in the election campaign Cotton along with other corporate executives threw their support to Burnquist. The prospect of a state administration dominated by the Townley organization was too horrible to contemplate. From a corporate standpoint, state-owned and state-operated flour mills, packing plants, terminal elevators, insurance systems, and banks threatened the very existence of vital Twin Cities interests — and the ongoing success of the Nonpartisan League in North Dakota was anything but reassuring. The terror inspired by Townleyism along Minnesota's main streets was equally intense. A Nonpartisan League triumph, small-town elites feared, would undermine both their economic and social status.

So far as anyone could tell, the undeclared war against the league launched in late 1917 failed to retard its momentum. Between September 1917 and late winter of 1918, state membership rose from thirty thousand to fifty thousand. By this time, too, the league had created an organizational structure in Minnesota capable of waging an aggressive campaign in the 1918 state elections. Precinct caucuses held on February 22 — a patriotic holiday — selected delegates to legislative district conventions that in turn chose delegates to attend the state convention, scheduled to convene in St. Paul on March 20. If contemporary NPL claims are credible, very few league members failed to attend their precinct caucuses, and enthusiasm for the cause was abundant. [3]

In planning convention proceedings and routines, the NPL leadership ran a proverbial tight ship. Clearly the convention was expected to ratify without argument leadership decisions both with respect to candidate endorsements and platform; this was the subliminal meaning of the popular NPL slogan "We'll Stick," which was emblazoned on buttons worn by delegates to the convention. A day before the state convention assembled, forty-eight local leaders, representing all but nineteen of Minnesota's legislative districts, met in St. Paul to select a state ticket — apparently no nominations from the floor were anticipated. The nineteen unrepresented districts included mostly urban and iron range areas where the endorsement initiative was left to organized labor. [4]

With one notable exception, convention planning was comparatively flawless. The exception was inviting Governor Burnquist to address the delegates. Perhaps the leadership regarded this as a move that would embarrass the governor. If so, it miscalculated. Instead of politely declining on the grounds of other commitments, Burnquist responded with an open letter — which the antileague press gleefully featured shortly before the convention opened — coupling a brusque refusal of the invitation with a recapitulation of the charges currently being leveled against the NPL by the organization's bitterest enemies.

League leaders, Burnquist charged, had "been closely connected with the lawless I.W.W. and with Red Socialists." They had "catered to that faction of labor which has violated the law and been opposed to compliance with just orders of duly constituted authority," an unsubtle reference to the streetcar strike. "The cheering and applauding of the unpatriotic utterances of Senator La Follette" at the 1917 Producers and Consumers Convention had "put a stamp of disloyalty on [the league] that can never be erased." Arthur Le Sueur, manager of the Minnesota NPL in whose name the Burnquist invitation had been extended, was "the attorney who defended the murderers in the I.W.W. trouble on the Range two years ago." The governor placed himself unambiguously on the side of the angels:

> He who in normal times needlessly arrays class against class is most often the ambitious demagogue, but any individual who will do so when our nation is in a life-and-death struggle is knowingly or unknowingly a traitor to his state and to his country.
> . . . [F]or me there are during this war but two parties, one composed of the loyalists and the other of the disloyalists. [5]

Whether or not Townley and his associates realized it, the Burnquist letter placed the NPL on the defensive. For the remainder of the campaign Minnesota loyalists would regard the missive as one of the most effective indictments of the NPL in print. However, it is not evident that any suspicion that this was so dampened the spirit of the NPL state convention. From beginning to end, a spirit of evangelical enthusiasm animated the assembly. At the same time convention managers succeeded through platform declarations, speeches, and visual images in articulating four major themes.

The first was the basic Nonpartisan League program with its core demand that the middleman sector of the agricultural economy be brought under effective government control. The second was unreserved and unqualified support of the war, affirmed by exhortations on behalf of Liberty bonds and the Red Cross and a conspicuous display of American flags. Appearances on the speaker's platform of several officials of the national administration, along with a friendly message from George Creel, implied that the president reposed confidence in the patriotic loyalty of the Nonpartisan League.[6]

The third theme affirmed NPL and trade-union solidarity. While addressing the convention's closing rally, Townley, pausing, posed a question to the agricultural sector of his audience: "Farmers of Minnesota, is there any hatred in your hearts toward organized labor?" The country people responded with an emphatic "No!" He then asked those willing to "pledge . . . allegiance to the workers of the city" to stand. Thousands of farmers rose, a gesture generating "tumultuous" applause. Townley then asked the workers "likewise [to] pledge . . . allegiance to the farmers" by standing. "In an instant the rest of the packed auditorium was on its feet, while hats sailed in the air amid deafening cheers." The highly visible presence near the front of the auditorium of a uniformed street railway employee — ostensibly a locked-out TCRTC worker — with his wife at his side and a small baby in his arms enhanced the dramatic effect. As Morlan put it, "The impossible in American politics, a farmer-labor alliance, was coming to pass." The fourth theme was a demand for a restoration of the country's lost civil liberties. "It will avail little to win a war for democracy abroad," proclaimed Lindbergh, "if in the prosecution of that war all . . . traditional rights and privileges . . . have been surrendered and abrogated."

The endorsement of Charles A. Lindbergh, Sr., for governor was the most important action taken by the NPL convention. Lindbergh accepted and shortly filed as a candidate for the Republican nomination, which placed him in direct confrontation with Burnquist. In the weeks that followed, Lindbergh's loyalty emerged as the predominant issue in the primary election campaign. The ex-congressman's detractors firmly believed him to be unpatriotic; Knute Nelson, for example, declared that Lindbergh was "as disloyal as can be." Although

*Charles A. Lindbergh, Sr.,
about 1920*

some NPL supporters suspected that Lindbergh's preoccupation with a conspiratorial "money trust" was a trifle obsessive, none of them questioned his loyalty; for them the defeat of Burnquist was the paramount concern. Another group of supporters regarded Lindbergh as a great popular tribune called to lead the farmers of Minnesota out of bondage; their enthusiasm for his candidacy was unbounded. [7]

Part of Lindbergh's problem was a refusal to employ patriotism as a political weapon. Shortly after U.S. entry into the war, he dispatched the following revealing letter to Burnquist:

> In no sense am I in search of a job, but if our Nation needs me in any capacity in connection with the war, I will be ready to serve. I have a special work that I am more than anxious to complete, but no one is entitled to excuse if emergency calls.
>
> I do not care to have the papers publish anything about it. I mereley [sic] wish you to understand that in these days of trial we must all be ready and willing to do our most, and I am of course. [8]

*Lindbergh (holding flag at right) cam-
paigning at Thief River Falls, 1918*

*Effigy of Lindbergh hanging from a
telephone pole in Stanton, 1918*

Burnquist chose not to accept Lindbergh's offer, which left him free to complete his "special work." Although the letter contains no clue illuminating the nature of the project, Lindbergh most certainly was referring to his book, which would be published in July 1917, entitled: *Why Is Your Country at War and What Happens to You after the War and Related Subjects.* From the standpoint of Lindbergh's political future, nonpublication of this opus would have been merciful. Although the author proclaimed the solemn obligation of every American to support the war effort, the overall message was confusing, combining as it did allegations that "a certain 'inner circle'" had maneuvered American entry with affirmations that the conflict had "now become a war for freedom."[9]

The book also abounded with statements vulnerable to out-of-context quotation. The most notable example was the passage: "We should spurn as contemptible to the idea of democracy the oft-heralded statement of 'Stand by the President,' in the sense of its present frequent use because it is too often used as a guise to deceive." As quoted by Lindbergh's opponents the statement read: "We should spurn as contemptible to the idea of democracy the oft-heralded statement of 'Stand by the President.'"

There is little doubt that distortion of this passage convinced many Minnesota voters that Lindbergh, indeed, regarded "standing by the president" as "contemptible." On the hustings the candidate valiantly sought to nourish a contrary impression. To those who would and could hear, he proclaimed that adoption of the Nonpartisan League program was a patriotic necessity. Modern war, he argued, relied as much on efficient production as on effective military action, a reality that America's allies had acknowledged by placing essential industry under tight government control. Russia's failure to do so, he contended, had precipitated that nation's collapse. "There is," Lindbergh declared, "only one remedy, and that is to have the government conscript industry." Of all the organizations in the country, he continued, the Nonpartisan League was the only one "backing up President Wilson in his fight with the politicians and profiteers." He added that "if there should be any firing squads . . . they should first seek out these traitors."[10]

Lindbergh's allusion to firing squads was inspired by a McGee indiscretion of a few weeks earlier that seriously embarrassed the Burnquist reelection campaign. On April 19 the commissioner was in

Washington testifying before the Senate Committee on Military Affairs in support of a bill calling for the trial by military courts of persons accused of sedition, a bill based on the assumption that civilian courts were not doing their job. In the course of his appearance McGee made a series of controversial statements:

> The United States Department of Justice in Minnesota has been a ghastly failure. The United States District Attorney in Minnesota is patriotic but he lacks a fighting stomach.
>
> A Non-Partisan League lecturer is a traitor every time. In other words, no matter what he says or does, a League worker is a traitor.
>
> Where we made a mistake was in not establishing a firing squad in the first days of the war. We should now get busy and have that firing squad working overtime. Wait until the long casualty lists begin to come in and the Minnesota woods will not be dense enough to hide the traitors who will meet punishment for their crimes. These men who are fighting our soldiers and stabbing them in the back are going to die.
>
> . . . The disloyal element in Minnesota is largely among the German-Swedish people. The nation blundered at the start of the war in not dealing severely with these vipers. [11]

The impact of McGee's remarks was not helpful to either the Burnquist campaign or the safety commission. An Otter Tail County Republican activist complained to Knute Nelson that McGee was "doing more to promote the union of the farmer & labor vote than a thousand Townleys could do." On behalf of the Scandinavian Women Suffrage Association, Nanny Mattson Jaeger forwarded a statement to Libby expressing regret that a safety commission member had "made a statement reflecting on the loyalty of a class of citizens to which we naturally belong." Several members of the Minneapolis City Council demanded McGee's ouster from the MCPS, but a majority bloc declined to go this far. Meanwhile, according to Morlan, "a wave of protest" swept over the state. [12]

Several federal officials also reacted negatively. In responding to a letter from Lind (written on the day McGee appeared before the committee) in which Lind had characterized McGee as "bitter and unreasoning," Attorney General Gregory commented: "I have never met [McGee] personally, but fully agree with your description of him and feel that while in Washington he did a great injustice to the people of your State." Gregory added that Lind was mistaken in believing that McGee had "the ear" of John Lord O'Brian, the assistant attorney general in charge of sedition. "Mr. O'Brian never saw Judge

McGee except on one occasion," wrote Gregory, "and the impression left upon him by [McGee] was exactly that entertained by you and myself." [13]

From the standpoint of both the MCPS and the Burnquist campaign, the damage caused by McGee's remarks clearly had to be addressed. In responding to Jaeger, Libby raised the possibility that McGee had been misquoted and would offer a convincing explanation when he returned from Washington — of this Libby was "positive." Moreover, Libby added, allowance had to be made for the great sacrifices being put forth by the McGee family. Two sons and a daughter were in France, and McGee had suspended his law practice to serve on the safety commission and as fuel administrator. [14]

Burnquist's reaction to the McGee testimony was more critical than Libby's. In the course of an interview with representatives of the Minneapolis City Council, the governor flatly stated that he disagreed with McGee's inflammatory rhetoric, had disagreed with him in the past, and would encourage him to exercise more restraint in the future. However, no plans to dismiss McGee were under consideration. [15]

For his part, McGee issued a lengthy statement that in effect reiterated most of the points made in his original testimony. But he insisted that he had not impugned Swedish-American loyalty; some of his best friends, including Burnquist, were of Swedish origin. McGee theorized that an exchange between himself and a group of reporters following the hearing had generated a distorted impression that he had characterized German-Swedish people as disloyal. In the course of this exchange, McGee had referred to Chisago — a "Swedish" county — and Brown — a "German" one — as areas where disloyalty was rife, a reference that the reporters somehow transformed into the offensive but totally false quotation. On the military courts issue, however, the press had quoted him accurately and he was not prepared to retreat a single inch from his hard-line position. As he put it, "The certainty of conviction of the guilty before such a court with a prompt appearance of the guilty before the firing squad would have had and would still have a most restraining influence on the disloyal, seditious and traitorous." [16]

Townley's own appearance before the Senate Committee on Military Affairs on May 1 may have been more helpful to the Burnquist campaign in overcoming the hostile reaction to McGee's remarks than the efforts put forth by the governor's supporters. This appearance was scheduled at Townley's request for the purpose of answering McGee's charges against the Nonpartisan League. Unfortunately for the league president, senators hostile to the NPL — and well briefed on the case against it — dominated the proceedings. At the outset, however, Townley gained one concession: the privilege of answering McGee's remarks as reported in the newspapers rather than as carried in the printed record that McGee had edited following delivery of his testimony. As the military affairs chairman put it: "A man can not make a charge and publish it broadcast and then shut your mouth by a withdrawal of it." [17]

Helpful as this concession may have been, the hearing did not eventuate in a Townley triumph. As a defense of NPL loyalty he pointed to the magnificent performance of North Dakota — a league-dominated state — in the Second Liberty Loan, a subscription that exceeded the quota by 73 percent. An unfriendly senator blunted Townley's argument by shifting the focus: How many bonds had the NPL as an organization purchased? Townley was obliged to acknowledge no NPL participation in the first two and a subscription of merely five thousand dollars to the third. [18]

The loyalty of the NPL leadership was another issue of concern to the senators. Quotations were cited from Lindbergh's book suggesting that corporate pressure on behalf of Liberty bonds was in part a ploy by the rich to shift the burden of paying for the war onto the backs of the poor — a line that Lindbergh and the league had long since abandoned but that had been in vogue a year earlier when the Lindbergh book was published. Again, Townley found himself on the defensive. In response to a question concerning one of the quotations from the book, he replied: "I think it is a very foolish and unjustifiable statement to be made at the present time."

At another point in the hearing Townley attempted to underscore NPL loyalty by citing the superpatriotic affirmations adopted in September 1917 at the Producers and Consumers Convention and those written into the March 1918 state platform. Again hostile questioning placed him on the defensive. A plank in the 1917 platform endorsed "industrial democracy" as it was being implemented in Russia; the 1918 manifesto reiterated support of the concept without linking it to Russia. Ignoring the reality that the Russian regime of September 1917 was the provisional government that would be overthrown by the Bolsheviks a few weeks later, Senator James A. Reed, Democrat of Missouri, argued that the 1917 plank proved that the Nonpartisan

League was sympathetic to bolshevism. Townley heatedly denied the charge, declaring that in his view the present Russian regime — the Bolshevik-dominated one — was pro-German and that "no one in our organization interprets the condition in Russia today as industrial democracy."[19]

Another NPL tactic distressing to the senators was the organization's persistent and strident attacks on "profiteers" in particular and corporations generally. This line, the lawmakers believed, was dividing the nation at a time when unity was imperative. On this point, however, Townley held firmly to his ground, freely acknowledging his belief that the United States suffered domination by an "industrial autocracy." He cited a passage from Woodrow Wilson's book *New Freedom* that read: "The masters of the Government of the United States are the combined capitalists and manufacturers of the United States." Townley asserted that he had "never said anything along that line stronger than that." Senator John W. Weeks of Massachusetts, a Republican, refused to be impressed, noting that the statement was not made in time of war.

On balance the Townley hearing as reported in the predominantly anti-NPL press was more helpful to Burnquist than to Lindbergh. For one thing, it diverted some attention away from McGee's testimony. For another, it reinforced doubts about the loyalty of the Townley circle. Nevertheless, Burnquist managers were not inclined to let down their guard. The resentments stirred by McGee were not easily set aside, and Nonpartisan League rallies, where they could be held, were attracting huge crowds. In early June Senator Nelson received an alarming message from a veteran Duluth Republican who described the situation as desperate. "The Loyalty issue," he wrote, "is the only thing that will save Burnquist."[20]

Nelson was of the same mind. About two weeks before the primary he issued a statement in support of Burnquist that laid particular emphasis on loyalty. "[T]he exigency of the war," declared Nelson,

> makes me especially interested in the nomination and re-election of Governor Burnquist. He has proved himself a veritable Rock of Gibralter in maintaining law and order, in sustaining the spirit of loyalty and patriotism, and in faithfully supporting our federal government in the war. . . . [T]o defeat Governor Burnquist under these circumstances . . . would be taking a backward step in the path of patriotism and loyalty.[21]

Anti-Lindbergh poster circulated during the primary campaign for governor, 1918

Even the most obtuse Minnesota voter in 1918 must have suspected MCPS involvement in the Burnquist renomination and reelection campaign. Nevertheless, a degree of caution both on the part of the commission and the governor was appropriate. The safety commission, after all, was a public agency, created and funded by the legislature, and hence by tradition if not by law barred from overt participation in electoral contests. However, the commission was adept at participating while maintaining the fiction of nonparticipation. Its contribution to Burnquist's renomination and reelection campaign was clearly more significant than that of the regular Republican organization, which had been in a state of disarray since the defeat of the Eberhart machine in 1914. [22]

The Burnquist strategy facilitated overt MCPS participation in the campaign. At the outset the governor announced that he intended "to make no political speeches during the primary," but he promised to "accept, as far as possible, those invitations to deliver patriotic addresses" that he had received. The safety commission was, of course, in an excellent position to spawn such invitations. On May 4 it asked the directors of the county safety commissions to enlist in a gigantic offensive against "kaiserism at home and abroad." The rallies organized by promoters of this offensive provided a forum for the governor that he utilized to the fullest. He also honored his promise to stress "patriotism" rather than "politics." In a speech delivered on the eve of the primary election, he referred to the need to prevent a "disintegration of our forces through ill-advised contests at home or through advocating the formation of such factions as to prejudice the different elements of our state against each other by reason of occupation or location." [23]

Along with providing forums for the delivery of Burnquist's patriotic homilies, the MCPS committed its publicity apparatus to promotion of the Burnquist image. Virtually every issue of *Minnesota in the War* carried articles extolling the governor's wartime leadership. Persons desiring copies of Burnquist's reply to Le Sueur for distribution as a campaign document could secure them by contacting Libby. [24] MCPS releases to the press cautiously avoided references to the gubernatorial race, but some came perilously close to advocacy of Burnquist's renomination. A statement issued a little more than two weeks before the primary and carried by many newspapers is illustrative:

Minnesotans are sure to study the matter carefully before they go on record as being opposed to any public man who has done his full official and patriotic duty and to register such a fact before a critical world. . . . The line is drawn and the issue is clean cut between the friends of disloyalty, half-hearted and selfish patriotism and the friends of one hundred per cent Americanism, that is pure and unadulterated by any personal or political interest of any kind. [25]

The safety commission's publicity apparatus focused particular attention on Scandinavian voters, especially after McGee's ill-advised remarks to the senate committee. Nicolay Grevstad, who had been monitoring the Scandinavian-language press for the MCPS since August 1917, had largely accomplished his mission of persuading editors of newspapers published in Swedish, Danish, and Norwegian to provide their readers with a "correct" interpretation of the war. As 1918 advanced he assumed responsibility for mobilizing Scandinavian journalistic support for the Burnquist and Knute Nelson reelection campaigns. [26]

Since Grevstad owed his position with the MCPS to Nelson, most of his efforts focused on the senator's campaign. Not that Nelson needed much assistance. The one certainty at the outset of the 1918 senatorial campaign was that Nelson would be reelected. His sole primary opponent, James A. Peterson, was handicapped by a federal court conviction on a sedition charge. Thanks to the friendship of leading Minnesota Democrats, Nelson also was spared the inconvenience of a Democratic opponent. In addition, the Nonpartisan League state convention refrained from endorsing a senatorial candidate, although late in the fall campaign league newspapers unofficially rallied to Willis G. Calderwood, Nelson's only opponent. Calderwood — who in the parlance of the time was known as a radical Prohibitionist — was running on the National ticket, which was backed by a coalition of erstwhile Prohibitionists, a Bull Moose remnant that had separated itself from Theodore Roosevelt on issues of foreign policy, and a group of prowar Socialists that had repudiated the party's antiwar stand.

The senator's glowing reelection prospects notwithstanding, the safety commission evidently perceived activity on his behalf as potentially helpful. A Nelson victory of more than landslide proportions promised to boost Burnquist's fortunes, particularly since it was known that Nelson supported the governor's renomination. From Grevstad's standpoint, Scandinavian honor also was at stake. An advocacy piece, most certainly composed by him and appearing in Norwegian-language papers shortly before the primary, strongly emphasized this point.

An overwhelming majority of Norwegian votes [for Nelson] is not sufficient. He ought to receive all of them. Unfortunately his opponent is a person of Norwegian blood who has been convicted of treasonable activity. . . . Lingering suspicions of Scandinavian loyalty in this war still persist, and one can be sure that the voting behavior of Scandinavian voting precincts will be closely watched. [27]

The Grevstad effort to achieve monopoly control over the editorial policy of the Scandinavian-language press fell short of fulfillment. In February 1918 the Nonpartisan League negotiated an agreement with Sigvard Rødvik, a left-wing Norwegian journalist, that placed Rødvik on the NPL payroll as a reporter and editorialist responsible for establishing liaison with the Norwegian- and Danish-language press. Before long the Rødvik byline became familiar to readers of this press. Newspapers that opposed the NPL in their own editorial columns frequently accepted the correspondent's material, which for the most part communicated the NPL message. Both Nelson and Grevstad were alarmed. By August, according to a Grevstad computation, about twenty-six papers were publishing Rødvik's articles every week. The Rødvik factor, Grevstad complained, had transformed "practically the entire Norwegian and Danish press . . . into a League press agency." Unhappily, nothing could be done to correct this situation. Grevstad did call "the attention of the Safety Commission to the activity of the League in the Norwegian press," but he learned that his superiors were powerless to act "unless charges of sedition" could be filed — and Rødvik was too shrewd to fall into such a trap. The only remaining recourse was to engage the NPL journalist in open competition. [28]

Along with making its publicity apparatus available to the Burnquist and Nelson campaigns, the safety commission also defended Burnquist's claim to exclusive possession of the nation's patriotic symbols. In early April, Libby received a disturbing report that Herman Berg, chairman of the Rush City Third Liberty Loan and also a league-endorsed candidate for the legislature, was "making political capital" out of his Liberty loan chairmanship "to the detriment of the drive." From Libby's standpoint this was intolerable: apparently whatever political capital inhered in Liberty loan campaigns belonged to the Burnquist camp. However, the director of the Chisago County drive did not share this perspective. He explained that Berg had been appointed Rush City chairman because the surrounding community was a "hotbed" of Nonpartisan League and Socialist enthusiasm and hence potentially more receptive to Berg's salesmanship than to that of an anti-NPL loyalist. [29]

To the safety commission, the NPL tactic of decking automobiles with American flags and Nonpartisan League banners was equally objectionable. Unfortunately, the flag and banner tactic was perfectly legal, and mob action against NPL paraders was clearly a violation of law. The safety commission dealt with the dilemma by ignoring NPL complaints about attacks on the parades. On at least one occasion it also offered comfort and reassurance to a worried citizen who feared that his participation in a vigilante caper had placed him on the wrong side of the law.

The story told by the citizen in question, a Blue Earth hardware merchant, was a familiar one. On June 13 a motorcade carrying a troupe of Faribault County leaguers entered Blue Earth with each vehicle in the parade decked with a Lindbergh banner and an American flag. Blue Earth "loyalists" requested the paraders to remove one or the other of the two emblems. This the leaguers refused to do, whereupon the "loyalists" agreed to a division of labor. One group undertook to remove the Lindbergh banners, another the flag. Since the hardware merchant had "a pair of . . . boys in the service," he chose to join the flag removers. The mission was accomplished, but following its completion the hardware merchant began to worry about the possibility of being prosecuted. Libby assured him that he had nothing to fear. The commissioner-secretary was "quite sure that . . . no jury in the world would hold you liable for the instance reported." [30]

By primary election norms, voter turnout on June 17 was remarkable. The vote garnered by the four candidates for governor — two Republicans and two Democrats — totaled 382,600; only in one final (as distinguished from a primary) election had the total exceeded this figure. The Republican share accounted for 349,951 of the total: 199,325 for Burnquist and 150,626 for Lindbergh. The Democratic contenders — W. L. Comstock the "liberal" and Fred G. Wheaton the "conservative" — split the remaining 32,649 votes almost evenly, with Wheaton winning the nomination by a margin of 629 votes. Some observers believed that if Comstock had won, a Democratic-NPL coalition might have been negotiated. As it was, Wheaton resisted any coalition arrangement, whether with the NPL or the Burnquist camp. [31]

Burnquist advocates hailed the outcome as a resounding victory for loyalty and patriotism.[32] The *St. Paul Daily News,* which had declined to endorse either GOP contender, ridiculed this line of reasoning. Noting that Lindbergh had polled three votes for every four cast for the governor, the paper commented:

> Something like 60 per cent loyalty for Minnesota isn't anything to . wave flags about. But such a standard . . . is . . . utterly false. . . . [T]he great mass of the Lindbergh vote was as loyal as the Burnquist vote, but . . . it voiced an emphatic PROTEST against real wrongs as well as fancied grievances.[33]

Despite Burnquist's success in the primary, the Nonpartisan League remained determined to contest the governor's reelection. With the status quo ante issue still pending, so did organized labor. A delegate assembly representing most of the state's unions met in St. Paul on August 25 for the purpose of initiating trade-union participation in the fall election. By prearrangement, an NPL convention met on the same day in another hall. Following brief deliberation, a joint committee recommended the endorsement of David H. Evans, a Tracy farmer and hardware merchant, for governor and Tom Davis, a flamboyant attorney who practiced his profession in Marshall, for attorney general. Both parent bodies heartily accepted these recommendations, and the two endorsees proceeded to legitimate their candidacies by petition. Initially they had planned to file as "Independents," but a ruling by the secretary of state against such a designation obliged them to adopt the "Farmer-Labor" label. This did not mean that the Farmer-Labor party as such was now in existence. The strategy of ultimately winning power through capture of the Minnesota Republican party was still in place and would be attempted again in 1920.[34]

The naming of Evans — whose obscurity statewide matched Lindbergh's prominence — was in part motivated by a desire to defuse the loyalty issue. A Wilson Democrat who had supported Comstock in the primary campaign, Evans possessed a set of patriotic credentials not vulnerable to serious challenge. As a member of the Lyon County Safety Commission's marketing committee, he actually was affiliated with the MCPS organizational network; he had also gained local prominence as a Liberty bond and Red Cross promoter. Although not a Lindbergh supporter in the primary contest, he had earned NPL gratitude by making a grove on his farm available for a league rally after Tracy authorities blocked efforts by Townley organizers to secure a meeting hall within the city. But he was not a member of the

Nonpartisan League, and his active support of Wilson in the presidential campaigns of 1912 and 1916 had earned him the right to claim that he was really "standing by the president."[35]

Nevertheless, the Burnquist campaign continued to press the loyalty issue. Largely ignoring Evans, the governor's advocates concentrated their fire on Arthur Le Sueur, manager of the Minnesota branch of the NPL. Unfortunately for the league, Le Sueur was extremely vulnerable. Among the items seized by authorities during the 1917 raids on IWW headquarters throughout the country was a letter dated April 5, 1917, from Le Sueur to his client, William D. Haywood, the notorious IWW leader. Among other things the letter expressed a hope that Haywood would not "start anything until the year has expired." It then added the following incriminating comment: "This damned war business is going to make it mighty hard to do good organization work or good radical work of any kind, but I think the fight should be now centered against spy bills and conscription."[36]

Le Sueur attempted to neutralize the damaging impact of this "infamous" letter by pointing out that it was written before the declaration of war. He also announced his own conversion to conscription. Such an explanation availed little. The very fact that the letter disclosed a Le Sueur relationship with an individual as notorious as Haywood was devastating enough to keep the loyalty issue alive.[37]

Following his primary defeat, Lindbergh did not sink into obscurity. In early September it was learned that the ex-congressman had been appointed to the War Industries Board. For a period of about two weeks this appointment was surrounded by confusion. Knute Nelson maintained that, although Lindbergh was being considered for the post, he had not been appointed and in all probability would not be. Citing incontrovertible evidence to the contrary — including a letter of appointment signed by the president, the appointee's letter of acceptance, and his journey to Washington to be sworn in — Bruce L. Larson, Lindbergh's biographer, has established that he had, indeed, been named. Precisely who inspired the appointment was another moot point. Conventional belief held George Creel responsible, a theory denied by Lindbergh. However, Larson has argued persuasively that Creel initiated the appointment.[38]

Whoever was responsible, the logic supporting the Lindbergh appointment is clear. For nearly a year the national administration had courted the Nonpartisan League on the theory that in dealing with Townleyism co-option was preferable to proscription. Moreover,

Lindbergh's ideas concerning economic mobilization, while somewhat in advance of administration thinking, were in the main consistent with the dominant trend in administration policy. Throughout the primary campaign he had vigorously supported the Wilsonian food and agricultural programs.

This logic failed to impress Lindbergh's many adversaries in Minnesota. Announcement of the appointment evoked a storm of protest from both Main Street commercial bodies and individuals. A Rice County official wondered, "What will the boys 'over there' say?" The publicity director of the Minnesota Republican State Central Committee could "think of no act since the sinking of the Lusitania that would outrage the feelings of our people more than the appointment of Mr. Lindbergh." A telegram dispatched to Commissioner March by a group of twenty-five Litchfield residents asserted: "In view of the disloyal record of Mr. Lindberg [*sic*], we must believe that every loyal citizen of this community would feel humiliated and discouraged in working for our common war activities."[39]

Officials of the Minnesota branch of the American Protective League were equally distressed. Recently they had received instructions to monitor the activities of the National Nonpartisan League. Now (September 11),

> the newspapers are full of reports that the infamous C. A. Lindberg, Non-Partisan leader, Pro-German, and pro-everything else except Pro-American is slated for a "job" on the war Activities [*sic*] Board and that nothing short of the refusal [to cooperate] of the loyal men appointed to supervise the next Liberty Loan . . . will prevent his appointment. [40]

In a letter to Senator Nelson, former Congressman Frank M. Eddy, a zealous loyalist Republican, feared that the appointment boded ill for the future as well as for Burnquist's reelection prospects.

> [T]he loyal men of Minnesota who in the recent primaries devoted their time, money and energy to saving the state from Lindberghism, socialism and pro-germanism would like a solution of the Administration's action and are wondering if after the war problems are to be settled by men of the Lindbergh-Townley stripe?
>
> If so what in hell are we fighting for? . . . No matter what others may tell you we have a hard fight on our hands to put Burnquist across this fall. [41]

In the face of the intense pressure mounted by his adversaries and cleverly orchestrated by Senator Nelson, Lindbergh withdrew from the fray. His resignation letter of September 11 took the high road. Lindbergh realized the administration's difficulty in coping with "emergencies" such as those created by his opponents, adding that it was not "so important that I should have the honor of serving my country in a responsible position." He further stated that he would "express no spirit of resentment against the objectors," but he contrasted the loyalty of his own following with that of persons who threatened noncooperation with the Liberty loan program if he assumed the post in question. [42]

Privately Lindbergh articulated his resentment more candidly. To his daughter he excoriated "certain well understood forces, who were willing to subvert their loyalty to selfish personal ends." The principal villains, he charged, were officials of "the Federal Reserve Bank of the 9th District, as well as the Reserve Banks in other sections of the country" who desired his exclusion "from any position where I might be able to deal effectively with economic and industrial problems."

Meanwhile, the dismal gubernatorial campaign ground on and on. Although loyalty remained a dominant factor, the turning of the tide on the western front reduced fear of the dreaded German threat, depriving the loyalty issue of some of its bite. A widespread ban on public meetings following outbreak of the influenza epidemic limited campaign activity. Caring for the victims of the devastating Cloquet–Moose Lake fires diverted the attention of many from politics. Finally, symptoms of a gathering backlash against the excesses of the loyalty campaign began to appear.

In late October an unexpected development introduced a new factor into the race for u.s. senator. Ostensibly, Senator Nelson had consented to run for reelection on the assumption that no Democratic candidate would challenge his bid for a fifth term. Throughout the summer and into the fall, Nelson's managers represented him as being Wilson's choice, a tactic not entirely agreeable to Democrats who looked to John Lind for leadership. On October 23 Lind confounded Nelson supporters by releasing the text of a telegram from the Democratic National Committee "strongly" endorsing Calderwood, the National party candidate, and calling Calderwood's election "of the utmost importance not only in the matter of supporting [the president's] conduct of the war but also for the purpose of cooperating in the reconstruction policies and progressive measures . . . which will follow cessation of hostilities." [43]

No one believed that this development seriously threatened Nelson's reelection, but any reduction of his anticipated margin diminished the efficacy of his coattails. Moreover, the announcement laid the foundation for an informal alliance between the Calderwood and Evans campaigns. The Nonpartisan League stopped short of endorsing Calderwood, but its official newspaper carried friendly allusions to his candidacy; since Calderwood was the administration's candidate, this tactic implied a linkage between Evans and the national administration. A vituperative editorial in the *Minneapolis Tribune* reflected the view of the Burnquist camp:

> Nonpartisanship, Socialism, political Prohibition and John Lind Democracy have struck hands . . . in support of W. G. Calderwood for the Senate. . . . What a composite of class politics, sedition and intrigue! . . . This combination will also gather to itself all the pro-German, Bolsheviki, i.w.w. and uncatalogued flotsam and jetsam of the state. [44]

The Evans-Calderwood entente received its decisive test on Election Day, November 5. As expected, Burnquist won reelection, polling 166,618 votes out of a total of 369,866 cast, far short of a majority. Four candidates shared the remaining 203,248 votes. David Evans polled 111,966; Fred Wheaton, the Democrat, 76,838; L. P. Berot, the Socialist, 7,795; and Olaf O. Stageberg, the National candidate (and technically Calderwood's running mate), 6,649. In the senatorial race, the Nelson-Calderwood split was about 60–40: Nelson polled 206,428, and Calderwood, 137,334. Significantly, in the nine counties where Calderwood prevailed, Evans commanded a plurality; the other counties returning Evans pluralities awarded Calderwood a respectable vote. Ironically, Calderwood — a statewide symbol of the prohibition movement — did exceedingly well in counties with larger German-American populations, thanks presumably to Nelson's prominent identification with the loyalty crusade. Ethnic self-respect, it seems, could at times prevail over a thirst for beer. [45]

The most remarkable aspect of the 1918 election was the size of the Evans vote. Notwithstanding the candidate's comparative obscurity, his entry onto the ballot via the petition route, and the unrelenting "loyalist" assault, Evans garnered about 30 percent of the total gubernatorial vote. Clearly the coalition of angry grain farmers, frustrated trade unionists, and disaffected ethnics forged during the primary campaign was holding together. Meanwhile, even though Burnquist commanded only about 45 percent of the vote, his supporters professed to derive satisfaction from a second triumph for loyalty and patriotism.

Passage into History

D efeat of the Nonpartisan League achieved one of the commission's principal goals in 1918. The status quo ante issue was still pending, but Burnquist's decision not to oppose the jurisdiction of the National War Labor Board left the commission little to do on behalf of the closed nonunion shop. Moreover, comfort could be derived from the probability that the new Republican Congress would exercise a check on "Bolsheviki" tendencies within the national administration.

Germany's capitulation of November 11 further reduced the commission's sphere of activity. The armistice did not, however, automatically terminate the MCPS mandate, which extended three months after ratification of a peace treaty, or sooner if so ordered by the governor or legislature. Moreover, failure of the United States Senate to ratify the Treaty of Versailles in the autumn of 1919 meant that the country remained technically at war with Germany until 1921, when passage of a joint congressional resolution terminated the state of war. [1]

Nevertheless, the commission was undergoing a process of gradual termination. Burnquist's 1919 inaugural message favored the MCPS with a glowing review that was pitched in the past tense, indicating completion of the agency's mission. On the other hand, the governor was not ready to order its liquidation. Federal officials had asked the states to maintain their councils of defense intact on the chance that they might contribute to the demobilization effort. [2]

A demobilization role apparently did not emerge for the Minnesota commission. In 1919 the commissioners met only three times, and then primarily for the purpose of closing up shop. On January 14 they declared "all orders . . . now in force" inoperative as of February 5 "unless the Commission is otherwise instructed by the Legislature." The commissioners cited two reasons for this decision: the conditions

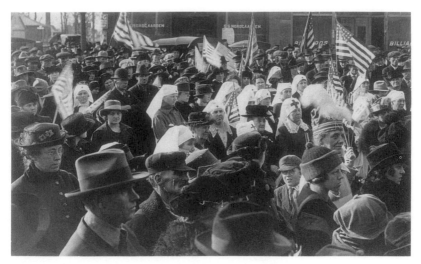

Armistice Day celebration, Madison, November 1918

imposed on Germany by the armistice made "a renewal of the war practically impossible," and the legislature was in session and in a position "to continue said orders or some of them in force after the date hereinafter suggested."[3]

On February 4 the commissioners modified the January 14 order, denying that the enactment was intended "to affect the status of the Home Guard, Motor Corps and Peace Officers" and noting that "measures are now pending in the Legislature relating thereto." Burnquist partisans had introduced a package of bills calculated to strengthen the state's military arm. The first called for a permanent Motor Corps within the National Guard to replace the provisional one operating under Home Guard auspices; the second provided for the recruitment of a Negro battalion, a move evidently designed to allow the Home Guard unit raised in the St. Paul black community in April 1918 to be taken into the National Guard; and the third proposed an extensive revision of the military code, including an enhancement of the authority of the adjutant general and the governor over the military forces.[4]

This program aroused strong opposition, all the more so because proponents stressed the usefulness of the Motor Corps bill in combating "red socialism" and "professional agitators." Nonpartisan League representatives relived memories of disrupted rallies, and labor advocates were haunted by the specter of uniformed strikebreakers. The National Guard, which was a powerful lobbying force, also saw its prerogatives threatened. By early February the doom of the Burnquist program was not a foregone conclusion, but at best it had only a fighting chance. The safety commission action of February 4 was an effort to preserve the legal basis of the Home Guard and the peace officer corps while the Motor Corps bill was still pending. As matters turned out, both the Motor Corps and military revision bills suffered defeat, and the remaining measure was weakened by an amendment that permitted rather than required the recruitment of a Negro battalion.[5]

While the fate of Burnquist's military program hung in the balance, an immediate legislative termination of the MCPS emerged as a possibility. A bill introduced by Representative William A. Pittenger of Duluth proposing abolition of the safety commission reached the floor for a vote on April 14. During a brief debate preceding the tally, no one offered an impassioned defense of the commission and, according to legislative observer Buell, "no one gave it a brown roast." Supporters argued that the work of the commission was completed and that its unexpended funds could serve better purposes. An amendment adopted in the course of the debate requiring return of these funds to the state treasury reinforced the latter argument. When the vote was taken, 107 legislators voted for the bill and only 12 against.[6]

A variety of motives influenced the 107 "abolitionists." Members of the NPL and labor blocs — some thirty-four in number — welcomed any opportunity to chastise the MCPS, and others were undoubtedly lured by the prospect of enhancing the state treasury. Still others may have been voicing a protest against MCPS liquor policy. Some perceived that since the commission had been in a state of "in[n]ocuous desuetude" for some time, early retirement seemed appropriate.[7]

An interesting aspect of the vote was the solidarity with which Iron Range legislators — "conservatives" as well as "laborites" — supported the Pittenger bill. One can safely assume that this reflected the existence of an entente between those legislators and several Twin Cities labor representatives — among them Thomas McGrath and Leo J. Gleason — who broke with the labor movement to vote against the tonnage tax. As a quid pro quo, range legislators backed a workers' compensation bill and, apparently, abolition of the safety commission.[8]

Favorable Senate action on the Pittenger bill might have moderated the labor movement's anger at McGrath and his colleagues by showing that their entente with the steel interests had produced a small return. Contrary to expectations, however, the upper house voted overwhelmingly to retain the safety commission. Deliberation on the bill precipitated "one of the hottest debates of the session," Buell reported. In a fiery speech George Sullivan of Stillwater questioned the motives of the Pittenger bill's supporters, "practically branding as disloyal all who opposed him, the 107 House members included." Andrew Devold of Minneapolis was equally strident in defending the measure, accusing the safety commission of having "used its autocratic power against labor in defiance of the United States government." Nor was this its only offense. It had sown discord both within country and city and had made a mockery of the nation's free speech tradition. The spectacle of Minnesota being "ruled by such a blackguard outfit" compelled Devold to vent his feelings of outrage. [9]

Some of the senators opposing the bill — including John D. Sullivan of St. Cloud — contended that the safety commission "had done much good, that it would wind up its affairs very soon anyway, and that to pass this bill now would be to slap the Commission in the face and encourage unrest and disloyalty." The combined impact of George Sullivan's intimidating rhetoric and the quieter persuasiveness of other opponents helped doom the Pittenger bill in the Senate. After the debate several senators announced a reversal of position. James A. Carley informed his colleagues, "I have now changed my mind. I am going to vote to keep the commission."

Only thirteen senators, most of them members of the NPL-labor bloc, voted aye on the bill. Forty-eight voted nay, and six were not recorded. Unlike their House counterparts, conservative members of the St. Louis County delegation cast negative votes. Whatever deals may have been negotiated between Iron Range conservatives and Twin Cities laborites in the House apparently did not involve members of the Senate. [10]

The Senate's emphatic refusal to acquiesce in the termination of the safety commission carried more symbolic than practical significance. Even though Burnquist retained the power to reactivate the MCPS, he did not do so — despite the anti-Red hysteria gripping Minnesota and the nation in 1919. Protectors of the state's power structures were becoming acutely aware of the political vulnerability of the state administration and were relying on other agencies, some public, others private, to guard their vital interests.

With each passing postwar month, several of these agencies were demonstrating enhanced efficacy. The Minneapolis Citizens Alliance, now freed from the threat of interference from the War Labor Board and Mayor Van Lear (who lost his bid for reelection in November 1918) and loyally backed by Hennepin County Sheriff Otto Langum, was better equipped than ever to block the advance of trade unionism. Under the attorney generalship of A. Mitchell Palmer, who joined the Wilson cabinet in March 1919, the U.S. Department of Justice was pursuing radicalism with new zeal. In southern Minnesota a small corps of county attorneys was successfully prosecuting Townley and Joseph Gilbert on charges of conspiracy to discourage enlistments in the armed forces, and the St. Louis county attorney was utilizing the 1917 syndicalism law to break the back of Finnish radicalism. [11]

The reputation of the Burnquist administration suffered a decline following the armistice, however, and many Minnesotans made it clear that they detested the safety commission. Although Burnquist's reelection was hailed by his supporters as a triumph for Americanism, the size and distribution of the NPL-labor vote suggested that a new political coalition had profoundly altered partisan alignments in Minnesota. The NPL legislative campaign also fell short of gaining control of either house, but several candidates endorsed by the league defeated entrenched conservatives. A few of these new legislators would later achieve prominence within the Farmer-Labor party, notably, Henry Arens of Jordan, Michael Boylan of Virginia, and Herman Schmechel of Fairfax.

So far as impressions of the safety commission were concerned, McGee was a large part of the problem. The perception that he had unfairly attacked the loyalty of German and Swedish Americans before the Senate military affairs committee in April 1918 was not soon forgotten nor easily forgiven, and his performance as state fuel administrator did not command universal admiration. Unfortunately for the reputation of the MCPS, in the minds of many McGee epitomized the commission. Such an impression may have done a grave injustice to March, Weiss, and Cashman, but, given McGee's image as the commission's dominant personality, it was inevitable.

The Burnquist fortunes continued their downward slide through 1919. Observers who had hailed the advanced progressivism of the

1917 inaugural were deeply disappointed by its 1919 counterpart, a message focusing on the urgent need to combat "Bolshevism" and socialism. [12] Meanwhile, NPL and labor activists were maintaining a high level of organizational activity, a reality nourishing Republican fears that the next Nonpartisan League effort to capture the GOP might succeed.

The death of Congressman Carl C. Van Dyke in May created an opportunity to test the political waters in mid-1919. The Republican nominating convention was enlivened by the candidacy of Oscar E. Keller, a staunch friend of organized labor. After losing to Carl W. Cummins, a St. Paul attorney, Keller launched an independent campaign on a platform calling for government ownership of transportation and communication systems, the right of labor to organize, old age pensions, and government-backed health insurance. On July 1 he won a substantial victory, polling 11,958 to 8,691 for Cummins and 6,245 for Richard D. O'Brien, the Democratic candidate. [13]

If Keller's coup reinforced GOP pessimism, intraparty acrimony on the issue of iron-ore taxation was calculated to induce panic. Over the years a growing number of people had become convinced that the mining companies were not carrying their fair share of the state's tax burden. Iron ore was an irreplaceable resource, the removal of which warranted compensation to the state over and above the regular taxes paid by the mining companies. In 1919 the clamor for a tonnage tax grew louder than ever, and the legislature rejected several tonnage tax bills by a narrow margin. Predictably, however, the issue would be resurrected at the first opportunity. [14]

Such an opportunity presented itself during a special legislative session that was called in late summer of 1919 to consider the Nineteenth Amendment, which gave women the right to vote. The amendment was easily ratified, but contrary to Burnquist's wishes the legislators also took up the mining tax issue and by impressive margins passed a tonnage tax. Burnquist vetoed the measure and blocked legislative recourse to an override by submitting his message after the special session adjourned. Public reaction was overwhelmingly negative. The *Minneapolis Journal,* hitherto a staunch defender of Burnquist, characterized the veto as a "mistake in judgment," given the powerful demand for a tonnage tax and the resentment generated by the impossibility of attempting an override. [15]

The erosion of Burnquist's base of support encouraged a proliferation of gubernatorial candidacies. Initially Gunnar Björnson professed not to be impressed. "The crop of candidates for governor . . . is going to be a bumper one," he wrote in January 1920:

> They grow like weeds and thrive like sow-thistle. . . .
>
> And they seem to substantially agree on one thing and that is that they all want to see the Nonpartisan League laid out cold. . . .
>
> But there is one thing that all these candidates have forgotten to come out for, in spite of all their loyalty and all their patriotism.
>
> Not a single one of them has come out against the practice of lynching Minnesota citizens. . . .
>
> Not many, if any, citizens . . . have been killed outright by mob violence, but very many have been lynched in one way or another.
>
> Men have been whipped, pounded, driven out and their property despoiled by mobs.
>
> Meetings have been stopped and speakers silenced without any warrant of law.
>
> The principle of free speech has had a hard time being heard in this state during the last two or three years.
>
> Here is an issue for a big man to go before the people on.[16]

Björnson's hope that issues relating to freedom of speech and assembly would emerge as factors in the forthcoming campaign for governor materialized. Henrik Shipstead, the Glenwood dentist who filed for the Republican gubernatorial nomination after receiving NPL and labor endorsements in March, adopted "government by law" as one of his major campaign themes. Speaking at Glencoe on May 19, Shipstead attacked the MCPS for its "lawless" ways. He recalled a confrontation between himself and an unidentified county safety commissioner who had supported the banning of a Nonpartisan League rally in the community. After securing an admission from the commissioner that free speech and assembly enjoyed constitutional protection, Shipstead asked, "Do you mean to come and tell me that a few men appointed by the governor of the State of Minnesota, can overturn the law and constitution?" At this point, according to Shipstead, the conversation proceeded as follows:

> Safety commissioner: Well, *admitting* that I was wrong [in banning meetings], I have *done* it; and don't you think that as a good loyal American citizen you ought to back me up?
>
> Shipstead: . . . You fellows have violated, have broken, the law: and I cannot back you up!
>
> Safety commissioner: Well, aren't you going to stand by the business men of this town?[17]

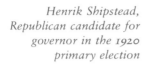

*Henrik Shipstead,
Republican candidate for
governor in the 1920
primary election*

Shipstead's candidacy generated considerable fear within the state Republican establishment. His ability to simplify complex issues without distorting their essence, his commanding presence on the stump, his record as a loyal supporter of the war effort, and his subordination of the "socialistic" planks in the NPL platform to the "government by law" theme exerted an appeal going beyond the NPL and labor constituencies that had endorsed him. Moreover, his challenge to the renomination of Andrew Volstead in the 1918 primary had given that veteran congressman the closest call of his long career. [18]

Another threat worrying the Republican establishment was the multitude of anti-NPL candidacies that surfaced in early 1920. With the certainty that league members would "stick" on primary election day, the possibility of a Shipstead victory (via a mere plurality) over a host of anti-NPL contenders was strong. To avoid such a debacle, state GOP leaders convened an "elimination convention" on May 8 for the purpose of achieving consensus on a gubernatorial candidate and drafting a platform. State Auditor Preus won the endorsement for governor, and the platform called for "a fair and equitable tonnage tax law on iron ore," a proposition strongly opposed by a vocal minority of the delegates. [19]

The Preus campaign avoided the excesses that had marred the Burnquist effort in 1918. To be sure, the candidate identified "Townleyism" as the "one big issue in this campaign" and as "a political cult that would take away from us our property and our homes"; but he did not choose to oppose this "cult" by excluding it from participation in the political process. Significantly, too, the Preus campaign largely ignored Shipstead's sharp attacks on the safety commission. The campaign also successfully courted the support of conservative Democrats. Years later, Preus commented that in 1920 "it would have been utterly impossible to defeat the Nonpartisan League if it hadn't been for the Democrats who left their party and went into the Republican party to vote the Republican ticket." In this connection Preus selected Thomas O'Brien and Pierce Butler for honorable mention. [20]

In the June 21 primary, Preus prevailed over Shipstead by a margin of fewer than 8,000 votes out of more than 320,000 cast in the GOP column. Attorney General Hilton was renominated by an even narrower margin, polling 118,932 votes to 117,799 for Thomas V. Sullivan, the NPL-endorsed candidate. Shipstead carried fifty-four of the state's eighty-six counties, an impressive advance over the thirty carried by Lindbergh in 1918 but not enough to overcome the Preus advantage in the remaining thirty-two. [21]

The NPL leadership decided to contest the final election by filing an independent ticket by petition, a move endorsed in July by a hastily called convention. Again Shipstead was chosen to run for governor, and the other candidates on the defeated NPL ticket were urged to file for the offices they originally had contested. Although the odds were heavily weighted against the election of independent tickets nominated by petition, the Preus managers did not take the election of their candidate for granted. Shipstead was popular, the times were volatile, and the Minnesota electorate was an unpredictable flock whose political behavior often departed from conventional norms. [22]

The Preus people laid particular stress in the fall campaign on a few issues calculated to win the votes of marginal NPL supporters. Hoping to weaken Shipstead's strong hold on the rural vote, "leading anti-League Republicans . . . suddenly became ardent proponents of cooperative marketing enterprises," wrote Morlan. Agricultural discontent, Preus acknowledged, was rooted in the disparity between what a farmer received for his commodities and the price he had to pay for consumer goods. The fifty-dollar suit in which Preus was attired had been fabricated from five dollars worth of wool.

According to Preus, two responses to the disparity problem were being articulated in the current state campaign. The Nonpartisan League approach was government ownership — a solution deserving rejection because it was "socialistic." The Republican answer was legislation designed to strengthen the position of agricultural cooperatives in the marketplace. Preus also enthusiastically embraced the tonnage tax proposal in the Republican platform, a measure that he pledged would command high priority in his program. [23]

Although Preus's warm endorsement of agricultural cooperatives and the tonnage tax helped to garner votes, Warren G. Harding's long coattails may have helped more: in the presidential race Harding carried every county in Minnesota over Democrat James M. Cox. In the contest for governor Preus defeated Shipstead by a plurality of 134,423 votes, which was considerably larger than many political pundits had anticipated. A second NPL bid for power had been foiled, but the league's substantial constituency remained a force to be reckoned with in state politics. [24]

On the day Preus was elected governor — November 2, 1920 — the safety commission was still vegetating in the state of "in[n]ocuous desuetude" into which it had fallen in early 1919. Following its close brush with death at the hands of the legislature in April 1919, it assembled twice: on May 13, 1919, and on December 15, 1920, when the commissioners finally closed up shop.

Both sessions focused on liquidation rather than fresh initiatives. At their May 13 meeting the commissioners accepted an allotment of surplus motor trucks from the war department, turning them over to Highway Commissioner Charles M. Babcock for allocation among the counties. They also authorized the payment of bills, including one submitted by the Northern Information Bureau, the employers' espionage agency. In the months that followed, Libby was the sole official on watch at MCPS headquarters; Tighe had been eliminated from the payroll on January 1, 1919, and the dismantling of the commission's publicity apparatus terminated Henke and Grevstad. [25]

Libby handled correspondence and became preoccupied with the work of the Minnesota War Records Commission, an agency created "to provide for the collection and preservation . . . of all available material relating to Minnesota's participation in the world war." Initiated by the MCPS in October 1918, the commission was awarded permanent status by the legislature the following spring. As a first step in activating the commission, Burnquist appointed Solon J. Buck, superintendent of the Minnesota Historical Society, as chairman, and Franklin F. Holbrook as director. Other commission members included Gideon S. Ives, former lieutenant governor and president of the Minnesota Historical Society; Lester B. Shippee and Willis M. West of the University of Minnesota history department; John D. Hicks, then a member of the Hamline University history faculty; Herschel V. Jones of the *Minneapolis Journal;* Adjutant General Rhinow; and Gustaf Lindquist, Burnquist's secretary. Several of these appointees served only briefly. Shippee, West, and Hicks are not listed in the commission's 1921 roster, but contact with the academic community was maintained by the appointment of Guy S. Ford, a well-known historian and dean of the University of Minnesota graduate school. Libby served on the War Records Commission until completion of its mission in 1927.[26]

At their December 15 meeting the safety commissioners instructed Libby to assemble all MCPS records for transfer to the War Records Commission; voted a repeal of the orders establishing the Home Guard and providing for the appointment of peace officers; and transferred funds in the MCPS account to appropriate state agencies. Libby was continued on salary until April 1, 1921, by which time the commission's business was to be completed. Near the close of the session, Burnquist remarked that this probably was the last meeting of the MCPS — a probability that the commissioners apparently accepted without complaint, and one that materialized.[27]

The official *Report of Minnesota Commission of Public Safety,* issued in 1919, did not underestimate the importance of the commission's role in the war effort. In early 1919, according to the report, it was difficult "to realize the indifference, pacifist sentiment and even opposition to the war which prevailed in some parts of Minnesota" two years earlier. The country was now celebrating a glorious victory attributable in part to the patriotic efforts of the people of Minnesota, and the commission modestly accepted a share of the credit for this miraculous transition. Its approach to the loyalty program had been two-pronged, a judicious mix of persuasion and coercion. In dealing with persons whose support of the war was lukewarm or marginal, it had undertaken "to kindle the back fires of patriotism" by promoting intensive educational campaigns. "With the leaders [of suspect causes] it [had] used the mailed fist."[28]

The commission had also initiated a myriad of creative activities, among them promotion of food production and conservation; eradication of the common barberry bush, the nemesis of wheat and other cereals; farm labor and crop censuses; recruitment of labor for farm and factory; measures for the welfare of men in the military services and their families; emergency relief for the victims of disaster; Americanization programs; and regulation of the liquor trade.[29]

A few of these claims are both credible and commendable. These would include MCPS assistance to Minnesota servicemen and the emergency relief provided the victims of such disasters as the Tyler tornado and the Cloquet–Moose Lake fires. Setting up the machinery that permitted military personnel stationed outside of Minnesota to vote in the 1918 primary (Order 31) and general elections (Order 46) was a positive action. So were the orders designed to minimize the threat of forest fires. Finally, from the standpoint of fiscal restraint, the commission's performance was astounding. On December 31, 1918, the million dollar appropriation awarded by the 1917 legislature retained a balance of $241,251.21, and of the approximately $767,000 spent, more than $488,000 had been allocated to "Soldiers' Pay and Sustenance." In other words, the princely sum of $278,495.01 financed the entire MCPS enterprise through the end of 1918.

This modest level of expenditure raises an interesting question: How could so much be accomplished with so few dollars? True, the commissioners served without pay, but Tighe, Pardee, Henke, Libby (in his capacity as secretary), the short-term intelligence operatives, and the secretaries were all on the payroll. Part of the answer would seem to be that the commissioners were accomplished "piggybackers." The only expense incurred in commissioning agents affiliated with the Minnesota branch of the American Protective League as peace officers was the price of a badge for each agent. Undoubtedly this adoption enhanced APL clout, but it is not clear that it clothed the MCPS with supervisory authority over league operatives.

To credit the safety commissioners with a few virtuous deeds is not to imply that they were innocent of serious mischief. Waging covert war on the national administration's labor policy while pretending that state policy was essentially in line with that of the National War Labor Board could be called brazen hypocrisy. Placing the commission's publicity apparatus at the disposal of Burnquist's 1918 reelection campaign was by itself a serious ethical breach, but seeking to exclude the Nonpartisan League from the state's political process while tacitly acknowledging NPL legitimacy by declining to institute legal action against the organization was much worse. In fairness, the commissioners could not be charged with direct responsibility for every vigilante action perpetrated within the state; their benign toleration of these atrocities, however, prompted Gunnar Björnson to wonder if "the mob was a new form of law and order enforcement."[30] The harassment of alleged idlers and bond slackers as authorized by Orders 37 and 44 was equally indefensible.

Notwithstanding its quiet demise following a prolonged period of inactivity, the Minnesota Commission of Public Safety remains firmly embedded in Minnesota's historical memory. In the postwar years, responsibility for most of the excesses of the 1917–18 loyalty crusade was laid at its doorstep; as public reaction against American involvement in the Great War escalated, the image of the commission as a ruthless dictatorship perpetrating a reign of terror gained wider credibility.

Much of this opprobrium was deserved, but not all. That the climate of the war years would have fostered chauvinistic excess without the safety commission is a safe conjecture. Moreover, the commission was too underfunded and inefficient to accomplish all the "evil" attributed to it. Nor was it able to transform the potential for dictatorship inherent in the MCPS statute into reality. With the resources at its disposal the commission could intimidate putative enemies of the established order and of the American war effort (the distinction between the two was usually hopelessly blurred), but it lacked the capacity to assume dictatorial control of the state's governmental processes. Similarly, it could flood the state with inflammatory propaganda, but it was unable to prevent dissemination of comment critical of the MCPS operation in the columns of NPL and labor papers. The commission had the power to intimidate journalists proportionate to journalism's amenability to intimidation, but press censorship was a federal prerogative.

During the summer of 1917, a cooperative relationship between the MCPS and the federal mobilization effort appeared to be evolving. By December, three more or less related developments contributed to an abrupt reversal of this trend. First of all, the MCPS resolutely refused to accept federal mediation in the Twin Cities railway strike. Second, the national administration negotiated a truce with Townley shortly after the MCPS had launched a campaign designed to exclude the Nonpartisan League from the state's political process. Third, the Lind and Ames tenure on the commission ended, Lind's by resignation and Ames's by dismissal. Given Lind's standing with the national administration, his departure seriously compromised the prospect of maintaining a cooperative federal-state relationship.

Throughout 1918 the commission concentrated mainly on reelecting Burnquist, monitoring the liquor trade, intimidating idlers, coercing bond slackers, and shaming aliens who had delayed naturalization. At the same time it maintained a pretense of loyal cooperation with federal authorities. In this case, however, a wide gap separated pretense and reality. The stalemate on labor policy continued; the MCPS doggedly resisted pressures from the Council of National Defense to reorganize itself into a more representative body; and there was no meeting of minds between federal officialdom and the MCPS on the question of NPL loyalty. Under these circumstances, federal mobilization in Minnesota increasingly bypassed the MCPS in favor of direct links with state and local agencies not under MCPS supervision.

Following the decline of the MCPS as a functioning agency in early 1919, supporters of the commission undoubtedly hoped that memories of its wartime role would fade. This, of course, was a vain hope; too many groups within the state nourished real and fancied grievances against the commission. Moreover, the brief but tragic career of John F. McGee on the federal bench, preceded by a protracted confirmation battle, perpetuated awareness of the safety commission and, more particularly, of McGee's role in the loyalty crusade.

Early in the Harding administration, Congress received a proposal to expand the federal judiciary at the district court level. Almost immediately McGee became a candidate for the additional judgeship that would be awarded to Minnesota. Realizing that a McGee candidacy would be controversial, Senator Nelson, McGee's chief sponsor, mounted a campaign to assure its consummation before the opposition could coalesce. The key to Nelson's strategy was to persuade his Minnesota colleague, Senator Kellogg, to join him in recommending McGee to President Harding. Under the long-standing tradition of "senatorial courtesy," a president was bound by recommendations of senators of his own party when appointing federal judges whose jurisdictions were located in the senators' states. [31]

Acting on this strategy, the McGee camp persuaded a prestigious group of individuals, including Burnquist, Edward E. Smith, the editors of the *Minneapolis Journal* and *Minneapolis Tribune,* and several Citizens Alliance leaders, to exert pressure on Kellogg to join the McGee cause. Nelson also hoped that undue publicity regarding McGee's candidacy could be avoided until Kellogg was committed. [32]

Unhappily for McGee, the Nelson strategy soon unraveled. A judicial expansion bill passed the Senate in June 1921 but encountered repeated delays in the House of Representatives — delays that stalled final enactment until mid-September 1922. In part the stalemate was due to disagreement concerning details, but Nelson believed that other motives were paramount. "Volstead," he confided to McGee on June 13, 1922, "is obstructing and holding back as much as he can." Congressman Andrew Volstead, who was chairman of the House Judiciary Committee and as such a key manager of the congressional calendar, was facing a tough reelection campaign that would not be assisted by identification with McGee. [33]

Kellogg, too, remained uncommitted. Like Volstead he was seeking reelection. Moreover, the junior senator was being deluged with recommendations on behalf of other candidates. In response to these pressures, Kellogg remained (as Nelson put it) "entirely noncommittal and noncommunicative." Nelson also suspected that his colleague had been "instrumental in trotting out [Charles] Loring," a future associate justice of the Minnesota Supreme Court, as an aspirant for the prospective post. [34]

While House action on the judgeship bill was going nowhere, several candidacies emerged for the post that would be created by enactment of the bill. At first advocates of these candidacies focused on their aspirants' virtues, omitting any mention of McGee. As rumors of Nelson's sponsorship of McGee gained credibility, supporters of the other contenders occasionally alluded to the former safety commissioner's shortcomings. A St. Paul attorney professed respect for McGee "as a lawyer" but doubted his temperamental fitness for a federal judgeship. [35]

By the spring of 1922, the controversy surrounding McGee's bid for the projected federal judgeship had become an excursion into the history of the safety commission. On April 9, the executive council of the Minnesota Federation of Labor adopted a resolution strongly opposing the proposed appointment on the basis of McGee's MCPS record. On April 12 the Minneapolis Trades and Labor Assembly passed an even stronger resolution, including quotes of the more damaging excerpts from McGee's testimony before the Senate military affairs committee four years earlier. Nelson scornfully dismissed both protests. In his words, the leaders of the two bodies were "evidently of Bolshevik leanings."[36]

A communication from Edward J. Lee, a Minneapolis attorney and longtime Nelson supporter, should have been more sobering. Lee warned the senator on April 15:

> I do not think you really know how unpopular Judge McGee is in Minnesota. His unpopularity is particularly accentuated in . . . Saint Paul and Minneapolis. . . . [A]t the Odin Club [a luncheon club open by election to Minneapolis Scandinavian-American professional men] . . . the possible appointment of Judge McGee is being very severely criticized. . . .
>
> [McGee] last basked in the limelight of publicity by reason of his appointments under Governor Burnquist. Today . . . Burnquist is almost forgotten politically in Minnesota and one of the things that brought about that . . . was his unfortunate appointment of Judge McGee.

A month later a poll of the members of the Hennepin County Bar Association confirmed Lee's analysis. Of the 299 votes cast, McGee received only 48. McGee refused to be impressed. The Hennepin association, he explained to Nelson, was not a representative body but one commanding the allegiance of the "Bolshevik" faction of the Hennepin County bar.[37]

Managers of the 1922 Republican state campaign obviously were more impressed than McGee by evidence that his candidacy was in trouble. In the summer the drive to secure the appointment appeared to lose some of its thrust. Under heavy attack by Henrik Shipstead, his Farmer-Labor opponent, and Democratic candidate Anna Dickie Olesen, Kellogg decided to defer action on the appointment until after the election. Meanwhile, domestic bereavement along with the infirmities of old age slowed Nelson's pace. On August 8 his wife of fifty-five years, Nicholina Jacobson Nelson, died following a long illness. McGee served as an honorary pallbearer at her funeral, an

Farmer-Labor candidate card in 1922, the first year in which the Farmer-Labor bloc entered its own ticket in the general election

indication of the intimate personal relationship between the senator and McGee.[38]

The November election produced a near disaster for the Minnesota Republican party. Shipstead decisively defeated Kellogg in the senate race, and Preus won reelection to the governorship by a scant plurality of 14,277 votes over Magnus Johnson, the Farmer-Labor contender. Two of the state's Republican congressmen, Andrew Volstead and Halvor Steenerson, suffered defeat at the hands of their Farmer-Labor challengers. The Farmer-Labor bloc in the state legislature also increased its representation by ten members.[39]

Although this outcome was by no means a mandate for McGee's elevation to the federal bench, it opened the way for McGee's appointment and confirmation during the short congressional session that assembled in early December and automatically expired on March 4, 1923. The judicial expansion bill was already law, and as a lame-duck senator Kellogg was not in a position to counteract his colleague's influence with the administration even if he had wished to do so.

With Harding's nomination of McGee in place, the Senate, meeting in executive (secret) session, took up the confirmation question a few days before its mandatory adjournment. Information provided by observers presumably familiar with the proceedings indicated that the debate was extremely acrimonious. According to the *St. Paul Daily News,* Republican progressives waged a "bitter fight" against McGee. Nonpartisan League legislators in St. Paul also took notice. In early March Andrew Devold and others introduced a joint resolution strongly protesting the McGee appointment, but the measure did not come to a vote before the U.S. Senate resolved the issue. [40]

On March 2 the Senate by unanimous consent resolved to remove "the injunction of secrecy . . . from certain votes and proceedings" relating to the confirmation issue, a move opening the way for a final vote. Forty-six senators voted for confirmation, eleven voted nay, and the remaining thirty-nine were not recorded. Kellogg voted aye, but Nelson, who was incapacitated by serious illness, was recorded in the not voting category. Obviously the senior senator's absence in the final hours of deliberation did not detract from the credit due him for the outcome. "Under the circumstances," Smith wrote Nelson, "this was a particularly good piece of work and is a high compliment to your standing with the Administration and with the Senate." [41]

Of the eleven anti-McGee senators, six were Republicans and five were Democrats. The six Republicans (Smith W. Brookhart of Iowa, Arthur Capper of Kansas, Hiram W. Johnson of California, La Follette of Wisconsin, Peter Norbeck of South Dakota, and George W. Norris of Nebraska) were all members of the Senate's progressive Republican bloc, a group that through the 1920s subjected the Harding-Coolidge policies to withering criticism.

Although McGee's confirmation produced considerable satisfaction within his camp, some of his backers feared that he might lash out at his critics. Nelson cautioned him to act prudently and to avoid calling attention to what was brought out against him in the executive session. Kellogg also warned him to refrain from public criticism of those who had opposed confirmation. Such advice, McGee informed Nelson, was wholly unnecessary. He, McGee, understood the rules of proper judicial behavior. [42]

Tragically from a human standpoint, the fulfillment that McGee expected to achieve on the bench proved to be elusive. On February 15, 1925, less than two years after his appointment, he took his own life. A lengthy handwritten suicide note indicated that for some time McGee had suffered a high state of agitation. An overwhelmingly heavy workload had induced stress that inhibited sleep and rendered him unable to focus his mind on the complex issues posed by the cases on his calendar. His physicians had warned him that he faced complete physical and mental collapse unless he reduced his rigorous work schedule. Unable to accept either option, McGee chose self-destruction. "I wonder if it is worth while to lead the strenuous life I have led, particularly since 1917 in April?" he queried. A general lack of appreciation of the immense sacrifices he had endured in the service of his country had strengthened a growing conviction that life was not worth living. [43]

A statement issued by one of his physicians shortly after the tragedy validated suspicions raised by McGee's farewell note. According to the physician, McGee had indeed suffered stress and anguish beyond the point of human endurance. His suicide was attributable to "a temporary form of insanity in which he was absolutely irresponsible for what he did." [44]

Like McGee's struggle to establish a career on the federal bench, Burnquist's quest for further elective office pointed up the disadvantages inherent in association with the MCPS. When Burnquist surrendered the governorship to Preus in January 1921 at the age of forty-one, retirement from electoral politics was not on his personal agenda, but the road to a comeback was exceedingly rough. In the 1920s he made repeated attempts to win the Republican nomination for one office or another — for the U.S. Senate in the special election of 1923 called to fill the vacancy created by the death of Knute Nelson, for the same post in 1928, and for the governorship in 1930 — and each time voters in the Republican primary decisively rejected him. Not until 1938 — a year of strong voter reaction against farmer-laborism — was Burnquist able to win a statewide election, this time as attorney general. Fortunately for his place in history, his sixteen-year tenure in that office was considerably less stormy than his last two terms as governor. Accolades rather than brickbats accompanied his final retirement from public life in 1955. [45]

In the years of Burnquist's exile, the safety commission as the institutional embodiment of the hated loyalty crusade was a symbol cherished by the Nonpartisan League and its successor, the Minnesota Farmer-Labor party. It was, in fact, a symbol of considerable importance in sustaining Farmer-Labor cohesion. At its base the Farmer-Labor party was an uneasy coalition of trade unionists, radical farmers, and disaffected ethnics, the solidarity of which was under continuing threat by divergence of opinion on fundamental issues both within and among the three groups. The interests of agriculture and organized labor frequently collided, and the party's ethnic component included voters whose suspicion of Farmer-Labor radicalism was easily aroused. Shared memories of safety commission "oppression" constituted one of the most important factors counteracting the centrifugal forces threatening party unity.

Although the Farmer-Labor party failed to win the governorship in the 1920s, it managed to elect two U.S. senators along with three congressmen and to achieve the status of Minnesota's second party, a feat attributable in part to successful exploitation of the safety commission symbol. In the late 1920s, however, Farmer-Labor fortunes fell into a temporary slump, a trend coinciding with a slight decline in the potency of issues linked to the loyalty crusade. The coming of the Great Depression, coupled with the leadership of Floyd B. Olson, sparked a Farmer-Labor revival extending from Olson's first election to the governorship in 1930 until Elmer A. Benson's decisive defeat for that office in 1938. In office Olson and Benson assigned highest priority to depression-related issues, but Olson's campaigns reminded voters that Raymond P. Chase, the 1930 Republican gubernatorial candidate, and Earle Brown, Olson's 1932 GOP adversary, had been conspicuously identified with the wartime loyalty crusade. Chase was manager of the Red-baiting campaign against Shipstead in 1920, and Brown served as an official of the American Protective League in 1918. [46]

In the late 1930s the utility of the safety commission symbol as a Farmer-Labor issue declined precipitously. By then, conservative Minnesota Republicans appeared more committed to an antiwar stance than did a Farmer-Labor party whose left wing was linked to the Soviet-sponsored popular front (a Communist-Socialist-liberal coalition). Before the Hitler-Stalin pact of August 1939, this front called for active resistance to Nazi expansion by force of arms if necessary. [47] This program attracted only limited support in Minnesota, where memories of World War I reinforced opposition to involvement

Laying the cornerstone for Deutsches Haus, Rice and Aurora streets, St. Paul, 1920. This German-American cultural center, which was renamed German House in 1935 and American House in 1942, stood at the site until 1960.

in the impending European war at almost any cost. Unfortunately, perhaps, this stance also inhibited recognition of nazism's demonic potentialities. In any case, from Pearl Harbor through vj day the determination to avoid another loyalty crusade held. World War II propaganda in Minnesota as elsewhere depicted German culture as morally flawed, but politicians and the press scrupulously avoided questioning the patriotism of the state's large German-American community.

Along with a determination not to repeat the stupidities of the World War I loyalty crusade, other factors contributed to a more harmonious home front in World War II than in the earlier conflict. By the 1940s labor-management relations had achieved a stability totally lacking in 1917–18. So had the relationship between the grain trade and the farmers' movement. And the support that World War II commanded both from the political Left and Right minimized the danger of linkage between one ideology or the other and patriotism or the lack of it. [48]

Beginning in the 1940s, custody of the MCPS legacy passed from politicians to historians and biographers. Historians of the Nonpartisan League, among others, devoted considerable space to commission activities, as did the biographers of Charles Lindbergh, Floyd Olson, and Hjalmar Petersen. The rising interest in ethnic history in the late 1960s and through the 1970s encouraged further investigation of MCPS history. June Drenning Holmquist, editor of the comprehensive history of the state's ethnic groups published in 1981, characterized the commission's loyalty campaign as a "blatant Minnesota example of legalized discrimination." This statement more or less defines the consensus developed by historians and others who have evaluated the role of the safety commission during the Great War. Historian Steven J. Keillor, for example, wrote that the commission was "martial law in bureaucratic form."[49]

Thus, decades after the Minnesota Commission of Public Safety passed from the scene, unmourned and unloved, it continued to fill a unique niche in the historical consciousness of informed Minnesotans. Perhaps the most important impact of the commission's zealous ways was to sensitize the state's political culture to the dangers inherent in liberating government from the constitutional restraints limiting the exercise of power. Even Ambrose Tighe developed serious misgivings about the performance of the agency he had helped to create: "The ruthlessness of the Commission's procedure," he confided to John Lind, "shows if further evidence was required, how dangerous it is to vest even good men with arbitrary power."[50] This judgment admirably identifies the unintended legacy bequeathed by the commission to the people of Minnesota.

Notes

PREFACE

1. Minnesota Secretary of State, *Session Laws,* 1917, chap. 261, p. 374.
2. Apr. 4, 1917, p. 16.
3. Quoted in the *Star Tribune* (Minneapolis), July 27, 1990, p. 4A.

CHAPTER 1. *The Setting*

1. Walter Lord, *The Good Years: From 1900 to the First World War* (New York: Harper and Brothers, 1960), ix.
2. See esp. Arthur S. Link, "What Happened to the Progressive Movement in the 1920's?" *American Historical Review* 64 (July 1959): 833–51.
3. Arthur S. Link, *Woodrow Wilson and the Progressive Era, 1910–1917* (New York: Harper and Brothers, 1954), 66–80.
4. Here and below, Link, *Woodrow Wilson,* 223–51. The 1916 campaign is discussed at greater length in Link, *Wilson: Campaigns for Progressivism and Peace, 1916–1917* (Princeton, N.J.: Princeton University Press, 1965).
5. For an analysis of the politics of the 1890s, see Carl H. Chrislock, "A Cycle in the History of Minnesota Republicanism," *Minnesota History* 39 (Fall 1964): 93–110.
6. Here and below, Carl H. Chrislock, *The Progressive Era in Minnesota: 1899–1918* (St. Paul: Minnesota Historical Society, 1971), 15–17, 26–28.
7. Surveys of Minnesota political history from 1900 to 1915 include Chrislock, *Progressive Era,* 1–88; William Watts Folwell, *A History of Minnesota,* rev. ed. (St. Paul: Minnesota Historical Society, 1969), 3:241–94; Winifred G. Helmes, *John A. Johnson: The People's Governor* (Minneapolis: University of Minnesota Press, 1949); and George M. Stephenson, *John Lind of Minnesota* (Minneapolis: University of Minnesota Press, 1935).
8. Here and below, Helmes, *John A. Johnson,* 177–84, 212–13. For an interpretation of the stance of business elites on progressivism — an interpretation stressing progressive reform as an instrument for achieving stability, predictability, and order — see Robert H. Wiebe, *Businessmen and Reform: A Study of the Progressive Movement* (Cambridge, Mass.: Harvard University Press, 1962).
9. Chrislock, *Progressive Era,* 14–17.
10. Here and below, Helmes, *John A. Johnson,* 211–13.
11. Charles B. Cheney, *The Story of Minnesota Politics: High Lights of Half a Century of Political Reporting* (reprinted from the *Minneapolis Morning Tribune;* n.p., March 1947), 43.

12. Here and below, Henry F. Pringle, *The Life and Times of William Howard Taft* (New York: Farrar and Rinehart, 1939), 442–57.

13. Sept. 18, 1909, p. 6.

14. Roger E. Wyman, "Insurgency in Minnesota: The Defeat of James A. Tawney in 1910," *Minnesota History* 40 (Fall 1967): 317–29.

15. June 18, 1912, p. 16. For a detailed account of the campaign of 1912, see Chrislock, *Progressive Era,* 47–58.

16. Here and below, Bruce M. White et al., comps., *Minnesota Votes: Election Returns by County for Presidents, Senators, Congressmen, and Governors, 1857–1977* (St. Paul: Minnesota Historical Society, 1977), 18, 179–80.

17. Link, *Woodrow Wilson,* 22, 24.

18. *Minnesota Politics,* 42 (quotation); Charles R. Adrian, "The Origin of Minnesota's Nonpartisan Legislature," *Minnesota History* 33 (Winter 1952): 155–63.

19. For a brief survey of the state's woman suffrage movement, see Marjorie Bingham, "Keeping at It: Minnesota Women," in *Minnesota in a Century of Change: The State and Its People Since 1900,* ed. Clifford E. Clark, Jr. (St. Paul: Minnesota Historical Society Press, 1989), 441–42.

20. *Minnesota Politics,* 37. On the 1914 campaign, see Chrislock, *Progressive Era,* 61–65, 77–83.

21. Quoted in Chrislock, *Progressive Era,* 85.

22. For an account of the county option battle in the 1915 session, see Cheney, *Minnesota Politics,* 35–37.

23. *Minneapolis Journal,* Apr. 22, 1915, p. 14; *St. Paul Pioneer Press,* Apr. 23, 1915, p. 8.

24. For an excellent account of the struggle for control of the grain trade in the early twentieth century, see Theodore Saloutos and John D. Hicks, *Agricultural Discontent in the Middle West, 1900–1939* (Madison: University of Wisconsin Press, 1951).

25. Saloutos and Hicks, *Agricultural Discontent,* 135, 137; Chrislock, *Progressive Era,* 107–8; *Commercial West* (Minneapolis), Mar. 22, 1913, p. 7.

26. Robert L. Morlan, *Political Prairie Fire: The Nonpartisan League, 1915–1922* (Minneapolis: University of Minnesota Press, 1955; St. Paul: Minnesota Historical Society Press, Borealis Books, 1985), 49–50, 87–89.

27. Walter E. Quigley, "Out Where the West Begins," typed manuscript in the collection of the Minnesota Historical Society (MHS), 25; W. E. Verity to Frank B. Kellogg, Nov. 11, 1916, Frank B. Kellogg Papers, MHS.

28. On Van Lear, see David Paul Nord, "Minneapolis and the Pragmatic Socialism of Thomas Van Lear," *Minnesota History* 45 (Spring 1976): 2–10, and "Hothouse Socialism: Minneapolis, 1910–1925," in *Socialism in the Heartland: The Midwestern Experience, 1900–1925,* ed. Donald T. Critchlow (Notre Dame, Ind.: University of Notre Dame Press, 1986), 133–66.

29. On the 1907 strike, see Neil Betten, "Strike on the Mesabi — 1907," *Minnesota History* 40 (Fall 1967): 340–47; Hyman Berman, "Education for Work and Labor Solidarity: The Immigrant Miners and Radicalism on the Mesabi Range," typescript in MHS, 38–46.

30. John E. Haynes, "Revolt of the 'Timber Beasts': I.W.W. Lumber Strike in Minnesota," *Minnesota History* 42 (Spring 1971): 166.

31. Minnesota State Federation of Labor, *Proceedings of the Thirty-Third Convention* (N.p.: The Federation, 1915), 21.

32. Rayback, *A History of American Labor* (New York: Macmillan Company, 1966), 258 (quotations); Chrislock, *Progressive Era,* 117.

33. George H. Mayer, *The Political Career of Floyd B. Olson* (Minneapolis: University of Minnesota Press, 1951; St. Paul: Minnesota Historical Society Press, Borealis

Books, 1987), 184; here and below, "The Twin Cities," *Fortune,* April 1936, p. 193.

34. Kirk Jeffrey, "The Major Manufacturers: From Food and Forest Products to High Technology," in *Century of Change,* ed. Clark, 232–59.

35. *Brown County Journal* (New Ulm), Aug. 8, 1914, p. 4.

36. Translation in *Brown County Journal,* Sept. 12, 1914, p. 4.

37. Chrislock, *Progressive Era,* 70–71, 95–98.

38. Carl H. Chrislock, *Ethnicity Challenged: The Upper Midwest Norwegian-American Experience in World War I,* Norwegian-American Historical Association, Topical Studies, vol. 3 (Northfield, Minn., 1981), 29–55.

39. A tally of the birthplace of "Fathers of Persons Enumerated" in the 1905 state census is carried in Minnesota Secretary of State, *Legislative Manual, 1907,* 528–31. See also *They Chose Minnesota: A Survey of the State's Ethnic Groups,* ed. June Drenning Holmquist (St. Paul: Minnesota Historical Society Press, 1981), esp. 335–40, 381–88.

40. *Minneapolis Journal,* May 29, 1915, p. 4, June 8, 1916, p. 14.

41. Edward Goldbeck letter to the *Minneapolis Journal,* July 16, 1916, Editorial section, p. 2.

42. *Blue Earth County Enterprise* (Mapleton), Oct. 13, 1916, p. 4.

43. *Labor World* (Duluth), June 26, 1915, p. 4.

44. Stimson was quoted in the *Labor World* on Feb. 5, 1916. On organized labor's neutralist orientation, see also *Minnesota Union Advocate* (St. Paul), Jan. 7, p. 3, Apr. 28, p. 4, June 23, p. 4, July 28, p. 4, Sept. 1, p. 1 — all 1916; *New Times* (Minneapolis), July 23, 1915 (*New Times* was a Socialist weekly). See also L. Stinton, recording secretary of the Minneapolis Trades and Labor Assembly, to Knute Nelson, Aug. 26, 1915, Knute Nelson Papers, MHS.

45. *War and the Intellectuals: Essays by Randolph S. Bourne, 1915–1919,* ed. Carl Resek (New York: Harper and Row, 1964), 5.

46. Franklin F. Holbrook and Livia Appel, *Minnesota in the War with Germany* (St. Paul: Minnesota Historical Society, 1928), 1:26–27 (quotation on 27).

47. Oct. 23, 1915, p. 4.

48. Here and below, Chrislock, *Progressive Era,* 119–29.

CHAPTER 2. *A Promise Unfulfilled*

1. Jan. 2, 1917, p. 1.

2. *St. Paul Daily News,* Jan. 1, 1917, p. 7; Minnesota, *House Journal,* 1917, p. 7.

3. In mid-December a prominent supporter of Burnquist suggested that the governor's upcoming inaugural message include a short paragraph "paying some attention to the marketing . . . of farm products." According to the correspondent, "These fellows" — an obvious reference to Nonpartisan League organizers — were "making a great stir among the farmers" (W. F. Schilling to Burnquist, Dec. 16, 1916, Joseph A. A. Burnquist Papers, MHS). For the text of the address, see *St. Paul Daily News,* Jan. 3, 1917, p. 4, and Burnquist, *Inaugural Message of Gov. J. A. A. Burnquist to the Legislature of Minnesota, 1917* ([St. Paul, 1917]).

4. "A Political Letter Home" by "State Committeeman," *St. Paul Daily News,* Jan. 7, 1917, Sports section, p. 4.

5. The report was based on a dispatch from the German Overseas News agency.

6. *St. Paul Pioneer Press,* Jan. 7, sec. 1, p. 1, Jan. 9, p. 6 — both 1917; *St. Paul Daily News,* Feb. 16, 1917, p. 1.

7. Feb. 3, 1917, p. 7, 8.

8. *Minneota Mascot,* Oct. 19, 1917, p. 1.

9. *Prairie Rebel: The Public Life of William Lemke* (Lincoln: University of Nebraska Press, 1963), 57.

10. *House Journal,* 1917, p. 67. See also text of Equity leadership communication to the membership expressing satisfaction with committee appointments: *St. Paul Daily News,* Jan. 15, 1917, p. 5.

11. *House Journal,* 1917, p. 191–92.

12. *House Journal,* 1917, p. 276–77.

13. *St. Paul Daily News,* Apr. 1, 1917, p. 1–2.

14. *St. Paul Daily News,* Feb. 16, p. 5, Feb. 22, p. 4, Feb. 25, p. 3, Mar. 4, p. 5, Mar. 22, p. 4, Mar. 23, p. 21, Mar. 31, p. 3, Apr. 1, p. 1, Apr. 5, p. 8 — all 1917; *House Journal,* 1917, p. 1874–78. See also Carl J. Buell, *The Minnesota Legislature of 1917* ([St. Paul, 1917]), 90–91.

15. Minnesota Secretary of State, *Session Laws,* 1917, chap. 280, p. 418, chap. 284, p. 421, chap. 377, p. 535; *St. Paul Daily News,* Mar. 1, p. 5, Mar. 7, p. 5, Apr. 2, p. 5 — all 1917; *House Journal,* 1917, p. 618, 735, 978 (quotation), 1366; Minnesota, *Senate Journal,* 1917, p. 1263.

16. Neil Betten, "Riot, Revolution, Repression in the Iron Range Strike of 1916," *Minnesota History* 41 (Summer 1968): 82–94; Peter Rachleff, "Turning Points in the Labor Movement: Three Key Conflicts," in *Century of Change,* ed. Clark, 196–202.

17. *St. Paul Daily News,* Aug. 1, p. 1, July 27, p. 6 (quotation) — both 1916; *Labor World,* July 22, p. 1–2, Aug. 19, p. 1, Sept. 23, p. 6 — all 1916; *Union Labor Bulletin* (Minneapolis), September 1916, p. 9. The report was carried in full by the *Duluth News Tribune,* Aug. 17, 1916, p. 8.

18. For a full and outstanding account of the strike, see Haynes, "Revolt of 'Timber Beasts,' " 163–74.

19. Here and below, Haynes, "Revolt of 'Timber Beasts,'" 170–71 (quotations on both pages).

20. Here and below, Haynes, "Revolt of 'Timber Beasts,'" 171–74 (quotations on 171, 173).

21. *St. Paul Pioneer Press,* Jan. 7, 1917, sec. 2, p. 1.

22. *St. Paul Daily News,* Jan. 3, 1917, p. 4 (quotation); Chrislock, *Progressive Era,* 120–21.

23. *Senate Journal,* 1917, p. 62; *St. Paul Daily News,* Jan. 12, 1917, p. 14.

24. Here and below, *Senate Journal,* 1917, p. 89 (quotation), 123, 124, 134, 135, 136.

25. Buell, *Minnesota Legislature of 1917,* 82.

26. *House Journal,* 1917, p. 187–88, 215; Buell, *Minnesota Legislature of 1917,* 82, 83 (quotations on both pages); *St. Paul Daily News,* Jan. 28, 1917, p. 8.

27. Haynes, "Revolt of 'Timber Beasts,'" 165. A stenographic copy of the hearings, entitled "Labor Troubles in Northern Minnesota, January 30, 1917," is in the John Lind Papers, MHS.

28. Buell, *Minnesota Legislature of 1917,* 83.

29. Here and below, *Senate Journal,* 1917, p. 267, 325, 641. See also Buell, *Minnesota Legislature of 1917,* 18–20; he gives the text of the Duxbury bill on p. 20.

30. *House Journal,* 1917, p. 1458, 1796; Buell, *Minnesota Legislature of 1917,* 83–84 (quotation on 84).

31. Here and below, *House Journal,* 1917, p. 25, 649, 1311–13.

32. *Senate Journal,* 1917, p. 1070, 1174–75, 1626–27; Buell, *Minnesota Legislature of 1917,* 78–80. The text of the bill is given in *Session Laws,* 1917, chap. 493, p. 832–33.

33. *Minnesota Legislature of 1917,* 107. For a summary of the session, see the *St. Paul Daily News,* Apr. 19, 1917, p. 5.

CHAPTER 3. *A Package of Three Bills*

1. Here and below, Link, *Progressivism and Peace,* 290–308.

2. Link flatly stated: "There was in mid-February virtually no articulate popular desire for participation in the war" (*Progressivism and Peace,* 307).

3. *New Times,* Feb. 10, 1917, p. 1, 2.

4. *Minneapolis Tribune,* Feb. 6, 1917, p. 10; John S. McLain to Knute Nelson, Feb. 16, 1917, Nelson Papers; *New Times,* Feb. 17, 1917, p. 1; *Union Labor Bulletin,* February 1917, p. 4; Holbrook and Appel, *Minnesota,* 1:43–44 (quotation on 44).

5. Here and below, Holbrook and Appel, *Minnesota,* 1:38–39 (quotations), 43–44; Knute Nelson to President Wilson, Feb. 21, 1917, copy in Nelson Papers. Under Feb. 3, 1917, the Nelson Papers include a copy of the pledge required to qualify for membership in the Minneapolis Loyalty League. See also the *St. Paul Daily News,* Feb. 9, 1917, p. 4.

6. *St. Paul Daily News,* Feb. 12, 1917, p. 5; *Minneapolis Journal,* Feb. 11, 1917, sec. 1, p. 1, 3.

7. *St. Paul Daily News,* Mar. 4, 1917, p. 1.

8. Here and below, Link, *Progressivism and Peace,* 342–63 (quotations on 354, 362).

9. *St. Paul Daily News,* Mar. 4, p. 1, Mar. 11, p. 5 — both 1917.

10. Charles W. Farnham to Burnquist, Mar. 7, 1917, Burnquist to Farnham, Mar. 8, 1917, Farnham to Burnquist, Mar. 9, 12, 1917, Burnquist to Farnham, Mar. 13, 1917, Farnham to Burnquist, Mar. 19, 1917 — all in file 648a, Governor's Records, Minnesota State Archives, MHS.

11. Hall Alexander to *St. Paul Daily News,* Mar. 11, 1917, p. 6. Commenting editorially on the patriotic league, the *Daily News* observed that league members had "been, in their way, as intensely pro-Ally as some other of your citizens have been pro-German" (Mar. 15, 1917, p. 6).

12. *House Journal,* 1917, p. 326 (quotation), 1070, 1071; *Senate Journal,* 1917, p. 84, 277 (quotation), 1437.

13. Buell, *Minnesota Legislature of 1917,* 94; *Senate Journal,* 1917, p. 278. The bill passed the House on Mar. 22 by a unanimous vote: *House Journal,* 1917, p. 1071.

14. Link, *Progressivism and Peace,* 393–96, 408 (quotations on 396, 408). Of the impact of the Russian Revolution on Wilson, Link pointed out: "It must be said with some emphasis that there is no evidence that events in Petrograd had any direct influence on his later decision for war with Germany. The most that can be said is that the Russian Revolution might possibly have facilitated his final decision" (396).

15. *Minneapolis Journal,* Mar. 21, 1917, p. 10; *St. Paul Daily News,* Mar. 26, 1917, p. 5 (quotations).

16. Mar. 25, 1917, p. 6.

17. *St. Paul Daily News,* Mar. 24, p. 1, Mar. 27, p. 1, Apr. 1, p. 1 (quotation) — all 1917.

18. *New Ulm Review,* Apr. 4, Apr. 11, 1917.

19. Minnesota Commission of Public Safety (MCPS), *Report* ([St. Paul, 1919]), 31.

20. Five candidates competed for the fifth district Republican nomination in June 1918. Walter H. Newton won, polling 11,484 votes. Lundeen, who came in second, received 9,946 votes: *Legislative Manual,* 1919, p. 254.

21. *St. Paul Daily News,* Apr. 6, p. 13, Apr. 7, p. 1 (quotation) — both 1917.

22. Mrs. E. J. Hoxie to Burnquist, Apr. 3, 1917, file 648a, Governor's Records. The letter writer referred to the mass execution at Mankato of thirty-eight Dakota Indians involved in the war of 1862 (Kenneth Carley, *The Sioux Uprising of 1862* [St. Paul: Minnesota Historical Society, 1976], 68–75).

23. Mar. 3, 1917, p. 4.

24. Apr. 4, 1917, p. 1.

25. *St. Paul Daily News,* Mar. 29, p. 1, Apr. 4, p. 1, Apr. 12, p. 1 — all 1917.

26. Here and below, *Senate Journal,* 1917, p. 892, 1022–23; *Session Laws,* 1917, chap. 215, p. 311–12 (quotations).

27. *Senate Journal,* 1917, p. 889; *Minneapolis Journal,* Mar. 24, 1917, p. 2; *St. Paul Daily News,* Mar. 24, 1917, p. 2 (quotation). On Mar. 26 the *Minneapolis Journal* strongly endorsed the concept embodied in the bill. According to the *Journal,* the states were responsible for "handling . . . hostile aliens or disloyal citizens within their own borders." Minnesota had "many aliens . . . men who have not been here long enough to become naturalized and to imbibe a love for America stronger than their love for their native lands" (p. 12).

28. *Senate Journal,* 1917, p. 1036–37; *St. Paul Daily News,* Mar. 31, 1917, p. 1–2; *Minneapolis Journal,* Apr. 4, 1917, p. 16.

29. *St. Paul Daily News,* Apr. 3, 1917, p. 6.

30. *St. Paul Daily News,* Apr. 4, 1917, p. 1; *Minneapolis Tribune,* Apr. 4, 1917, p. 1.

31. *House Journal,* 1917, p. 1265, 1468–69.

32. *Minneapolis Tribune,* Apr. 6, 1917, p. 9; *St. Paul Daily News,* Apr. 5, 1917, p. 1, 5. The term *copperhead* was used in the Civil War to denote northerners who sympathized with the Confederacy; it was later applied generally to people suspected of disloyalty.

33. *House Journal,* 1917, p. 1469; *Minneapolis Tribune,* Apr. 6, 1917, p. 9 (quotation).

34. Charles W. Ames to Burnquist, Apr. 6, 1917, file 648a, Governor's Records.

35. *Minneapolis Journal,* Apr. 7, 1917, p. 1 (quotation); *St. Paul Daily News,* Apr. 7, 1917, p. 1.

36. *Senate Journal,* 1917, p. 1187–88; *House Journal,* 1917, p. 1488–89.

37. *Senate Journal,* 1917, p. 1192–96 (quotations on 1194–95); *St. Paul Daily News,* Apr. 10, 1917, p. 1. Units of the guard were called into duty for service at the border during General John J. Pershing's expedition into Mexico in pursuit of Francisco (Pancho) Villa. Holbrook and Appel, *Minnesota,* 1:29–31; Link, *Woodrow Wilson,* 136–44.

38. McGee to Nelson, Apr. 11, 1917, Nelson Papers.

39. *Senate Journal,* 1917, p. 1197–98; *Minneapolis Journal,* Apr. 10, 1917, p. 2 (quotations).

40. Newton D. Baker to Burnquist, Apr. 9, 1917, file 648a, Governor's Records; Robert H. Ferrell, *Woodrow Wilson and World War I* (New York: Harper and Row, 1985), 102–3. On Apr. 20, Burnquist informed Baker that the Minnesota Commission of Public Safety was in place.

41. Here and below, *House Journal,* 1917, p. 1614–16.

42. *St. Paul Daily News,* Apr. 13, 1917, p. 6 (quotations). According to *New Times,* Devold "left the House Chamber before the vote was taken" (Apr. 14, 1917, p. 1).

43. Here and below, *House Journal,* 1917, p. 1616–19.

44. *Senate Journal,* 1917, p. 1325–26, 1347, 1446, 1559.

45. *Senate Journal,* 1917, p. 1326 (quotation). According to C. A. French, editor of the *Monticello News,* Senator Sullivan questioned Burnquist's loyalty in a speech the next summer at an Anoka patriotic rally: French to Burnquist, Aug. 13, 1917, Burnquist Papers.

46. *Senate Journal,* 1917, p. 1426–29 (quotation on 1427); *House Journal,* 1917, p. 1709–12.

47. *Senate Journal,* 1917, p. 1428–29, 1446, 1504–5.

48. *St. Paul Daily News,* Apr. 14, 1917, p. 3.

49. *House Journal,* 1917, p. 1685–86.

50. *Senate Journal,* 1917, p. 1559; *Session Laws,* 1917, chap. 435, p. 651–52, chap. 463, p. 764–65.

51. Folwell, *Minnesota,* 3:556.

52. Here and below, *St. Paul Daily News,* Apr. 14, 1917, p. 1.

53. Apr. 10, 1917, p. 1.

54. Quoted in Charles Hirschfeld, "Nationalist Progressivism and World War I," *Mid-America* 45 (July 1963): 146-47.

55. John Washburn to Nelson, Sept. 1, 1916, George M. Gillette to Nelson, Sept. 7, 1916 — both in Nelson Papers.

56. Sept. 9, 1916, p. 7.

57. McGee to Nelson, Nov. 15, 1916, Nelson Papers.

CHAPTER 4. *The Original Commission*

1. *Minneapolis Journal,* Apr. 13, 1917, p. 2.

2. *Minneapolis Tribune,* Apr. 19, 1917, p. 1; *Minneapolis Journal,* Apr. 19, 1917, p. 1.

3. Here and below, *Minneapolis Tribune,* Apr. 20, 1917, p. 1.

4. *St. Paul Dispatch,* Apr. 18, p. 1, Apr. 19, p. 1 (quotation) — both 1917.

5. *St. Paul Dispatch,* Apr. 19, 1917, p. 8; *Minneapolis Journal,* Apr. 19, 1917, p. 1.

6. For biographical data on Burnquist, see Joseph A. A. Burnquist, ed., *Minnesota and Its People* (Chicago: S. J. Clarke Publishing Co., 1924), 3:540–43; Theodore Christianson, *Minnesota; The Land of Sky-Tinted Waters; A History of the State and Its People* (Chicago: American Historical Society, 1935), 2:355; *Who's Who in Minnesota,* comp. C. N. Cornwall (Minneapolis: Minnesota Editorial Association, 1941), 822–23. The front section of the 1955 *Legislative Manual* carries a sketch of Burnquist's career, which terminated with his retirement as attorney general in January 1955. This sketch stresses Burnquist's support of social justice measures and makes no reference to the safety commission.

7. *Legislative Manual,* 1919, p. 190, 620.

8. Lynn Haines, *The Minnesota Legislature of* 1911 (Minneapolis: N.p., 1911), 42–47.

9. This conclusion is based on Neill's relatively strong showing in counties where opposition to county option was strong (*Legislative Manual,* 1913, p. 342–43). Until 1972, candidates for governor and lieutenant governor in Minnesota ran on separate tickets (*Legislative Manual,* 1973–74, p. 450).

10. Here and below, Chrislock, *Progressive Era,* 51, 61–65, 77–81; *Legislative Manual,* 1913, p. 504–7.

11. R. I. Holcombe and William H. Bingham, *Compendium of History and Biography of Polk County, Minnesota* (Minneapolis: W. H. Bingham and Co., 1916), 169; *Legislative Manual,* 1915, p. 186–87.

12. *Legislative Manual,* 1915, p. 534–37; Chrislock, *Progressive Era,* 85–86.

13. *Brown County Journal,* Mar. 4, 1916, p. 2.

14. Edward MacGaffey, "A Pattern for Progress: The Minnesota Children's Code," *Minnesota History* 41 (Spring 1969): 229–36 (quotation on 229).

15. Berman, "Education for Work," 47–55; Betten, "Riot, Revolution, Repression," 88, 91, 94, and "Strike on the Mesabi," 346.

16. The full text of the Department of Labor report was carried in the *Labor World,* Aug. 19, 1916, p. 1. Proceedings of the 1916 MFL convention, held in Hibbing, were carried in *Union Labor Bulletin,* July 1916, p. 5–7, 14. See also *Labor World* front-page editorial, Aug. 12, 1916.

17. In advance of the election, one Republican activist predicted that "the Union Labor vote will be cast almost solidly against [Burnquist]." However, he won a stunning victory. See Chrislock, *Progressive Era,* 120–22 (quotation on 121).

18. For biographical data on Smith, see Henry A. Castle, *Minnesota: Its Story and Biography* (Chicago: Lewis Publishing Co., 1915), 3:1763–64. See also in memorium sketch by Clifford L. Hilton in front section of *Legislative Manual,* 1919.

19. Here and below, Stephenson, *John Lind,* 3–27, 42–43, 57–58, 66–68; White et al., comps., *Minnesota Votes,* 78.

20. Here and below, Stephenson, *John Lind,* 83–139, 140–90.

21. Here and below, Stephenson, *John Lind,* 191–205.

22. Here and below, Stephenson, *John Lind,* 205–9. Stephenson devotes five chapters to Lind's Mexican mission: p. 208–329.

23. Stephenson, *John Lind,* 330–32.

24. Stephenson, *John Lind,* 334; Tighe to Lind (citing a Lind statement from an earlier letter), Feb. 13, 1918, John Lind Papers, MHS.

25. Chrislock, *Ethnicity Challenged,* 63.

26. Telegram from McGee to Harry A. Garfield, Mar. 11, 1918, file 206, Main Files, Minnesota Commission of Public Safety Papers, Minnesota State Archives, MHS.

27. For biographical data on McGee, see Marion D. Shutter and J. S. McLain, eds., *Progressive Men of Minnesota* (Minneapolis: Minneapolis Journal, 1897), 500–501 (quotation on 500); Hiram F. Stevens, ed., *History of the Bench and Bar of Minnesota* (Minneapolis: Legal Publishing and Engraving Co., 1904), 1:154.

28. See, for example, McGee to Nelson, Mar. 7, 11, 29, 1916, Nelson Papers; McGee to Senator Moses E. Clapp, Feb. 14, 1916, copy in Jacob A. O. Preus Papers, MHS; McGee to Congressman George R. Smith, Mar. 1, 1916, copy in Nelson Papers. In all of these letters McGee stridently attacked supporters of the Gore-McLemore resolutions.

29. For biographical data on Charles Gordon Ames, father of the safety commissioner and of Alice Ames Winter, director of the MCPS Women's Auxiliary Committee, see Allen Johnson, ed., *Dictionary of American Biography* (New York: Charles Scribner's Sons, 1964), 1:241–42; Alice Ames Winter, ed., *Charles Gordon Ames: A Spiritual Autobiography* (Boston: Houghton Mifflin Co., 1913).

30. For biographical data on Charles W. Ames, see Burnquist, ed., *Minnesota and Its People,* 3:30–35; Christianson, *Minnesota,* 4:13–15; Castle, *Minnesota: Story and Biography,* 1:285, 2:975–76.

31. *St. Paul Pioneer Press,* Apr. 4, 1921, p. 1, 2.

32. For biographical data on March, see *Who's Who in Minnesota,* 345; *Minneapolis Star-Journal,* Aug. 28, 1945, p. 1; *St. Paul Dispatch,* Aug. 28, 1945, p. 11.

33. For biographical data on Weiss, see Burnquist, ed., *Minnesota,* 4:525–26; *Duluth Daily News-Tribune,* Nov. 28, 1938, p. 1, 4; *Duluth Herald,* Nov. 28, 1938, p. 1.

34. Stephenson, *John Lind,* 205–6; Arthur S. Link, *Wilson: The Road to the White House* (Princeton, N.J.: Princeton University Press, 1947), 445 n. 70.

35. For biographical data on Tighe, see Albert Nelson Marquis, ed., *The Book of Minnesotans* (Chicago: A. N. Marquis, 1907), 513–14; *St. Paul Pioneer Press,* Nov. 12, 1928, p. 7. The book written by Tighe was *The Development of the Roman Constitution* (New York: American Book Co., 1886).

36. *Legislative Manual,* 1913, p. 359.

37. Here and below, *Papers and Proceedings of the Sixth Annual Meeting of the Minnesota Academy of Social Sciences,* ed. Jeremiah S. Young ([Mankato]: Free Press Printing Co., 1913), 21–33 (quotations on 31, 33).

38. Burnquist to Qvale, Apr. 25, 1917, Burnquist Papers.

39. *Union Labor Bulletin,* June 1917, p. 4.

40. *Labor World,* May 12, p. 2, June 30, p. 4 — both 1917; Ferrell, *Woodrow Wilson,* 102–3.

41. Ambrose Tighe, "The Legal Theory of the Minnesota 'Safety Commission' Act," *Minnesota Law Review* 3 (December 1918): 13.

42. Ames to Burnquist, Jan. 11, 1921, Burnquist Papers. In this letter, written shortly after Burnquist left office and shortly before Ames's death, the latter asked Burnquist to explain why he, Ames, had been summarily dismissed from the commission in December 1917. Burnquist's reply did not cast any further light on the matter (Burnquist to Ames, Jan. 12, 1921, Burnquist Papers).

43. Tighe to Lind, Feb. 13, 1918, Lind Papers.

44. Quoted in Stephenson, *John Lind,* 324.

45. Lind to Burnquist, May 16, 1917, Burnquist Papers.

46. Here and below, McGee to Nelson, May 31, 1917, Nelson Papers.

47. *New Ulm Review,* June 6, 1917, p. 4.

CHAPTER 5. *Getting Down to Business*

1. MCPS Minutes, Apr. 23, 1917, MCPS Papers.

2. Here and below, *Session Laws,* 1917, chap. 261, p. 373–77. The full text of the statute is also carried in MCPS, *Report,* 55–57.

3. McGee to Nelson, Apr. 11, 1917, Nelson Papers; here and below, Tighe, "Legal Theory," 7, 10.

4. Tighe, "Legal Theory," 10–11.

5. Tighe, "Legal Theory," 11–12.

6. Tighe, "Legal Theory," 13.

7. Quoted in Tighe, "Legal Theory," 14.

8. Tighe, "Legal Theory," 14, 16; MCPS Minutes, Apr. 30, 1918; MCPS, *Report,* 114.

9. MCPS Minutes, Apr. 24, 1917. On Pardee's career, see *St. Paul Dispatch,* Apr. 10, 1930, p. 10.

10. Pardee to Lincoln Steffens, July 5, 1917, file 108, Main Files.

11. Pardee to E. M. Morgan, July 24, 1917, file 108, Main Files.

12. Pardee to S. H. Bingham, May 25, 1917, file 108, memorandum, Pardee to MCPS, May 12, 1917, file 107 — both in Main Files.

13. The by-laws, both in original and amended form, are carried in MCPS, *Report,* 70–71.

14. MCPS Minutes, May 29, 1917.

15. MCPS Minutes, Apr. 24, 1917.

16. MCPS, *Report,* 72–73 (text of Order 1); *Proceedings of the City Council of . . . Minneapolis,* 1917, p. 293–94, 314–15.

17. MCPS Minutes, Apr. 25, 1917; MCPS, *Report,* 73–74 (text of Order 2).

18. Memorandum, A. F. Woods to Burnquist, undated, filed under April 1917, Woods telegrams to potential appointees, Apr. 7, 1917, Burnquist to Woods, Apr. 13, 1917 — all in Burnquist Papers.

19. MCPS Minutes, Apr. 25, 1917.

20. MCPS Minutes, Apr. 28, 1917; MCPS, *Report,* 74–75 (text of Order 3). Strictly speaking, Fred B. Wood was adjutant general when the Home Guard was organized. However, Rhinow, who assumed the title of military secretary to the governor in May 1917, appears to have been in charge. On Sept. 1, 1917, Rhinow formally replaced Wood as adjutant general (*Legislative Manual,* 1919, p. 282, 716).

21. MCPS Minutes, May 29, May 14, 1917; MCPS, *Report,* 165, 75–76 (quotations on 165, 76).

22. MCPS Minutes, July 17, 1917.

23. McGee to Congressman Clarence B. Miller, May 28, 1917, Nelson Papers;

William Crozier to McGee, July 10, 1917, attached to McGee to Burnquist, July 14, 1917, Burnquist Papers.

24. MCPS Minutes, July 17, 1917; Joseph Chapman to Burnquist, Apr. 10, 1917, Burnquist to Chapman, Apr. 11, 1917 — both in file 648a, Governor's Records; Libby to Rhinow, Feb. 20, 1918 (quotation), memorandum, Rhinow to MCPS, Feb. 19, 1918 (quotation) — both in file 50, Main Files.

25. MCPS Minutes, May 10, 1917.

26. MCPS, *Report,* 74–75 (quotations); MCPS Minutes, May 29, 1917.

27. McGee to Miller, May 22, 1917, Nelson Papers; MCPS Minutes, May 24, 1917.

28. Undated memorandum to MCPS, filed under Apr. 15, 1918, file 50, Main Files; MCPS, *Report,* 13 (quotation).

29. MCPS Minutes, May 7, 1917.

30. Form letter dated May 2, 1917, attached to G. H. Richards to Pardee, May 3, 1917, file 109, Main Files.

31. Burnquist, ed., *Minnesota and Its People,* 4:259–60; Marquis, ed., *Book of Minnesotans,* 415–16; Castle, *Minnesota Story and Biography,* 2:1101; Walter Van Brunt, ed., *Duluth and St. Louis County, Minnesota* (Chicago: American Historical Society, 1921), 3:1077–78; *Legislative Manual,* 1917, p. 626.

32. Marquis, ed., *Book of Minnesotans,* 478; biographical sketch of Cotton at beginning of Donald R. Cotton Papers, MHS; Pardee to County Directors, June 13, 1917 (quotation), file 107, Main Files.

33. MCPS, *Report,* 226, 237, 266, 270, 272, 278; W. F. Toensing, comp., *Minnesota Congressmen, Legislators, and Other Elected State Officials: An Alphabetical Checklist, 1849–1971* (St. Paul: Minnesota Historical Society, 1971), 1606; Christianson, *Minnesota,* 4:613–14.

34. Here and below, Pardee to Director, May 23, 1917 (quotations), file 107, Main Files. For a complete roster of county and local MCPS officials, see MCPS, *Report,* 174–309.

35. MCPS Minutes, Apr. 28, 1917; "Report of Meeting of Representatives . . . ," May 5, 1917, file 96, Main Files; MCPS Minutes, May 10, 1917.

36. Here and below, MCPS Minutes, May 21 (quotation), May 24, June 19, 1917.

37. Burnquist, "To the Farmers of Minnesota," June 1, 1917 (quotation), MCPS to County Director, June 1, 1917, Pardee to Township Chairmen, undated — all in file 124, Main Files.

38. Pardee to E. Dana Durand, June 8, 25, 1917, John J. Wagner to Pardee, July 18, 30, Aug. 5, 1917 — all in file 124, Main Files.

39. Pardee to County Director, June 29, 1917, file 107, Main Files.

40. Quotations in Pardee to County Directors, June 13, 1917 (draft copy), file 107, Main Files. A summary of conference proceedings is given in MCPS Minutes, June 19, 1917.

41. Donald R. Cotton to W. E. Hall, Apr. 11, 1918, Cotton Papers.

42. Here and below, *Who's Who among Minnesota Women,* compiled and published by Mary Dillon Foster (1924), 347; *Minneapolis Morning Tribune,* Apr. 6, 1944, p. 10; *Minnesota Clubwoman* 60 (March 1978), [p. 6].

43. "A Versatile Woman Leader," *Minneapolis: Metropolis of the Northwest,* August 1928, p. 27.

44. MCPS to Mrs. Thomas G. [Alice Ames] Winter, May 22, 25, 1917, file 56, Main Files.

45. Alice Ames Winter to M. M. Booth, undated, file 56, Main Files.

46. Pardee to A. Winter, June 20, 1917, file 56, Main Files.

47. Pardee to Robert L. Pollock, May 25, 1917 (quotation), file 102, to A. D. Stewart, July 7, 1917, file 110, to R. A. Ziebarth, July 19, 1917, file 110 — all in Main Files.

48. MCPS Minutes, May 29, 1917.

49. MCPS Minutes, June 5, 1917.

50. Baker to Burnquist, May 26, 1917, file 71, Main Files.

51. Bovey to Burnquist, June 6, 1917, Burnquist Papers.

52. Telegrams, Trades and Laborer Assembly of Minneapolis and Hennepin County to Newton D. Baker, June 8, 1917, W. S. Gifford, Council of National Defense, to Trades and Laborer Assembly, June 15, 1917 – both in file 102, Main Files.

53. Van Lear to Burnquist, June 21, 1917, file 102, Main Files; *Proceedings of the City Council*, 1917, June 15, July 13, 1917, p. 449, 518–19, 548.

54. The full text of the Booth decision is carried in MCPS, *Report,* 57–65.

55. MCPS Minutes, June 7, 1917.

56. O. H. O'Neill to Pardee, June 9, 1917, Pardee to O'Neill, June 11, 1917, O'Neill to Pardee, June 12, 1917 – all in file 102, Main Files.

57. Libby to R. B. Brower, Sept. 21, 1917, Libby to C. Rosenmeier, Dec. 8, 1917 – both in file 102, Main Files.

58. MCPS Minutes, June 19, 1917.

CHAPTER 6. *Rooting Out Disloyalty*

1. McGee to Pardee, July 12, 1917, file 71, Main Files.

2. A. MacMurphy to Burnquist, Apr. 5, 1917, Mrs. B. Langtry to Burnquist, Apr. 8, 1917 – both in file 648a, Governor's Records.

3. Charles E. Houston to Burnquist, Apr. 11, 1917, Burnquist to Houston, Apr. 12, 1917 – both in file 648a, Governor's Records.

4. Here and below, MCPS Minutes, May 7, 10, 14, 21, 1917.

5. MCPS Minutes, May 24, 29 (quotation), 1917. For McGee version of confrontation with Lind, see McGee to Nelson, May 31, 1917, Nelson Papers.

6. For example, on May 14 McGee presented MCPS with excerpts from a speech delivered by Elizabeth Gurley Flynn at a recent IWW meeting in Minneapolis.

7. McGee to C. B. Miller, May 22, 1917, copy in Nelson Papers; telegrams, *New York World* to Burnquist, Burnquist to *New York World* – both May 30, 1917, file 648a, Governor's Records.

8. MCPS Minutes, May 21, 29, 1917.

9. Since Winter's operation was covert, his appointment was not publicized. For Winter's understanding of the appointment, see T. Winter to Pardee, June 30, 1917, Pardee folder, Agents' Reports to T. G. Winter – hereafter cited as TGW Reports – in the MCPS Papers. Even before his appointment Winter had supplied information on "suspicious" characters and activities: see T. Winter to Pardee, June 27, 1917, "T" folder, TGW Reports.

10. B. J. Randolph to T. Winter, July 25, 1917, Randolph folder, TGW Reports.

11. T. Winter to W. J. Smith, Oct. 14, 1917, Randolph folder, TGW Reports.

12. O. R. Hatfield to Pardee, July 26, 1917, file 116, Main Files.

13. Here and below, T. Winter to Pardee, July 28, 1917, Pardee folder, TGW Reports. A clipping of the article is attached to this letter.

14. Pardee to T. Winter, July 30, 1917, Pardee folder, TGW Reports. A cordial letter from Pardee to H. B. R. Briggs of the *St. Paul Daily News* suggests a warm Pardee relationship with the editorial staff of that paper: Pardee to Briggs, Aug. 19, 1917, file 102, Main Files.

15. Undated report (early June), CMR folder, TGW Reports.

16. Report dated June 2, 1917, VSS folder, TGW Reports; *Brown County Journal,* June 9, 1917, p. 1; report dated June 5, 1917, WGS folder, TGW Reports.

17. Report dated June 1, 1917, DJG folder, TGW Reports; reports dated May 31, June 1, 1917, CH folder, TGW Reports.

18. Reports dated June 22, 23, 1917, DJG folder, TGW Reports.

19. Reports dated June 5, 6, 1917, DJG folder, TGW Reports; *Minneapolis Daily News,* June 13, 19, 1917, clippings in vol. 65, MCPS Scrapbooks, MCPS Papers.

20. Telegram, J. C. Barr (representing a group of Cuyuna Range mining executives) to C. H. March, June 9, 1917, Burnquist Papers; draft memorandum, MCPS to Attorney General of the United States, undated, file 54, Main Files.

21. Reports dated June 9, 4, 1917, DJG folder, TGW Reports.

22. Report dated June 10, 1917, DJG folder, TGW Reports; Douglas J. Ollila, "Defects in the Melting Pot: Finnish-American Response to the Loyalty Issue 1917–1920," reprint from *Turun Historiallinen Arkisto* 31:397–413, esp. 398–99.

23. Report dated June 11, 1917, DJG folder, TGW Reports.

24. Jones to Burnquist, June 18, 1917, Burnquist Papers.

25. MCPS Minutes, June 19, 1917; Gillette to Burnquist, June 20, 1917, Burnquist Papers.

26. Here and below, report dated June 18, 1917, CH folder, TGW Reports.

27. Here and below, reports dated June 19–23, 1917, CH folder, TGW Reports.

28. MCPS Minutes, June 20, 1917.

29. Here and below, "Special Meeting of the Commission with Iron Range Officials," report dated June 21, 1917, file 106, Main Files.

30. MCPS Minutes, June 26, 1917. The text of the ordinance is given in MCPS, *Report,* 154–55.

31. "Assembly of Sheriffs," brochure containing minutes of meeting held Aug. 15, 1917, p. 3, file 90, Main Files. In commenting on the Minnesota statute prohibiting speech or writing calculated to interfere with enlistments, U.S. Attorney Alfred Jaques pointed out: "This act is much more stringent than any law of Congress relating to literature of this character" (Jaques to Pardee, May 17, 1917, file 55, Main Files). Perhaps this judgment would not have been correct after Congress enacted the sedition law of 1918.

32. Hatfield to T. Winter, June 26, 1917, Hatfield folder, TGW Reports.

33. The following account of the Boyd rally is taken from the report dated July 13, 1917, GWS folder, TGW Reports.

34. Undated memorandum, Carl Ahlteen folder, TGW Reports; here and below, CH folder, especially memorandums of June 10, 11, 24, 1917, TGW Reports.

35. Reports dated June 13, 15, 16, 18 (quotations), 19–24, 1917, DJG folder, TGW Reports.

36. Reports dated June 26 (quotation), 27, 1917, DJG folder, TGW Reports; *Duluth News Tribune,* June 30, 1917.

37. Reports dated June 18, 19, 21, 1917, DJG folder, TGW Reports.

38. Hatfield to T. Winter, July 12, 17, 1917, Hatfield folder, TGW Reports.

39. Pardee to T. Winter, July 19, 1917, Pardee folder, TGW Reports.

40. MCPS Minutes, June 7, 1917; Chrislock, *Ethnicity Challenged,* 101–4; here and below, reports dated June 18 (quotations), 19, 1917, CUP folder, TGW Reports.

41. Nelson to McGee, June 7, 1917, file 103, Main Files.

42. MCPS Minutes, Aug. 1, 7, Oct. 9, Dec. 12, 1917; *Park Region Echo* (Alexandria), Mar. 12, 1918, p. 1; Chrislock, *Ethnicity Challenged,* 103. For a detailed and sympathetic chronicle of Carl Wold's career, see the *Park Region Echo* for Nov. 6, 1918, p. 1.

43. MCPS Minutes, July 11, 1917; William E. Matsen, "William S. Schaper, War Hysteria, and the Price of Academic Freedom," *Minnesota History* 51 (Winter 1988): 131–37. The role of the safety commission in the Schaper case was and remains

controversial. University President Marion L. Burton told Schaper that the MCPS sent the regents a letter, in Matsen's words, "regarding faculty members suspected of having anti-American sentiments" (p. 131). However, in communicating with Schaper on Oct. 19, 1917, John Lind denied the existence of such a letter, a version accepted by Schaper. Matsen regarded Lind's denial with skepticism, characterizing it as "misinformation" (p. 132 n. 4). Perhaps the July 11 MCPS Minutes provide a clue as to what really happened. One can assume that McGee, whose zeal for pursuing "seditionists" was unbounded, interpreted reference of the "facts" regarding the loyalty of University faculty "back to him" as a mandate to contact such regents as Fred Snyder, either by letter or oral communication, and that Burton and others regarded McGee, even though he acted on his own, as the authoritative voice of the safety commission.

44. Hatfield to Pardee, July 18, 1917, file 116, Main Files.

CHAPTER 7. *July 25 and Its Aftermath*

1. *Brown County Journal,* July 28, 1917, p. 1 (quotations). Although the *Journal,* unlike its rival, the *New Ulm Review,* was out of sympathy with the purposes of the rally, its coverage appears fair and balanced. For the *Review* account, see issue of Aug. 1, 1917, p. 1. For a considerably less than sympathetic account, see *Minneapolis Journal,* July 26, 1917, p. 1, 2.

2. Here and below, *Brown County Journal,* July 28, 1917, p. 2. The *St. Paul Daily News,* July 26, 1917, p. 1, also carried quotes from Pfaender's remarks.

3. *Minneapolis Journal,* July 26, 1917, p. 2; *New Ulm Review,* Aug. 1, 1917, p. 2.

4. The following account of the Bemidji mob action is taken from the report dated July 25, 1917, DJG folder, TGW Reports. For another account, see S. C. Bailey to Burnquist, July 25, 1917, Burnquist Papers. See also Art Lee, "Hometown Hysteria: Bemidji at the Start of World War I," *Minnesota History* 49 (Summer 1984): 65–75.

5. *Princeton Union,* July 26, 1917, p. 4.

6. *Princeton Union,* Aug. 16, 1917, p. 4; quoted in *Labor World,* Aug. 25, 1917, p. 3.

7. *New Ulm Review,* Aug. 1, 1917, p. 1; somewhat illogically, the *Review* in its next issue complained of journalistic concentration on New Ulm: see Aug. 8, p. 4; *Princeton Union,* Aug. 9, 1917, p. 4.

8. Here and below, MCPS Minutes, Aug. 1, 7, 1917; MCPS, *Report,* 48. Berg was apparently dropped from the commission's investigation in its early stages.

9. Here and below, Tighe to Lyndon A. Smith, Aug. 13, 1917, file 136, Main Files.

10. MCPS Minutes, Aug. 14, 1917. For a safety commission version of this meeting, see MCPS, *Report,* 49.

11. MCPS, *Report,* 49–50.

12. MCPS Minutes, Aug. 21, 1917.

13. *St. Paul Daily News,* Aug. 22, 1917, p. 1, 2; *Minneapolis Journal,* Aug. 22, 1917, p. 1, 2 (quotation).

14. *New Ulm Review,* June 27, p. 4, July 11, p. 6 — both 1917; Viereck to Burnquist, June 15, 1917, Burnquist to Viereck, June 21, 1917 — both in Burnquist Papers.

15. *New Ulm Review,* Aug. 29, 1917, p. 6.

16. *St. Paul Daily News,* Aug. 22, 1917, p. 1, 2.

17. *New Times,* Aug. 4, 1917.

18. Reports dated July 26, 19, 1917, DJG folder, Pardee to T. Winter, July 19, 1917, Pardee folder — all in TGW Reports.

19. Graham M. Torrance to Burnquist, July 24, 1917, file 648a, Governor's Records; report dated July 24, 1917, DJG folder, TGW Reports. In this report DJG cast considerable doubt on the theory that the fire had been deliberately set.

20. Burnquist to S. C. Bailey, July 28, 1917, Burnquist Papers; MCPS Minutes, July 3, 1917; MCPS to Wisconsin Council of Defense, July 25, 1917, Wisconsin file, Main Files. See also William F. Houk to Burnquist, July 30 (clipped to W. D. Bailey to Burnquist, July 25, 1917), file 648a, Governor's Records. Houk reported no evidence of agitation.

21. Lind to Thomas W. Gregory, July 26, 1917, Lind Papers.

22. R. L. Downing to Ralph A. Stone, July 30, 1917, Stone to Burnquist, Aug. 1, 1917 — both in Burnquist Papers; Victor H. Gran to Burnquist, July 2, 1917, and his letter to the MCPS on the same date, file 171, Main Files.

23. MCPS Minutes, July 24, 1917; Lind to Gregory, July 26, 1917, Lind Papers.

24. Charles S. Ward, "The Minnesota Commission of Public Safety in World War One: Its Formation and Activities" (Master's thesis, University of Minnesota, 1965), p. 69; Folwell, *Minnesota,* 3:568.

25. William B. Wilson to Lind, quoted in Lind to Tighe, July 31, 1917, Lind Papers.

26. Lind to Wilson, quoted in Lind to Tighe, July 31, 1917, Lind Papers.

27. Ward, "Minnesota Commission," 70–71.

28. Tighe to Burnquist, July 31, 1917, Lind Papers.

29. MCPS Minutes, Aug. 14, 1917; H. C. Peterson and Gilbert C. Fite, *Opponents of War, 1917–1918* (Madison: University of Wisconsin Press, 1957), 62; *Duluth News Tribune,* Aug. 21, 1917, p. 3.

30. *Minneapolis Journal,* Sept. 6, 1917, p. 1; *Minneapolis Morning Tribune,* Sept. 6, 1917, p. 1 (quotation).

31. *St. Paul Dispatch,* Sept. 8, 1917, p. 6; *Minneapolis Journal,* Sept. 8, 1917, p. 4.

32. *Fergus Falls Free Press,* Sept. 19, 1917.

33. Quoted in Peterson and Fite, *Opponents of War,* 60.

34. *Minneapolis Journal,* Sept. 22, 1917, p. 5; *New Times,* Sept. 29, 1917, p. 1.

35. Here and below, MCPS Minutes, Sept. 25, 1917.

36. Here and below, Peterson and Fite, *Opponents of War,* 74–75 (quotations); Chrislock, *Progressive Era,* 138.

37. *New Times,* June 30, 1917, p. 1; here and below, Chrislock, *Progressive Era,* 138, 149.

38. *New Times,* July 28, Aug. 4, 1917; Van Lear to Burnquist, Aug. 24, 1917, and attached "Mayor's Statement Concerning Meeting of People's Council," Burnquist Papers.

39. *St. Paul Dispatch,* Aug. 24, 1917, p. 10.

40. MCPS Minutes, Aug. 21, 28, 1917.

41. *New Times,* Sept. 1, 1917, p. 1; *Labor World,* Sept. 8, 1917, p. 1. For Burnquist's order, issued as a telegram to Sheriff Langum, see MCPS, *Report,* 33.

42. Here and below, Peterson and Fite, *Opponents of War,* 77–78 (quotations on 77).

43. Peterson and Fite, *Opponents of War,* 80.

44. MCPS Minutes, Aug. 1, 14, 21, 1917; Pardee to Sheriffs, Aug. 28, 1917, file 107, Main Files.

45. Here and below, *Brown County Journal,* Sept. 8, 1917, p. 1 (quotations); *New Ulm Review,* Sept. 5, p. 1, Sept. 12, p. 1, 2 — both 1917.

46. MCPS Minutes, Sept. 4, 1917; here and below, Agnes L. Peterson to Pardee, Aug. 26, 1917 (quotations), file 108, Main Files.

47. Here and below, reports dated Aug. 23, 24, 19, 1917, WGS folder, TGW Reports.

48. WGS report dated Aug. 20, 1917 (quotation), No. 83 report dated Aug. 20, 1917 — both in Ackerman [*sic*] folder, TGW Reports.

49. *Brown County Journal,* Sept. 15, 22, 1917, p. 1; MCPS Minutes, Sept. 18, 1917.

50. The following material on the hearing is taken from *Brown County Journal,*

Oct. 6, 1917, p. 1, 2 (quotation). Both New Ulm papers gave the hearing full coverage: see *Brown County Journal,* Sept. 29, p. 1, 8, Oct. 6, p. 1, 2 — both 1917; *New Ulm Review,* Oct. 3, 1917, p. 1, 2. A transcript of the hearing ("Transcript of Testimony and Proceedings: In the Matter of Charges Filed against L. A. Fritchie [*sic*], Albert Pfaender, and Louis G. Vogel, of New Ulm, Minn.") is filed under Petitions and Transcripts of Testimony in Investigations, MCPS Papers. See also Holbrook and Appel, *Minnesota,* 2:40–43.

51. Quoted in Holbrook and Appel, *Minnesota,* 2:41–42; *New Ulm Review,* Dec. 5, 1917, p. 1; *Brown County Journal,* Dec. 8, 1917, p. 6. Burnquist's decision to reinstate Vogel may also have been influenced by a letter he received from Frank Clague, Redwood Falls attorney and future congressman, strongly recommending reinstatement. Clague asserted that Vogel's participation in the rally had been less extensive than originally believed (Clague to Burnquist, Oct. 9, 1917, Burnquist Papers).

52. MCPS Minutes, Nov. 20, 1917, Tighe to Board of Trustees, Martin Luther College, Nov. 21, 1917, file 136, Main Files.

53. H. Klatt to Tighe, Nov. 23, 1917, Tighe to Martin Luther College, Jan. 2, 1918, Klatt to MCPS, Dec. 31, 1917, Tighe to Klatt, Jan. 9, 1918, G. E. Bergemann to Tighe, Jan. 16, 1918 — all in file 136, Main Files.

54. Tighe to Bergemann, Jan. 24, 1918, file 136, Main Files.

55. Bergemann to Tighe, Jan. 25, 30, 1918, file 136, Main Files.

56. The MCPS Minutes for July 9, 1918, record the following: Communication received "From Louis G. Vogel . . . asking reimbursement in the amount of $372.75 for alleged personal expenses incurred incident to removal hearing recommended by the Commission. On motion it was agreed that the request be denied."

CHAPTER 8. *The Nonpartisan League under Fire*

1. MCPS Minutes, Aug. 1, 1917.

2. Here and below, "Assembly of Sheriffs," 2, file 90, Main Files.

3. "General Plan of Organization of County Units of the Minnesota Motor Reserve," undated typescript filed under August 1917, file 107, Main Files.

4. MCPS, *Report,* 13; *How Minnesota Gave to the United States the First Military Motor Corps,* designed by Capt. Leonard Cary (Minneapolis: Bancroft Printing Co., 1919), 28, 81–85, 97–110; *Minneapolis Journal,* Oct. 27, 1918, p. 1, 4; Francis M. Carroll and Franklin R. Raiter, *The Fires of Autumn: The Cloquet-Moose Lake Disaster of 1918* (St. Paul: Minnesota Historical Society Press, 1990), 70, 104–5, 108.

5. "Assembly of Sheriffs," 3–4.

6. Einar Hoidale to Pardee, Aug. 24, 1917 (quotations), file 103, Main Files. The opening files of the Cotton Papers include considerable material about the American Protective League.

7. MCPS Minutes, Aug. 21, 1917; Pardee to County Director, Aug. 22, 1917, file 107, Main Files.

8. Weiss memorandum, May 14, 1917, file 103, W. C. Handy to Weiss, June 18, 1917, file 72 — both in Main Files.

9. Pardee to County Directors, Aug. 23, 1917, file 107, Main Files; MCPS Minutes, Sept. 25, 1917.

10. MCPS Minutes, Aug. 1, 1917.

11. Here and below, Chrislock, *Ethnicity Challenged,* 68–69; MCPS Minutes, Aug. 14, 1917.

12. Nelson to Grevstad, Aug. 27, 1917, in Nicolay A. Grevstad Papers, Norwegian-American Historical Association Archive, Northfield, Minn.

13. Pardee to Weiss, July 11, 1917, Weiss to Pardee, July 12, Aug. 1, 1917 – all in file 72, Main Files.

14. Weiss to Pardee, Aug. 10, Aug. 3 (quotations), 1917, file 72, Main Files; MCPS Minutes, Aug. 28, 1917.

15. MCPS Minutes, Aug. 7, 14, 1917; here and below, Holbrook and Appel, *Minnesota*, 2:68–72.

16. C. W. Henke to Editor, Sept. 20, 1917, file 107, Henke to March, Nov. 14, 1917, file 70 – both in Main Files.

17. For biographical data on Libby, see Marquis, ed., *Book of Minnesotans*, 308; Franklyn Curtiss-Wedge and William Jay Whipple, comps., *The History of Winona County, Minnesota* (Chicago: H. C. Cooper, Jr., 1913), 2:927–28. See also Libby to County Director, Oct. 4, 1917, file 107, Main Files.

18. MCPS Minutes, Sept. 18, Oct. 25, 1917; Pardee to T. Winter, Aug. 6, 1917, Pardee folder, TGW Reports; McDonald to Nelson, Aug. 7, 1917 (quotation), Nelson Papers. Shortly before terminating Pinkerton, the commission provided T. Winter with additional agents: Pardee to T. Winter, Sept. 4, 1917, Pardee folder, TGW Reports.

19. *Martin County Sentinel* (Fairmont), Feb. 2, 1917; Snyder to Nelson, Aug. 18, 1917, Nelson Papers.

20. Morlan, *Political Prairie Fire*, 127–28 (quotation on 128). Given the scope of its activity – including publication of a journal accorded a mass circulation – the fake league involved a substantial expenditure of money. Testimony given in a lawsuit litigated in 1920 identified "several prominent Twin Cities businessmen, bankers, and railroad officials" along with Gustaf Lindquist, Burnquist's confidant and secretary, as its sponsors (Morlan, 128).

21. Teigan to Mrs. August Baumgarten, Mar. 6, 1917, microfilm edition, National Nonpartisan League (NNPL) Papers, MHS; Morlan, *Political Prairie Fire*, 110.

22. Baumgarten to Teigan, June 7, 1917, NNPL Papers.

23. Teigan to Baumgarten, June 16, 1917, NNPL Papers.

24. Teigan to Baumgarten, July 3, 1917, NNPL Papers.

25. The statement is quoted in Morlan, *Political Prairie Fire*, 136–37.

26. Address of Jan. 8, 1918, reprinted in *The Messages and Papers of Woodrow Wilson*, ed. Albert Shaw (New York: George H. Doran Co., 1924), 1:464–72 (quotation on 468).

27. The full quotation from which the phrase is excerpted reads: "Professional politicians of the socialist or Non-partisan league stamp, who sought to win votes at their country's cost by pandering to a treasonable sentiment" (MCPS, *Report*, 32).

28. Report dated June 16, 1917, "T" folder, TGW Reports. The report was based on the text of a speech carried on June 16 in *Gaa Paa*, a radical Norwegian-language weekly published in Minneapolis that was friendly to the Nonpartisan League.

29. Filed under June 21, 1917, Burnquist Papers. For extensive quotes from a Townley speech delivered at Jamestown, N. Dak., see Morlan, *Political Prairie Fire*, 138–39.

30. Here and below, Morlan, *Political Prairie Fire*, 141–42 (quotations on 141).

31. Morlan, *Political Prairie Fire*, 142–43 (quotations).

32. The following account of the La Follette incident, including quotations from his speech, is based primarily on Belle Case La Follette and Fola La Follette, *Robert M. La Follette* (New York: Macmillan Co., 1953), 2:762–69. Other accounts may be found in Morlan, *Political Prairie Fire*, 142–45; Chrislock, *Progressive Era*, 149–51; Herbert E. Gaston, *The Nonpartisan League* (New York: Harcourt, Brace and Howe, 1920), 209–11. The various stenographic accounts taken during the speech do not differ materially. The federal district attorney received the MCPS version with thanks but indicated that the entire conference was "covered quite fully" by special agents

of the Department of Justice: Jaques to MCPS, Sept. 27, 1917, file 135, Main Files.

33. La Follette and La Follette, *Robert M. La Follette,* 2:770; here and below, Morlan, *Political Prairie Fire,* 145.

34. *Minneota Mascot,* Sept. 28, 1917.

35. MCPS Minutes, Sept. 25, 1917.

36. Here and below, "Testimony of A. C. Townley, President of the Nonpartisan League, Taken in the Office of Governor Burnquist at a Meeting of the Public Safety Commission," Sept. 25, 1917, file 135, Main Files.

37. "Testimony of A. C. Townley," sec. 2, p. 3.

38. "Testimony of A. C. Townley," sec. 1, p. 12–13.

39. Here and below, MCPS Minutes, Sept. 25, 1917.

40. MCPS Minutes, Sept. 26, Oct. 2, 1917.

41. La Follette and La Follette, *Robert M. La Follette,* 2:776, 911, 927–31; William O'Brien (a temporary MCPS operative) to MCPS, Oct. 16, 1917, file 148, Main Files. Reporting on a Townley meeting in Marshall, O'Brien remarked that "Townley spoke in his usual strain . . . but said nothing that wasn't well covered. . . . It wasn't what he said, but the way he said it, that showed his real self."

42. Ames to MCPS, Feb. 25, 1918, file 1, Main Files. A few days before submitting this preliminary report, Ames replied to a query about NPL loyalty by pointing to North Dakota's failure to meet its quota on the First Liberty Loan: Ames to Charles F. Serline, Feb. 22, 1918, file 68, Main Files.

43. Smith to Burnquist, Oct. 11, 1917, file 94, Main Files.

44. The following account of the St. Paul meeting is taken from the *Duluth News Tribune,* Oct. 8, 1917, p. 1, 12. See also Morlan, *Political Prairie Fire,* 146–47.

45. Telegram, Nelson to President Wilson, Oct. 20, 1917, Nelson Papers; *Nonpartisan Leader* (St. Paul), Apr. 1, 1918, p. 13, quoting *Houghton Gazette* (Houghton, Mich.) of Jan. 27, 1918. Chapman was in Houghton addressing a group of bankers.

46. Here and below, Morlan, *Political Prairie Fire,* 147 (quotations), 149.

47. Nelson to Creel, Apr. 8, 1918, Nelson Papers. The printed text of Creel's reply is filed with Nelson's letter.

48. Libby to Stewart, May 25, 1918, file 135, Main Files.

49. Libby to Wilson, Oct. 2, 1917, Libby to county directors in fifteen counties, same date — both in file 135, Main Files.

50. E. A. Siddall to Burnquist, Jan. 5, 1918, Burnquist to Siddall, Jan. 7, 1918 — both in file 648a, Governor's Records.

51. Butterfield Commercial Club to Burnquist, Feb. 23, 1918, Burnquist to J. Brogger, Feb. 27, 1918 — both in file 648a, Governor's Records.

52. Here and below, Morlan, *Political Prairie Fire,* 162–63 (quotations).

53. *Minnesota in the War,* Mar. 30, 1918, p. 2.

54. Morlan, *Political Prairie Fire,* 159; Gaston, *Nonpartisan League,* 231.

55. John R. Serrin to Nelson, Jan. 31, 1917 (quotation), Nelson Papers (Serrin was appointed director of the Pope County Safety Commission a few months later); Morlan, *Political Prairie Fire,* 116–20. For a reflection of the "status fears" inspired by the Nonpartisan League on Main Street, see editorial from an unidentified North Dakota newspaper quoted in Saloutos and Hicks, *Agricultural Discontent,* 159.

56. Sterling to MCPS, July 5, 1918, file 135, Main Files.

CHAPTER 9. *The Button War*

1. Pardee to A. F. Ferguson, Aug. 14, 1917, file 108, Main Files.

2. David Paul Nord, "Hothouse Socialism in Minneapolis," in *Socialism in the Heartland,* ed. Donald T. Critchlow (Notre Dame, Ind.: University of Notre Dame Press, 1986), 144.

3. Here and below, George W. Lawson, *History of Labor in Minnesota* (St. Paul: Minnesota State Federation of Labor, 1955), 34–35.

4. Here and below, Lawson, *History of Labor,* 36–37.

5. *Labor World,* July 28, 1917.

6. Lawson, *History of Labor,* 37–38 (quotation on 38); Nord, "Hothouse Socialism," 145.

7. Here and below, W. C. Robertson to Knute Nelson, Jan. 16, 1918, Nelson Papers.

8. Nord, "Hothouse Socialism," 145 (quotations); *Union Labor Bulletin,* August 1917, p. 22.

9. *Labor World,* Sept. 1, p. 1, 3, Sept. 15, p. 1 — both 1917.

10. *Mesaba Ore and Hibbing News,* Sept. 28, 1917 (quotation); *Duluth News Tribune,* Oct. 8, 1917, p. 12.

11. Here and below, William Millikan, "Defenders of Business: The Minneapolis Civic and Commerce Association *versus* Labor during W.W.I.," *Minnesota History* 50 (Spring 1986): 2–17 (quotations on 13).

12. As the months passed the Wilson administration moved closer to labor's interpretation, and there is some evidence that the streetcar strike may have reinforced this trend: see A. Viola Smith (Department of Labor official) to Lind, Dec. 12, 1917, file 69, Main Files.

13. George Lawson's version was fully communicated in an interview with William C. Koch, a colleague of Donald Cotton in the St. Paul branch of the War Industries Board. For a reconstruction of this interview, see Koch to Cotton, Feb. 8, 1918, p. 1–2, Cotton Papers.

14. Here and below, Millikan, "Defenders of Business," 10–11.

15. Here and below, Millikan, "Defenders of Business," 11–12 (newspaper quoted on 11).

16. MCPS Minutes, Oct. 9, 1917.

17. Here and below, MCPS Minutes, Oct. 11, 12, 1917.

18. *Commercial West,* Oct. 13, 1917, p. 8; *New Times,* Oct. 13, 1917, p. 1; *Union Labor Bulletin,* Oct. 1917, p. 6 (quotation), 8.

19. Millikan, "Defenders of Business," 12. The *Union Labor Bulletin* noted complaints "that foremen at different stations [were treating union men] unfairly and that non-union employes [were] taunting the union men and . . . making life miserable for them" (November 1917, p. 8).

20. Ora A. Hilton, *The Minnesota Commission of Public Safety in World War I, 1917–1919,* Oklahoma Agricultural and Mechanical College, Bulletin, vol. 48, no. 14 (Stillwater, Okla., 1951), 20 n. 49.

21. MCPS Minutes, Nov. 2, 1917.

22. Millikan, "Defenders of Business," 12–13; MCPS Minutes, Nov. 6, 1917.

23. "Report of Special Committee," Nov. 19, 1917, file 206, Main Files.

24. MCPS Minutes, Nov. 20, 1917; Millikan, "Defenders of Business," 13. An extract from a hearing before the committee ("Extract from Street Car Controversy"), ostensibly documenting the union representative's acceptance of a ban on buttons, is in file 75, Main Files.

25. Here and below, MCPS Minutes, Nov. 20, 1917.

26. There is an interesting variance between the official MCPS minutes and the

printed version of McGee's resolution in the commission's published report. The minutes fail to indicate that Lind's motion to lay McGee's resolution on the table — a motion adopted by the commission — was taken off the table for passage. The report simply states that McGee's resolution "carried" (MCPS, *Report,* 147).

27. Koch to Cotton, Feb. 8, 1918, p. 2–3; Millikan, "Defenders of Business," 13.

28. MCPS Minutes, Nov. 27, 1917. The recommendations that Order 16 refers to as having been adopted on Nov. 19 were actually passed on Nov. 20.

29. December 1917, p. 17.

30. *Gaa Paa,* Dec. 8, 1917; Chrislock, *Progressive Era,* 158.

31. Millikan, "Defenders of Business," 14–15.

32. Chrislock, *Progressive Era,* 158; James Manahan, *Trials of a Lawyer* (Minneapolis: N.p., 1933), 224–32.

33. Toensing, comp., *Minnesota Congressmen,* 63, 76.

34. Stevens to Nelson, Dec. 22, 1917, Nelson Papers.

35. Here and below, Millikan, "Defenders of Business," 14–15 (Lowry quotation on 14); MCPS, *Report,* 40 (Burnquist quotation). Ironically, at least one union transmitted its request for intervention through Senator Nelson, who was lobbying vigorously against federal intrusion into the controversy: see Nelson to Louis F. Post, Dec. 7, 1917, Nelson Papers. See also telegram, Nelson and Kellogg to Burnquist, Dec. 7, 1917, Wilson to Nelson, Dec. 7, 1917, Nelson to A. M. Robertson (TCRTC vice-president), Dec. 4, 1917 — all in Nelson Papers.

36. Telegram, Baker to Burnquist, Dec. 4, 1917, copy in Nelson Papers; MCPS, *Report,* 41 (Burnquist quotation). Burnquist replied in a similar vein to Samuel Gompers, who also had urged federal mediation: MCPS, *Report,* 41.

37. On Dec. 4, Burnquist wired Ames "substantially" as quoted: copy in Nelson Papers, Dec. 4, 1917.

38. Tumulty to Nelson, Dec. 11, 1917, Nelson Papers. The *St. Paul Daily News* deplored the dismissal of Ames, which it attributed to his participation in the conference with Baker, Kellogg, and Van Dyke that led to Baker's request that the button order be suspended. The newspaper noted that the meeting included a balance of the different points of view in the dispute: Kellogg oriented to management, Van Dyke to labor, Baker representing the federal government, and Ames appropriately speaking for the MCPS. (*St. Paul Daily News,* Dec. 7, 1917, p. 6; a clipping of the editorial is filed in the Charles W. Ames Papers, MHS.)

39. Telegram, Captain Ten Broek to Nelson, Dec. 5, 1917, Nelson Papers.

40. McGee to Nelson, Dec. 5, 1917, quoting McGee telegrams to Baker and William G. McAdoo (secretary of the treasury), Nelson Papers; here and below, Millikan, "Defenders of Business," 15–16.

41. Copies of the correspondence are in the Nelson Papers, Dec. 13–14, 1917.

42. MCPS, *Report,* 41.

43. Lowry to Nelson, Dec. 21, 1917, Nelson Papers.

44. President's Mediation Commission Report, copy in the Lind Papers under Feb. 14, 1918; Tighe to Burnquist, Mar. 13, 1918, file 136, Main Files. The Council of National Defense asked the MCPS to urge compliance with the mediation recommendations: Millikan, "Defenders of Business," 17; MCPS Minutes, Mar. 5, 1918.

45. *Union Labor Bulletin,* December 1917, p. 17.

46. Lind to Harthill, Oct. 20, 1917, attached to A. L. Kercher (Lind's secretary) to Libby, Oct. 31, 1917, file 69, Main Files.

47. Harthill to Lind, Oct. 23, 1917, attached to Kercher to Libby, Oct. 31, 1917, file 69, Main Files.

48. Quoted in McGee to Nelson, Dec. 5, 1917, Nelson Papers.

49. Handwritten reply on letter from William W. Folwell to Lind, Nov. 19, 1924, Folwell Papers, MHS.

50. Lind to Burnquist, Dec. 7, 11, 1917, Burnquist Papers.

51. Lind to Burnquist, Jan. 7, 1918, Burnquist Papers.

52. Burnquist to Lind, Jan. 9, 1918, March to Lind, Jan. 12, 1918 — both in Lind Papers.

53. Tighe to Lind, Feb. 13, 1918, Lind Papers.

54. Quotation found in Tighe to Lind, Feb. 13, 1918, Lind Papers, referring to a statement made in an earlier Lind letter to Tighe; Burnquist to Lind, Mar. 16, 1918, Lind Papers. For biographical detail on Cashman, see *St. Paul Dispatch,* Dec. 15, 1933, p. 1, 5.

55. Certificate of appointment, Lind Papers, Jan. 24, 1918; Stephenson, *John Lind,* 333.

56. Nord, "Hothouse Socialism," 149.

57. Text of Mahoney address to 1923 Farmer-Labor conference, in *Third-Party Footprints: An Anthology from Writings and Speeches of Midwest Radicals,* ed. James M. Youngdale (Minneapolis: Ross and Haines, 1966), 190. Lowry felt impelled to respond to the recruitment complaint when it was voiced by Republican Congressman Sydney Anderson of Minnesota's first district: MCPS Minutes, Mar. 5, 1918.

CHAPTER 10. *Bread, Booze, and Bonds*

1. *Proceedings of the City Council,* 1917, p. 270, 337, 344, 486, 497, 834. Dight, a physician by profession, is best known for his identification with the eugenics movement of the 1920s; see Gary Phelps, "The Eugenics Crusade of Charles Fremont Dight," *Minnesota History* 49 (Fall 1984): 99–108.

2. MCPS Minutes, June 26, 1917; draft, MCPS to Boards of County Commissioners, June 28, 1917, file 107, Main Files.

3. Here and below, MCPS, *Report,* 16–17; MCPS Minutes, Oct. 25, 1917.

4. MCPS Minutes, Apr. 30, Jan. 8, 1918.

5. Carl J. Buell, *The Minnesota Legislature of 1919* ([St. Paul, 1919]), 106; here and below, *St. Paul Daily News,* Aug. 1, 1917, p. 6.

6. Here and below, MCPS Minutes, July 3, 16, Nov. 2, 1917.

7. MCPS, *Report,* 82–87 (quotation on 83).

8. "Report and Recommendation of the Committee on Cost of Living," Aug. 28, 1917, p. 1–3 (quotations on 2, 3), file 124, Main Files; MCPS Minutes, same date; here and below, MCPS, *Report,* 89, 103–4.

9. MCPS Minutes, Nov. 6, 1917.

10. MCPS Minutes, Dec. 4, 1917; here and below, MCPS, *Report,* 92–93, 104.

11. MCPS Minutes, Feb. 26, 1918; MCPS, *Report,* 103–5 (quotations).

12. Ward to Lind, Mar. 1, 1918, Lind to March, Mar. 6, 1918 — both in Lind Papers.

13. Here and below, MCPS, *Report,* 19; MCPS Minutes, July 3, 11, 16, 17 (quotation), Aug. 1, 14, Nov. 2, 1917; McGee to Burnquist, Aug. 1, 1917, Burnquist Papers.

14. "Responsibility for the Movement of Anthracite in Minnesota in the Fuel Year April 1st, 1918 to February 1st, 1919," Mar. 25, 1919, file 71, Main Files.

15. Joseph T. Garry to Burnquist, Sept. 17, 1918, file 648a, Governor's Records. A Duluth resident informed Burnquist that he, Burnquist, had "been a very loyal Governor but [believed] some people on the Safety Commission . . . don't consider anybody except possibly the big interests. . . . Your Mr. McGee has certainly got himself and everybody connected with him in pretty bad. Even here in Duluth it is carry your own coal and there is a great deal of feeling against him" (John J. Lane to Burnquist, Aug. 22, 1918, file 648a, Governor's Records).

16. Lindquist to Garry, Sept. 18, 1918, file 648a, Governor's Records.

17. Full texts of the commission's orders are given in MCPS, *Report,* 72–142.

18. J. C. Barr to MCPS, Nov. 1, 1917, file 110, Main Files.

19. MCPS Minutes, July 16, 1917.

20. MCPS, *Report,* 36.

21. MCPS Minutes, July 24, Aug. 28, Sept. 4, 11 (quotation), 1917.

22. Here and below, MCPS Minutes, Sept. 12 (quotations), Aug. 6, 1917.

23. MCPS Minutes, Sept. 18, Oct. 16, 25, 1917; MCPS, *Report,* 80–82.

24. McGee to *Masonic Observer,* Dec. 29, 1917, file 110, Main Files.

25. MCPS Minutes, Feb. 5, 1918; MCPS, *Report,* 161.

26. Packet of letters re Forest Lake dated September 1917, file 110, Main Files; MCPS Minutes, Sept. 18, 1917 (quotation); Rochester petition dated Apr. 2, Libby to Gooding, Apr. 11, Gooding to Libby, Apr. 12, Libby to Gooding, Apr. 18 — all 1918, all in file 110, Main Files.

27. N. I. Lowry to Libby, May 3 (quotation), Mrs. John C. Killner to MCPS, Oct. 19, Libby to Mayor, Oct. 24 — all 1918, all in file 110, Main Files.

28. Notwithstanding a massive volume of complaints concerning liquor violations in Springfield, the MCPS declined to act. According to Libby, the MCPS had "authority to act only when a military situation is proven," and no military need was apparent (Libby to Alexander Seifert, Apr. 24, 1918, file 110, Main Files).

29. Here and below, MCPS Minutes, Dec. 5, 1917, Jan. 8, May 14, 1918, MCPS, *Report,* 90–91, 116 (quotations on 91).

30. MCPS Minutes, June 27, 1918; MCPS, *Report,* 41–42.

31. State ex rel. Burnquist v. District Court Second Judicial District, 141 *Minn.* 1 (quotation on 15).

32. MCPS Minutes, Sept. 24, 1918; MCPS, *Report,* 132–35.

33. MCPS Minutes, Apr. 30, 1918. Apparently one motive for the order was to facilitate enforcement of liquor decrees: Libby to E. H. Nicholas, Apr. 29, 1918, file 110, Main Files.

34. Here and below, MCPS Minutes, Dec. 11, 1917, Jan. 15, 30, 1918, MCPS, *Report,* 94–95, 97–99, 36–37.

35. Here and below, MCPS Minutes, July 30, Aug. 13, 1918. Possible action with respect to Red Lake County was discussed on Aug. 6. McGee introduced a motion calling for total prohibition in the county, and Weiss moved to amend by applying the Martin-Pipestone precedent. Only Weiss and March voted aye, whereupon the original motion passed by a vote of six to one with Weiss voting nay; however, the motion was not immediately incorporated into an order.

36. MCPS, *Report,* 122–23.

37. Chrislock, *Progressive Era,* 87; Cheney, *Minnesota Politics,* 35–37.

38. "To the Banks, Bankers and Trust Companies of the Ninth Federal Reserve District," Oct. 2, 1917, file 68, Main Files.

39. Holbrook and Appel, *Minnesota,* 2:193–200.

40. George F. Porter to State Councils of Defense, Aug. 13, Sept. 22, 1917, file 68, Main Files; MCPS Minutes, Sept. 18, 1917.

41. "To Our Comrades in the Second Liberty Loan Campaign," Sept. 28, 1917, file 68, Main Files.

42. Cashman to Henke, Oct. 22, 1917, file 101, Main Files.

43. Ames to Thomas H. Sullivan, Oct. 12, 1917, file 101, Main Files.

44. Ames to Hess, Oct. 12, 1917, file 101, Main Files.

45. Hess to Ames, Oct. 30, 1917, Henke to Hess, Nov. 1, 1917 — both in file 101, Main Files.

46. MCPS Minutes, Oct. 11, 1917; telegram, Henke to Porter, Dec. 5, 1917, file 101, Libby to Ames, Feb. 7, 1918, file 68 — both in Main Files; Holbrook and Appel, *Minnesota,* 2:202–3.

47. Jan. 26, 1918, p. 5.
48. Holbrook and Appel, *Minnesota,* 2:202–3.

CHAPTER II. *Mobilizing Minnesota Women*

1. Alice Ames Winter to Pardee, Aug. 1, 1917, Fisher to M. M. Booth (MCPS clerk-secretary), Sept. 20, 1917, Fisher to Libby, Aug. 7, 1918 — all in file 56, Main Files.
2. MCPS, *Report,* 310–17, carries a complete roster of the Winter organization.
3. See "Report for First Six Months of Work," Nov. 15, 1917, detailing organizational structure and early accomplishments, file 56, Main Files (hereafter cited as Nov. 15 Report).
4. A. Winter to Booth, June 28, 1917, file 56, Pardee to County Director, July 23, 1917, file 107 — both in Main Files.
5. Nov. 15 Report.
6. Here and below, see biographical material in Biography Project files, Reference Library, MHS.
7. Anna Augusta Helmholtz Phelan, *The Social Philosophy of William Morris* (Durham, N.C.: Duke University Press, 1927).
8. Dolores De Bower Johnson, "Anna Dickie Olesen: Senate Candidate," in *Women of Minnesota: Selected Biographical Essays,* ed. Barbara Stuhler and Gretchen Kreuter (St. Paul: Minnesota Historical Society Press, 1977), 231.
9. A. Winter to Pardee, Aug. 3, 1917, file 56, Main Files.
10. "Resume of Work for the Month of July," file 56, Main Files; Ferrell, *Woodrow Wilson,* 91–93 (quotations on 92 and 93).
11. Nov. 15 Report.
12. "Resume of Work," file 56, Main Files; Ferrell, *Woodrow Wilson,* 92.
13. Here and below, Women's Auxiliary Committee, "Report of County Chairmen for August 1917," attached to Burnquist proclamation filed under Sept. 21, 1917, file 56, Main Files.
14. A. Winter to Pardee, Aug. 4, 1917, file 56, Main Files.
15. Here and below, Nov. 15 Report.
16. A. Winter to County Chairmen, undated, file 56, Main Files; Nov. 15 Report.
17. Aug. 4, 1917, file 56, Main Files.
18. A. Winter to Madam Chairman, Apr. 30, 1918, "Resume of Office Work for . . . September [1917]" — both in file 56, Main Files.
19. A. Winter to Libby, Oct. 19, 1917, file 56, Main Files; MCPS Minutes, Sept. 18, 1917. A copy of Burnquist's proclamation is filed under Sept. 21, 1917, in file 56, Main Files.
20. "Report of Committee on Women in Industry," undated, file 56, Main Files.
21. Here and below, Ferrell, *Woodrow Wilson,* 62–63.
22. Philip D. Jordan, *The People's Health: A History of Public Health in Minnesota to 1948* (St. Paul: Minnesota Historical Society, 1953), 251–53.
23. Pardee to Mrs. A. (Clara) Ueland, June 6, 1917, and to Mrs. A. M. Burt, July 23, 1917 — both in file 73, Main Files.
24. Here and below, Jordan, *People's Health,* 254–56; MCPS Minutes, Oct. 16, Nov. 13, 20, 1917, Jan. 29, 1918. The Nov. 20 motion, introduced by Lind, approved the proposed social hygiene commission and "requested" the State Board of Health to cooperate with it and "to clothe such of its members or agents as it may select, with the powers of special health officers." The motion also promised to "consider" budgetary proposals from the new body.
25. MCPS, *Report,* 26.

26. Here and below, A. Winter to Burnquist and Weiss (identical letters), Mar. 15, 1918, file 56, Main Files. The commission endorsed the program and responded positively to the request for a paid stenographer: Libby to A. Winter, Mar. 27, 1918, file 56, Main Files.

27. Here and below, Jordan, *People's Health,* 383–84 (quotation on 384).

28. MCPS Minutes, June 27, 1918.

29. Here and below, Jordan, *People's Health,* 385 (quotation), 414.

30. Carroll and Raiter, *Fires of Autumn,* 112, 115, 123–24.

31. "Report of Work — Nov. 1–Dec. 1, 1918," file 56, Main Files.

32. A. Winter to Madam Chairman, Nov. 30, 1918, file 56, Main Files; Jordan, *People's Health,* 385 (quotation), 386.

33. A. Winter to Madam Chairman, undated letter filed under Dec. 18, 1918, file 56, Main Files.

34. A. Winter to Pardee and attached letter from Agnes Bobb Adsit to Winter, Aug. 3, 1917, file 56, Main Files.

35. Postcard, A. Winter to Booth, Apr. 13, 1918, Libby to A. Winter, Apr. 15, 1918 — both in file 56, Main Files.

36. A. Winter to Burnquist and Libby (identical letters), June 14, 1918, Libby to A. Winter, June 20, 1918, Anna H. Phelan and A. Winter to Madam Chairman, June 26, 1918 — all in file 56, Main Files.

37. A. Winter to Madam Chairman, Apr. 30, 1918, file 56, Main Files.

38. MCPS Minutes, Nov. 20, 1917; A. Winter to County Chairmen, Oct. 16, 1918, file 56, Main Files.

39. Pamphlet filed under Dec. 31, A. Winter to Madam Chairman, Nov. 30, 1918 — both in file 56, Main Files.

40. A. Winter to Libby, Oct. 26, 1918, file 56, Main Files; MCPS Minutes, Dec. 31, 1918, Jan. 14, 1919.

41. Lane to MCPS, Oct. 12, 1918, A. Winter to Libby, Oct. 26, 1918, Libby to A. Winter, Oct. 30, 1918 — all in file 56, Main Files.

42. Here and below, Legislative Committee of Minnesota Woman's Committee, Council of Defense, to Madam Chairman, Dec. 18, 1918, file 56, Main Files.

43. *Session Laws,* 1919, chap. 320, p. 337–38.

CHAPTER 12. *Defending the Status Quo Ante*

1. Henke to County Director, Dec. 10, 1917, file 107, Main Files.

2. Henke to March, Dec. 27, 1917, file 70, Main Files.

3. MCPS Minutes, Jan. 8, 1918, Cotton to Burnquist, Jan. 2, 1918, Cotton Papers; Henke to A. C. Rutledge, Jan. 11, 1918, file 145, Main Files.

4. Telegram, Libby to George F. Porter, Feb. 6, 1918, file 67, Main Files.

5. Memorandum, Winterbotham to Cotton, Feb. 6, 1918, Cotton Papers.

6. Cotton to Burnquist, Dec. 18, 1917, file 648a, Governor's Records; MCPS Minutes, Oct. 2, 9, 1917; W. E. Hall to Cotton, June 20, 1918, Cotton Papers.

7. Cotton to Burnquist, May 28, 29, Sept. 16, 1918, file 648a, Governor's Records; Cotton to Winterbotham, Apr. 29, Winterbotham to Cotton, June 10, 1918, Cotton to Winterbotham, June 14, 1918 — all in Cotton Papers.

8. Winterbotham to Cotton, Mar. 4, 1918 (quotation), Cotton to Strong, Mar. 6, 1918, Cotton to L. S. Gillette, June 8, 1918, telegram, Cotton to W. C. Koch, Apr. 9, 1918, Koch to Cotton, Feb. 8, 1918, p. 5 (quotation) — all in Cotton Papers.

9. Winterbotham to Cotton, Oct. 3, 11, 1918, Cotton to Winterbotham, Oct. 14, 1918 (quotations) — all in Cotton Papers.

10. Smith to MCPS, Feb. 14, 1918, S. W. Frasier to Smith, Feb. 20, 1918, Smith to Frasier, Feb. 23 (quotation), Mar. 19, 1918, Frasier to Porter, Mar. 13, 1918 (quotation) — all in file 67, Main Files. Less than a month before the armistice, the MCPS passed a motion requesting Public Examiner Andrew E. Fritz to systematize the work in the office: MCPS Minutes, Oct. 16, 1918.

11. Here and below, Henry F. Pringle, *The Life and Times of William Howard Taft* (New York: Farrar and Rinehart, 1939), 2:915–18 (quotations on 918).

12. Here and below, Pringle, *William Howard Taft,* 2:916.

13. Here and below, Pringle, *William Howard Taft,* 2:915–16.

14. Here and below, Chamberlain to Nelson, July 3, 1918, Nelson Papers.

15. Report of President's Mediation Commission and associated CPI news release, Feb. 14, 15, 1918, Lind Papers; MCPS Minutes, Feb. 27, 1918; Koch to Cotton, Feb. 7, 1918, Cotton Papers.

16. Here and below, Minnesota State Board of Arbitration, "Report for Biennium 1917 and 1918" (printed as Exhibit C in Minnesota State Board of Arbitration, *Biennial Report, 1919–1920* [St. Paul: 1921], 13–21) and "Daily Diary . . . Entries for April 8 to June 17, 1918" — both in Minnesota State Board of Arbitration Papers, Minnesota State Archives, MHS; MCPS Minutes, Apr. 16, 1918; MCPS, *Report,* 108–9 (quotations). The arbitration board recognized the variance between federal and state labor policy: see "Report for Biennium 1917 and 1918."

17. Here and below, Herbert R. Brougham and Raymond G. Swing, "Report of an Investigation of the Minneapolis Steel and Machinery Company," file 75, Main Files (hereafter cited as Brougham and Swing Report). This report covers considerably more than the troubles between Minneapolis Steel and Machinery and International Association of Machinists Local 91. It is a comprehensive account of the labor turmoil afflicting Minneapolis in the summer of 1918. Brougham and Swing interviewed Lawson on July 28: Brougham and Swing Report, 20–21. After he left government service in 1919, Raymond Swing returned to journalism and achieved national prominence as a foreign correspondent during World War II.

18. Brougham and Swing Report, 3–4; Lawson, *History of Labor,* 41–45.

19. McGrath to Raymond F. Schroeder, June 8, 1918, copy in Brougham and Swing Report, 24 (quotations); Minnesota State Board of Arbitration Memo, docket 196, National War Labor Board Papers, National Archives, Washington, D.C.

20. Horace Lowry to Minnesota State Board of Arbitration, June 10, 1918, copy in Brougham and Swing Report, 26.

21. Award issued by arbitration board, copy in Brougham and Swing Report, 29–30 (quotations on 29).

22. Lowry to Minnesota State Board of Arbitration, June 13, 1918, copy in Brougham and Swing Report, 27; Brougham and Swing Report, 28.

23. Here and below, Brougham and Swing Report, 6–7.

24. Copy of article in Brougham and Swing Report, 32.

25. Telegram, Brougham and Swing to Lauck, Aug. 1, 1918, copy in Brougham and Swing Report, 33; Lauck to Swing, Aug. 1, 1918, copy in Brougham and Swing Report, 34; telegram, Frank Morrison to Jean A. Spielman, Sept. 10, 1918, Jean A. Spielman Papers, MHS.

26. A preliminary investigation of the Minneapolis Steel and Machinery labor policy disclosed that "said company claims and insists on being a non-union shop, and bases its present attitude on the authority of the declarations of principles as promulgated by the Public Safety Commission" (Brougham and Swing Report, 47).

27. Here and below, Brougham and Swing Report, 7–8.

28. Here and below, Brougham and Swing Report, 9–11, 14, 39 (quotations on 9 and 14).

29. Quotations here and below taken from statement drafted by Tighe, attached to Tighe to Libby, Oct. 14, 1918, p. 1, 3, 5, file 75, Main Files.

30. Tighe statement, attached to Tighe to Libby, Oct. 14, 1918, p. 5–6 (quotations on 5).

31. "National War Labor Board: Transcript of a Hearing Held in Minneapolis . . . on October 10, 1914," 83–84, docket 196, NWLB Papers.

32. "Employers' Objection and Plea to Jurisdiction," Oct. 17, 1918, docket 196, NWLB Papers.

33. The text of the brief is filed in docket 196, NWLB Papers.

34. Here and below, Tighe statement, attached to Tighe to Libby, Oct. 14, 1918.

35. Here and below, NWLB, "Award in Cases No. 46 and 196," NWLB Papers, 2, 6–7 (hereafter cited as NWLB Award); MCPS, *Report,* 109 (quotation from Order 30). A copy of this document is also in the Spielman Papers, attached to Lauck to Spielman, Nov. 25, 1918, and in file 648a, Governor's Records, attached to Lauck to Burnquist, Nov. 25, 1918.

36. NWLB Award, 8.

37. NWLB Award, 9–10.

38. Spielman et al. to Taft and Walsh, undated, docket 196, NWLB Papers.

39. "National War Labor Board: Transcript of a Hearing Held in Minneapolis . . . on Jan. 14, 1919," docket 196, NWLB Papers.

40. "Findings and Recommendations in re Local No. 91, International Association of Machinists . . . versus Minneapolis Steel & Machinery Co.," docket 46, NWLB Papers. A copy is also filed in the Spielman Papers under Apr. 23, 1919.

41. Robert K. Murray, *Red Scare: A Study in National Hysteria, 1919–1920* (Minneapolis: University of Minnesota Press, 1955), 105–21.

42. When Western Union refused to honor an NWLB award in mid-July 1918, "the upshot was authorization by Congress for President Wilson to take over the telegraph and telephone lines" (Pringle, *William Howard Taft,* 2:920).

CHAPTER 13. *Chauvinism at High Tide*

1. Ferrell, *Woodrow Wilson,* 53. The normative size of a division was forty thousand men.

2. July 13, 1918, p. 7.

3. Ferrell, *Woodrow Wilson,* 65–73.

4. Portions of Iowa proclamation found in Chrislock, *Ethnicity Challenged,* 81–82; other quotations in Peterson and Fite, *Opponents of War,* 213–14.

5. Quoted in Peterson and Fite, *Opponents of War,* 215.

6. T. Winter to Burnquist, Mar. 13, 1918, file 648a, Governor's Records, wherein Winter disclosed that he was departing for France to supervise distribution of Allied relief; MCPS Minutes, Jan. 15, 1918; Peterson and Fite, *Opponents of War,* 19 (quotations). Donald Cotton was active in the management of APL's Minnesota branch. See Cotton to Paul J. Kalman, Jan. 23, 1918, and Kalman to Cotton, Jan. 25, 1918, Cotton Papers, which disclosed that the expense of maintaining a Minneapolis office was around three hundred dollars a month. The St. Paul Association defrayed part of the expense incurred by the capital city branch.

7. MCPS Minutes, Feb. 27, 1918.

8. Weiss to McGee, Apr. 3, 1918, file 72, Main Files.

9. Libby to Boyce, July 10, 1918 (quotation), Boyce to Libby, July 11, 1918 — both in file 100, Main Files.

10. NIB reports of July 11, 18, 20, 25, 28, Oct. 4, 30, 1918, file 100, Main Files.

11. The original termination decision was taken on Oct. 8: Libby to Boyce, Oct. 9, 1918; however, at McGee's insistence it was lifted: Boyce to Libby, Dec. 5, 1918, Libby to Boyce, Dec. 6, 1918. The final termination was accomplished in late May 1919: Libby to Boyce, May 20, 1919 — all in file 100, Main Files.

12. Boyce to Libby, Oct. 4, 1918, NIB report, Oct. 4, 1918 — both in file 100, Main Files.

13. Here and below, Morlan, *Political Prairie Fire,* 167–71, 256–61, 336, 159; Folwell, *Minnesota,* 3:570–75.

14. Jens N. Landro to Burnquist, Feb. 18, 1918, file 648a, Governor's Records.

15. Herman Samuelson to Landro, Feb. 20, 1918, file 648a, Governor's Records.

16. A Meeker County parade, NPL supporters claimed, was twelve miles long. "The biggest meeting" assembled at Wegdahl (Chippewa County) on June 14, 1918: Morlan, *Political Prairie Fire,* 197.

17. C. W. Schultz to Burnquist, June 15, 1918, Gustaf Lindquist to Schultz, Aug. 6, 1918, A. Fredrickson (Brown county attorney) to Lindquist, Aug. 2, 1918 (quotation) — all in file 648a, Governor's Records.

18. S. H. Jenson to Burnquist, May 8, 1918, Burnquist to Louis P. Johnson (Lincoln county attorney), May 10, 1918 — both in file 648a, Governor's Records.

19. Johnson to Burnquist, May 18, 1918, file 648a, Governor's Records.

20. Anna Sulem to Burnquist, July 30, 1918, file 648a, Governor's Records.

21. Lindquist to Sulem, July 31, 1918, file 648a, Governor's Records.

22. Frank B. Kellogg to Burnquist, Apr. 19, 1918, enclosing a copy of the O'Brian to Kellogg letter: file 648a, Governor's Records.

23. MCPS, *Report,* 22–23.

24. Here and below, MCPS Minutes, Jan. 15, Feb. 5, 1918. The texts of Orders 23 and 25 are given in MCPS, *Report,* 97–98, 100–103.

25. Here and below, MCPS Minutes, Feb. 26, Mar. 5, 1918.

26. MCPS Minutes, Mar. 5, 1918.

27. Quoted in Chrislock, *Ethnicity Challenged,* 80–81. The quotation is a translation of the probate judge's speech appearing in a Norwegian version in *Lutheraneren* 2 (Feb. 20, 1918): 241; this periodical, the official organ of the Norwegian Lutheran Church in America, was published in Minneapolis.

28. Telegrams, Julius E. Haycraft to Burnquist, Apr. 9, 1918, W. F. Sanger to Burnquist, Apr. 12, 1918 — both in file 648a, Governor's Records. Haycraft was city attorney of Fairmont and a well-known former state legislator.

29. Burnquist to Sanger, Apr. 17, 1918, Burnquist to Haycraft, Apr. 18, 1918 — both in file 648a, Governor's Records.

30. Chrislock, *Ethnicity Challenged,* 81.

31. MCPS Minutes, Apr. 30, 1918; MCPS, *Report,* 115.

32. La Vern J. Rippley, "Conflict in the Classroom: Anti-Germanism in Minnesota Schools, 1917–19," *Minnesota History* 47 (Spring 1981): 170–83; MCPS Minutes, Sept. 12, 1917.

33. MCPS Minutes, Nov. 20, 1917.

34. MCPS Minutes, Nov. 6, 13, 1917. The resolution was adopted on Nov. 13.

35. Ames to C. F. Angell, Nov. 12, 1917, file 68, Main Files.

36. Ames to Libby, Mar. 20, 1918, file 68, Main Files.

37. Schulz to Burnquist, May 10, 1918, file 648a, Governor's Records.

38. For copies of both surveys, see Schulz to Burnquist, May 10, 1918, file 648a, Governor's Records.

39. Cited in *Brown County Journal,* June 28, 1919, p. 4.

40. Burnquist to Thomas P. Christensen, Oct. 29, 1918, file 648a, Governor's Records. By contrast, Ohio Governor James M. Cox, Democratic presidential nominee

in 1920, "urged the Ohio legislature to forbid instruction in German in elementary schools, public, private and parochial, because it was part of a German plot to gain loyalty of school children" (Ferrell, *Woodrow Wilson*, 205).

41. The foregoing is Schulz's version of what he told the St. Paul business leaders: Schulz to Busch, Nov. 4, 1918, attached to Busch to Burnquist, Oct. 28, 1918, copy in Lind Papers.

42. Apparently the Aronovici project was undertaken at Ames's initiative: Aronovici to Pardee, June 26, 1917, file 73, Main Files. A statement outlining Aronovici's goals is in file 73 under July 12, 1917.

43. Before completing his investigation, Aronovici submitted several preliminary recommendations: Pardee to Aronovici, Aug. 13, 1917, file 73, Main Files. Since these recommendations are not in the MCPS Papers, the account here and in following paragraphs is based on Aronovici's final report, submitted on Mar. 11, 1918: see Libby to Aronovici, Mar. 14, 1918, file 73, Main Files.

44. Here and below, MCPS Minutes, June 4, 1918; MCPS, *Report*, 117–18.

45. Paul Ahles to Hilton, June 29, 1918, file 51, Main Files.

46. Smith to Ahles, July 5, 1918, file 51, Main Files.

47. Libby to C. H. Ellison (Rochester city justice), July 30, 1918, Libby to Ed Chill, July 22, 1918 — both in file 51, Main Files.

48. Pfiffner to Major J. P. Snyder, July 18, 1918, file 50, Main Files.

49. Pfiffner to Snyder, Nov. 13, 1918, file 50, Main Files.

50. Libby to C. M. Miller, Aug. 20, 1918, file 51, Main Files.

51. Butler to Libby, Sept. 4, 1918, Alger, Smith and Co. to MCPS, Sept. 7, 1918 — both in file 51, Main Files.

52. MCPS Minutes, Aug. 24, 1918; MCPS, *Report*, 125–26.

53. Holbrook and Appel, *Minnesota*, 2:207.

54. E. Nelson to Burnquist, Oct. 10, 1918, Samuelson to Nelson, Oct. 12, 1918 — both in file 648a, Governor's Records.

55. F. D. Warden to Burnquist, Oct. 12, 1918, Samuelson to Warden, Oct. 14, 1918 — both in file 648a, Governor's Records.

56. Libby to C. W. Gordon, Oct. 12, 1918, Gordon to Libby, Oct. 14, 1918 — both in file 101, Main Files.

57. By mid-July *Commercial West* was questioning the wisdom of banning NPL meetings: issue of July 13, 1918, p. 8.

58. Both incidents are described in Chrislock, *Progressive Era*, 174.

59. The text is carried in *Minneota Mascot*, Oct. 11, 1918.

60. Editorial, Oct. 11, 1918.

CHAPTER 14. *The Campaign of 1918*

1. *Minneota Mascot*, Jan. 7, 1916.

2. See above, p. 179–80, 250–52.

3. Here and below, Morlan, *Political Prairie Fire*, 214, 381 n. 99, 187; Chrislock, *Progressive Era*, 145; Gaston, *Nonpartisan League*, 252.

4. Morlan, *Political Prairie Fire*, 188.

5. The full text of the Burnquist letter may be found — among other places — in the *Minneapolis Tribune*, Mar. 12, 1918, p. 1, 4.

6. Here and below, Morlan, *Political Prairie Fire*, 189–91 (quotations on 189, 191).

7. Bruce L. Larson, *Lindbergh of Minnesota: A Political Biography* (New York: Harcourt Brace Jovanovich, 1973), 252 (quotation); *Gaa Paa*, Mar. 23, 1918.

8. Lindbergh to Burnquist, undated but filed under May 1917, Burnquist Papers.

9. *Why Is Your Country at War and What Happens to You After the War and Related Subjects* (Washington, D.C.: [National Capital Press], 1917), 6, 117, 7; Chrislock, *Progressive Era,* 167.

10. *St. Paul Daily News,* May 9, 1918, p. 4.

11. Several versions of McGee's remarks, differing in minor details but not in substance, are extant. The foregoing is taken from Lynn Haines and Dora B. Haines, *The Lindberghs* (New York: Vanguard Press, 1931), 281–82.

12. A. C. Hatch to Nelson, Apr. 22, 1918, Nelson Papers; Mrs. Luth Jaeger to Libby, Apr. 27, 1918, file 71, Main Files; *Proceedings of the City Council of . . . Minneapolis,* 1918, p. 209; Morlan, *Political Prairie Fire,* 165. On May 10 the *Minneota Mascot* called for McGee's resignation.

13. Gregory to Lind, May 3, 1918, Lind Papers.

14. Libby to Jaeger, May 1, 1918, file 71, Main Files.

15. *Proceedings of the City Council,* 1918, p. 251–52. The report of the delegation that interviewed Burnquist noted: "The impression your committee gets from the Governor was that he resented Judge McGee's statement as much as your committee and the public in general" (p. 252).

16. *St. Paul Pioneer Press,* May 5, 1918, sec. 2, p. 4.

17. U.S. Senate, *Hearings before the Committee on Military Affairs,* 65th Cong., 2d sess., 1918, pt. 2: 71 (hereafter cited as Townley Hearing). A copy of this transcript is in file 135, Main Files.

18. Here and below, Townley Hearing, 70, 85 (quotation).

19. Here and below, Townley Hearing, 72–75, 99 (quotations on 75, 99).

20. L. M. Willcuts to Nelson, May 30, 1918, Nelson Papers.

21. Quoted in Chrislock, *Progressive Era,* 170.

22. The Nelson Papers contain substantial information about internal GOP difficulties. See Magnus Martinson to Frank B. Kellogg, Oct. 4, 1917, and Nelson to J. A. O. Preus, July 8, 1918, which suggests a lack of amiability between Burnquist and Nelson.

23. *St. Paul Daily News,* May 6, 1918, p. 2; *Fairmont Daily Sentinel,* May 4, 1918, p. 4; *St. Paul Daily News,* June 16, 1918, p. 12.

24. S. M. Sivertson to March, Apr. 6, 1918, Libby to Sivertson, Apr. 24, 1918 — both in file 135, Main Files.

25. This message appeared under the MCPS byline in many newspapers, including the *Morton Enterprise,* May 24, 1918, clipping in vol. 64, MCPS Scrapbooks.

26. Chrislock, *Ethnicity Challenged,* 109, 99–105.

27. Chrislock, *Ethnicity Challenged,* 103, quoting *Reform* (Eau Claire, Wis.), June 11, 1918.

28. Chrislock, *Ethnicity Challenged,* 110–15; Grevstad to Nelson, Aug. 27, 1918, Nelson Papers.

29. Libby to C. E. Van Nest, Apr. 4, 1918, Van Nest to Libby, Apr. 5, 1918 — both in file 101, Main Files.

30. J. M. Malmin to MCPS, June 13, 1918, Libby to Malmin, June 15, 1918 — both in file 135, Main Files.

31. *Legislative Manual,* 1919, p. 252–53; Chrislock, *Progressive Era,* 171.

32. *Commercial West,* June 22, 1918, p. 7.

33. *St. Paul Daily News,* June 18, 1918, p. 6.

34. Chrislock, *Progressive Era,* 172.

35. Gaston, *Nonpartisan League,* 261.

36. A copy of the letter is in the Burnquist Papers under Apr. 5, 1917.

37. For an editorial comment sympathetic to Le Sueur, see *Fergus Falls Free Press,* Oct. 2, 1918.

38. See Nelson correspondence (outgoing) for Sept. 11, 12, 1918, Nelson Papers; Larson, *Lindbergh,* 251.

39. Frank M. Kaisersatt to Nelson, Sept. 9, 1918, Sidney J. Huntley to Nelson, Sept. 10, 1918 — both in Nelson Papers; telegram, twenty-five Litchfield residents to March, Sept. 10, 1918, file 70, Main Files.

40. Patrick J. Russell to Nelson, Sept. 11, 1918, enclosing letter from Earle Brown, state inspector, APL, to all APL chiefs in the state (quotation), Nelson Papers.

41. Frank M. Eddy to Nelson, Sept. 8, 1918, Nelson Papers.

42. Here and below, Larson, *Lindbergh,* 252–53.

43. A printed facsimile of this telegram was extensively circulated throughout the state. A copy is filed under Oct. 28, 1918, in the Nelson Papers.

44. *Minneapolis Morning Tribune,* Oct. 29, 1918, p. 6. The editorial went on to excoriate John Lind as the "guiding spirit of this conspiracy."

45. For general election returns by county and precinct, see *Legislative Manual,* 1919, p. 514–682. For returns by county, see White et al., comps., *Minnesota Votes,* 35, 183–84.

CHAPTER 15. *Passage into History*

1. Ferrell, *Woodrow Wilson,* 230.

2. *Inaugural Message of Gov. J. A. A. Burnquist to the Legislature of Minnesota, 1919* ([St. Paul, 1919]), 4–9.

3. Here and below, MCPS Minutes, Jan. 14, Feb. 4, 1919, MCPS, *Report,* 141–42 (quotations).

4. Here and below, Buell, *Minnesota Legislature of 1919,* 75–81 (quotations below on 76, 77); *House Journal,* 1919, p. 78, 196–97; *Senate Journal,* 1919, p. 507; *The Appeal* (St. Paul), April 6, 13, 20, 1918.

5. Following lengthy debate on Feb. 13, the Motor Corps bill passed the House by a vote of eighty-five to forty-three (*House Journal,* 1919, p. 415–20). On Feb. 28 the Senate Committee on Military Affairs recommended passage of the bill (*Senate Journal,* 1919, p. 512), but it went no further in that body. A Senate bill calling for revision of the military code was indefinitely postponed on Mar. 28 (*Senate Journal,* 1919, p. 1044). The Negro battalion measure as enacted may be found in Minnesota Secretary of State, *Session Laws,* 1919, chap. 472, p. 628; an editorial critical of the bill appeared in *The Appeal,* Feb. 15, 1919.

6. *House Journal,* 1919, p. 20, 93, 1137, 1398, 1592–93; Buell, *Minnesota Legislature of 1919,* 81–83 (quotation on 83).

7. Buell used the term "inocuous [*sic*] desuetude" (p. 83) in quotes without attributing it to a specific source. Evidently one of the participants in the House debate on the Pittenger bill originated it.

8. Buell, *Minnesota Legislature of 1919,* 52–53.

9. Here and below, Buell, *Minnesota Legislature of 1919,* 82–83 (quotations).

10. *Senate Journal,* 1919, p. 1562–63. When the vote was taken on the majority report, only seven senators voted nay.

11. On the Citizens Alliance, see William Millikan, "Maintaining 'Law and Order': The Minneapolis Citizen's Alliance in the 1920s," *Minnesota History* 51 (Summer 1989): 219–33. On Palmer's anti-Red crusade, see Murray, *Red Scare,* 191–260. If Palmer relieved Minnesota authorities of some of their Red-chasing responsibilities, shifts in federal labor policy also generated happiness within conservative circles. In a letter to Herschel V. Jones of the *Minneapolis Journal,* Knute Nelson predicted that the "battle of the future" would pit organized labor against the American people.

"It is a pity," wrote Nelson, "that the President did not take the stand three years ago that he has lately taken. If he had we would not have had the trouble we are now having" (Nelson to Jones, Sept. 8, 1919, Nelson Papers). On the Townley trials, see Folwell, *Minnesota*, 3:571–75; Morlan, *Political Prairie Fire*, 160–61, 167–73, 256–61, 336–38. On the Iron Range trials, see Ollila, "Defects in Melting Pot," 405.

12. Burnquist, *Inaugural Message, 1919*, 3–4, 25–26 (quotation on 4); *Minneota Mascot*, Feb. 7, 1919.

13. Keller biography, *Legislative Manual*, 1921, p. 590–91; White et al., comps., *Minnesota Votes*, 102.

14. Buell, *Minnesota Legislature of 1919*, 47–58.

15. *Minneapolis Journal*, Sept. 20, 1919, p. 4.

16. *Minneota Mascot*, Jan. 16, 1920.

17. A transcript of the Glencoe speech is in the Henrik Shipstead Papers, MHS, under May 19, 1920. A complete text of Shipstead's acceptance speech was carried by the *Park Region Echo* on Apr. 14, 1920, p. 1, 5.

18. Following Shipstead's endorsement by the league, *Minneota Mascot* (Apr. 2, 1920) carried a lengthy editorial lauding but not endorsing him; the editorial laid particular stress on Shipstead's independence. For 1918 primary results, see *Legislative Manual*, 1919, p. 255.

19. *Minneapolis Journal*, May 8, 9, 1920, both p. 1; *Minneota Mascot*, May 14, 1920, p. 1 (quotation).

20. *Princeton Union*, May 13, 1920, p. 1; Preus, transcript of interview by Lucile Kane, 1960, p. 55, MHS.

21. *Legislative Manual*, 1921, p. 100–101.

22. Here and below, Morlan, *Political Prairie Fire*, 297.

23. *Minneota Mascot*, Oct. 15, 1920.

24. White et al., comps., *Minnesota Votes*, 19–20, 184–86.

25. MCPS Minutes, May 13, 1919.

26. *Legislative Manual*, 1919, p. 473, 1921, p. 323, 1927, p. 154; *Session Laws*, 1919, chap. 284, p. 293 (quotation).

27. MCPS Minutes, Dec. 15, 1920.

28. MCPS, *Report*, 31–32.

29. Here and below, MCPS, *Report*, 12–24, 45–47.

30. *Minneota Mascot*, Oct. 11, 1918.

31. Nelson to McGee, June 22, 1921, Nelson Papers.

32. McGee to Nelson, June 29, 1921, Nelson Papers.

33. Nelson to McGee, June 13, 1922, Nelson Papers.

34. Nelson to J. A. O. Preus, Apr. 17, 1922, Nelson Papers.

35. N. H. Clapp to Nelson, June 24, 1921, Nelson Papers.

36. George W. Lawson to Nelson, Dan W. Stevens to Nelson, both Apr. 14, 1922, Nelson to Edward J. Lee, Apr. 19, 1922 — all in Nelson Papers.

37. Lee to Nelson, Apr. 15 (quotation), May 17 (enclosing newspaper clipping), McGee to Nelson, May 17, 1922 — all in Nelson Papers.

38. Martin W. Odland, *The Life of Knute Nelson* (Minneapolis: Lund Press, 1926), 305–6.

39. White et al., comps., *Minnesota Votes*, 36, 105, 186–87; Chrislock, *Progressive Era*, 188.

40. *St. Paul Daily News*, Mar. 3, p. 3, Mar. 2, p. 9 — both 1923.

41. *Congressional Record*, 67th Cong., 4th sess., 1923, 64, pt. 5: 5125–26 (quotation on 5125); Smith to Nelson, Mar. 3, 1923, Nelson Papers.

42. Nelson to McGee, Mar. 3, 1923, McGee to Nelson, Mar. 5, 1923 — both in Nelson Papers.

43. *Minneapolis Journal,* Feb. 16, 1925, p. 1 (quotation), 8; *St. Paul Pioneer Press,* same date, p. 1.

44. *St. Paul Pioneer Press,* Feb. 17, 1925, p. 1, 3 (quotation).

45. *Legislative Manual,* 1925, p. 297, 1929, p. 190–91, 1931, p. 186–87, 1939, p. 215, 1955, front section.

46. Mayer, *Floyd B. Olson,* 51.

47. George W. Garlid, "The Antiwar Dilemma of the Farmer-Labor Party," *Minnesota History* 40 (Winter 1967): 365–74.

48. For a brief but persuasive analysis contrasting the climates of the two wars, see Steven J. Keillor, *Hjalmar Petersen of Minnesota: The Politics of Provincial Independence* (St. Paul: Minnesota Historical Society Press, 1987), 216–17.

49. Holmquist, ed., *They Chose Minnesota,* 10; Keillor, *Hjalmar Petersen,* 43. Morlan pointed out that "during the war [the commission's] word was law . . . and its standards of 'loyalty' the norm" (*Political Prairie Fire,* 129). Larson underscored the involvement of the commission in the persecution of Charles Lindbergh in 1918 (*Lindbergh,* 224, 234–35). Mayer noted that the agency was "top-heavy with zealous Republicans [who] encouraged summary action by local authorities to crush the [Nonpartisan] League" (*Floyd B. Olson,* 21). According to historian William E. Lass, the MCPS was a body "dominated by ultra conservatives [that] became a virtual government in its own right, employing its own agents and constabulary" (*Minnesota: A Bicentennial History* [New York: W. W. Norton, 1977], 179). Refer to the Bibliography for a listing of dissertations and articles relating to the safety commission.

50. Tighe to Lind, Feb. 13, 1918, Lind Papers.

Bibliography

A Note on Primary Sources

The Minnesota Commission of Public Safety Papers, a holding of the Minnesota State Archives, Minnesota Historical Society, served as the single most important source for this study. This collection is organized by subgroups, the largest being the Alien Registration and Declaration of Holdings files (which fill forty-eight boxes) and the Farm Crop and Labor Reports (twenty-five boxes). Among the other subgroups are Casualty Lists and Related Materials, Clippings Scrapbooks, Gold Star Roll, Mexican Border Service Bonus Correspondence and Vouchers, and Women's Committee of Ramsey County (Council of Home Defense) Americanization Survey Cards.

Of particular value for this study were the Main Files, which contain the bulk of the MCPS correspondence and related documents, divided into subject categories; the Commission Minutes, contained in three volumes; the Woman's Committee Records; Commission Correspondence, dating mostly from 1919–21 when the commission was winding down its work; Agents' Reports to T. G. Winter; Records of County Branches; Correspondence with Counties; and Survey of Women in Industry (Women Employed Outside of Home).

Another Minnesota State Archives holding of considerable value was the Governor's Records covering the years of the Burnquist administration (1915–21). The National War Labor Board Papers held by the National Archives in Washington, D.C., also yielded useful data with respect to the tensions between federal and Minnesota labor policies.

The following materials in the MHS Manuscripts Collection were thoroughly researched: the Joseph A. A. Burnquist Papers; the Donald R. Cotton Papers; the Frank B. Kellogg Papers; the John Lind Papers; the National Nonpartisan League Papers; the Jacob A. O. Preus Papers; the Henrik Shipstead Papers; and the Jean E. Spielman

Papers. The Nicolay A. Grevstad Papers, a holding of the Norwegian-American Historical Association Archive in Northfield, Minnesota, were also helpful. After the research for this book was substantially completed, the Minnesota Historical Society acquired the personal papers of Charles W. Ames. Although they were not used as a primary source for the writing of this book, a cursory review of the papers showed that they contain supporting material about Ames's work on the commission.

As the text's annotation suggests, the MHS Newspaper Collection was another valuable source. Contrary to an impression cultivated by the safety commission, the Minnesota press did not unanimously support all MCPS actions. Although the four leading Twin Cities dailies (the *Minneapolis Journal, Minneapolis Tribune, St. Paul Pioneer Press,* and *St. Paul Dispatch*) were generally supportive of the commission, the *St. Paul Daily News* frequently subjected it to scathing criticism. The English-language *New Ulm Review* and its German-language counterpart, the *New Ulm Post,* both edited by Albert Steinhauser, often assailed the commission in their editorial columns. Late in the war Gunnar Björnson's *Minneota Mascot* emerged as one of the MCPS's most incisive critics. Martin W. Odland's paper, the *Fergus Falls Free Press,* also responded to commission actions with considerable reserve.

From the time the commission was organized, the state's leading labor papers — chiefly the *Minnesota Union Advocate* (St. Paul), *Labor World* (Duluth), and *Labor Review* (Minneapolis) — complained of Governor Burnquist's failure to accord the trade unions representation on the commission; as the commission's response to the Twin Cities streetcar strike unfolded, the stance of these papers became increasingly hostile. The *Union Labor Bulletin* (Minneapolis), which purported to represent the conservative wing of the state's labor movement, also registered vigorous objection to the infamous "button order." Not surprisingly, the official Nonpartisan League press remained strongly critical of the commission from beginning to end.

Suggestions for Further Reading

Although the experience of the United States in World War I has evoked a vast literature, coverage of the activities of state and local councils of defense is relatively thin. This is an unfortunate gap. Stephen Vaughn has suggested that since some of the severest repression of civil liberties originated on the state and local level, the area deserves fuller exploration: see his *Holding Fast the Inner Lines: Democracy, Nationalism and the Committee on Public Information* (Chapel Hill, N.C.: University of North Carolina Press, 1980). A few articles merit citation: William J. Breen, "Mobilization and Cooperative Federalism: The Connecticut State Council of Defense, 1917–1919," *Historian* 42 (November 1979): 58–84, and "The North Carolina Council of Defense during World War I, 1917–1918," *North Carolina Historical Review* 50 (Winter 1973): 1–31; James H. Fowler II, "Tar and Feather Patriotism: The Suppression of Dissent in Oklahoma during World War One," *Chronicles of Oklahoma* 56 (Winter 1978–79): 409–30; Gerald Senn, "'Molders of Thought, Directors of Action': The Arkansas Council of Defense, 1917–1918," *Arkansas Historical Quarterly* 36 (Autumn 1977): 280–90; and Lawrence O. Christensen, "Missouri's Responses to World War I: The Missouri Council of Defense," *Midwest Review* 12 (1990): 34–44.

Coverage of MCPS history is somewhat more ample than that accorded other state councils. Ora A. Hilton, *The Minnesota Commission of Public Safety in World War I, 1917–1919*, Oklahoma Agricultural and Mechanical College, Bulletin, vol. 48, no. 14 (Stillwater, Okla., 1951), is a brief but excellent monograph focusing both on the New Ulm episode and the streetcar strike. In addition to the titles cited in chapter 15, note 49, and elsewhere in the text, two articles in *Minnesota History* illuminate specific facets of safety commission policy: Carol E. Jenson, "Loyalty as a Political Weapon: The 1918 Campaign in Minnesota," vol. 43 (Summer 1972): 42–57; and La Vern J. Rippley, "Conflict in the Classroom: Anti-Germanism in Minnesota Schools, 1917–19," vol. 47 (Spring 1981): 170–83. Carol E. Jenson, *Agrarian Pioneer in Civil Liberties: The Nonpartisan League in Minnesota during World War I* (New York: Garland, 1986); Willis H. Raff, "Coercion and Freedom in a War Situation: A Critical Analysis of Minnesota Culture during World War One" (Ph.D. diss., University of Minnesota, 1957); and Charles S. Ward, "The Minnesota Commission of Public Safety in World War One: Its Formation and Activities" (Master's thesis, University of Minnesota, 1965), are helpful contributions. Millard L. Gieske, *Minnesota Farmer-Laborism: The Third Party Alternative* (Minneapolis: University of Minnesota Press, 1979), notes the safety commission's role in the early history of the Nonpartisan League.

Coverage from a national perspective of the impact of World War I on the American home front is more extensive than on the state and local levels. David M. Kennedy, *Over Here: The First World War and American Society* (New York: Oxford University Press, 1980), fulfills the expectations inherent in the title. Robert D. Cuff, *The War Industries Board: Business-Government Relations during World War I (Baltimore: Johns Hopkins University Press, 1973)*, is widely regarded as a definitive study. Maurine W. Greenwald, *Women, War and Work: The Impact of World War I on Women Workers in the United States* (Westport, Conn.: Greenwood Press, 1980), focuses on women in the factories. Maxcy Robson Dickson, *The Food Front in World War I* (Washington, D.C.: American Council on Public Affairs, 1944), and Charles Gilbert, *American Financing of World War I* (Westport, Conn.: Greenwood Press, 1970), are valuable. George Creel, *How We Advertised America* (New York: Harper and Brothers, 1920), and Harold D. Lasswell, *Propaganda Technique in World War I* (New York: Alfred A. Knopf, 1927; Cambridge, Mass.: K. Paul, Trench, Trubner and Co., 1971), view the manipulation of public opinion from differing perspectives. Valerie Jean Conner, *The National War Labor Board: Stability, Social Justice, and the Voluntary State in World War I* (Chapel Hill: University of North Carolina Press, 1983), is an excellent account of federal labor policy, particularly in 1918. Most of these works have extensive bibliographies directing the reader to related studies on the topic.

Over the years, many studies of the World War I crusades against German Americans and radicals have appeared. Emerson Hough, *The Web: The Authorized History of the American Protective League* (Chicago: Reilly and Lee, 1919), is sympathetic to the APL; Joan M. Jensen, *The Price of Vigilance* (Chicago: Rand McNally, 1968), views the APL more critically. William Preston, Jr., *Aliens and Dissenters: Federal Suppression of Radicals, 1903–1933* (Cambridge, Mass.: Harvard University Press, 1963), demonstrates that antiradical crusades neither began nor ended in 1917–18. A highly recommended study of the German-American plight is Frederick C. Luebke, *Bonds of Loyalty: German-Americans and World War I* (DeKalb: Northern Illinois University Press, 1974). George Sylvester Viereck, *Spreading Germs of Hate* (New York: H. Liveright, 1930), views the anti-German crusade from the vantage point of a victim. In *World War I and the Origin of Civil Liberties in the United States* (New York: Norton, 1979), Paul L. Murphy suggested that the reaction of the victims of governmental repression during the war gave birth to "the politics of civil liberties" (p. 31). Robert K. Murray, *Red Scare: A Study in National Hysteria, 1919–1920* (Minneapolis: University of Minnesota Press, 1955), focuses primarily on the postwar period but explores the wartime roots of the hysteria.

Revisionist historians have done much to elevate the reputation of the IWW from where it stood in 1917–18. See especially, Melvyn Dubofsky, *We Shall Be All: A History of the Industrial Workers of the World* (Champaign: University of Illinois Press, 1988); Fred Thompson, *The I.W.W., Its First Seventy Years, 1905–1975* (Chicago: Industrial Workers of the World, 1976); and Donald E. Winters, Jr., *The Soul of the Wobblies: The I.W.W., Religion, and American Culture in the Progressive Era, 1905–1917* (Westport, Conn.: Greenwood Press, 1985).

Index

ᦈ

Picture Credits

The photographs and other illustrations used in this book appear through the courtesy of the institutions listed below. The names of the photographers, when known, are given in parentheses, as is additional information about the source of the item.

Frontispiece, pages 4, 6, 12, 19, 26 (Kenneth M. Wright), 27 (Lee Bros.), 32, 34, 45 (Lee Bros.), 50 (Fontaine Fox for the Wheeler Syndicate), 67 (*Minneapolis Journal*), 74 (Lee Bros.), 78 (Lee Bros.), 80, 83 (Lee Bros.), 94, 97, 107, 118 (Lee Bros.), 120 (*St. Paul Dispatch*), 134 (Golling-Hesse Studio), 145 (*Duluth News Tribune*), 151, 161, 162, 191, 195, 223, 228 (*Minneapolis Star-Journal*), 231 (*St. Paul Daily News*), 232, 236, 240, 262, 274, 278 (*St. Paul Dispatch*), 296 (Lee Bros.), 297 (both), 303, 315, 321, 330, 334 (C. P. Gibson) — Minnesota Historical Society

Page 41 (Sussman) — Hennepin County Historical Society, Minneapolis

Page 66 — Beltrami County Historical Society, Bemidji

Page 135 (both) — Brown County Historical Society, New Ulm

Page 214 — Pipestone County Historical Society, Pipestone